T0414339

SHAPING REMEMBRANCE FROM SHAKESPEARE TO MILTON

Whether situated in churches or circulating in more flexible, mobile works – manuscript or printed texts, jewels or rosaries, personal bequests or antique "rarities" – monuments were ubiquitous in post-Reformation England. In this period of religious change, the unsettled meanings of sacred sites and artifacts encouraged a new conception of remembrance and, with it, changed relationships between devotional and secular writings, arts, and identities. Beginning in the parish church, *Shaping Remembrance from Shakespeare to Milton* moves beyond that space to see remembrance as shaping dynamic systems within which early modern men and women experienced loss and recollection. Removing monuments from parochial or antiquarian concerns, this study reimagines them as pervasively involved with other commemorative works, not least the writings of our most canonical authors. These far-reaching, flexible chapters combine three critical strands – religion, materiality, and gender – to describe the arts of remembrance as material and textual remains of living webs of connection in which creators and creations are mutually involved.

PATRICIA PHILLIPPY is a professor of English Literature at Kingston University London. She has published widely in early modern literature and culture, with a special focus on women's writing. Her books include *Women, Death and Literature in Post-Reformation England* (2002) and *Painting Women: Cosmetics, Canvases, and Early Modern Culture* (2006). She has edited the writings of Elizabeth Cooke Hoby Russell as *The Writings of an English Sappho* (2011), and *A History of Early Modern Women's Writing* (2018).

SHAPING REMEMBRANCE FROM SHAKESPEARE TO MILTON

PATRICIA PHILLIPPY

Kingston University London

CAMBRIDGE
UNIVERSITY PRESS

University Printing House, Cambridge CB2 8BS, United Kingdom

One Liberty Plaza, 20th Floor, New York, NY 10006, USA

477 Williamstown Road, Port Melbourne, VIC 3207, Australia

314–321, 3rd Floor, Plot 3, Splendor Forum, Jasola District Centre, New Delhi – 110025, India

79 Anson Road, #06–04/06, Singapore 079906

Cambridge University Press is part of the University of Cambridge.

It furthers the University's mission by disseminating knowledge in the pursuit of education, learning, and research at the highest international levels of excellence.

www.cambridge.org
Information on this title: www.cambridge.org/9781108422987
DOI: 10.1017/9781108394697

First published 2018

Printed in the United Kingdom by TJ International Ltd. Padstow Cornwall

A catalogue record for this publication is available from the British Library.

ISBN 978-1-108-42298-7 Hardback

for Fouad,
a rarity lost and found

Contents

Illustrations

Color plates can be found between pages 178 and 179.

Acknowledgments

This project began nearly a decade ago, and the generosity of many individuals and institutions has contributed to its completion. In its earliest days, support from the Program to Enhance Scholarly and Creative Activities at Texas A&M University enabled me to travel to England and make my way – often following circuitous pathways – to visit and photograph monuments in parish churches. I am grateful for the goodwill and hospitality of numerous members of these parishes, who were always eager to talk about their monumental residents. At Boughton House, Crispin Powell generously shared his expertise and knowledge of the Montagu archives. Robert Yorke of the College of Arms helped me to unravel some of the mysteries of the manuscript box at Barnwell in the earliest moments of my research.

I have benefitted from the generous comments of colleagues who have read parts of the book or, in some cases, the whole manuscript. Margaret J. M. Ezell provided her reliably astute and insightful commentary on the project throughout and helped me to mold my argument. Julia Reinhard Lupton contributed, directly and indirectly, to my treatment of Shakespeare in the chapters that follow, and I have learned a great deal from her during a friendship of three decades. Jaime Goodrich, Sarah C. E. Ross, and Jessica Malay read individual chapters and offered provocative and productive comments on my handling of women's works. Colleagues at Kingston University London have read or heard various pieces of this project over several years, and their engagement with my work has been a great help. My relocation to the United Kingdom in 2010 made this project possible, and I must acknowledge the Faculty of Arts and Social Sciences at Kingston for bringing me here and for encouraging this research. My thanks go particularly to Andrew Teverson, Head of the School of Arts, Culture and Communication at Kingston, for his generosity in supporting the publication of color images in this book.

A Leverhulme Trust Research Fellowship in 2015–2016 enabled me to finish writing the book.

As always, my greatest debt of gratitude goes to my family. Iman Khadija Berrahou was more than a casual reader of most of these chapters and offered excellent companionship as we photographed the Dudley and Bradstreet monuments in Boston and North Andover.

I dedicate this book to my husband, Fouad Berrahou. His patience and belief in me and my work – and his willingness to share with me the cartography of commemoration in the remotest corners of the United Kingdom – enabled this project to reach its end.

Abbreviations

BCP	Church of England, Book of Common Prayer
BL	British Library, London
BM	Historical Manuscripts Commission. *Report on the Manuscripts of Lord Montagu of Beaulieu.* 2 vols. London: HMSO, 1900.
Bod	Bodleian Library, Oxford
Borthwick	Borthwick Institute for Archives, University of York
BQ	Historical Manuscripts Commission. *Report on the Manuscripts of the Duke of Buccleuch and Queensberry.* 3 vols. London: HMSO, 1809.
Hunt	Huntington Library, San Marino, CA
NRO	Northampton Record Office, Northampton
ODNB	*The Oxford Dictionary of National Biography: In Association with the British Academy: From the Earliest Times to the Year 2000.* ed. Matthew H. C. G. Harrison and Brian Howard. Oxford University Press, 2004. Online edition, 2008.
OED	*Oxford English Dictionary.* 2nd edition. Oxford University Press, 1989.
TNA	The National Archives, Kew

Introduction
An Amber Casket

> While a viper crawled among the weeping branches of the Heliads, a drop of amber flowed onto the creature in its path. As it marveled to find itself stuck fast in the viscous liquid, it stiffened, bound of a sudden by congealed ice. Be not proud, Cleopatra, of your royal sepulcher, if a viper lies in a nobler tomb.
>
> – Martial[1]

Writing in the late fifteenth century, the humanist Giovanni Pontano recalled a diminutive monument presented to King Alfonso of Naples by the merchant and antiquarian, Cyriac of Ancona: a piece of amber that contained a fly with its wings open; "a thing so small," he wrote, "but one whose rarity rendered it most great in the eyes of the king" ("succino eum donovit quo pansis alis musca includebatur, parva immo pusilla sane res, at raritas apud principem").[2]

I begin with Cyriac's memorable gift to offer a parable, a figuration, and a myth that, collectively, define the central concerns of this study. The inclusion and its textual transmission tell a story of the anxiety and ambivalence attending the retrieval and reuse of remnants of the past. The artifact presents figuration of the phenomenal interrelations of subjects and objects, particularly as religion creates communities that join the faithful with each other and with the material accessories of belief.[3] The mythic origins of amber, finally, are rooted in women's mourning and commemoration, positing a suggestive alignment of femininity with

[1] Martial, *Epigrams*, 4:59: "Flentibus Heliadum ramis dum vipera repit, / fluxit in obstantem sucina gutta feram: / quae dum miratur pingui se rore teneri, / concreto riguit vincta repente gelu. / ne tibi regali placeas, Cleopatra, sepulchro, / vipera si tumulo nobiliore iacet."

[2] Pontano, *Opere*, fols. y5^{v}-y6^{r}. For a modern Latin-Italian edition, see Pontano, *I libri delle virtu sociali*, 212–13. On Pontano, see Hersey, *Alfonso II*; and Welch, "Public Magnificence." On Ciriaco de' Pizzicolli (Cyriac of Ancona) (1391–1452), see Bodnar and Foss, eds., *Cyriac of Ancona*; Saxl, "Classical Inscription"; and Kokole, "Cyriacus of Ancona."

[3] I adopt Braidotti's definition of figuration throughout as "no metaphor" but a representation that expresses materially embedded subject positions: see *Nomadic Subjects*, 10–11.

materiality that invites one to see gender as both embodied in and produced by memorial acts and objects.

This book explores the visual, textual, and material monuments that characterize the culture of remembrance in post-Reformation England. In the chapters following, I investigate how commemorative objects and texts were used in innovative ways to preserve memory; negotiate shifts in religious belief and practice; and craft personal, national, and confessional narratives in the century stretching from the Elizabethan Settlement to the English Civil War. Whether situated in churches or circulating in more flexible, mobile works – manuscript and printed texts, needlework, jewels and rosaries, personal bequests, or antique "rarities" – monuments were ubiquitous in post-Reformation England. Beginning in the sacred space of the parish church, this study moves beyond that location to argue that in this period of religious change, the unsettled meanings of sacred sites and objects encouraged a new conception of remembrance and, with it, changed relationships between devotional and secular writings, arts, and identities.

The amber inclusion preserved in Pontano's text is emblematic of Renaissance antiquarianism itself, a project initiated by "the founding father of archaeology," Cyriac, and his humanist redactors and continued, albeit with different motives, in the chorographic activities of the English Society of Antiquaries a century later.[4] The relic is a morsel to whet the appetite for greater riches promised by archaeological and mercantile enterprises in the Mediterranean world. Like the object, Cyriac's drawings and transcriptions of classical monuments made during his travels throughout the region document the wondrous but woefully ephemeral traces of a past available only in fragments. Writing from Heraklion in October 1445, Cyriac admires one such marvelous fragment in terms that suggest his attraction to the inclusion (see Figure I.1). He begins by transcribing the object's Greek inscription – an epitaph commemorating its maker – and goes on to describe the "wondrous beauty" of "a splendid crystalline signet seal the size of a thumb that is engraved in deep relief with a bust of helmeted Alexander of Macedon, the marvelous workmanship of the artisan Eutyches."[5] This tiny, translucent object, like the inclusion, artfully encloses a figure that hovers between myth and ancient

[4] Bodnar and Foss, eds., *Cyriac of Ancona*, ix. On the Society of Antiquaries, see Evans, *History;* Woolf, *Social Circulation*, esp. 141–82; Schyler, "Antiquaries"; Harris, *Untimely* Matter, 95–118; and Parry, *Trophies of Time.*

[5] Quoted and translated in Bodnar and Foss, eds., *Cyriac of Ancona*, 196–9.

Figure I.1 Roman Gem with Portrait of Pallas Athena by Eutyches (first century AD). © bpk / Antikensammlung, SMB (inv. no. FG2305).

matter; the signet created by a skillful engraver, the inclusion by a more mysterious art. These remnants of "untimely matter" permeated early modernity, spectral tokens of the transience of artifacts and the impenetrability of their meanings.[6] This semiotic threat was poignantly realized in Cyriac's misreading of the figure on Eutyches' intaglio: not Alexander but Athena. Although Cyriac visited and recorded the intact Temple of Hadrian at Cyzicus in 1431 (see Figure I.2), he reported despairingly that it was in ruins when he returned thirteen years later.[7] The loss of antiquities prompted the feverish collection of inscriptions and epitaphs: Cyriac's work alone, compiled in his *Commentarii*, filled six manuscript volumes. Inspired by the desire to preserve fragile remains, Cyriac's textual monuments were themselves lost in 1514, when the Sforza library in Pesaro housing the only holograph copies was devoured by fire.[8]

While Cyriac and the Italian antiquarians following him aimed to preserve the remnants of a remote classical past, English antiquarians were

[6] Harris, *Untimely Matter*, 11–12.
[7] See Saxl, "Classical Inscription," 32; and Ashmole, "Cyriac of Ancona."
[8] Saxl, "Classical Inscription," 19; and Ashmole, "Cyriac of Ancona," 26.

Figure I.2 Bartolomeo Fonzio, "Collectanea Epigraphica" (late fifteenth century), Temple of Hadrian at Cyzicus, after Cyriac of Ancona.
The Bodleian Libraries, The University of Oxford. MS. Lat. Misc. d.85, fols. 133^{v}–134^{r}.

motivated by the loss of monuments closer to home. In 1600, Francis Tate recounted to the Society of Antiquaries an event some twenty years earlier, when servants plowing a field in Norfolk "found a vault, and therein a man lying buried, and a booke with bosses on his brest; the body and the booke being touched fel into dust."[9] This grim archaeology suggests time's ability to erase subjects and objects, monumental texts and tombs alike. Tate's tale of inadvertent disinterment is an exception among more violent and jarring exhumations. In 1549, the Pardon Chapel at St. Paul's, "whose Monuments in number and curious workmanship passed all that were in the Cathedral," was pulled down by Edward Seymour, Duke of Somerset, "and the materials carried to the Strand, toward the building of that stately fabrick called Senate House."[10] "The bones of the dead, couched up in a Charnill," John Stow writes, "(by report of him who paid for the cariage) were convied from thence into Finsbery fielde, amounting to more then one thousand cart loades."[11] Prompted by "the woefull experience" of iconoclasm, William Dugdale recorded "what Monuments [he] could" in St. Paul's, "that the Shadows of them, with their inscriptions, might be

[9] Hearne, *Collection*, vol. I, 217–18. [10] Dugdale, *History of St. Paul's*, 132.
[11] Stow, *Survay* (1598), 268.

preserved for posteritie, forasmuch as the things themselves were so neer unto ruine."[12] As Alexandra Walsham writes, Dugdale hoped "to pictorially repossess spaces that had been desecrated [and] to commemorate a structure . . . facing a sentence of execution."[13]

Against the threat of iconoclasm and archaeological dismay that prompted and beset early modern antiquarianism, Cyriac's inclusion is an optimistic emblem of recovery and preservation that resonates in secular and spiritual registers. An "eternal sepulcher," the inclusion promises that one might fix memory in material form. "We see, how Flies and Spiders, and the like, get a Sepulcher in Amber," Francis Bacon muses, "more Durable, than the Monument, and Embalming of the Body of any King."[14] As Girolamo Cardano puts it, the "flies, ants, little fish, leaves, scrapings – captured by the tenacious moistness of the amber . . . cannot decay, and shine out from their eternal tomb, a grander one than the Mausoleum Artemisia built."[15] Yet if the inclusion is a figure of entombment, it is also a sign of salvation. To the early modern world, amber was a substance capable of quasi-miraculous works, valued for its curative properties, mysteriously endowed with a magnetism that could coach matter into motion, and emitting a sweet smell that enhanced the religious experience of worshippers in fragrant incense and rosaries.[16] Its mythic origins lay in an act of commemoration, often repeated in representations of women's mourning and remembrance: the sisters of Phaethon, grieving at their brother's tomb, were transformed into poplars whose tears fell into a nearby river and hardened into amber.[17] For Pontano, the material was inherently precious and potent, displaying its power in its miraculous preservation of the fly, a translation of the humble to the exalted. The inclusion is a tomb where a body sleeps, perhaps awaiting resurrection. It is a sacramental: as the Catholic Eucharist contains the body of Christ, or a relic enfolds the essence of the saint, the inclusion's meager body is preserved in a supernatural operation that mimics and encodes divine grace.

[12] Dugdale, *History of St. Paul's*, fol. A3^{v}. [13] Walsham, "'Like Fragments,'" 98.

[14] Gilbert, *De magnete*, 47; and Bacon, *Sylva Sylvarum*, 33. [15] Cardano, *De subtiltate*, 307.

[16] De Acosta's *Naturall and Morall Historie*, 287, describes the qualities of amber as "sweete and medicinall . . . and a good perfume." See also Pliny, *Historie*, 607–9; Gilbert, *De magnete*; and Cardano, *De subtiltate*, 304–5. On rosaries, see King, "'Beads'"; TNA PROB 11/24/113, fol. 67^{r}, for Katherine Styles's bequest in 1530 of a "payer of beades of white aumber"; and Salter, *Six Renaissance Men*, 117–29, for commentary. An amber rosary hangs on the wall behind the subjects in Jan van Eyck's *Arnolfini Wedding*

[17] Ovid, *Metamorphoses*, 2:319–65. The myth gained authority for early modern readers through Pliny's reiteration, *Historie*, 607–8. For discussion, see Kelley, "Amber."

Amber's enigmatic properties made it a popular image in religious polemics. In Reformation Europe, Protestants and Catholics alike saw amber as figuring collective religious experience. For Anabaptist Ulisse Aldrovandi, human flesh "involved in the vanities of the world, does not lack the softness of pleasures, but at the time of the resurrection, having been hardened by divine heat, it will appear the image of amber." Alternatively, creatures involved in amber, like Cyriac's fly, are heretical avatars "engulfed by the stickiness of transgressions." Amber's magnetism figures Christ's, who "burning with the heat of his love draws vain sinners to himself."[18] Severin Goebel compares the prophets and apostles to "poor fishermen, just like those who gather amber that has been cast on the shore"; the Christian community, in this figure, is comprised of bits of amber, transformed to solidity by the frigid seas of God's law and redeemed on the tranquil shore of God's mercy.[19] When a piece of amber larger than the body of an ox ("una massa di quest Electro, ò ambra, maggiore del corpo di un bue") washed ashore in Buchan, Scotland, in 1546, the Italian expatriate Petruccio Ubaldini reported that the shepherds who found it, smelling a sweet odor pervading the air, took it to the local priest to use as incense ("à ridirlo al prete della loro prossima Chiesa allegramente, mostrandogli d'haver ritrovato una cosa cosi utile come l'incenso per la sua Chiesa").[20] William Camden's account of the episode sixty years later displaces Ubaldini's superstitious shepherds' adornment of the Catholic Mass with a sober, if unsure, natural history: "A mighty masse likewise of Ambar as big as the body of an horse, was not many yeers since cast upon this shore. The learned ... supposed that it was a certaine juice or liquor which distilleth out of trees in Britaine, and runneth downe into the sea, and is therein hardned."[21]

It is in the context of religious debate that Cyriac's inclusion entered England. Dedicating his collection of daily devotions, *The Key of Knowledge*, in 1572, Puritan Thomas Achelley borrowed Cyriac's rarity as an emblem for his book:

> Pontanus in his 19. Chapiter *de magnificentia* ... maketh mention of one Anconitanus, that presented unto Alphonsus, King of Calabria, a Box of

[18] Aldrovandi, *Musaeum*, 414–15; translated King, "'Beads,'" 165. This discussion is greatly indebted to King's research.

[19] Goebel, *Pia commonefactio*, n.p.; quoted and translated King, "'Beads,'" 156.

[20] Ubaldini, *Descrittione del Rigno di Scoti*, 52.

[21] Camden, *Britain [Britannia]* (1610), fol. Dddd6^v.

> Amber, very curiously and artificially wrought, which being opened by the King: had nothing else but a fly enclosed within.[22]

Achelley's attempt to deploy the object as a figure for his text grows tortured when he insists that his book agrees in one respect with the amber box but differs from it in another. "It agreeth . . . in baseness," he reasons:

> but it differreth onely from the Amber Box, which proffered a glosing and beautiful show to the outward view, and yet had nothing with in it but a thing of nought. Whereunto the thing that I offer is clean contrary, for it yieldeth no glorious nor glistering glose nor any colour of delight unto the eye: notwithstanding . . . the matter therein contained shall suffice to commend it without the help of any external ornaments.[23]

Achelley's book reverses the structure and symbolism of its defining image. The "glose" of Cyriac's curious box holds a meaningless triviality. Achelley's modest text, by contrast, is "a thing of nought" that nonetheless contains the key of knowledge. Against the idolatrous surface of a box that is merely a tomb, Achelley's devotions are a humble fly, a lowly embodiment of the reformed faith's sincere essence.

Misreading the inclusion as a box, Achelley indicts the object's "glose" as distorting and denying the somber but instructive *memento mori* within. His indictment echoes the nervousness of his reformed countrymen with regard to religious idols and images, whose "bewytchyng . . . colors enticeth the ignorant."[24] This concern, implicit in Achelley's dedication, becomes explicit in the devotions that follow: thus he praises the "poore flock" of true believers who serve God "in lowlines and purenesse of hart, ab[an]doning all the rabble of Romayne traditions, and idolatrous ceremonies."[25] Once the Reformation troubled the link between outward form and inner essence in religious objects and images – a movement of which the international debate on transubstantiation is archetypical – icons were condemned as empty idols.[26] Achelley's vocabulary is symptomatic of iconoclasm: the words "curious," "wrought," and "artificial" held potentially diabolical meanings in post-Reformation England, while "glose"

[22] Achelley, *Key of Knowledge*, sig. B7^{r-v}. Achelley was a minor poet and dramatist: see Freeman, "Writings."

[23] Achelley, *Key of Knowledge*, sig. B8^{v}-C1^{r}.

[24] Church of England, *Homyly agaynst peryll of Idolatry*, fols. 61^{v} and 16^{v}.

[25] Achelley, *Key of Knowledge*, 62–3.

[26] On iconoclasm, see Duffy, *Stripping of the Altars*; Aston, *Broken Idols*; and O'Connell, *Idolatrous Eye*; and MacCulloch, *Reformation*, 558–63. For a summary of the vast literature on transubstantiation, see Wallace, *Long European Reformation*, 82–114.

carried the sense of flattery, deceit, false show, and pretense.[27] The opulent exterior of the amber box renders it an idolatrous tomb, as worthy of destruction by the iconoclast's hammer as the statues of saints. If Pontano's inclusion shimmers with the promise of miraculous salvation, Achelley's amber casket is an icon turned idol; a false sacrament signaling death.

Pontano's textual recollection and Achelley's recovery of the inclusion suggest the improvisational character of religious and commemorative practices following the repudiation of Catholic rites and beliefs. In redefining the relationship of the living to the dead, the English Reformation required a new understanding of monuments and memorial sites: when the monumental cartography of chapels and chantries no longer mapped the recitation of prayers for the dead, focus shifted from the spiritual efficacy of remembrance toward a proliferation of its material displays.[28] Although we often envision post-Reformation churches as whitewashed and austere, most were busy with commemorative objects in all media. Churches were galleries crowded and densely hung with monuments of marble, brass, wood, vellum, and glass. Memorials were painted on walls and pillars of churches, and manuscript poems, pinned to the pall during funerals, were posted on or near monuments, creating sites for spontaneous poetic rivalries, parodies, and debut publications by new poets. Memorial glass sparkled in the windows and hung from pillars. Textiles donated in remembrance of the dead hung from pulpits and adorned chapel walls. With the loss of the familiar Catholic rituals and liturgy attending remembrance, memorial sites became improvisational, open-ended spaces, while new Protestant practices, themselves continually in flux, created locations for "the meeting-up of histories," to borrow Doreen Massey's terms, "a simultaneity of stories-so-far."[29] Church interiors were dynamic sites of interaction between subjects and objects and between the living and the dead, where acts of memory were continually reenacted with unpredictable results as congregations and beliefs changed over time. The image of the speaking stone was a staple of post-Reformation epitaphs, instructing readers to perform any number of impromptu memorial

[27] Acrasia's Bower of Bliss exemplifies this corrupt (most often Catholic) imagery pervasive in Spenser's poem: see Spenser, *Faerie Queene*, in *Poetical Works*, 2:12. All subsequent references to Spenser's works are to this edition. On "glose," see *OED*; and on its usage in Shakespeare's and Wilkins's *Pericles*, see Chapter 5.

[28] I am indebted to Scodel, *English Poetic Epitaph*, 21, who notes that the removal of sacred images in the Reformation led to the proliferation of monuments. I build on this research by expanding the scope of my study to embrace a wide variety of texts, artifacts, and practices.

[29] Massey, *For Space*, 4 and 11.

gestures: "tread soft," "trace his tombe," "sit downe and thinke," "reade theis lynes," "looke on this vault."[30] Church buildings and fabric were profoundly polychronic and multi-temporal.[31] The recovery or retention of Catholic sites and objects within Protestant churches influenced parishioners who erected memorials, and those who experienced them as (sometimes unwelcome) attendants to worship.

This book takes account of post-Reformation monuments erected in sacred spaces as a starting point for exploring how changed notions of remembrance within religious beliefs and practices permeate and influence the secular sphere. Enfolded in the confessional movements of the Reformation, the term "remembrance" also inflects secular experience and expression.[32] These modulations in sense and context are interwoven throughout my study, moving and expanding my focus beyond that explored in more exclusive approaches to monuments.[33] Rather than pursuing documentary concerns, I remove monuments from limited antiquarian and parochial interests to locate them in provocative relationships with early modern texts, from masques, poems, and plays to religious and devotional writings. I reimagine monuments as profoundly and pervasively involved with other commemorative works, not least literary works by our most canonical authors. From this perspective, Shakespeare's Marina (a daughter lost and found in *Pericles*) and Milton's Sabrina (Genius of the Severn in *Comus*) both incarnate the losses registered in monuments and the recoveries to which they aspire.[34]

[30] Stow, *Survey* (1633), 789; 792; and Mosse, *Monumental Effigies of Sussex*, 151.

[31] Harris, *Untimely Matter*, 3.

[32] Studies in early modern memory inform my discussion throughout. See Carruthers, *Book of Memory*; Yates, *Art of Memory*; Hiscock, *Reading Memory*; Summit, *Memory's Library*; Gordon, *Writing Early Modern London*; Bolzoni, *Gallery of Memory;* Beecher and Williams, eds., *Ars Reminiscendi;* and Engel, Loughnane, and Williams, eds., *Memory Arts*. See also Gordon and Rist, "Introduction," in *Arts of Remembrance*, who note of the omnipresent arts of remembrance in early modern culture, "In their material diversity, these works testify to a habit . . . that sees in the created object the enactment of remembrance" (1).

[33] This study supplements two recent studies of early modern monuments. See Llewellyn, *Funeral Monuments*, for an authoritative, comprehensive account which locates church monuments within the historiography of English art; and see Sherlock, *Monuments and Memory*, which studies the material culture of memory in sixteenth- and seventeenth-century England in a narrower range of monuments.

[34] Shakespeare and Wilkins, *Pericles*, ed. Gossett; and Milton, *Maske*, in *Complete Works, Volume III: The Shorter Poems*, ed. Lewalski and Haan. All subsequent references to *Pericles* are to this edition unless otherwise noted. All subsequent references to Milton's works are to this edition unless otherwise noted.

This interdisciplinary study considers the sacred and secular aspects of remembrance as they influence artifacts, texts, and the individuals who created and experienced them. As such, this work is aligned with scholarship in historical phenomenology, making use of the flexibility of this approach not only to accommodate history and theory, but also to join the three critical strands of inquiry – religion, materiality, and gender – that combine within and mutually structure this project.[35] Pursuing phenomenology's blending of subject and object into its inflection by "new materialism," moreover, I adapt Rosi Braidotti's view of the posthuman subject as "constituted through embedded and embodied sets of interrelations," and I emphasize the centrality of acts of remembrance – of oneself and of others – to ensure "the inner coherence" of the self.[36] Thus, I situate "remembrance" between subject and object, life and death, exploring the dynamic networks in which early modern men and women experienced loss and recollection. The arts of remembrance, then, are the material and textual remains of living webs of connection – "the close-woven fabric of the true world," as Maurice Merleau-Ponty puts it – in which creators and creations are enmeshed.[37] Accordingly, these chapters present a series of linked cartographies of discrete locations within the interrelational field of early modern remembrance.[38] These maps strive to be accurate and precise in capturing the situated character of memorial works and, in doing so, to chart the changing terrain of post-Reformation remembrance. For example, when John Milton eulogizes the Marchioness of Winchester with the assurance, "This rich Marble doth enterr," his printed monument – uprooted from the literal site of burial – relies upon successive acts of reading and remembrance to instantiate presence. Supported by the scaffolding of shared

[35] Works aligned with this method include Smith, "Premodern Sexualities"; Smith, *Phenomenal Shakespeare*; Paster and Floyd-Wilson, eds., *Reading the Body*; Harris, *Untimely Matter*; Shannon, *Accommodated Animal*; Curran and Kearney, "Introduction," and all the articles in *Criticism*'s special issue, *Shakespeare and Phenomenology*. Lupton, "Macbeth's Martlets," 365, offers an inclusive description of the strand of phenomenology deployed in my project: "Phenomenology attends to how the world of things manifests itself in a single flow of emergent and continuous processes that dissolve (human) subjects and (nonhuman) objects in shared fields of causation, movement, ambience, intentionality, and perception."

[36] Braidotti, *Posthuman*, 99. Curran and Kearney, "Introduction," 357, note the confluence of phenomenology with anti-dualist theorists including Deleuze, whose work has been foundational for "Deleuzian feminists" such as Rosi Braidotti and Elizabeth Grosz. See also Braidotti, *Metamorphoses*, 111. While I make use of concepts derived from critical posthumanism, I agree with Campana and Maisano, *Renaissance Posthumanism*, 3, that "ideas of the human as at once embedded and embodied in, evolving with, and de-centered amid a weird tangle of animals, environments and vital materiality" are to be found in the early modern period.

[37] Merleau-Ponty, *Visible and Invisible*, 5–6.

[38] See Braidotti, "Critical Cartography."

literacy, printed monuments rewrite pre-Reformation communal prayers for the dead with the collective memory and interiority created by the book.[39]

As Ken Jackson and Arthur Marotti have argued, the "religious turn" in early modern studies "was determined in large part by the 'theological turn' in phenomenology."[40] In this study, I delineate connections between Reformation theological debates and their representations in monumental and commemorative forms. Exploring "material religion," in Hamling and Richardson's term, I aim to account for changing relationships between worshippers and sacred objects, ceremonies, and sites, demonstrating the various ways in which post-Reformation monuments and memorial artifacts were created in the lingering shadow of discarded sacraments and icons.[41]

In the period's contested views of the sacraments, remembrance was advanced as the foundation of reformed definitions: the bread and wine of the Protestant Communion did not confer grace but were "signe[s] of remembrance" to confirm salvation.[42] If religious beliefs made use of remembrance in doctrinal reform, memorial arts and practices, in turn, adopted religious terms to navigate the passage from life to death to commemoration. Set in the threshold between the physical and spiritual, inscribed within a religion understood as "a reality both within and beyond the phenomenal world," post-Reformation monuments express their subjects' numinous passages in visual, textual, and figurative terms borrowed from and set in conversation with the Word.[43] The shifting currents of religious beliefs stir the pool of images given to personal commemoration

[39] Milton, "Epitaph," line 1. See Chapter 6.

[40] Jackson, "All is True," 469; and see Jackson and Marotti, "Turn to Religion." For discussions of contemporary postsecularity, see Habermas, "Notes"; and, in relation to feminism and the posthuman, Braidotti, "In Spite," summarized in *Posthuman*, 27–31. For postsecularity in early modern studies, see Walsh, "'A Priestly Farewell'"; Beckwith, "Stephen Greenblatt's *Hamlet*"; Aers, "New Historicism"; Hammill and Lupton, eds., *Political Theology*; and Loewenstein and Witmore, eds., *Shakespeare and Early Modern Religion*.

[41] Hamling and Richardson, eds., *Everyday Objects*, 231; and see relevant discussions, 232–88. See also Gayk, *Image, Text and Religious Reform*; and Aston, *Broken Idols*, for projects aligned with my own.

[42] Hooker, *Lawes*, 158. Interpretations of the sacraments as commemorative are not exclusively Protestant, nor is there an absolute distinction between Catholic and Protestant views. See Beckwith, "Stephen Greenblatt's *Hamlet*," 261–7, who argues that the English church's version of the Eucharist involved an incarnational understanding of presence that rejected "bare memorialism"; and see Chapter 1. On the persistence of sacramental thought in the post-Reformation, see Schwartz, *Sacramental Poetics*; Parker, "What a Piece of Work": Beckwith, *Shakespeare and the Grammar of Forgiveness*; Knapp, *Shakespeare's Tribe;* and Burnham and Giaccherini, eds., *Poetics of Transubstantiation*.

[43] Jackson and Marotti, "Turn to Religion," 169.

in waves that move in various, unpredictable directions. Thus, for example, when Blanche Parry commissioned a joint memorial for herself and her monarch, Elizabeth I, she prolonged the life of Catholic sacraments and ceremonies, subsuming their memory in a new form: the queen's effigy was placed in the chancel precisely where the statue of the church's patron, St. Faith, once stood.[44] Regardless of devotional allegiances, commemorative practices carry traces of the sacred, whether in displacing and rewriting discarded pre-Reformation beliefs or in aligning commemoration with typologies seen as transcending early modern theological and doctrinal divisions.[45] Indeed, four centuries after the Reformation, the typological affinity, on both sides of the theological divide, between the sacrament and communicants inflects Merleau-Ponty's doctrinally precise analogy for the sensory experience of the phenomenal world:

> Just as the sacrament not only symbolizes . . . an operation of Grace, but is also the real presence of God, which it causes to occupy a fragment of space and communicates to those who eat of the consecrated bread, provided that they are inwardly prepared, in the same way the sensible has not only a motor and vital significance, but is nothing other than a certain way of being in the world suggested to us from some point in space, and seized and acted upon by our body, provided that it is capable of doing so, so that sensation is literally a form of communion.[46]

The fact that nearly every clause of Merleau-Ponty's description of the sacrament, from the nature of real presence to the processes assuring preparedness, was at the center of sometimes bitter disputes during the Reformation alerts us to the distance between our "certain way of being in the world" and that of early modern subjects. The analogy indexes the contingency of our identities and desires – even the ecumenical will to reconcile differences and bridge divides.

Phenomenology's "dual embrace" of subject and object, as Kevin Curran and James Kearney note, "provides a way to address material culture, to attend to the things of the early modern world without losing sight of the fact that there is no intelligible object world divorced from the subject."[47]

[44] See Richardson, *Mistress Blanche*, 143–8. See Chapter 6.
[45] For an incisive reading of Renaissance typology, see Lupton, *Afterlives*.
[46] Merleau-Ponty, *Phenomenology of Perception*, 246.
[47] Curran and Kearney, "Introduction," 359. Key texts in "the material turn" include Hamling and Richardson, eds., *Everyday Objects*; de Grazia, Quilligan and Stallybrass, eds., *Subject and Object*;

Five decades ago, Thomas M. Greene observed that "the image that propelled the humanist Renaissance and still determines our perception of it was the archaeological, necromantic metaphor of *disinterment*, a digging up that was also a resuscitation or a reincarnation or a rebirth."[48] Since then, Greene's cogent association between the humanist anticipation of rebirth in every disinterment and the critical aspiration to "speak with the dead" has both preserved and refined the archaeological metaphor.[49] We now strive for an "archival reconstruction" of the "politics of location," an excavation not of artifacts but of ecosystems, "a version of phenomenology [that] attempts to be historically relative and politically aware."[50] A central concern throughout this study is the relationship between material objects and subjects as mutual partners in acts and performances of memory. If commemoration, as Andrew Jones notes, "is paradigmatic of the kind of connective practices which tie together people and things," offering "a framework for remembering itself," the effort to interpret post-Reformation memorial practices by calling attention to the place of material objects within them suggests a means to accommodate the multiple media and forms of interconnected "textualities" that are the subject of this book.[51]

These chapters expand consideration of commemorative textualities beyond their location in sacred sites, reading them in relation to other memorial projects in both sacred and secular spheres. As the purpose of memorial sites within Reformation churches changed, the meanings of monuments occupying these spaces also became unfixed and vulnerable. Beyond church walls, meanwhile, the Renaissance encounter with the ruins of the classical and medieval past sets the recovered object at the heart of the period's conflicted projects of building national identity and codifying religious orthodoxy. Throughout this book, I remain mindful of antiquarianism in an international context, and I draw parallels between the antiquarian retrieval of secular relics and the English Reformation's encounter with the discarded monuments and relics of the Catholic past. Thus, I explore how reclamations of ancient or foreign objects strove to

Jones and Stallybrass, *Renaissance Clothing*; Bruster, "New Materialism"; Appadurai, ed., *Social Life of Things*; and more recently and critically, Harris, "New New Historicism's *Wunderkammer*"; and Gordon and Rist, eds., *Arts of Remembrance*.

48 Greene, "Petrarch," 206. 49 Greenblatt, *Shakespearean Negotiations*, 1.

50 See Smith, "Phenomophobia," 483; Smith, *Key of Green*, 8; and Braidotti, *Nomadic Subjects*, 14–15. For archaeological approaches to literary and material culture, see Schwyzer, *Archaeologies*; Gaimster and Gilchrist, eds., *Archaeology;* and Hines, *Voices of the Past.*

51 Jones, *Memory*, 46. See also Frye, *Pens and Needles*, for a critical treatment of material textualities.

reinterpret them as familiar, naturalized relics in support of newly framed cultural and national histories. When, for instance, John Tradescant the younger published his catalog of the "collection of rarities" amassed by his father, he did so, he claimed, as "an honour to our Nation." The cabinet included among many treasures "Pohatan, King of Virginia's habit all embroidered with shells," "Henry the 8 his stirrups," and "Divers sorts of Ambers, with {Flyes Spiders} naturall." On his death, the collection – a hotly contested inheritance – passed to Elias Ashmole and subsequently formed the foundation of the museum at Oxford that carries his name.[52]

This book attends to women's authorship of memorial artifacts and texts by bringing together a body of women's writing that demonstrates diverse encounters with the arts of remembrance. Whether commissioning sculptural tombs or leaving instructions for their creation in their wills, scripting and circulating memorials in manuscript or print, or bequeathing artifacts as tokens of remembrance, post-Reformation women made wide use of the rich creative site of commemoration. Through performances of remembrance, women were able to cement political and dynastic ties and advance religious agendas. Tracing connections between apparently disparate commemorative works reveals dense networks of social and family alliance, religious society, patronage, and political activism preserved but often overlooked in the memorials that women created for themselves and others. To approach these interrelated works, I develop the idea of "monumental circles," collaborative creative networks that invite us to consider women's productions alongside men's and to seek points of contact and contrast between men's and women's commemorative artifacts and texts. Ann Montagu's monumental "Letters, Prayers, and Poems," for instance, resides in conversation with the Puritan faith of her male relatives and religious instructors, yet it displays a complex exchange between female matter and religious belief that results in a distinctly feminine art of memory.[53]

In bringing this archive of women's commemorative writings and monuments to light, this study contributes to the recovery of women's writing that has redefined the critical view and canon of early modern studies in the past four decades. My intervention in this criticism proceeds in two directions. First, I advance the burgeoning criticism on material

[52] Tradescant, *Museum Trandescantianum*, fol. a3^r; and 36 and 47. Subsequent citations appear parenthetically. See Chapter 4 for discussion.
[53] See Chapter 2 for discussion.

cultures and the history of the book by scrutinizing media beyond the manuscript and printed book as sites of women's textual production. Thus I enlarge the idea of authorship to include translations, transcriptions, and commissions.[54] Second, my focus on the material objects and practices of women's commemoration confronts the common equation of materiality and femininity, a formula with origins in antiquity, transmitted by the *contemptus mundi* of medieval Christianity, and renewed by the denigration of matter in the reformation of the sacraments. Central to my project is an idea of the female body as fluid and nonessential, an idea of subjectivity as constituted within an embedded and enfleshed materialism.[55] As such, one aim of this book is to refine the contemporary critical embrace of the "situational model" of women's writing by way of a vitalist materialist view of the female subject as constituted by interactions between the gendered body and its social, cultural, natural, and spiritual environments.[56] Bringing to bear upon this model the understanding of figurations as composing, in Braidotti's terms, "a living map [of] highly specific geo-political and historical locations; history tattooed on your body," enables more nuanced and precise cartographies that capture the embodied, relational, and transformative situations of women's literate production.[57] Women's works present female bodies, in life and in death, not as passive objects but as subjects enmeshed in webs of relations that extend into the afterlife through monumental texts, artifacts, and legacies. Influenced by Reformation redefinitions of the sacrament, moreover, women's monumental writings and artifacts undertake a redemptive treatment of the female body as matter infused with spirit; a "re-membrance," to borrow Sarah Beckwith's phrase, enabled by the notion of the permeable borders of women's bodies within the material world surrounding them.[58] While this image is frequently deployed by male writers to represent feminine mourning and complaint, as the myth of Phaethon's sisters reminds us, women's commemorative writing regularly employs evolutionary, processual images of dispersal and

[54] For similar projects, see Ezell, *Social Authorship*; Frye, *Pens and Needles;* Goodrich, *Faithful Translators*; Pender and Smith, eds., *Material Cultures*; Malay, ed., *Anne Clifford*; and Wray, "Memory."

[55] The first formulation follows Grosz, *Volatile Bodies*; the second, Braidotti, *Metamorphoses*.

[56] The situational view of women's literary production is adopted by most critics in the field and advocated in the major theoretical collections, including Knoppers, ed., *Cambridge Companion*; Bicks and Summit, eds., *History;* and Suzuki, ed., *History*. Goodrich, "Reconsidering," has productively brought intersectional theory to bear upon this model, with which new materialism (s) generally are aligned.

[57] Braidotti, *Nomadic Subjects*, 10–11.

[58] Beckwith, *Shakespeare and the Grammar of Forgiveness*, 106.

recovery – of ruin and remembrance – to preserve traces of their agency in networks of lived experience.

In the post-Reformation world, death was "a porous threshold."[59] Nowhere is this expressed in more fascinating complexity than in Shakespeare's late plays. In each of the three romances explored in this study, characters pass through this threshold, traversing the spaces between life and death with astonishing ease. The liminal passages of Innogen and Posthumus, Pericles and Marina, Hermione and the necromantic Paulina argue, as Braidotti puts it, that "the spectacle of our death is written obliquely into the script of our temporality, not as a barrier but as a condition of possibility."[60] The skull haunting Holbein's *Ambassadors* (1533), in this view, is not merely a *memento mori* but also a point of departure. If we, and the protagonists of Shakespeare's late plays, are "virtual corpse[s]," we anticipate the generative, transformative movement from the potential to the actual – from the foreknowledge of death to its realization.[61] Holbein's skull is not the absolute limit of his subjects' existence; it is a spectral sign of remembrance, falling obliquely between the observer and the objects perceived, calling us to mark not merely death but the lives affirmed by the brilliant tissue of accessories within which the sitters are enmeshed.

Braidotti's posthuman vision of death, grounded in the immanence of a vital, material subject, challenges the early modern Christian faith in the transcendence of an immortal soul. Nonetheless, my readings of Shakespeare's late plays stress the negotiations of these works with the materiality of death and remembrance as phenomena at which the limits of the human become especially fraught. Glossing Merleau-Ponty's idea of the intertwining of subject and object – the crisscrossing of self and world that is the condition of human experience – Judith Butler writes, "it is quite possible . . . to pursue positions of mastery or self-loss that try to do away with this intertwining, but such pursuits are always partially foiled or struggle constantly against being foiled."[62] One might see the entanglements of the late plays as staging series of such attempts, from Pericles's sea voyage of self-forgetting, to Leontes's delusional domestic tyranny, to the demi-deaths and resurrections of Innogen, Marina, Thaisa, and Hermione. Yet these adventures resolve themselves in the loosening of knots of

[59] Braidotti, *Posthuman*, 95. [60] Braidotti, *Posthuman*, 95. [61] Braidotti, *Posthuman*, 98.
[62] Butler, "Merleau-Ponty," 203–4; and see Jackson, "All is True," 422–5, for the relevance of this passage to his reading of the "haptic rhetoric" of the late plays.

entrelacement as the romance plot calms itself by forging, instead, ties that bind. Sojourns at and across the borders of the human and nonhuman, the living and the dead, end optimistically in the recovery of communities, households, interrelations of kin and kin.

Resonant, certainly, in these rehabilitations are the religious struggles, antipathies, passions, and reconciliations of the Reformation. In each of the romances I study here, a submerged religious or sacramental subtext enables regenerative, reconciliatory outcomes. In my view, Shakespeare utilizes the familiar tropes, images, and experiences of post-Reformation religion across the confessional divide. Itself a strategy of intertwining, Shakespeare's spiritual hybridity works, as Brian Walsh writes, "to braid together disparate spiritual traditions and doctrines."[63] While *Cymbeline*, I argue, makes use of a heretical (that is, Catholic) sacrament to "disanimate" Innogen, she is resurrected under the regenerative sign of Protestant communion.[64] *Pericles* calls the Catholic poet Gower to "stand i' th' gaps" not only between his medieval tale and Shakespeare's audience, but between the Catholic and Protestant ceremonies exploited, in equal measure, throughout the play.[65] Paulina's faith-awakening performance at the close of *The Winter's Tale* is a syncretistic blend of Calvinist reliance on faith alone and proto-Arminian ritual that would reach its height under Archbishop Laud. As Thomas Betteridge suggests, a "post-confessional" Shakespeare attempts a semantic recovery in the late plays as they "look back to a pre-confessional world in which liturgical words, the language of faith, united rather than divided Christians."[66] Symptomatic of the hybrid spiritualities of the late plays, I suggest, is the porous threshold of death through which characters – Innogen, Thaisa, Marina, Hermione – come and go. As if marking the communal lapses and retrievals of religious faith, truth, and identity that constitute the seismic upheavals of the Reformation world, the late plays perform rituals of remembrance staged in the gaps, blurring the borders between the phenomenal world and the alien nation of the dead.

My reading of Shakespeare's romances through the lens of remembrance brings to the fore the features of the more conventionally commemorative works and subjects treated in this study. The plots of dispersal and recollection and patterns of loss and recovery that run through

[63] Walsh, "'A Priestly Farewell,'" 81. See also Mayer, *Shakespeare's Hybrid Faith*; and Hunt, "Syncretistic Religion."

[64] On disanimation, see Shannon, *Accommodated Animal*, 225.

[65] Shakespeare and Wilkins, *Pericles*, 4.4.8.

[66] Betteridge, "Writing Faithfully," 225.

Shakespeare's late plays are characteristic of the innovative approaches to remembrance in the wake of the passage from the old religion to the new. Mystical sleeps and wondrous resurrections are marked by monuments – tombs, tokens, statues, books, and tablets – and attended by deities, ghostly visitations, prophecies, myths, and histories that cause characters and audiences alike to waver between belief and disbelief. Shakespeare's romances embody and exploit the post-Reformation renaissance of remembrance and, with it, the ambivalent retrieval of beliefs and knowledge, marked by astonishing transmissions of objects overtaxed with uncertain, polyvalent meanings. They irresistibly invite recovery, reuse, and renewal.

The figuration and parable of Cyriac's inclusion encapsulate the main interests and approach of this study, and from it I derive the design of my book. As for the myth of amber's feminine origins, it informs women's representations and self-representations in commemorative works interwoven throughout these chapters. At the same time, I recognize that gender encloses each act of remembrance, regardless of the sex of its author. The myth of Phaethon's sisters glosses the transformations of bodies in death as fleshly borders blend with earth, and the processes of commemoration when the body is replaced by the monumental marble of the tomb.

As an object that captures the processual exchanges between the creature and the world, Cyriac's inclusion, moreover, offers a concise figuration of the phenomenal interrelations that sustain negotiations between subject and object, life and death, in remembrance. Natural philosophers in the period observed that the malleable properties of amber – neither liquid nor solid, both prehistoric and ephemeral – rendered the substance indeterminate; a threshold between binaries defining the natural world. Neither fully animate nor inanimate, neither living nor dead, the enclosed being and the viscous substance enfolding it illustrate the embodied and embedded nature of subjectivity, as well as the networks of loss and recovery in which post-Reformation commemoration takes part.[67] In its transmission from Pontano's treatise on magnificence to Achelley's Puritan book of devotions – a progress in which sacramental essence is displaced in a reformed distrust of surfaces – Cyriac's relic demonstrates how memorial artifacts embed and, in turn, influence changing religious beliefs. Elaborating the potency of objects within the doctrinal and confessional shifts

[67] See, for example, Aldrovandi, *Musaeum*, 403–18; and Cardano, *De subtiltate*, 306–7.

from the old religion to the new, Part I of this study, "Signes of Remembrance," examines how the Protestant reconceptualization of the sacraments influences commemoration in sacred and secular works. In each of these chapters, remembrance is predicated upon "a sacramental poetics," the displacement of religious mystery into secular forms that point toward and recall that disallowed substance.[68] The three chapters of Part I are closely interconnected and, paradigmatically, follow the movement of this project, from a close reading of a memorial program erected in a parish church, to a study of a commemorative manuscript by a woman writer, to a chapter on Shakespeare's late play, *Cymbeline*.

Chapter 1, "'A Mousoleum for a Flie': Sidney Montagu and the Sacramental Sign" recovers a repertoire of religious beliefs enclosed in a remarkable memorial for a three-year-old child. Following Henry Montagu's death in 1625, his father installed a memorial comprised of three objects in Barnwell All Saints Church. In addition to an alabaster monument, the memorial program incorporated a thirteenth-century piscina (a basin for washing Communion vessels) and a painted wooden triptych containing a manuscript sheet, "Upon the Birth and death of his deere sonne." This chapter interprets the texts and imagery of the Barnwell monument, illustrating the blending of confessional and political identities and personal, deeply felt emotions in an array of interconnected object whose meanings – both latent and created – move in multiple directions. Investing memorial artifacts with the qualities attributed to the sacraments, Montagu develops and defends a private idolatry in which secular objects acquire the aura of the sacred. While the Barnwell monument engrafts commemoration on the sacramental signs of remembrance, the manuscript triptych turns from the sacramental to the superstitious. Locating commemoration uneasily between private idolatry and communal worship, Montagu's memorial displays the divisions between and the cooperation of religious faith, personal belief, and sacred objects, images, and practices as they move into secular spheres.

Chapter 2 examines how Puritan beliefs are enclosed in memorial texts and objects created by members of the Montagu "monumental circle," placing questions of gender at the center of my discussion. I consider the little-known manuscript, "Letters, Prayers, and Poems," written by Ann Montagu in 1637 and the literary legacies of her mother-in-law, Elizabeth Harington Montagu, alongside the monumental project of union collectively pursued by Elizabeth Montagu's six sons. The Montagu men

[68] Schwartz, *Sacramental Poetics*, 13–17.

intertwine secular and Pauline figurations of secular and spiritual union to construct "permanent memory-traces" celebrating fraternal fellowship.[69] By contrast, Ann Montagu's manuscript engages remembrance within a Puritan conception of the sacrament as a multiplicity of signs experienced through remembrance and interpretation. This processual, evolving sacrament is mirrored in Ann Montagu's evolving art of memory, where scattered signs, bodies, and texts are purposefully recollected and unified. I trace a similar process of dispersal and recollection through the passage of Elizabeth Montagu's legacies, including manuscripts shared by members of the Montagu monumental circle across generations. The Montagu women's commemorative processes make use of the productive intermingling of the female subject, sacramental matter, and the material text to knit together an intergenerational society of saints.

Chapter 3, "Innogen's Needle: Remembrance and Romance in *Cymbeline,*" maps this course of dispersal and recollection onto the romance adventures of Innogen, and explores a similar model of feminine subjectivity in Innogen's fluid blending of subject, sacrament, and text. I explore the perceived intermingling of sacramental matter, femininity, and idolatry in Jachimo's voyeuristic violation of Innogen's chamber, a space where competing views of the nature of the sacrament and ornamentation of the altar blend sacred and secular themes in the allusive density of Innogen's textualities. Reading the chamber's decoration and furniture alongside probate and church inventories, I argue that Jachimo's intrusion translates the chamber into a chantry and entombs Innogen by crafting her as a figuration of the idolatrous Catholic sacrament. A second scene of entombment in the pastoral world of Wales, however, corrects Innogen's necrophilic chamber, placing her in a porous threshold between life and death, where Protestant figures of spiritual diffusion and reincorporation are mobilized to enliven her. Representing Innogen's viscous embodiment of subject, sacrament, and text, Shakespeare answers Jachimo's deadening images by moving his heroine from the sacrament of death to that of life. Embodying, as Merleau-Ponty writes, a "texture that returns to itself and conforms to itself" – a wondrous essence – Innogen claims a regenerative power to control the "contingency [and] chaos" of *Cymbeline*.[70]

The parable of material losses and recoveries scripted by Cyriac's inclusion brings into critical focus the anxieties attending post-Reformation retrievals and reuses of the classical and medieval past. The precarious state of Church of England buildings and the monuments that they housed

[69] Freud, "A Note Upon the 'Mystic Writing Pad."

[70] Merleau-Ponty, *Visible and Invisible*, 146.

profoundly affected the antiquarian project in England, rendering it as much a sacred as a secular undertaking. In Part II of this study, "Monuments of Antiquitie," I turn my attention from sacramental poetics toward antiquarianism, recognizing as I do so the close imbrication of the two spheres of activity. Each of these three chapters examines aspects of commemoration as they pertain not primarily or exclusively to private loss and remembrance, but to monuments that enfold or seek to control social, political, and cultural memories and identities.

Chapter 4, "'The grave is but a Cabinet': Remembrance and Recreation in Post-Reformation London," sets the commemorative strategies of post-Reformation cabinets of curiosities alongside those employed by antiquarians and chorographers, teasing out the connections between the means by which the two genres craft cultural memory. I align John Stow's reclamation of John Gower's monument, erected by the poet before his death in 1408 in the priory of St. Mary Overie (now Southwark Cathedral), with the processes and values guiding reclamations of relics and rarities in the Tradescant collection of curiosities, the "Ark," amassed by two generations of John Tradescants in their Lambeth home. Developing the argument that acts of remembrance are simultaneously acts of recreation, I show how Stow's repossession of Gower's remains and the Tradescants' acquisition of rarities both evade the factual confines of history to reside instead in the evolving field of memory, exploiting its capacity to renew objects and beliefs across time. Binding the two projects is a commitment to immanence rather than transcendence: thus Stow explores the embedding of Gower's virtual corpse in the living cartography of the cathedral's evolving present tense, while the Tradescants' aggressive ravishment of the animal world occurs alongside the retrieval of rarities and botanical specimens that reanimate the Ark's menagerie.[71] The chapter describes a poetics of wonder traversing these projects that preserves the mystery of beliefs and objects (both Catholic and natural) but transforms this aura within "an economy of astonishment."[72] Negotiating pre- and post-Reformation rituals of remembrance, Stow and the Tradescants cultivate narratives that affirm the continuities between past and present and aspire to control remembrance in perpetuity.

Chapter 5, "Shakespearean Reliquaries: *Pericles* and the Ark of Wonder," follows the poetics of wonder outlined in Chapter 4 into the rich seascape of *Pericles*, replete with monuments true and false, to examine Shakespeare's engagement with his collaborator – not George Wilkins, but

[71] Braidotti, *Posthuman*, 98. [72] Daston and Park, *Wonder*, 276.

the "ancient Gower," who rises from the ashes to narrate a plot from his *Confessio Amantis*.[73] I examine *Pericles* as a play of enclosures – cabinets, coffers, chests, and cenotaphs – which give shape to the action and the frame tale as the episodic plot is crafted in the enclosures of Gower's choruses. A tale of literary primogeniture, *Pericles* affirms Shakespeare's performance as heir to moral Gower within a romance of recovery that depends upon reading the play's female characters as both rarities entombed in deadening interiors and as wondrous vessels themselves, stored with good or ill; a reading that aligns femininity with monumentality. Accordingly, I follow Thaisa's coffin from its disposal at sea to its retrieval in the play's cabinet of curiosities, Cerimon's closet, where this "maker's" creative and recreative sovereignty figures that of Gower, the "maker" of the story in the cabinets of his choruses.[74] Exploring Gower's increasingly sophisticated metrical interventions as points of contact between the twin makers Gower and Shakespeare, I trace the transference of this narrative sovereignty in the last acts of *Pericles* from Gower to Shakespeare's Marina. The bearer of "most clear remembrance," Marina is a fluid, nomadic narrator in whose peregrinations the play's shifting, unstable monuments, finally, gain ground.[75] In Marina's embodiment of "Patience gazing on kings' graves," Shakespeare renews Gower's poetics of wonder to affirm the continuing relevance of past things to the cultural present and to display the regenerative art of making an old tale new.[76]

Chapter 6, "'Chain'd up in Alabaster': Awakening Remembrance in *The Winter's Tale* and *Comus*," explores a poetics of proximity common in printed epitaphs, in which authors falsely insist upon composition and performance in the presence of the grave. I suggest that figures of "marmorization" – transformations of bodies into stone – offer succinct figurations of this relocation of traditional rites of remembrance to the textual memory of print. I compare two scenes of the comingling of flesh and stone: Paulina's awakening of Hermione in *The Winter's Tale*, and Sabrina's release of Milton's Lady from her fusion to Comus's enchanted chair in *A Maske Presented at Ludlow Castle, 1634*. This comparison is framed by readings of a monument erected by Blanche Parry (Keeper of Queen Elizabeth I's jewels and books), and the productions of a monumental circle comprised of Alice Spencer, Countess of Derby (patron of Edmund Spenser and John Milton), and her female descendants.

[73] Shakespeare and Wilkins, *Pericles*, Chorus 1.2.
[74] Shakespeare and Wilkins, *Pericles*, 3.2.44 and 4.4.3.
[75] Shakespeare and Wilkins, *Pericles*, 5.3.12.
[76] Shakespeare and Wilkins, *Pericles*, 5.1.129.

Employing a hybrid methodology, I blend historical phenomenology and corporeal feminism in this chapter, treating these biform figures both within the cultural environment of the rise of literacy and as figurations of a female subject for whom the borders between body and world are fluid, unfixed, and permeable. Shakespeare and Milton locate these scenes of reanimation between truth and falsehood, and between spectacle and silence, in terms that parallel the migration of remembrance from embodiment to print. If the hybrid women of *The Winter's Tale* and *Comus* become specters haunting the interiority of the reader's imagination, however, their embodiment in Parry's and Spencer's monumental projects recovers their voices by imagining the subject, in death as in life, as insistently material.

I conclude with a brief comparison of two works that stand at the beginning and the end of the period studied in this book, a ballad commemorating the death of Henry VII, alternatively attributed to John Skelton and Stephen Hawes, and the commemorative works of America's "tenth muse," Anne Bradstreet. Considering the confluence of print and privacy, religious and secular arts of remembrance, and the distances traversed by these authors in crafting personal and national narratives of the past, I map this project's transmission of early modern models of remembrance from old worlds to new.

PART I

"Signes of Remembrance"

CHAPTER 1

"A Mousoleum for a Flie"
Sidney Montagu and the Sacramental Sign

> Nay of all monuments that parents can leave behind them, there is none (as one saith) like to a vertuous son.
>
> – Robert Hill[1]

> [T]he bodies of Flies, Pismires, and the like, which are said oft-times to be included in Amber, are not real but representative. If so ... Cardans Mousoleum for a Flie [is] a meer phansie. But hereunto we know not how to assent, as having met with some whose reals made good their representments.
>
> – Sir Thomas Browne[2]

A Cartography of Belief

In a spirited condemnation of religious images and idols, the 1563 *Homyly agaynst Peryll of Idolatry* sets forth stunning catalogs of the materials with which pre-Reformation churches in England were beautified. "The corruption of these latter days hath brought to the Church infinite multitudes of ymages," the sermon complains. Church doctors have decked all parts of the church:

> with golde and sylver, paynted with colours, set them with stone and pearle, clothed them with sylkes and precious vestures, phantasing untruely that to be the chiefe deckyng and adornyng of the Temple of God, and that all people shoulde be the more moved to the due reverence of the same.[3]

Poised uncertainly in the difficult succession of Edwardian reform, Marian restoration, and a nascent Elizabethan Settlement, the sermon brings to the mind's eye the rich inventory of materials it seeks to dispel. Vexations

[1] Hill, "Epistle Dedicatorie," in Perkins, *Godly and Learned Exposition ... upon the Revelation*, fol. A2^{v}.
[2] Browne, *Pseudodoxia epidemica*, 82, referring to Cardano's *De subtilitate*, 307. See Introduction.
[3] Church of England, *Homyly agaynst Peryll of Idolatry*, fol. 12^{v}. Subsequent citations are to this edition and appear parenthetically.

of the eye abound: parishioners, bedazzled and perplexed by fraudulent idols, are led into "the pit of dampnable Idolatry" by bishops, "blynded by the bewytchyng of Images, lyke blynde guydes of the blynde" (fol. 61ᵛ). While concerned with stemming the "phantasing" of idolatry, the sermon also seeks to control overzealous iconoclasts, "lest private persons uppon colour of destroying of Images should make any sturre or disturbance in the common wealthe," taking into their own hands "the redresse of suche publique enormities [that] appertayneth to the Magistrates, and suche as in authoritie onlye" (fol. 19ʳ). The sermon treats laypeople alternatively as sheep, easily led or misled by clergy, and as wolves, liable to ravage the fabric of the church.

The homily's conflicted approach to vision and blindness – at once revealing the dangers of idolatry and concealing the violence of iconoclasm – and to pastoral care and censure bespeak anxieties traversing this turbulent era toward sacred objects and the sacred spaces where religion was performed. The laity had been remote witnesses to the Catholic Mass, which was conducted by priests behind screens that divided the chancel from the nave. The reformed liturgy, by contrast, viewed the church as a community of like-minded souls and encouraged religious fellowship and conformity in words rather than images. While distinctions between pre- and post-Reformation liturgies were far from absolute, English Protestants, from Puritans to high churchmen, saw the laity's participation in Communion as a fundamental departure from Catholic practice.[4] Queen Elizabeth's first Royal Injunctions, issued in 1559, ordered that "the holy table" should be:

> set in the place where the altar stood . . . saving when the Communion of the Sacrament is to be distributed; at which time the same shall be so placed in good sort within the chancel, as whereby the minister may be more conveniently heard of the communicants in his prayer and ministration, and the communicants also more conveniently and in more number communicate with the said minister.[5]

At the end of Elizabeth's reign, Richard Hooker's *Lawes of Ecclesiasticall Politie* codified the nature of Church of England buildings as public places whose architecture and fabric were suited to the communal celebration of

[4] See Duffy, *Stripping of the Altars*; Whiting, *Reformation*, 3–21; and Addleshaw, *High Church Tradition*.

[5] See "Royal Injunctions of Queen Elizabeth I, 1559," in Frere and Kennedy, eds., *Visitation Articles*, vol. III, 27–8. See Aston, "Public Worship," on resistance to church reforms, including the removal of chancel screens.

Protestant sacraments. "It behooveth that the place where God should be served by the whole Church," he writes, "be a publique place, for the avoiding of privie conventicles, which covered with pretense of religion, may serve unto dangerous practices."[6] As the altar was replaced by "the Lord's board,"[7] around which parishioners took Communion together, the chancel was no longer a privie conventicle but became instead a "communion room."[8]

The resilient, ever-changing Church of England building is a monument to the steadfast, long-suffering body of the English faithful. The century and a half following Henry VIII's split with Rome consisted of oscillating periods of embellishment and defacement of church buildings and fabric. Rood screens, altars, and images destroyed under Edward VI were restored by Mary. Widespread iconoclasm in 1559 was calmed by Elizabeth's "vexed (and state-legislated) imbrication of image and word," maintained for half a century by royal and clerical equivocation with regard to "things indifferent."[9] From Hooker to Laud, the high church defense of ceremony and splendor led to beautifications that were, in turn, undone by iconoclasts incited by parliamentary ordinances of the 1640s sentencing "all monuments of superstition and idolatry" to destruction.[10]

In post-Reformation churches, discarded materials and mysteries were often recovered, and sometimes redeployed. From the Puritan perspective, the return of repudiated practices, images, and objects revealed the dangerous persistence of traditional devotion. William Perkins's *Reformed Catholicke*, published a year before Hooker's *Lawes of Ecclesiasticall Politie*, identifies areas of agreement between Catholicism and the reformed faith, but concludes, finally, that the "union of two religions can never be made more then the Union of light and darknes."[11] For Hooker, the danger lay

[6] Hooker, *Lawes*, 20. [7] Nicholas Ridley, quoted in Yule, "James VI and I," 187.
[8] Yule, "James VI and I," 193.
[9] Fleming, "Wounded Walls," 16. See, for example, Hooker, *Lawes*, 25, 157, and 162.
[10] England and Wales, Parliament, Ordinance ... 28 August 1643, fol. A2r. On the high church movement from Hooker to Laud, see Addleshaw, *High Church Tradition*.
[11] Perkins, *Reformed Catholicke*, title page and fol. ¶2r. There are numerous points of agreement between Hooker and Perkins, but ultimately Hooker's *via media* asserted more continuities between the old religion and the new than Perkins would allow. See Lake, *Anglicans and Puritans?*, 145–97; and MacCulloch, *Reformation*, esp. 382–93 and 502–28. Sidney Montagu was Perkins's student at Christ College, Cambridge, and was a conforming Calvinist; at once a Puritan and a Royalist who sought a *via media* in his political career. Chapter 2 discusses the moderate Puritanism shared by the Montagus. In this chapter, I am interested in Protestant tenets held in common at key moments of doctrinal definition and recognizable by individuals approaching memorial objects. Thus I move from the early Elizabethan period to the Civil War, and doctrinally between Hooker and Perkins, while remaining attentive to contextual and theological differences.

not in recovered rites and objects themselves but in the easily clouded understanding of worshippers. Thus the poison that "privie conventicles" presented lay not in unorthodox practices per se, but in breeding suspicion and fear of "those actions, which," according to Hooker, "in them selves [are] holy."[12] Mindful of "how dull, how heavie & almost how without sense the greatest part of the common multitude everie where is," Hooker retrieves abandoned ceremonies in terms whose subtlety may have escaped the laity:

> Are we to forsake any true opinion because Idolaters have maintained it? . . . Not therefore whatsoever idolaters have either thought or done, but let whatsoever they have either thought or done *idolatriouslie, be so farre-forth* abhorred. For of that which is good even in evill things God is author.[13]

Artifacts of God's authorship were commonly unearthed in Church of England buildings, often in providential circumstances and with supernatural implications. The divine influence of consecration pervades Simon Gunton's harrowing account of the destruction of Peterborough Cathedral in 1643, a force that ensured the miraculous preservation of some artifacts and avenged the destruction of others. "There was some good from that evil," Gunton concludes, when the high altar was demolished because of its "Popery, and superstition" and two ancient chests were revealed, "in each of which were the Bones of a man [and] a plate of lead in each chest whereon the name of a person was engraven."[14] A discovery in St. Ann Blackfriars after the Great Fire similarly affirmed God's authorship of good even in evil things, uncovering objects whose careers map the shifting course of post-Reformation belief. In the cellar, workmen found "a kind of Cupboard" where four pots of pewter contained "four humane Heads, unconsumed, preserved, as it seems, by Art." John Strype examined one of these caskets, "inscribed in a scrawling Character (which might be used in the times of King Henry VIII.) J. CORNELIUS," and surmised the heads were those of "some zealous Priests or Friers, executed for Treason . . . for denying the King's Supremacy." The artifacts were sold; one to an apothecary, another to the parish clerk who "got Money by shewing of it." "It is probable," Strype speculates, "they were at last . . . conveyed abroad; and now become Holy Relicks."[15]

[12] Hooker, *Lawes*, 20. [13] Hooker, *Lawes*, 183 and 21–2.

[14] Gunton, *History*, 98. Subsequent citations are to page numbers in this edition and appear parenthetically. Gunton was a priest at Peterborough during the iconoclasm of 1643. He died in 1676, and *History* was published posthumously from his manuscripts.

[15] Strype, *Survey*, 2.3.191. For similar recoveries set in the context of early modern antiquarianism, see Woolf, *Social Circulation*, 221–56.

The monument erected by Sir Sidney Montagu in the chancel of the parish church of Barnwell All Saints following his son's death in 1625 is an object preserved against all odds (see Figure 1.1). The reformed conversion of chancels into sites for communal worship often meant that funeral monuments installed in those desirable locations were dismantled and moved.[16] The chancel housing the tomb of three-year-old Henry Montagu was spared when the congregation merged with that of nearby St. Andrew's in 1821 and All Saints was pulled down four years later.[17] In the remains of the church today – a small, intimate room appropriate for a toddler's tomb – an alabaster obelisk rises above Henry Montagu's erect effigy. Two additional elements of the memorial program are entombed behind unmarked wood panels near the altar. In one cupboard is a thirteenth-century piscina (see Figure 1.2), where the consecrated wine remaining after Communion was washed into the consecrated ground of the churchyard. A second cupboard on the adjacent wall contains a painted wooden box bearing the word *Posteris* – to Posterity – in gold lettering on the exterior panels (see Figure 1.3). This triptych opens to reveal painted interior wings (see Figure 1.4) and, mounted on the back panel, a single manuscript sheet entitled "Upon the Birth and death of his deere sonne, Henry Mountagu, S[i]r Sidney Mountagu, Knight, Anno D[omi]ni 1627" (see Plate 1).

Montagu's memorial program exploits the interplay of revelation and concealment and of private and communal worship emergent in post-Reformation ideas of the sacraments and the sacred spaces where they were celebrated. Although the Barnwell piscina and manuscript box were enclosed in paneling decades after the program's installation,[18] Montagu situates his program between secular and sacred, public and private concerns. He does so, first, by investing memorial artifacts with the qualities attributed to the Protestant sacraments, and, secondly, by developing and

[16] See Yule, "James VI and I," 201; and on the disinterment and removal of bones more generally, see Schwyzer, *Archaeologies*, 108–50.

[17] See Bridges, *History … of Northamptonshire*, vol. II, 214–16, on the former church building; and see Pevsner and Cherry, *Northamptonshire*, 102, on the current structure.

[18] The paneling was installed by Ralph Montagu, 1st Duke of Montagu (d. 1709). Although his motives are undocumented, he was renowned for the renovations of his houses in Northamptonshire and Bloomsbury. He may have intended, therefore, to beautify the church rather than to conceal the manuscript box and piscina. See *ODNB*; and Wise, *Montagus*, 37–46 and 76–87. Owing to the concealment of the manuscript box, there has not been any published scholarship to date on either Montagu's textual monument or the memorial as a unified program. The sculptural monument has also been neglected by scholarship, having received only a passing comment in Llewellyn, "'[An] Impe entombed,'" 60; Llewellyn, *Funeral Monuments*, 359; and Esdaile, *English Church Monuments*, 123.

Figure 1.1 William Wright (attrib.), Monument for Henry Montagu (1626). Barnwell All Saints.
Author's photograph.

Figure 1.2 Piscina (thirteenth century). Barnwell All Saints. Author'sphotograph.

Figure 1.3 Manuscript box (exterior) (1627). Barnwell All Saints. Author's photograph.

Figure 1.4 Manuscript box (interior) (1627). Barnwell All Saints. Author's photograph.

defending a private idolatry, a "superstition," in which secular objects acquire the aura of the sacred.

Approaching the Barnwell memorial as both a product of and an artifact within the chancel's cartography of evolving beliefs, this chapter responds to a repertoire of religious beliefs embedded in Montagu's memorial program. This recovery of an unknown child's diminutive tomb – a task that is itself, perhaps, a mausoleum for a fly – studies the material "incarnation" of beliefs in a particular time and place, and at a specific moment within local and national theological debate and definition.[19] Set between sacred and secular concerns, monuments trouble the relationship between religion and a secularism that has, until recently, dominated contemporary treatments of early modern culture and beliefs. It is symptomatic of our critical tendency to subsume religious difference within secular familiarity that current observers, centuries later, appear so easily to understand

[19] See Appadurai, "Introduction," in *Social Life of Things*, 3–62, who sees objects as sites "where collectively shared values are incarnated" (30); and see Gordon and Rist, "Introduction," in *Arts of Remembrance*, 4, for the view of artifacts as "reveal[ing] the extent to which theology, so often seen as an abstraction, found material expression in remembrance."

projects such as Montagu's. His memorial is recognizable, even mundane: building a monument to paternal fondness, Montagu remembers the life and mourns the death of "a wittie and hopeful child, tender and deere in the sight of his parents."[20] Yet our ease with the project's sentiment should not obscure the temporal strangeness of its encounter with the "reservoir of foundational stories, tropes, and exegetical habits" that Graham Hammill and Julia Reinhard Lupton see as characteristic of "religion not fully reducible to culture." "Not only an element in culture," they argue, religion is a force that "instantiates discourses of value that aim to transcend culture, by creating trans-group alliances and affiliations around shared narratives, commandments, and principles."[21] Montagu reaches backward to root his monumental matter in sacred images and objects shaped by New Testament faith, and forward to embed his son's memory in the corporate body of the perpetual Church. Considered on its own terms, his project demonstrates how, for post-Reformation men and women, as David Aers writes, "narratives and memories of 'the time-bound and material world'" – the tragic drowning of a three-year-old boy – could "be ordered toward and around . . . the sacramental sign."[22]

The first section of this chapter explores how Montagu's memorial program incorporates the Protestant understanding of the sacraments as "signes of remembrance" in order to evade the threat of idolatry with a

[20] Quotations from the Barnwell memorial are transcribed from the objects on site. Sidney Montagu claims authorship of the manuscript and responsibility for the monument, but the execution of the stone monument, and thus the authorship of its iconography, is less certain. The Barnwell manuscript and Montagu's "Valida Consolatio" (BL MS Add 28560) display the same hand, confirming that Montagu authored and executed both. He or his wife may have painted the images on the Barnwell manuscript box and parchment,or employed an arms painter to do so. A second version of the manuscript survives in the Northamptonshire Record Office (NRO, uncatalogued): see n74. I am indebted to Crispin Powell for directing my attention to the NRO copy. The monument was attributed to Gerard Christmas by Esdaile, *English Church Monuments*, 123, but this is persuasively challenged by White, *Biographical Dictionary*, 18–20. On stylistic grounds, William Wright is probably the sculptor: see White, *Biographical Dictionary*, 155. The painting on the monument base is evidently done by a professional. On the activities of arms painters in the counties, see Wagner and Squibb, "Deputy Heralds." I am grateful to Robert Yorke for providing a copy of this article and for his generous comments on the manuscript box.

As collaborative works, monuments often cannot be attributed with certainty to individual authors, and therefore they challenge claims of authorial intention. In the absence of documentation, Montagu's motives cannot be retrieved. My reading of the Barnwell program does not rest upon asserting his intentions. Rather, my aim is to describe a repertoire of conventional religious and affective signs embedded in monumental objects that were recognized as taking part in the theological and doctrinal debates surrounding the creation of the memorial.

[21] Hammill and Lupton, "Sovereigns," 1.

[22] Aers, "New Historicism," 250, quoting Gallagher and Greenblatt, *Practicing New Historicism*, 81. See also Schwartz, *Sacramental Poetics*, 9, which demonstrates that "the Eucharist is a rich site for investigation about the infusion of sacramentality into the secular world."

discretionary insight capable of perceiving essential grace within the sacred object.[23] His memorial is a gesture of religious fellowship and, at the same time, a private performance enacted in the shadow of idolatry. Creating a "dead and dombe Image" (*Homyly*, fol. 42^{v}) of his son, Montagu laments a personal loss. Yet he understands the signs of the sacrament as outward reflections of inward grace – as Perkins teaches, the sacrament's "spirituall and internall actions" shape its "sensible and externall" parts – and he turns this faith toward preserving his son's memory.[24]

In Section 2, I focus on Montagu's manuscript box, describing his turn from the sacramental to the superstitious in this object as typical of the way religious faith and personal belief blend in the period as sacred objects, images, and practices move into secular spheres. Locating remembrance between privacy and community, Montagu's memory box suggests how, in the larger polity, spiritual and political identities crystallize in dynamic interrelations between individuals, sacred artifacts, and their secular shadows.

Negotiating the sacred object in his act of commemoration, Montagu is able to "make good his representment" of his son's brief incarnation with his "real": divine grace embodied in the incarnate savior. In the imagery of his memorial program, erected in the Communion room at Barnwell, two fallen sons – one real, the other representative – are remembered and resurrected by loving fathers.

1 The cranie of the eye

Simon Gunton recounts an episode during the destruction of Peterborough Cathedral that illustrates the centrality of vision not only to idolatry but also to iconoclasm. Upon seeing "the Picture of our Saviour seated on a Throne," several soldiers cried out, "This is the Idol they worship and adore," and ruined the image with musket fire. "The odiousness of this Act," Gunton supposes,

[23] Perkins, *Reformed Catholicke*, 370. Hooker offers a similar definition of the sacrament as a "signe of remembrance": see *Lawes*, 158. Interpretations of the sacraments as commemorative are not exclusively Protestant, but reformers, following Calvin, stressed this aspect of sacramental matter as a way of asserting God's real presence while at the same time denying transubstantiation. See Perkins, *Reformed Catholicke*, 185–204; and see Philips, *Reformation of Images;* Sheehan, "Altars of Idols"; and Wooding, "Remembrance." On commemoration and incarnationalism for Church of England conformists, see Addleshaw, *High Church Tradition*, 177–84.

[24] Perkins, *Golden Chaine*, 111; and see Figure 3.4. See also Hooker, *Lawes*, 128: "as the soule doth organise the body, so the inward grace of the sacraments may teacheth what serveth best for their outward form."

> gave occasion to a common Fame very rife at that time ... That divine Vengeance had signally seised on some of the principal Actors, That one was struck blind upon the place by a Re-bound of his Bullet; That another dyed mad a little after; neither of which I can certainly attest ... I could never find any other judgment befall them then, but that of a mad blind Zeal, wherewith these persons were certainly possest. (*History*, 334–5)

When the soldiers exchange the "blynde zeal" of idolatry (*Homyly*, fol. 28^{r}) for the "mad blind Zeal" of iconoclasm, their punishment is to suffer the literal loss of sight and sense that their violence figuratively enacts. Gunton's equivocation about the truth of the tale may acknowledge the fact that this judgment, if true, affirms the potency of the dead image whose supposed impotence prompted the soldiers' attack.

Nearly a century after the Elizabethan *Homyly agaynst Peryll of Idolatry* was introduced at the pulpit and in print, the essence of sacred images and objects remained mysterious, and their efficacy continued to be contested. When Hooker insists that God is the author "of that which is good even in evill things," he relies upon the discretionary insight of clergymen, if not parishioners, to recognize the value of ceremonies, including those wrongly rejected as idolatrous. The early Elizabethan effort to shift the focus of proscriptions on idols from object to subject – from "the material church" where "filthy and dead images" have no place, to the banished *behavior* of image worship, "though [images] be of themselves things indifferent" (*Homyly*, fol. 21^{r}) – sought to sever the potent link between essence and matter in Catholic sacraments and images.[25] Yet the assumed power of sacred objects lingered well after their repudiation. While the *Homyly* asserts that images are not "wicked of them selves" (fol. 65^{r}), it vexes all images displayed in sacred sites as inciting the viewer to the "spiritual fornication" (fol. 66^{v}) of idolatry. "As a shadowe foloweth the bodye when the sunne shyneth," the sermon reasons, "so Idolatry foloweth and cleaveth to the publique hanging of Images in Churches and Temples" (fols. 65$^{r\text{-}v}$).[26] The idolater's love affair with the dead object recasts the Christian body, "the Holy Temple and lively ymage of God" (fol. 21^{r}), as an effigy of the beloved. So strong is the sway of this desire to reanimate the dead that the *Homyly*, citing "the .8. Chapter in the Booke of Wysdome," locates the origin of idolatry in "a blinde love of a fond father, framing for his comfort an Image of his sonne, being dead, so at the last

[25] Aston, *England's Iconoclasts*, 320–4, demonstrates that Elizabeth's personal edits of the *Homyly* largely redefined idols as "things indifferent."

[26] See Sheehan, "Sacred and Profane."

men fell to the worshipping of the Image of him whom they did know to bee dead" (fol. 66r).[27] Perkins numbers among images approved by God those that "serve to keepe in memorie friends deceased whome we reverence," but traces the origin of their abuse to "the Romane Church." "For in the daies after the Apostles," he explains, "men used privately to keep the pictures of their friends departed: and this practice after crept into the open congregation, and at last superstition getting head, images began to be worshipped."[28]

While idolaters err in deifying images and objects, iconoclasts commit a similar offense. Their violence is not directed toward benign objects but toward those whose potency – albeit more representative than real – must be utterly overthrown. The iconoclast's engagement with the image responds to the object's power with open force or parodic inversion: in the church at Yaxley, Gunton reports, soldiers "break open the Church doors, piss in the Font, and then baptize a horse and mare, using the solemn words of Baptism, and signing them with the sign of the cross" (*History*, 337). "False feigned" monuments, whose mimicry of life seemed to assert an occult connection between living subject and dead object, were equally vulnerable to attack.[29] Sir Humphrey Orme, for example, "outlived his own Monument, and lived to see him self carried in Effigie on a souldiers back, to the publick Market-place, there to be sported withal, a Crew of Souldiers going before in procession, some with Surplices, some with Organ pipes, to make up the solemnity" (Gunton, *History*, 336).

The site of these interactions between subject and object is "the cranie of the eye," as Richard Brathwait calls it; a material threshold where the rays emitted by the eye mingle with those emitted by the object.[30] "As the eye of all other Sences is most needful, so of all others it is most hurtfull," Brathwait warns, since "there is no passage more easie for the entry of vice."[31] Embodied in the eye, vision approximates touch, a notion captured in Andrea Alciato's uncanny image of the seeing hand (see Figure 1.5). Illustrating the motto, "Νῆφε, καὶ μέμνησ᾽ἀπιστεῖν. ἄρθρα ταῦτα τῶν φρενῶν" (Be sober and remember not to be too rashly credulous: these are the limbs of the mind), the disembodied hand figures the

[27] The apocryphal *Book of Wisdom* was ubiquitously cited by medieval writers to locate the origins of idolatry in euhemerism. See Cooke, "Euhemerism"; and Gayk, *Image, Text, and Religious Reform*, 126–34.

[28] Perkins, *Reformed Catholicke*, 170–1.

[29] Elizabeth I, *Proclamation* (1560). For discussion, see Marshall, *Beliefs and the Dead*, 169–77.

[30] Brathwait, *Essaies*, 3. [31] Brathwait, *Essaies*, 3.

Figure 1.5 Andrea Alciato, *Emblematum libellus* (Venice: Aldus, 1546), sig. 28v.

naive mistaking of appearances for truths: "*Ecce oculata manus credens id quod videt*" (Behold the hand with the eye, believing what it sees).[32] Alciato's contrast between the credulity of the seeing hand and the sobriety of the limbs of the mind is cast by Brathwait as the opposition of bodily vision to spiritual insight: "It is against reason, that the greater light should be extinguished by the lesser; the eye of the soule, by the eye of the bodie."[33] The overcoming of this greater light by the lesser is the unschooled passion that precipitates idolatry: "to desyre an Image of God commeth of infidelitie," the *Homyly* teaches, "thynking not God to be present except they might see some signe or ymage of him" (fol. 43r). The fondness of idolatry is a symptom of the faulty, credulous eye, prone to mistaking the dead image for the living God.

Sidney Montagu's monument for his son is informed by Reformation discourse of idolatry, at whose center is the distracted eye, easily taken in by surfaces and suffering a metamorphopsia that amounts to "the blyndnes of false superstition" (*Homyly*, fol. 36v). Henry Montagu's effigy – a life-sized portrait of a lovely boy – is one such surface. The image of his son threatens to possess Montagu's eye and obstruct his view, preventing him from seeing beyond the fact of the body buried beneath the tomb. Read in this way, the tomb is merely a monument to the lost body, one that finds a poignant counterpart in the response of Montagu's brother, Henry, Earl of Manchester, to a son's conversion to Catholicism. "[Your] Letter I take

[32] Alciato, *Emblematum libellus*, sig. 28v. [33] Brathwait, *Essaies*, 5.

into my hands," Manchester writes to his son Walter, "as he did the Urne of his sonnes ashes to shed over it *veras lachrymas*." If the beam in Montagu's eye is a father's idolatrous longing for the dead flesh of his son, the mote blurring Manchester's vision is a father's awareness of the eternal death of a son's immortal soul, the irrevocable surrender of a "lost child."[34]

In another text, however, Montagu achieves something of his brother's spiritual insight, prescribing a cure for the despair caused by a blindness that approximates death. Montagu presented a manuscript meditation, "Valida Consolatio" (see Figure 1.6) to his mother, Elizabeth Harington Montagu, on New Year's Day, 1614, offering "a cordiall for th[e] common disease" of despair (fol. 2[r]) and specific consolation for the blindness that she experienced in her old age.[35] To comfort his mother, Montagu casts the body and its senses as "things indifferent" when measured against the spiritual insight that leads to true comfort: "But in the want or privation of the outward thinges or outward senses consists neither miseries nor consolation," he assures his mother, since "you have the inward sight of light of the soule, you have attained this stronge Consolacion" (fol. 3[r]).

To illustrate this consolation grounded in the "inward sight of light," Montagu turns to an Old Testament episode that condenses the themes of blindness and insight in the context of idolatry:

> If wee had all the pleasures and happiness that this life could afforde... yet we were but miserable whensoever wee remembered the hand writing before Belshazzar, *mene mene tekell eupharsin*, that our daies were nombred, that our joys should have an end, here was a discomfort enough to make every joint of us to tremble in our greatest joletie. (fols. 8[r-v])

Like Alciato's seeing hand, the disembodied finger that writes on Belshazzar's palace wall urges sobriety and caution.[36] The script appears as a material witness to the king's iconoclastic removal of golden vessels from the temple of Jerusalem to furnish his feast, where he and his guests idolatrously toast "gods of silver, and gold, of brass, iron, wood, and stone, which see not, nor hear, nor know" (Daniel 5:18). At the sight of this menacing apparition, Belshazzar is filled with the dread of an unspeakable foreknowledge: "his thoughts troubled him, so that the joints of his loins

[34] Montagu, *Coppy of a Letter Sent*, 11 and 20. Manchester was the author of one of the period's most popular arts of dying, printed shortly after the death of his namesake at Barnwell. See his *Contemplatio mortis [Manchester al mondo]*.

[35] BL Add MS 28560, fol. 5[r]. Subsequent citations appear parenthetically.

[36] Daniel 5.5. All biblical citations are to the King James Version (1611) and appear parenthetically.

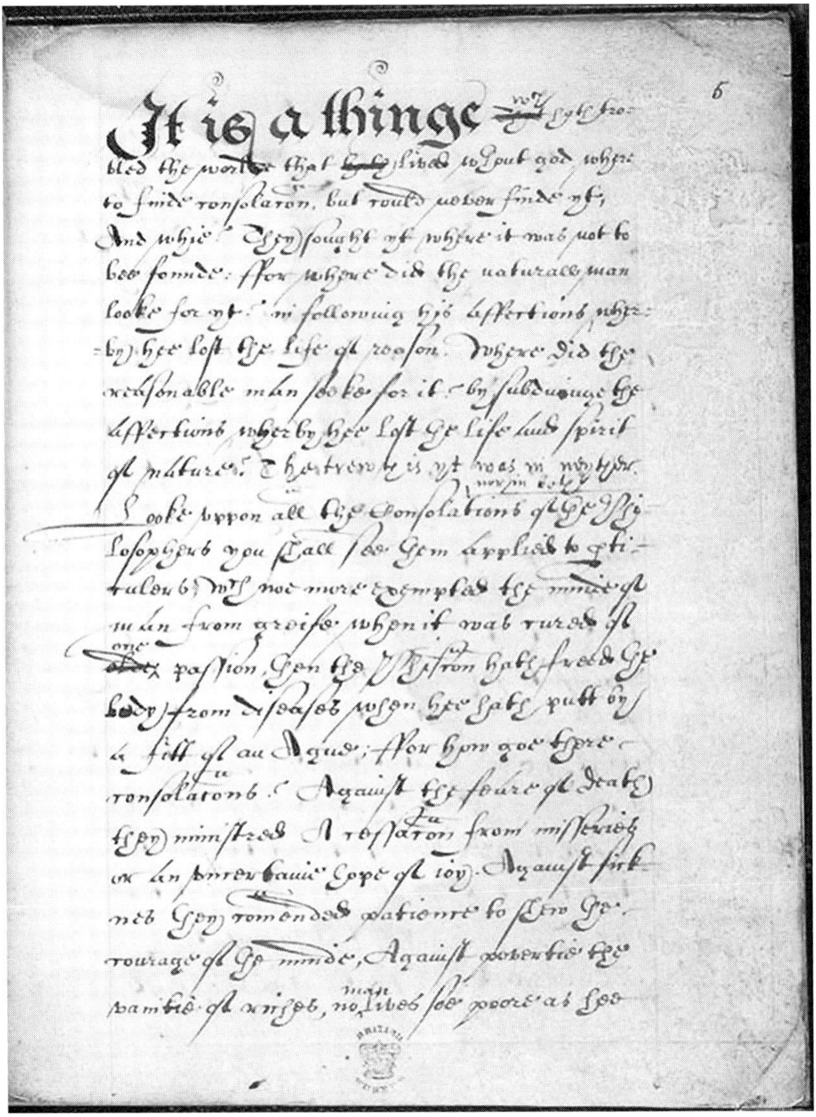

6

It is a thinge [illegible] hath tro-
bled the worlde that they liued wthout god where
to finde consolacon, but could never finde yt,
And why? They sought yt where it was not to
bee founde: ffor where did the naturall man
looke for yt? in following his affections where-
-by hee lost the life of reason. Where did the
reasonable man seeke for it? by subdueinge the
affections whereby hee lost the life and spirit
of nature. The trewth is yt was in neither.
Looke uppon all the Consolations of the Philosophers you shall see them applied to parti-
culers wch noe more exempted the minde of
man from greife when it was cured of
one passion, then the Phisition hath freed the
body from diseases when hee hath putt by
a fitt of an Ague; ffor how goe there
consolatons? Against the feare of death
they ministred a cessation from miseries
or an uncertaine hope of ioy. Against sick-
nes they commended patience to shew the
courage of the minde, Against povertie the
vanitie of riches, noe man liues soe poore as hee

Figure 1.6 Sydney Mountagu, "Valida Consolatio" (1614), fol. 6r.
© The British Library Board. Add MS 28560.

were loosed, and his knees smote one against another" (Daniel 5:6). Appearing as undeniable matter, written "over against the candlestick upon the plaister of the wall" (Daniel 5:5), this icon responds to the material practices of iconoclasm and idolatry in which Belshazzar indulges, repaying these deadening acts by foretelling the death that the king (knowingly) has earned. When the natural wisdom of the court astrologers cannot decipher the text, Daniel's "light and understanding and excellent wisdom" easily penetrate the intractable figure to reveal its meaning and to remind Belshazzar of what he already knows: "thou knewest all this, but hast lifted up thyself against the Lord of heaven" (Daniel 5:14, 21–2).[37]

Adapting the Old Testament text to his handbook of Christian comfort, Montagu encourages his mother to allay her sorrow by reading with spiritual insight the text inscribed on her heart, to recognize in Daniel's typological inward light her own "inward sight of light." For Montagu, this sacred sign is above all a sign of remembrance: the implicit power of the sacred object becomes explicit in Daniel's interpretation. In exchange for Belshazzar's false comfort, the proceeds of the bodily eye, Montagu posits true consolation as the certainty of salvation lodged in the mind's eye as it recalls and meditates on God's scripted word.

The Barnwell monument embeds this notion of inward sight, replacing the statue's blind eyes with the trace of divinity animating the "Temple and lively ymage of God" (*Homyly*, fol. 21^{r}) that the effigy recalls. Although the eyes of Henry Montagu's effigy are now vacant, they were originally painted, alert and forward looking, to enhance the liveliness of the lifeless portrait.[38] The apparent idolatry in the painted face, either of the living or dead, condemned effigies as counterfeits. When the *Homyly* complains, "as lyttle gyrles playe with lyttle puppettes, so be these decked Images greate puppettes for olde fooles to playe with" (fol. 77^{v}), it is hard not to see Henry Montagu's effigy as a doll, animated to provide his grieving father an imitation of life. "Valida Consolatio," however, glosses Montagu's project at Barnwell by endorsing the spiritual insight that translates loss to gain, corruptible flesh to sainthood. The blind eyes of

[37] For discussion of the episode in Daniel, see Fleming, "Wounded Walls," 19–20.

[38] An estimate for repairs to the monument dated July 26, 1989, now in the Barnwell All Saints Church Survey, CARE 28/302, File 902, Doc. 902.1, states that it was not possible at that time to detect whether the effigy displayed original polychrome, although some of the heraldry did. The estimate recommends repainting. There is no record that this work was done, but the contrast of bright coloring on the effigy and the natural stone of the face suggests repainting. For a detailed discussion of the use of polychrome in relation to iconoclastic suspicion of visual imagery, see Llewellyn, *Funeral Monuments*, 237–69.

Figure 1.7 William Wright (attrib.), Monument for Henry Montagu (detail) (1626). All Saints Barnwell. Author's photograph.

the Barnwell effigy invite this spiritual insight, the judgment required to discern the good that proceeds from evil things, whether a mother's blindness or a son's premature death. Understanding monuments as signs of remembrance that "may with choice and discretion be used,"[39] Montagu presents the effigy not as a portrait, but as a figuration of his son's salvation.

Around this figure, an allusive iconography transforms the child's death from tragedy to comedy (see Figure 1.7). In the central register, Henry's effigy stands upright on a base embellished with waves, recalling the boy's death by drowning and figuring his salvation through Baptism. He holds a scroll whose motto, "Lord, give me of that water," quotes the Samaritan

[39] Hooker, *Lawes*, 152. Perkins distinguishes between approved images for "civill use" and their idolatrous abuse: see *Reformed Catholicke*, 168–82. His argument that memorial images are approved by God may be construed as permitting "civil," secular monuments, used with discretion, to be installed in sacred sites.

woman's request for living water in John 4:15. Below the effigy's feet is a gold cup, encircled by a paraphrase of Psalm 51:12, "Poure on me the joy of thy salvation." The final iconographical elements appear on either side of this object, also amid the waters: a large, disembodied foot is carved on either side of the pedestal, the first inscribed, "Not my feete only," and the second continuing the quotation from John 13:9, "But also my hands and head." The inscriptions allude to the *pedilavium*, the Gospel episode in which Jesus washes the disciples' feet at the Last Supper. When Peter refuses to allow Jesus to perform this servile act, he learns that cleansing is a condition of salvation and insists, overzealously, that his hands and head should also be washed.

The saint's disembodied feet, like Alciato's seeing hand, give material form to the interaction of body and spirit, sight and insight, within the transformational processes of religion and remembrance. They interrogate and ultimately validate the use of monumental effigies as prompts to memory. Alluding to the *pedilavium*, they recall the incarnate savior on whose words and actions the sacraments and rites of the church are modeled. As such, the feet are both emblematic and effigial, calling to mind the absent-present body of Christ in the precise moment when the water used in the *pedilavium* becomes the spiritual water of Baptism ("If I wash thee not, thou hast no part with me," Jesus tells Peter in John 13:8) and the bread and wine of the Last Supper become, for the first time, the sanctified body of Christ in the Eucharist. Memorializing his son, Montagu also commemorates the Son of God, whose humanity substantiates the tomb containing the material remnant of Henry Montagu's brief incarnation.

St. Peter's sculpted feet continue the monument's theme of salvation by water, and also introduce into its iconography a doctrinal debate that, for parents in post-Reformation England, was a matter of life and death. Reformed exegeses of the *pedilavium* saw its central image as figuring carnal sin. Calvin explains, "all the affections and cares, which are worldly, are called the feete metaphorycallye," while Erasmus goes further to argue that "feete [represent] the affeccions of minde."[40] If the feet represent the blemishes of sin, they implicate even the "tender and deere" three-year-old mourned at Barnwell: as Calvin reminds us, the *pedilavium* demonstrates above all else that Peter (and, by extension, all mankind) "was wholly polluted naturally with filthines."[41] St. Peter's feet recall the carnal spots of original sin that taint even the most innocent child.

[40] Calvin, *Harmonie*, 312; and Erasmus, *Paraphrase*, 88.

[41] Calvin, *Harmonie*, 312.

Figure 1.8 Unknown artist, Monument for Anthony and Anne Everard (detail) (1611), Great Waltham. Author's photograph.

With this image of original sin, Montagu extends the monument's meditation on Baptism by engaging the Reformation debate on the status of the sacrament as a prerequisite to salvation. "Wee denie that Baptisme is of absolute necessitie to salvation," Perkins writes, since "Sacraments doe not conferre grace, but rather confirme grace, when GOD hath conferred the same."[42] Hooker agrees: since "grace is not absolutely tied to sacraments ... [God] will not deprive them of inward grace because necessity depriveth them of outward sacraments."[43] A pair of twins, "Anonymus & Richard," locked in an eternal embrace on their parents' tomb (see Figure 1.8), embodies this faith in Baptism and hope of God's mercy: one was baptized and christened before his death, the other not, but both are believed to have been saved.[44]

Henry Montagu certainly was baptized as an infant, and baptized again in the pond that took his life. Yet the contested status of the sacrament permeates his memorial. George Jay's invocation of the example of Belshazzar in his funeral sermon for three-year-old Mary Villiers expresses the notional link between the dead objects of idolatry and the death sentence of original sin, evaded by the child who "baptized her selfe with her owne teares." Looking on her corpse,

[42] Perkins, *Golden Chaine*, 114

[43] Hooker, *Lawes*, 135. Perkins is confident in the salvation of "Infants already elected," regardless of whether they die before or after birth: see *Golden Chaine*, 152. For a useful discussion, see Marshall, *Beliefs and the Dead*, 188–99.

[44] See Coster, "'Tokens of Innocence,'" for the argument that attitudes gradually shifted in the period toward viewing unbaptized children as saved.

> wee should stand all like Belshazzar when hee saw the hand-writing upon the wal ... so that the joints of our loines should be loose, & our knees smite against one another to think upon this harmelesse innocent, that here hath suffered for one sinne, and that sin none of her owne.[45]

The saturation of Montagu's monument in the imagery of Baptism responds to the hollow materiality of objects severed from divine presence. God is not confined to mere matter, and the water of Baptism cannot, in itself, confer grace. Water, as base matter, is a swollen pond where a toddler's lifeless body floats; a vacancy that asserts, with the iconoclast, the impotence of rites and things. Yet Montagu's program hopes to infuse the monumental stone with the essence of its subject and with the image, if not the fact, of spiritual power. The child depicted on the tomb, standing like a saint in his niche, is the resurrected Henry Montagu, seeming – like his Savior – to walk on water. The refashioning of the dead flesh into an alabaster saint is a figuration of the soul's transformation from sin to salvation in the complementary sacraments of Baptism and Communion. The effigy is the tangible remnant of an invisible presence and grace, perceived only by the mind's eye.

The apparent inspiration for this merger of the two sacraments in the monument's iconography is the piscina installed near the altar at Barnwell (see Figure 1.2), an object whose shape, function, and dimensions suggest its incorporation into Montagu's memorial program. A focal point for rival views of the sanctity of the sacraments' material remains, this sacred sink draining into the consecrated ground of the churchyard was a receptacle for holy water with which the priest washed before the Catholic Mass and where liturgical vessels were washed, with remnants of consecrated wine, afterward. While piscinae were commonly used in the Catholic Mass, the Reformation refusal of transubstantiation gradually made them obsolete. Not until 1662 does the Book of Common Prayer distinguish between the disposal of consecrated and unconsecrated bread and wine, and the lack of uniformity in Church of England services in the period makes it difficult to gauge perceptions of the piscina at Barnwell when Montagu erected his monument nearby.[46]

What is clear, however, is that the piscina is a monument in its own right, set within the chancel's cartography of belief, inviting Montagu to recover and redeploy this relic in commemorating his son. By association

[45] Jay, *Sermon*, 45. On the connections between original sin and idolatry, see Zimmerman, *Early Modern Corpse*, 24–60.

[46] See BCP (1662), fol. G5ʳ. On the piscina, see Whiting, *Reformation*, 106–8.

with the biblical pools that share its name, the piscina recalls the union of essence and matter in the body of Christ. "In thys fontaygne," the *Legenda aurea* explains of the curative pool at Bethesda, "is lyvyng water . . . that the samarytane requyred of our lord to have of the holy pecyne."[47] The water of the piscina at Barnwell is, notionally, the water of salvation to which the motto on the scroll in Henry Montagu's hand alludes. The gold cup depicted on the monument is an accessory of the baptismal font and the piscina, both located nearby. Montagu's monument, like the piscina, asserts the cooperation of Baptism and Communion in the drama of salvation, and attempts the merger of essence and object of which the piscina is a sign. The effigy embodies resurrection as matter infused with grace. Embedding this belief within a defense of spiritual insight – an argument for the discretionary eye, capable of retrieving the good in repudiated rites and objects – the Barnwell monument gives shape to paternal grief in a fond icon that stops just short of idolatry.

2 Dumb Ceremonies, Silent Rites

In imitation of Christ, English monarchs from Henry VII to James II, including the two whom Sidney Montagu served as Master of Requests, performed an annual *pedilavium*, the Royal Maundy, ceremonially washing the feet of poor subjects on Maundy Thursday (see Figure 1.9). This commemoration of the events of the Last Supper derived its name from the *mandatum*, the "new commandment" given by Christ on that occasion, "that ye love one another; as I have loved you" (John 13:34).[48] The rite's association with sacramental matter was implicit, and worries about its apparent Catholicism were often voiced after the Reformation. A foreign observer of the Royal Maundy performed by Elizabeth I in 1565 reported, "After she had washed the poor women's feet, she deliberately traced a very large and well-defined cross and kissed it to the sorrow of many persons who witnessed it and of others who would not attend the ceremony, but to the joy of others."[49]

For those who found the spectacle sorrowful, the queen's crossing the poor women's feet came close to an idolatrous worship of the "signe or ymage" of God (*Homyly*, fol. 43^{r}), an illicit materialization of the sacred with which the Barnwell iconography also struggles. At this early moment

[47] Voragine, *Legenda aurea*, fol. 370^{v}. The healing at the pool of Bethesda appears in John 5:1–18.
[48] See Levin, "'Would I Could,'" and McManus, "Queen Elizabeth," 43–66.
[49] Guzman da Silva, quoted in Levin, "'Would I Could,'" 203.

Figure 1.9 Levina Teerlinc, *Royal Maundy* (1565).
Creative Commons CCO (public domain).

in the Elizabethan Settlement, those who greeted the act with joy may have hoped to see a resurgence of Catholicism, evidence of which was also found in the queen's chapel and the retention of Marian ceremonies in her churches.[50] In 1566, Elizabeth's ambassador to France, Sir Thomas Hoby, wrote to his brother-in-law William Cecil reporting a French schoolmaster's observation that Church of England services use "alters, organes, crosses, copes, surplices ... contrarie to the maner of all refourmed Churches," and, more disturbingly, that "your queene doest maintaine in despite of all your refourmed ministers suche thinges which men tearme abuses of the Churche of Roome." "The crosse, alter, and organe be

[50] Elizabeth's equivocation in the "Royal Injunctions of 1559" about the location of the communion table is one example of this retention of traditional forms and ceremonies: see n5.

alwaies in the accustomed place in your Queenes chappell," he claims, "which must needes argue a chaunge shortly within your Realme." Horrified, Hoby confides that he has had "manie conflictes ... with sundrie aswell Papists as Protestants about the same, not a little to my greef to heare."[51] When he writes to Queen Elizabeth the same day, Hoby's reformed fervor is very much on show. An episode of the French king's following "an Idoll on foote, carried in the Bishoppes hands under a canopie about the Citie... seemed not altogether unpunished at Goddes hands" when news that in Pamiers, "there were slaine by the Protestants in their defense CCC Papists at the least." He concludes by wishing the queen "a longe and most prosperous raigne to the maintenance of the good and godlie and rooting out of all superstition and Idolatrie."[52]

As Hoby's foreign encounters imply, sacred objects and rites in the hands of the ruling elite bore profoundly political meanings, offering familiar supports borrowed from religious practice for performances of statecraft. Hooker's first principle, of course, in his *Lawes of Ecclesiasticall Politie* is that "Religion ... is the stay of all wel ordered common-wealths." "Let Politie," accordingly, "acknowledge it selfe indebted to religion."[53] Hoby's parable of the massacre at Pamiers, moreover, demonstrates that when sacred matters bleed into secular affairs, faith and superstition are two sides of the same coin. The Royal Maundy and the ritual of the king's touch, by which anointed monarchs were believed to be capable of curing scrofula, were conducted with elaborate ceremony, particularly during Elizabeth's reign when the pressures of religious instability and the queen's femininity required her to assert her identity as "God's substitute."[54] Despite the monarch's assumption of Christ-like humility in the Maundy, however, the ritual ultimately underwrote "the maintenance of power and the class distinctions that Jesus's *mandatum* sought to erase."[55] The feet of the poor women participating in the ceremony were washed in sweet water by no less than three court officers prior to the queen's kneeling to wash, cross, and kiss them.[56] Lacking the theatrical talents of his predecessor, James reluctantly but pragmatically continued to perform both the Royal Maundy and the king's touch, but refused to make the sign of the cross. "He says that neither he nor any other King can have power to heal scrofula," the Venetian secretary wrote, "for the age of miracles has

[51] TNA SP 70/84, fol. 202ʳ. [52] TNA SP 70/84, fols. 200ʳ–201ʳ. [53] Hooker, *Lawes*, 1–2.

[54] See Levin, "'Would I Could;'" McManus, "Queen Elizabeth;" and Shakespeare, *Richard II*, 1.2.250.

[55] McManus, "Queen Elizabeth," 46. [56] McManus, "Queen Elizabeth," 45–8.

past . . . However, he will have the full ceremony, so as not to loose this prerogative, which belongs to the Kings of England."[57] If performances of sacred kingship displayed secular power and wealth, some subjects approached them with a mixture of faith and pragmatism akin to the monarch's. A maid healed by Elizabeth's touch was compelled to sell the gold angel she wore as a token of the miracle, "yet she remained well."[58] The lingering presence of the sacred sign, the healing hand, remained as a permanent mark on her flesh despite the loss of its material emblem.

The political alliance of pragmatism and belief had a troubled legacy following Henry VIII's dissolution of the monasteries, which decimated religious houses and razed many monuments in the process to create a generation of newly made men – among them Thomas Hoby's half-brother, Philip, and Sidney Montagu's grandfather, Edward – who received former monastic properties as private holdings.[59] If the Royal Maundy and king's touch occupied one extreme on the spectrum of faith and pragmatism attending post-Reformation sovereignty, the dispensation of the king's "Justice and Grace" occupied the other.[60] Sidney Montagu played a central role in this process as one of four Masters of Requests serving first James and then Charles.[61] The Masters were officers of the Court of Requests, but their primary role was to accompany the king to receive requests from petitioners.[62] After several stages of triage, petitions were presented in periodic audiences during which the Master, "remain[ed] on his knees as representing the subject petitioning the king."[63] Conversely, the Master represented the monarch to petitioners, performing the royal will either by letter or with the king's seal. Despite this bureaucratic assembly line, an aura of divine right

[57] Giovanni Carlo Scaramelli, quoted in McManus, "Queen Elizabeth," 65.

[58] William Tooker, quoted in McManus, "Queen Elizabeth," 44; and see the surrounding discussion, 43–6, on the resale of royal gifts.

[59] Sir Philip Hoby (d. 1558) received Bisham Abbey and a house in Blackfriars that he willed to Thomas at his death: see Victoria County History, *Berkshire*, vol. III, 139–52. Chief Justice Edward Montagu (d. 1557) received properties belonging to the late monastery of Thorney: see Victoria County History, *Northampton*, vol. III, 101–9; and Gunton, *History*, 66–7. On the destruction of monuments during the dissolution, see Marshall, *Beliefs and the Dead*, 88–9.

[60] So Sir Julius Caesar divided petitions to the king in his "Notes touching suits" of July 1604: see Hoyle, "Masters of Requests," 563.

[61] Sidney Montagu was appointed master extraordinary in February 1616, and was knighted in July. He became one of the four masters in ordinary in 1618. From 1616 to 1639 he received an annuity of £100 for his service. See Institute of Historical Research, "Office Holders, Masters of Requests."

[62] Hoyle, "Masters of Requests," 563.

[63] BL Add MS 15632, "Proceedings," fol. 45^{r}; see also Hoyle, "Masters of Requests," 557.

surrounded the bestowal of royal favor. In *Basilikon doron*, James advises Prince Henry, "be in your giving accesse so open and affable to every ranke of honest persons . . . to make their own sutes to you themselves, and not to employ the great Lords their intercessours: for intercession to Saints is Papistry."[64] In James's Protestant fiction of direct access, royal will becomes divine.

To minds less absolute than Hoby's, the sights and rites of sacred kingship were equivocal, requiring a discretionary eye, and quotidian ceremonies often involved secular tokens that seemed endowed with the power of the sacred object. Hooker equates the operations of sacred and secular rites by recalling the domestic *pedilavium* performed by the woman in Luke 7 who washes Jesus's feet with her tears:

> Doth not our Lord Jesus Christ himself impute the omission of some courteous Ceremonies even in domesticall intertainement to a colder degree of loving affection? . . . Wherefore the usuall dumb Ceremonies of common life are in request or dislike according to that they import, even so religion having likewise her silent rites, the chiefest rule whereby to judge of their qualitie is that which they meane or betoken.[65]

In this alignment of the dumb ceremonies of common life with religion's silent rites, the ambiguous sign – sacred and secular, partaking equally of faith and superstition – hovers between the material object and its memorial trace. It is this sign that the memory box at Barnwell adopts, interrogates, and adores.

While the alabaster monument at Barnwell is informed by the sacramental features of the piscina, the third component of the Barnwell program, Sidney Montagu's manuscript, "Upon the Birth and death of his deere sonne," responds to the secular imagery on the monument's obelisk. When Henry Montagu drowned, his death was catastrophic since it signaled a rupture in dynastic succession. Yet this crisis was short-lived: before Henry's monument was finished in August 1626, his mother, Paulina Pepys Montagu, had given birth to a second son who would survive his father, eventually becoming the 1st Earl of Sandwich.[66] The texts of Montagu's monument allude to this fact, diverting dynastic concerns toward personal sorrow and loss:

[64] James I, *Basilikon doron*, 46. [65] Hooker, *Lawes*, 158–9.

[66] Henry's elder brother also drowned, but at sea during the Battle of Solebay in 1672, which ended an illustrious career as Lord Admiral for Charles II. See *ODNB*.

Here under lyeth
interred Henry Montagu,
Esq., Then onely sonne of
S[i]r Sidney Mountagu, K[nigh]t:
(one of the Masters of
Requests to the Ma[jes]ties
of King James) and
King Charles) and of
Dame Paulina his wife
third daught[e]r of John
Pepys of Cottonham
in the County of Cambridge,
Esq.: A wittie & hope=
full child, tender &
deere in the sight of
his parents & much
lamented of his freinds.

The inscription is remarkable in noting that the child was *then*, briefly, Montagu's only son. With dynastic continuity restored, the epitaph attends instead to the devastation of "freinds." The manuscript, however, unfolds the obelisk's heraldry to script the child's genealogy. "The coates [of] Armes over the Childes *Statua*," Montagu explains, "are his Ancestores of the fathers side ascent and theire Matches. The coate first in ascent from the *Statua*, are his father and mother." Naming the child's grandparents, Sir Edward Montagu and Elizabeth Harington, the manuscript records the careers of Edward's sons, including Sidney: "These six brothers, *12º Reg Jaco* were of the Parliament at one time; *James*, Lord Bishoppe of Bath and *Welles* of the higher howse, and the other five of the howse of *Commons.*" While the text offers a verbal reproduction of the obelisk's heraldry, the painted images of the manuscript and triptych visually reproduce the tomb's sculptural imagery: coats of arms, hearts of black, and "true-love knottes" (see Figure 1.4 and Plate 1).

Amid otherwise dry enumerations of dynastic alliances, Montagu's pedigree remembers his mother with unusual affection. Elizabeth Harington Montagu was "a most religious, wise & vertuous ladie, of a cheerefull spirit, of admiredd hospitalitie during 17 years of her widdowhood . . . and bequeathed many greate and pious Legacies at her death." Lady Montagu's will, written a decade before her grandson's death, includes a legacy that informs the iconography of the Barnwell tomb: to each of her sons she gave "as a mothers remembrance, a guilte standinge cup of the value of twentie poundes . . . desiring that this posie maye be engraven about every of them, *Lorde give mee of that water, that I never more thirst.* John 4."[67] Henry Montagu's effigy carries the same "word," a grandmother's remembrance, on the scroll in his hand, while the gold cup at his feet is at once a

[67] TNA PROB 11/131/760, fol. 425^r. The same "word" is engraved on gold rings bestowed to Lady Montagu's sons-in-law. See Chapter 2.

sacramental and a secular sign. Embedding his mother's memory in the memorial program, moreover, Montagu acknowledges her role in fostering her grandson's birth. Henry's mother, Paulina Pepys, was a maidservant to Lady Montagu and the recipient of a generous bequest, including "the bedde whereupon she usually lyes with the coverlet and the rest of the ffurniture which belonges thereto, and five paires of sheets . . . and the little blacke coffer also, which standes in my closet, with such trifles as are in it." Lady Montagu's final bequest was to Sidney, who lived with his mother until her death: "all of my money, jewels, plate, household stuff, chattels, goods, and what else whatsoever unbequeathed . . . I give and bequeath to my sonne Sidney Mountague; to furnishe him towards howsekeeping."[68] Lady Montagu, a posthumous witness to Sidney Montagu's marriage to Paulina Pepys, is remembered in the private subtext of the memorial for her grandson.

Montagu's mapping of his son's death onto his dynastic record in the manuscript, however, struggles with the child's effective exclusion from that story. Henry Montagu did not have the chance to grow into virtue: the deeds celebrated by the manuscript are those of adult men. Although they are continually referred to the child by Montagu's insistent use of the possessive ("*his* grandfather . . . *his* great grandfather . . . *his* greate grandfathers father"), the pedigree paradoxically elides Henry's existence altogether. In his autobiographical entry, Montagu writes:

> ***Sidney*** the sixth sonne now living . . . one of the master of Requestes to his Ma[jes]tie [King James]; in w[hi]ch place hee still continueth by the favour of king *Charles* whom god long preserve, whoe by *Paulina Pepys* . . . hath issue *Eliza* and *Edward*, whom god almightie blesse and preserve.

The manuscript devoted to the life and death of Henry Montagu argues that, in dynastic terms, his insignificant life is not worth mentioning. He is a child lost to history, generating but also standing entirely outside the genealogical record that glosses his life. Part pedigree and part work of mourning, the manuscript treats the child's death as a personal loss and a symbolic event, delivering to posterity a memory of parental bereavement that reiterates and deepens the emotion expressed in Montagu's monumental inscriptions.

As the generative but silent sign at the center of this dynastic account, Henry Montagu is a specter whose presence is realized through the material remnants of his brief life. Most striking among these is the child's christening gown–cum–winding sheet:

[68] TNA PROB 11/131/760, Will, fols. 426$^{r–v}$.

> The nethermost stone [of the monument] in forme of a sheet set w[i]th true-love knottes, resembled the lawne sheet which covered the Childes head at his funerall (beeing the same which covered him to his Christening) and was set with true-love knottes of black Ribbins made by divers of his friends.

This sign of the child's Baptism is transformed into the symbol of his death by a literal work of mourning, the addition of black ribbons crafted into truelove knots. Created and supplied by the Montagu family, the christening gown replaces the pre-Reformation chrisom, a linen cloth held in inventories of Catholic churches, disallowed as an idolatrous accessory of Baptism by the second Edwardian prayer book. In the pre-Reformation ceremony, the minister put the chrisom on the baptized child, saying, "Take this white vesture for a token of the innocencie, which by Gods grace in this holy sacrament of Baptisme, is geven unto thee."[69] An object carrying the memory of sacramental essence, Henry Montagu's linen sheet is so thoroughly endowed with meaning that Montagu is moved to represent it in the imagery of the monument, and again visually and textually in the manuscript.[70] The garment's truelove knots are homespun, secular symbols of immortality: each black ribbon twists infinitely upon itself. They balance and counter the sacramental symbols of spiritual immortality in the monument's iconography. The memory of this deeply intimate work of mourning, a textile monument to childhood, love, and loss, occupies the central place in the Barnwell program. The refashioning of this disallowed sacramental as a private token of remembrance summarizes the innovations attending the new understanding of sacraments as signs of remembrance, and the changed relationships between sacred and secular objects and rites in the wake of the Reformation.

This linen sheet is, literally and figuratively, a buried artifact, resurrected to remember and make permanent the bodily interment of the beloved child. Montagu's attachment to this object, his reluctance to surrender it to the grave, and his repeated recreations of the details of this material token of his son's incarnation express a father's blind devotion to his lost son, the original act of idolatry censured in the *Homyly agaynst Peryll of Idolatry*. The revival of the chrisom's idolatry in Henry Montagu's

[69] BCP (1549), fols. 179$^{r–v}$. The chrisom is dropped from the ceremony in BCP (1552), fols. P4^{v}–P6^{v}. On pre-Reformation church inventories of textiles, see Whiting, *Reformation*, 74–5.

[70] Montagu's manuscript states that the shroud is represented on the monument's "nethermost stone," but the truelove knots appear in the register above the effigy's niche. Since both the base and the urn atop the monument are decorated with painted ribbons, the base may depict arms originally painted or embroidered on the child's christening/funeral garment, or the whole monument may represent a shroud tied at the crown.

christening/funeral garment is glossed by a remarkable story told in the *Homyly*: when Epiphanius sees in the church a linen cloth painted with Christ's image, he "dyd teare it, and gave counsell to the kepers of the Church, that they should wynde a poore man that was dead in the sayd cloth and bury him" (fols. 23^{r-v}). This associative link between the painted idol and the winding sheet indicts Montagu's fetishistic treatment of the child's shroud, an overvalued object that joins physical corruption and the spiritual death of idolatrous desire.[71] When Montagu entombs the image of the winding sheet inside a wooden box of the same size as the niche where his son's effigy stands, the box becomes a coffin.

Although the manuscript repeats the parental grief expressed in the monument's inscriptions, Montagu attempts to read through the sorrowful palimpsest of the child's death to decipher the providential plot that can make sense of this brutal loss. Montagu's textual monument aims not merely to contain the idolatrous sign but to reimagine the memorial project by grounding it in the shared currency of sacred and secular signs. If the manuscript box is a grave, its opening promises a resurrection, if only at the fleshly hands of a mortal father.

The Barnwell monument forestalls idolatry by invoking a discretionary insight able to read the essence inside the object – to see in the dead effigy the animated symbol of resurrection. In his manuscript, Montagu explores a similar project but turns from the sacramental sign to the potent secular signs suffusing the story of his son's brief life. The four-line poem that begins and ends his meditation "Upon the Birth and death of his deere sonne" is an exercise in insightful reading:

> Midd may brought thee to a world of Flowers,
> But Aprill drown'd thee w[i]th to many Showers
> Ascens[i]on day baptis'd thee Christian
> Thursday rewasht thee to Ascend againe.

As Montagu uses the scripted pedigree to unfold the sculptural heraldry nearby, so he provides a marginal gloss to his poem that roots his imagery in historical record:

> Thursday 16. May. 1622. Borne.
> Much rayne falling Aprill: 1625 filled a Ponde w[hi]ch w[i]th a Scoopet beeing by was supposed the occasion of his end.
> Thursday Ascenc[i]on day Christened.
> Thursday 28. Aprill: 1625 dyed.

[71] On the fetish in early modern object theory, see Stallybrass and Jones, "Fetishisms"; and Parker, "What a Piece of Work."

All of the noteworthy events of Henry Montagu's short life occurred on a Thursday, a detail that Montagu sees as far from coincidental. Montagu's quatrain returns to the monument's iconography to link Baptism and death: his son is washed in Baptism on Holy Thursday, Ascension Day – a date that must have seemed in retrospect both poignant and providential – and "rewasht" in drowning. Montagu's formal choice of two rhyming couplets produces a shifting chronology of the child's life: Henry's death is reported both before his christening and again afterward, as though the two events were one. When read as proof of divine providence, however, these repetitions and reversals matter little. In a biography that elides the life, birth and death are near-simultaneous events, unfolding within a woefully small number of inescapable Thursdays. The child's life is as brief and crafted as a quatrain.

As it collapses Henry Montagu's life and death into a single commemorative moment and utterance, Montagu's poem and its gloss record a fatal transformation of inert matter into potent signs. His memorial is written in a highly personal symbolic lexicon culled from the objects attending his son's life and death. This emblematic exchange between object and sign transforms a mere thing into a "monument of superstition." These personal omens easily distract both eye and mind with a desire more difficult to counter, because more private and idiosyncratic, than the worship of religious idols. Such superstitions abound in the period, exploiting the juncture of the sacred and the secular. On her deathbed, the toddler Princess Mary Stuart amazed spectators when, "immediately before shee offered up her selfe a sweete Virgin-sacrifice . . . she cryed, *I goe, I goe.* The more strange did this appeare to us that now at the last (as if directed by supernaturall inspiration) shee did so aptly utter these, and none but these."[72] Like a prescient Desdemona, who foresees her shroud in her marriage sheets, Frances, Duchess of Lennox and Richmond, willed that her corpse should be "wrapt in those sheets wherein my lord and I first slept that night when we were married."[73] Potent secular signs permeate daily life in the post-Reformation polity, while the collapse of religion's "silent rites" signals chaos in the commonwealth. When the cathedral at Peterborough was made "a ruthful Spectacle, a very Chaos of Desolation and Confusion," Gunton reports, two events, remarkable for their strangeness, took place. Two boys climbed up to the empty bell tower and slid down the ropes, much to their peril, but "it pleased God by a strange and wonderful providence to preserve [them]." Shortly afterward,

[72] Leech, *Sermon*, 41. [73] See Shakespeare, *Othello*, 4.3.21–4; and Chester, *Marriage*, 133n7.

a "young lad" fell through the church rafters while "rifling jack daws nests to get their young" and died, "his pockets filled with those inauspicious birds. These two things happened much about the same time, and in the time of that publick Confusion and Disorder" (*History*, 337–8). If the miraculous salvation and ill-fated death of Peterborough's children are influenced by the vibrant ghost of the cathedral, so the manuscript entombed in a memory box at Barnwell is anchored in the potent absence of a vanished son.

As Montagu reproduces and glosses the signets that sealed his son's fate, counting and compiling meaningful Thursdays, he schools himself to submit to the will of God. At the same time, though, he practices a private idolatry, superstitiously crafting his son's life and death into an artifact that marks his absence and recalls his transient incarnation. The manuscript box argues that the personal details and private memories of the child's life – the wealth of meanings his small body accrued despite its brief existence – cannot be fully revealed in his emblematic tomb yet are profoundly worthy of record. Montagu protects his son's memorials from becoming merely illegible signs, concealed within the unfathomable fabric of the silent church and cancelled from the record of history. His creation of an icon of paternal bereavement hopes to ensure the survival of the fond *Statua* standing erect in its monumental niche and the fateful mementos stored in this "celle and closet of fancie," the manuscript box.[74]

True-Love Knottes

Sidney Montagu ends his manuscript with two proverbs, familiar citations that would have been signs of remembrance for discerning readers. From Ovid's *Metamorphoses*, Montagu borrows the tag, "*Et genus et proavos et quae non fecimus ipsi / Vix ea nostra voco* " ("For our birth, our ancestors, and things which we have not ourselves done – these things I can hardly call our own").[75] The last word of the memorial program turns from secular commentary on dynastic identity to scriptural reconsideration of

[74] Hooker, *Lawes*, 160. The widespread opinion, underlying early modern antiquarianism, that textual monuments were more durable than tombs may explain Montagu's supplement of the sculptural monument with the manuscript. However, the existence of a second manuscript in NRO may suggest the perceived vulnerability of the Barnwell manuscript itself. Written in simple italic and painted with less elaborate imagery, the NRO manuscript appears to be a copy of that installed in the church. The possibility that it was an earlier draft for use by an arms painter is less likely, given that the Barnwell manuscript is in Sidney Montagu's hand.

[75] Ovid, *Metamorphoses*, 13:140.

true fatherhood: "Behold what love the father hath shewed unto us, that we should be called the sonnes of God" (John 3:1).

These twin mottos play out Montagu's engagement with an imagined posterity and, in equal measure, his resistance to public display. The Ovidian challenge to ancestral identity and privilege interprets Henry Montagu's elision from the genealogical record of his dynasty. What, finally, might a child dead at the age of three (or his mourning father) call his own? If the veneration of ancestors cannot justify an ostentatious tomb for a mere child, Montagu advances the affective value of a tomb that commemorates promise unrealized and potential overturned. His monument is unapologetically a mausoleum for a fly. What Henry Montagu owned was a small number of days and objects attending an ordinary life that revealed themselves as significant only when that life was ended; tokens of memory containing his essence and conveying them, reluctantly, to posterity. The manuscript box is a body whose form follows the function of its soul. It turns in on itself like a truelove knot, hiding from view those treasures it also aims to reveal, as if these remnants and fragments too precious to share were vulnerable to depletion by use, or liable to be spoiled by an abrasive gaze.

Montagu's turn to the sacred text, though, returns his memorial project to the public space of Barnwell's chancel. If Henry Montagu can claim nothing from his heritage, and his dynasty could claim nothing from him, the verse from John reconsiders fatherhood in sacred rather than secular terms. The statement completes the competitive staging of paternities begun in the funeral monument, renewing the challenge posed by Henry Montagu's erect effigy as it walks, in imitation of Christ, triumphantly on water. It is hard to overlook the comparison between God's sacrifice of his son and Sidney Montagu's surrender of his. But here paternity is keyed to the collective: Henry Montagu's status as a son of God earns him a place among his ancestors – distinguished not by their rank or deeds but by their faith – and among the community of worshippers in the chancel where his monument stands. In its final moment, Montagu's memorial program remembers the promise of the *mandatum* and reimagines the privie conventicle, where a private death is mourned, as a Communion room, the site of collective remembrance of resurrected sons.

CHAPTER 2

Wondrous Work

Crafting Remembrance in the Montagu Archive

Every sacrament is the word of God made visible to the eye.

– William Perkins[1]

The bread is a remembrauncer unto us of christs body.

– Zacharias Ursinus[2]

A Wondrous Web

During his summer progress in July 1616, King James I paid homage to Elizabeth Harington Montagu, matriarch of the Northamptonshire family whose six sons were in royal service, the youngest, Sidney, having been knighted just nine days earlier (see Figure 2.1).[3] Sir Edward Montagu, the eldest, wrote to his brother James, Bishop of Winchester, reporting that when the king passed through Geddington Woods on July 29, he "killed there quickly a very fat buck; which, when it was dead, his Majesty called for me, and bade me send it to my mother, and tell her it was a buck of his killing and my keeping, and that would please her well." "I had above half an hour's speech with him," Montagu continues, "hand to hand, wherein he entered into discourse of my mother and all us brethren too long to write of. [He] wondered at . . . my mother's working, being stone blind." Accordingly, Montagu presented to the king ocular proof of Lady Montagu's wondrous work:

[1] Perkins, *Commentarie . . . [upon] Galatians*, 254. [2] Ursinus, *Summe of Christian Religion*, 756.

[3] Nichols, *Progresses . . . of King James*, vol. III, 180–1. On Sidney Montagu, see Chapter 1. Walter (d. 1615) was MP for Monmouthshire. James (d. 1618) was advanced to Bishop of Winchester in July 1616 and was instrumental in the appointment of his brother Henry (d. 1642) as Chief Justice of the King's Bench the same year. Henry became 1st Earl of Manchester in 1626. Charles (d. 1625) pursued a military career in Ireland and then returned to London as MP for Higham Ferrers. Edward (d. 1644) was MP for Northamptonshire from 1604 to 1621, when he became 1st Baron Montagu of Boughton. See *ODNB* for each; and see Thrush and Ferris, eds., *History of Parliament*, vol. V, 358–60, 362–80, and 381–6.

Figure 2.1 Unknown artist, *Portrait of Elizabeth Montagu* (before 1618), Boughton House.
By kind permission of the Duke of Buccleuch and Queensberry KBE.

> On Saturday, when I took my leave of his Majesty, having gotten a fine handkerchief of my mother's hemming, I told his Majesty that I had brought him the wonder to see; and he presently called for it, and showed it to all the Lords, and told them of another wonder I had told him of, that one nurse with one milk did suckle six of us.[4]

Elizabeth Montagu's handkerchief bespeaks the mystery of its maker's prodigious sight in working it and her prophetic foresight in uniting her sons in the fellowship of common milk.

These twin wonders – Lady Montagu's ability to see feelingly in her old age and her insistence as a younger mother that all of her sons should be suckled by the same nurse – enhance a portrait of the family as a single, unified body; a portrait that circulated widely. Dedicating the posthumous edition of William Perkins's commentary on St. John's Revelation to Lady Montagu's children, Robert Hill writes, "as the members of a body being once dismembred, they cannot possibly be joyned againe: so if naturall brethren be once unnaturally disjoyned, no glue will conjoyne them fast againe."[5]

[4] NRO, Montagu MS 3, fols. 180^{r}–1^{r}; printed in *BQ*, vol. I, 249.

[5] Hill, "Epistle Dedicatorie," in Perkins, *Godly and Learned Exposition ... [upon] the Revelation*, fol. $A2^{v}$. This second edition of Perkins's work includes a dedication by Thomas Pierson to Elizabeth Montagu (fols. ¶3^{r-v}). Hill's first edition was also dedicated to the Montagus: see Perkins, *Lectures*; and see Chapter 3. On Pierson's corrections of Hill's edition, see Eales, "Thomas Pierson," 82–3. Hill was James Montagu's chaplain: see Fielding, "Conformists," 32.

If the Montagus are "brethren by *nature* of one venter, *nation* of one country, *grace* of one spirit, *affection* of one heart,"[6] the handkerchief hemmed by Lady Montagu is a memento of the conjoined threads of the close-knit family and of the creative, female roots of that web in the shared venter and common milk.

The drama of union staged by the Montagus in the political arena and the royal court resonated with the king's dream of union, the birth of a "nation of one country" in the body of Great Britain. "What God hath conjoined let no man separate," James told Parliament on March 19, 1604: "I am the head and [the kingdom] is my body ... I hope therefore that no man will think that [the head] should have a divided or monstrous body."[7] Rhetorically and conceptually, the two projects of union were closely aligned, both partaking of the familiar genealogical imagery of "auncient *Stocke* and *Name*," as John Speed put it, and both surrounded by wonder and mystery.[8] Proponents of union celebrated "the miraculous and happie union of England and Scotland" in the mystical body of James; the providential return of Britannia "in the royall Person of our now-*Soveraigne*."[9] As God's design unfolded in James's monarchy, "most properly [was] performed that *propheticall promise* made unto the *Church of Christ*: *that Kings should become her nursing Fathers*."[10]

In Chapter 1, Sidney Montagu's memorial for his son revealed how religious beliefs were incarnated in commemorative projects in the wake of the evacuation of spiritual power from religious objects and rites. Montagu evades idolatry by investing his stone monument with the likeness of the Protestant sacraments, refigured not as mysteries but as "signes of remembrance."[11] In his manuscript, addressed to posterity, he convenes a company of ancestors around the absent son, locating his act of remembrance uneasily between private superstition and communal worship of the resurrected Son.

This chapter considers how memorial texts and objects created by members of the Montagu monumental circle are permeated by and promote the family's Puritan faith. I focus particularly on women's works:

[6] Hill, "Epistle Dedicatorie," in Perkins, *Godly and Learned Exposition ... [upon] the Revelation*, fol. A2^{v}.

[7] James I, *Works*, 488–9.

[8] Speed, *Theatre*, 896. On the project of union, see Harris, *Foreign Bodies*, 19–47.

[9] Cornwallis, *Miraculous and Happie Union*, fol. A1^{r}. On the king's mytical body, see Kantorowicz, *King's Two Bodies*; and Schwartz, *Sacramental Poetics*, 19–35.

[10] Speed, *Theatre*, 896 and 205.

[11] Perkins, *Reformed Catholicke*, 370.

Ann Montagu's manuscript "Letters, Prayers, and Poems," and the material and literary legacies of her mother-in-law, Elizabeth Harington Montagu. In line with recent criticism that considers Puritanism "as a form of religious culture,"[12] this chapter locates theological and ecclesiastical concerns within a body of texts and practices to explore networks of unity, sociability, and sacramentality traversing the "conforming Calvinism" of the Montagu family.[13] My study of the memorial projects of the Montagu women, moreover, enlarges the critical view of Puritanism as encouraging and promoting, rather than stifling, women's intellectual, political, and literary engagements and products.[14] This chapter contributes to these areas of critical concern in two ways. First, by aligning the materiality of the Montagu women's legacies with the material signs of the Puritan sacrament, I suggest that models of meditative reading associated with Puritanism may be enlarged to account for the refashioning of secular material culture in a sacred shape. Second, I argue that the Montagu women's memorials, while rooted in Puritan ideas of sociability and sacramentality, chart a course of dispersal and recollection – of signs, texts, and objects – that is strikingly different from the "permanent memory-traces" erected by the Montagu men. I argue, in other words, that while performances within this monumental circle share a common religious culture, gender plays a part in these commemorative acts in a discernible way.[15]

Section 1 of this chapter shows how the six sons of Elizabeth Montagu shape their project of union by weaving together the secular imagery of dynastic affiliation and its sacred counterpart, the Pauline idea of the church body, as expressed in the writings of Puritan ministers promoted by the family. Monumental and monolithic, the Montagu nation is embodied in a series of stable, unyielding structures that encrypt women's memories, co-opting and suppressing their generative presence.

Section 2 moves from the monuments of memory to its processes in Lady Ann Montagu's manuscript "Letters, Prayers, and Poems." Following Puritan theologians, Ann Montagu engages with the Puritan sacrament

[12] Cambers, "Reading," 800. Key texts on the culture of Puritanism are Lake, and Questier, *Antichrist's Lewd Hat*; and Durston and Eales, eds., *Culture of English Puritanism.* In this collection, Lake's "'Charitable Christian Hatred'" is particularly relevant to the politico-religious context of Northamptonshire, as is Lake and Stephens, *Scandal.*

[13] See Steere, "Calvinist Bishop"; and Lake, *Moderate Puritans.*

[14] Noteworthy titles are Harris and Scott-Baumann, eds., *Intellectual Culture;* White, "Women Writers"; Ross, *Women, Poetry and Politics*, esp. 1–62 and 135–218; Phillippy, "Living Stones"; and papers by contributors to the "Constructing Elizabeth Isham" project.

[15] For a related view, see Longfellow, "Take Unto Ye Words."

as a multiplicity of signs – the complex embodiment of the Word – encountered through remembrance and interpretation, processes central to the identity of the godly. Infused by this multifaceted sacrament, Ann Montagu's book embodies an evolving, progressive art of memory in which dispersed members – the broken body of Christ, or the dispersed and scattered saints – are meaningfully recollected and unified.

Section 3 follows this tissue of dispersal and reincorporation into Elizabeth Montagu's material and literary legacies, embodied in her Last Will and Testament and in manuscript miscellanies that passed through her hands to those of her descendants. Moving horizontally rather than vertically, and stressing process rather than object, these monuments convene a society of the saints across generations.[16] The "godlie familie" is repeatedly, continuously remade by these wondrous works.[17]

This chapter serves as an epilogue to the one preceding it, but also as a prologue to Chapter 3, which traces these networks of sacramentality and sociability in Shakespeare's *Cymbeline*. There, divisions in the body politic are represented as failed sacraments, ruptures that are repaired through the prophetic union of the redeemed believer with the resurrected spirit of "tender air."[18] On the eve of Christianity, *Cymbeline* plays out the processes by which the body politic appropriates sacramental, feminine textualities to craft the memory and matter of Britain.

1 A Band of Brothers

On the final day of the Hampton Court Conference, January 18, 1604, James Montagu wrote to his mother with as full an account of the proceedings as time would allow: "I am sure you have a longing to hear what becometh of this great Business between the Bishops and the Ministers. I cannot write you the Disputes, my Imployments at this time would not permit, but in short, on Saturday it began . . ."[19] Montagu was present throughout the three-day conference, where the direction of the Jacobean Church of England was set, and a new translation of the Bible under the monarch's name and a revised Book of Common Prayer were

[16] James, *Women's Voices*, 1–2, describes men's vision of the family as "vertical" and women's as "horizontal . . . incorporating [in their wills] siblings and their offspring, godchildren, indigent female relations, and assorted dependents."

[17] Pierson, "Epistle Dedicatorie," fol. ¶3^r.

[18] Shakespeare, *Cymbeline*, ed. Warren, 5.4.438. All references are to this edition unless otherwise noted.

[19] Sawyer, ed., *Memorial*, vol. II, 13.

ordered. As one of the translators of the King James Bible and the editor of the king's collected *Works* – which, "[in] the manner of God his setting forth his own *Workes*," reunited King James's "dismembered" textual remains "into one Body" – James Montagu contributed to installing James Stuart as head of the eccelesiastical body and the body politic.[20]

At Hampton Court, James Montagu took part in the "stir" about ceremonies, and his claim that the disputants expressed only lukewarm support for abolishing rituals may reflect his own diplomatic self-censorship:

> The King pleaded hard to have good Proof against the Ceremonies [but] there was not any of them that they could prove to be against the Word, but all of them confirmed by the Fathers, and that long before Popery. So that for the Ceremonies I suppose nothing will be altered. And truly the Doctors argued but weakly against them: So that all wondered they had no more to say against them.[21]

When, in the following year, the subscription to ceremonies in Northamptonshire resulted in the deprivation of sixteen "grave, learned and sober-minded ministers, for not observing certain ceremonies, long since by many disused," Puritans Richard Baldock and Henry Bridger, both patronized by Elizabeth Montagu, were among those deprived.[22] Edward Montagu's movement of a parliamentary petition to reinstate the ministers led to his being "put out of all commissions for his Majesty's service and [commanded] to depart into the country."[23] Noting his subject's apparently divided allegiance, the king remarked that although Montagu "smelt a littell of Puritanisme," he tolerated him "for love of all [the Montagu] family."[24] Montagu's exile continued until June, when his forgiveness was brokered by his brother James. "It seems now, by your letter," his mother wrote to him in July 1605, "that both by speech and writing you have submitted yourself to the King his command, and I trust in so good respect

[20] James I, *Works*, fol. d3^{v}. On the centrality of Puritans in the Tudor and Stuart politico-religious mainstream, see Collinson, *Religion of Protestants;* Tyacke, *Anti-Calvinists*; and Lake and Questier, "Puritans."

[21] Sawyer, ed., *Memorials*, vol. II, 14. A copy of the instructions to the Puritan clergy at Hampton Court with a detailed account of the debate on ceremonies is included in the Montagu papers: see *BM*, vol. I, 33–40.

[22] *BM*, vol. I, 42; Fielding, "Conformists," 24 and 63; and Thrush and Ferris, eds., *History of Parliament*, vol. V, 383. Bridger received a stipend of 20s in Elizabeth Montagu's will: see TNA PROB 11/131/760, fol. 426^{r}. On Montagu's parliamentary journals, see Cope, *Life of a Public Man.*

[23] *BM*, vol. I, 146. [24] NRO Montagu MS 3, fol. 118^{r}; printed in *BQ*, vol. I, 255–6.

that neither the King nor the Council shall have any further cause of exception against you, if reason may give them content."[25]

The "longing" with which Elizabeth, Lady Montagu, awaited news of events at the Hampton Court Conference bespeaks her mastery of the intricacies of doctrinal and liturgical change. More pressingly, it registers her hopes for the political success of the Puritan agenda through the "Christian magistracy" for which that she and her husband had prepared her sons.[26] In the last lines of her will, Lady Montagu would affirm as her lasting legacy her sons' royal service:

> [I pray] God to make [them] faythfull servant[s] to his majestie, who hath bene a moste gratious kinge to mee, his dayly poore Beadeswoman and to all my children, trusting they all will showe themselves his majesties loyall and faythfulle servants and subjects to their lives end.[27]

She may have been displeased by the outcome of the debate, "which held three hours at least," surrounding "Private Baptism by Women." The position formulated at Hampton Court was "that it should be administred by Ministers, yet in Private Houses, if occasion required [and] that whosoever else should baptise, should be under Punishment." While the policy specifically limited women's administration of the sacrament, Lady Montagu advanced her agenda by proxy.[28] On June 23, 1606, "Doctor Mountagew, Deane of his Majesties Chappell" baptized King James's newborn daughter Sophia.[29] Four days later, he wrote from Greenwich to his brother Sidney, residing at their mother's house, with news "of our Christening turned to a funeral," adding, "the Childe is buried this day in Westminster."[30]

For the Montagu brothers, the claims of membership in the body of the Puritan faithful, the natural fraternal body, and the body politic traversed their public and private acts of devotion and commemoration. Often these claims coalesced. Edward Montagu's "Act for the publick thanksgiving to Almighty God every year on the 5th Day of November" established a ceremony in parishes across England as "a perpetual remembrance . . . of God's miraculous and gracious deliverance of his church" in the body of

[25] *BM*, vol. I, 46. See Cope, *Life of a Public Man*, 36–42.
[26] See Fielding, "Conformists," 192–202; and Cope, *Life of a Public Man*, 12–13 and 74–6.
[27] TNA PROB 11/131/760, fol. 426^{v}.
[28] The new position was that "all those Questions that institute [Baptisme] to be done by Women [shall be] taken away." See Sawyer, ed., *Memorials*, vol. II, 14.
[29] See *Old Cheque-book*, 170.
[30] Bod Carte MS 74, item 187.

"the most great, learned and religious King."[31] Contending obligations were reconciled in the secular imagery of ancestral descent and the Pauline idea of the faithful, who "being many, are one body in Christ" (Romans 12:5) – figurative strands that intertwined. Thus, Thomas Fuller celebrates Edward Montagu's three sons as "Faire Branches of a Stock as faire," and Robert Hill rejoices "that from one honorable roote have issued so manie profitable branches to the Church."[32] Hill cites an example from Plutarch to celebrate the brothers' unity: "Scilurus at his death need not teach you concord, by giving to each of you a sheafe of arrows, which cannot well be broken whilst they are conjoined; for you by your amitie make your selves invincible."[33] Sidney Montagu took the exemplum to heart: the brothers, he writes, are "a bundle of arrows, which being sundered [are] easily broke ... yet if we hold together we shall be the stronger in ourselves and against others."[34] The wall monument erected in St. Margaret's, Barking, for Charles Montagu after his death in 1625 paints an evocative portrait of fraternal separation and incorporation (see Figure 2.2).[35] Alone in his tent, helmet and gauntlet set aside, this Christian knight rests head on hand. Yet he is guarded by sentinels, a page walks his masterless horse to stable, and his tent is one of many in a vast encampment. The scene evokes the fraternity of soldiers in battle: the "band of brothers" crafted by Shakespeare's Henry V at Agincourt and embodied in the fellowship of the Montagu men.[36] Placed at the still center of a busy, crowded scene, the knight is embedded, like a jewel in an elaborate setting, in vital connections. Waiting silently at the calm heart of the web, he is eternally enmeshed and included in living relations.

If Charles Montagu is a secular saint, the sacred motif was promulgated more broadly in the works of ministers supported by the family,

[31] Pickering, ed., *Statutes*, vol. VII, 145–7. In his will, Montagu established charitable donations to six parishes to be distributed annually during the Thanksgiving service to commemorate "that greate deliverance from the Powder Treason": see TNA PROB 11/196/404, fol. 366r.

[32] Fuller, *Davids Hainous Sinne*, sig. A2r; and Hill, "Epistle Dedicatorie," in Perkins, *Godly and Learned Exposition ... [upon] the Revelation*, fol. A2v.

[33] Hill, "Epistle Dedicatorie," in Perkins, *Godly and Learned Exposition ... [upon] the Revelation*, fol. A2v. Scilurus's story appears in Plutarch, *Philosophie*, 203.

[34] NRO Montagu MS 6, fol. 183r.

[35] Charles's will named his widow as his executor and bequeathed large sums to his three daughters, his only heirs: see TNA PROB 11/148/393. They probably commissioned the monument, but authorship of the program is uncertain. The workshop of William Cure II may have created the work, given their long affiliation with the Montagu family. Stylistic similarities between Montagu's armor-clad figure and the two knights on the monument for Philip and Thomas Hoby in Bisham, erected by the Cure workshop after 1566, support this attribution.

[36] Shakespeare, *Henry V*, 4.3.60.

Figure 2.2 Unknown sculptor (Cure workshop?), Mural monument for Sir Charles Montagu (after 1625).
St. Margaret's, Barking. Author's photograph.

particularly those associated with the "Puritan seminaries" of Cambridge University and the Kettering Lecture, where the chief patron, Edward Montagu, was a "usuall and ordinary frequent[er]."[37] Dedicating a volume of sermons preached in the lecture to Montagu, Robert Bolton celebrated his patron's confounding the "Powder-plots of all the powers of darkness" and his service to "our great Lord in Heaven and his Royal Deputie our highest Soveraigne upon earth."[38] In 1630, Joseph Bentham published *The Societie of the Saints*, a collection of sermons preached at the Kettering Lecture, dedicated to his patron's three sons and daughter. The work aimed "to agglutinate us into that so sweet Societie, which is with the Saints, with the Father, and with his sonne Jesus Christ."[39] In this agglutination, figures of union multiply. The "scattered Apostles and dispersed Christians" are "all one bread." They are "members of the one

[37] Bentham, *Christian Conflict*, A5^{v}. On the moderate Puritanism dominant in Elizabethan Cambridge, see Lake, *Moderate Puritans.* On the Montagus' connections with Cambridge, see Fielding, "Conformists," 24–32. James, Henry, and Sidney Montagu attended Christ's College, Cambridge, where William Perkins was their tutor: see Venn, ed., *Alumni cantabrigienses*, Part 1, vol. III, 201–3. Most of the ministers in the Montagu circle came from Cambridge, including: Joseph Bentham, Nicholas Estwick, Robert Hill, and Thomas Pierson: see Venn, Part 1, vol. I, 135; Part 1, vol. 2, VI and 272; and Part 1, vol. III, 331, respectively. On Bentham and the activities of the Kettering Lecture, see Fielding, "Conformists," 30–5 and 192–202; Lake, "Charitable Christian Hatred"; and Lake and Stephens, *Scandal*, 97–170.

[38] Bolton, *Some Generall Directions*, fols. A2^{v} and A4^{r}.

[39] Bentham, *Societie*, 2.

and self-same body," "stones of the same building," and "branches of the same vine . . . of which vine Christs godhead is the root, his manhood the stock, his graces the sappe, his servants the branches, and good works the grapes."[40] The members of the godly body are "knit together" and confirm their election by "receiving the Sacraments . . . which are holy tokens, visible signes of invisible graces."[41] So, too, the visible church is the earthly embodiment of the invisible church of the elect. The saints are "joyned, and compacted, not onely to the visible Church by certaine bands which are visible and dissoluble . . . but also by other ties, and ligaments, which are internall, invisible, and [in]dissoluble, to wit, the band of their eternall election in Christ."[42]

These principles also shape Bentham's manuscript memorial for his patron, "The Life of Lord Edward Montagu." Addressed to Montagu's eldest son, Bentham offers "a book of record to further your remembrance of the many worthy examples of your renowned Parents."[43] The manuscript convenes and reanimates a lost community of Montagu ancestors, but also resurrects a body of textual authorities. Bentham draws on "authentick records and credible relations."[44] The inscription on Lord Chief Justice Edward Montagu's funeral monument in Weekley is recorded alongside marginal citations of chronicle histories ("Stowe, at the end of Hen. 8, Speed Hen. 8"). His primary source is a work of "sound and sufficient authority," the Lord Chief Justice's funeral sermon, with its deathbed account culminating in Montagu's "depart[ing] this life most christianly, easily and happily."[45] As the voices of Bentham's sources blend with his, temporal shifts in the narrative and exchanges between the acts of reading and writing create a text that incorporates the universal, meditative features of godliness as both formal and thematic touchstones.

A similar incorporation pervades the Montagu brothers' monuments for their dead. "You hear how that God hath taken to himself my brother Walter Mountagu," Sidney Montagu wrote in March 1616, and imagining his brother's migration from the visible to the invisible church: "He hath broken the ice to us, and we must follow after."[46] Two years later, on July 21,

[40] Bentham, *Societie*, 3.
[41] Bentham, *Societie*, 145, 147 and 181; and see Lake, "'Charitable Christian Hatred,'" 152–3, on this imagery in Bentham's political theology.
[42] Bentham, *Societie*, 215.
[43] Bentham, *Societie*, fol. ¶2ᵛ.
[44] NRO Montagu MS 186, item 10, 1.
[45] NRO Montagu MS 186, item 10, 2–5. Bentham was vicar at Weekley from 1617–1630: see *ODNB*.
[46] *BQ*, vol. I, 247.

Figure 2.3 William Cure and Nicholas Johnson, Monument for James Montagu, Bishop of Winchester (1618). Bath Abbey.
Author's photograph.

Charles wrote to his elder brother, Edward, "This day, about 7 of the clock in the morning, God took my brother [James] to his rest. When breath was gone, I went to look for his will,"[47] a document in which James had carefully attended to arrangements for his memorial. "Yet my will is to have three hundred pounds bestowed uppon a Monument in the body of the church of Bathe," he states, "and for all other [funeral] chardges I would not have my Executors exceede the amount of foure hundred poundes."[48]

Five months after James's death, Charles made "Covenantes for the tombe . . . with William Cuer, citizen and free mason of London, and Nycholas Johnson, of the p[ar]ish of St. Savior in Southwark, in the countie of Surr[ey], carver." The contract commissioned "one tomb or monument of alabaster and touchstone with armes to be carved and engraven, and to be set in their proper colours and mettalls" (see Figure 2.3).[49] The primary place of arms in the contract is consistent with the period's understanding of monuments chiefly as genealogical records: the finished work, surmounted by "fower griffin heads upon their severall pedestals, representing the crests of the arms of the Montagues," is a monument to dynastic identity.[50] Above all, however, the Bath monument commemorates the indissoluble bonds of fraternal fellowship. The

[47] *BQ*, vol. I, 253. [48] TNA PROB 11/132/132, fol. 37^{r}.
[49] See Dingley, *History from Marble*, vol. II, 156–8, for "Articles of Indenture for the Erection of the Tomb of James Montague," dated November 25, 1618.
[50] Dingley, *History from Marble*, vol. II, 157.

Latin inscription, supplied, according to the covenant, by Charles Montagu, extends the ties binding the band of brothers across the porous threshold of death: "with due ceremonies," the epitaph reads, the four surviving Montagus, "eus cum justis ... Equites aurati, Fratri optime merito cum lachrimis posuerunt" (golden knights, with tears for a brother of the best merit, have buried him).[51]

Like Charles Montagu's monument, the Bath Abbey tomb locates remembrance between separation and union, and finally dissolves this false opposition. "The faithfull being dead," as Perkins writes, "continue members of [Christ's] family and have Christ Jesus dead and buried reckoned among them for their eldest brother."[52] This monument to fraternal unity is accompanied by a second memorial in wood, one that attempts to reinterpret the abbey as a memory palace. "His brother, Sir Henry Montagu, L[ord] C[hief] J[ustice]," a plaque near James's tomb reports, "erected the great West Doors in his memory."[53] In "a curious artifice," the arms of the two deceased brothers James and Walter are joined by a banner inscribed with the beginning of Psalm 133:1, "Ecce quam bonum et quam iucundum est" ("Behold, how good and how pleasant it is"). Visitors are called upon to supply the conclusion, drawing on their memories: "habitare fratres in unum" ("for brethren to dwell together in unity").[54]

Absent from Bath Abbey's commemoration of the Montagu brothers is the name of the mother. Patrilineal descent and royal service unite the brothers here, rather than the common venter and milk.[55] The secular project of union, grounded in "auncient *Stocke* and *Name*," subordinates and suppresses the woman's part: the venter is only a vessel transmitting a paternal legacy. Yet the sorrow uniting the fraternal mourners for James Montagu must have carried a trace of Elizabeth Montagu's memory. She died on May 19, 1618, just two months before her son, and was buried in the tomb prepared for her according to her husband's will seventeen years earlier. Joseph Bentham officiated at the funeral.[56]

[51] My thanks to Jaime Goodrich for her help with this translation.

[52] Perkins, *Godly and Learned Exposition ... [upon] the Revelation*, 20–1.

[53] From the plaque in Bath Abbey. [54] See Dingley, *History from Marble*, vol. I, xxvi.

[55] A Latin inscription on the Bath monument identifies James as Edward Montagu's fifth son ("Edwardi Montacuti de Boughton ... Filius quinto genitus") but does not name his mother. The couple's monument at Weekley is also dedicated entirely to genealogical record: see Wise, *Montagus*, 71–3.

[56] NRO Montagu MS 186, item 10, Bentham, "Life," 31. The letters surrounding Elizabeth Montagu's final illness and death express her sons' concern and sorrow: see *BQ*, vol. II, 251–2.

If the Montagu brothers' secular program easily submerged its female origins, the sacred imagery underpinning this project of union accommodated and encouraged women's participation. Joined in the religious culture of Puritanism, the Montagu women engaged in acts of commemoration and self-commemoration, conveying to their descendants the memory of their membership in the godly body. After the death of Edward Montagu's first wife, Elizabeth Jefferay, he erected a monument in the parish church of Chiddingly, fulfilling her dying wish (see Figure 2.4):

> Dame Elizabeth Mountagu . . . died the: 6: of December: 1611: at whose request to her said husband S[i]r Edward Mountagu in memory both of her discent and ofspringe,: this monument was erected and finished: 1612.[57]

The monument joins three generations of Jefferay women. The deceased mother, Alice, appears recumbent while her husband, John, adopts the "toothache" position nearby. Standing erect in niches beside them are the effigies of the surviving husband, Edward, and his departed wife, Elizabeth. In front of the monument, their only child, another Elizabeth, who survived her mother, kneels. While the depiction of generations of living and dead relatives on tombs was common across confessional divides and certainly was not unique to Puritanism, the iconography of the monument resonates with the principles espoused by the ministers of the Kettering Lecture and their patron. The tomb *is* unique in the period in its representation of figures standing erect:[58] the effigies of Edward and Elizabeth stand in niches traditionally reserved for the statues of saints. They embody the reformed society of the saints, a community embracing both the living and the dead. Subtracted from fellowship with his brothers, Edward Montagu here becomes a godly witness to the bands tying him to his wife, now a member of the invisible church, and the daughter who would outlive him. Although silenced by death, Elizabeth Jefferay expresses her will in this token of remembrance, relying on the conjoined bodies of marriage and faith that, on this occasion, approved the body's right to direct the head.

[57] From the monument. Attributions to William Cure II and Nicholas Johnson have been rejected by White, *Biographical Dictionary*, 47. Montagu recalls having erected the monument in his will: see TNA PROB 11/196/404, fol. 365^{r}.

[58] The other example of a standing figure in the period is the effigy of Peregrine Bertie at St. James Church: Spilsby, who stands atop a monument for his daughter, Catherine. She died in childbirth in 1610, so the erect effigies at Spilsby and Chiddingly are contemporaneous. The younger Elizabeth Montagu married Peregrine's son, Robert Bertie, in 1605. Since both families were firm Puritans, the standing effigies may signify the belief in the immediate enrollment of the godly in the invisible church upon death. Fourteen years later, Sidney Montagu depicted his son Henry standing erect in a niche: see Chapter 1.

Figure 2.4 Unknown sculptor (Cure workshop?), Monument for John and Alice Jefferay and Elizabeth Jefferay Montagu (1612). Chiddingly Parish Church
Author's photograph.

2 A Book of Goulde

The linen sheet that shrouded three-year old Henry Montagu at his funeral in 1625, "beeing the same which covered him to his Christening," was transformed from a sacramental token to a memorial by the addition of "true-love knottes of black Ribbins made by divers of his friends."[59] Although Sidney Montagu says no more about these "friends," the task was most likely undertaken by the boy's female relations. This silence invites us to situate "women's textualities," to adopt Susan Frye's evocative term within an extended familial network where women as well as men were productive and engaged.[60]

The fabric of the Montagu family's efforts to build their collective legacy is legible in exchanges between surviving texts and between texts and artifacts. Material texts – textiles, plate, monuments, and jewelry – permeate the Montagu archive, often in the service of remembrance. When Elizabeth Montagu writes to her son to request the loan of "hangings" needed to decorate her hall at Hemington, she refers to "a sute of hangings of the storie of Holifernes and Judithe" bequeathed by her aunt, Frances Sidney Radcliffe, Countess of Sussex, to Elizabeth's husband, Edward Montagu (see Plate 2).[61] The countess also perpetuated her memory by founding Lady Frances Sidney Sussex College at Cambridge, "a good and godly monument for the mayntenance of good learning." Her great-nephew, James Montagu, laid the cornerstone of this "Puritan seminary"[62] on formerly monastic grounds in 1595. His service as "Master, or rather nursing-father of Sidney College," launched his career as Dean of the Chapel Royal. Remembering this debt, he bequeathed "all [his] bookes in all places where they are" to the college at his death.[63]

The intertwining of the sacred in the secular is evident in the Montagus' material and textual remains. "Hospitality," as Julia Reinhard Lupton writes, "is phenomenology as social theater: a way of soliciting and orchestrating forms of appearing that gather humans [and] objects . . . in a single

[59] Quoted from the Barnwell manuscript. See Chapter 1.

[60] Frye, *Pens and Needles*. See also Ezell, "Elizabeth Isham's Books," 71–84, to which this discussion is greatly indebted.

[61] See NRO Montagu MS 3, fol. 69^{r}; and TNA PROB 11/74/331, fol. 249^{r}. The tapestries now hang in the reading room at Boughton House. I am indebted to Crispin Powell for noting the bequest in connection with Lady Montagu's letter.

[62] Fielding, "Conformists," 30.

[63] See TNA PROB 11/74/331, Will of Frances Radcliffe, Countess of Sussex, fol. 247^{r}. And see TNA PROB 11/132/132, Will of James Montagu, fol. 37^{v}; and Fuller, *History of the Worthies*, 284.

if self-divided ensemble of encounter, experience, and recognition."[64] In Elizabeth Montagu's social theater, secular forms are invariably inflected by the sacred: thus the apocryphal Judith, the scourge of God who seduces and beheads the tyrant Holofernes, takes shape in a rich tapestry – "an heirloome of the house" – adorning Elizabeth Montagu's walls as she orchestrates her encounters with noble guests.[65] When she bequeaths "to my sonne Sir Henry Capell the Book of goulde which I [meante] to my daughter his wife, prayinge him to bestowe it uppon his daughter Besse," her gift blends secular and sacred matter.[66] This compact book of devotions was set in a gold cover and hung on a gold chain from the waist.[67] The object's material richness figures the precious wisdom inside: half-text and half-jewel, the book's sacred script and its value as an accessory cooperate to convey Lady Montagu's memory to her granddaughter.

At the heart of the culture of Puritanism uniting the Montagu monumental circle was the exchange of books and material tokens of remembrance. Lady Montagu's bequest of her book of gold must have been the last in a series of loans and gifts of godly texts throughout her life. Like this book of gold, Ann Montagu's manuscript "Letters, Prayers, and Poems" uses the material text to embody a commemorative purpose.[68] And like Elizabeth Jefferay's eloquent tomb, the manuscript makes use of Puritan tenets to forge ties between generations and to transmit the author's memory to posterity.[69] Ann Montagu's text locates remembrance at the core of the Puritan sacrament, exploring a process of recollection,

[64] Lupton, "Macbeth's Martlets," 375.

[65] TNA PROB 11/131/760, fol. 425^r. "The Book of Judeth" was included among the "Apocrypha" of the King James Bible.

[66] TNA PROB 11/131/760, fol. 425^v. See also TNA 11/24/113, fol. 67^r for Katherine Styles's bequest "to John Chesemans doughter a book which was doctour Gawthorpe with clapses silver," a devotional work which, Salter surmises, was a gift from the author John Gunthorpe: see *Six Renaissance Men*, 122–4.

[67] James, *Women's Voices*, 87 and 266.

[68] Ann Montagu's manuscript is not titled or paginated; these were provided when the papers were bound in NRO Montagu MS 3, fols. 235–59. Two unrelated letters appear on fols. 233–4. The work proper begins with the dedicatory epistle to the Montagu children on fol. 235. The order of the manuscript from this point to the last page appears to be Lady Montagu's: the pages were stitched together, perhaps in preparation for binding, with seven needle marks visible on every page. All subsequent citations are parenthetical, citing stanza numbers in the central poem and folio numbers from NRO Montagu 3 for the minor poems and prose sections. Folio pages are numbered consecutively on either side; therefore, recto and verso are not indicated.

[69] Ann Montagu (1563–1648) was one of ten children of John Crouch of Corneybury (d. 1605). In 1625, she and her two sisters, "sole survivors of so numerous an offspring, out of reverence and love" erected a monument to their father's memory in Layston Church, Hertfordshire. See Gerish, "Cornybury," 151, for the Latin inscription and an English translation.

interpretation, and transformation in the sacrament that creates and recreates the godly subject and the community embracing her.

When Ann Crouch married Edward Montagu in 1625, she had been thrice widowed.[70] Having no children from previous marriages, she became "as a naturall mother," her husband recalls, to his four young children.[71] Twelve years later, she created a textual monument addressed to the 20-year-old son and heir, Edward, his two brothers, and a sister – the same children to whom Joseph Bentham's dedicates his *Societie of the Saints*.[72]

Ann Montagu was not only encouraged by Bentham's example to address her children in a devotional work. She incorporates the religious principles and politics espoused by her husband into both the form and content of her book, where they animate the "sweet communion" of the godly.[73] The work's central piece, 160 quatrains of original verse, rehearses the practical divinity taught in the Kettering Lecture. Her poem brings to life the model Puritan described in Bentham's *Societie of the Saints*. Rather than defending "fanaticall Separatists," Bentham defines Puritans as "practicing Protestants":

> such men, who daily reade the Scriptures, pray with their families, teach them the way to heaven, eschue … all knowne sinnes: spend the Lords daies holily in hearing Gods Word, prayer, meditation, conference, singing of Psalmes, … [are] diligent in their particular Callings, frame their lives according to Gods will revealed in his Word, &c.[74]

Lady Montagu also follows Bentham's method in his "Life of Lord Edward Montagu," adding to her original composition texts copied or adapted from printed works, specifically Puritan writers, and chiefly those trained at Cambridge.[75] Her "Cattychisme" is a verbatim copy of Joseph Hall's

[70] Ann was married first to Robert Wynchell, a painter stainer, second, to Richard Chamberlain, and third, to Sir Ralph Hare of Stow Bardolph. Her match with Montagu was brokered by her sister Margaret, Henry Montagu's third wife.

[71] See TNA PROB 11/196/404, Will of Edward Mountagu, fol. 365ʳ. These are the children of Edward Montagu's second wife, Frances Cotton. Edward waited twenty-four years after the birth of his daughter Elizabeth in 1593 for the arrival of his son and heir, a fact that he acknowledges in NRO Montagu MS 186, article 13, "Directions to my Sonne": "My Sonne, God of his grace gave you me in myne old age, when other thought to have possessed myne estate."

[72] See Bentham, *Societie*, fol. ¶2ʳ. Edward alone was the addressee of Bentham's "Life," but the four children were the recipients of a lost manuscript mentioned in the dedication to *Societie*.

[73] Bentham, *Societie*, fol. ¶4ᵛ. [74] Bentham, *Societie*, 29.

[75] Two of Ann's brothers matriculated from Cambridge, Richard in 1585 and Thomas in 1582: see Venn, ed., *Alumni cantabrigienses*, Part 1, vol. III, 426. Her major sources, Joseph Hall and William Attersoll, were Cambridge divines: see *ODNB* for both. Hall became chaplain for Prince Henry in 1608, which brought him into contact with James Montagu.

Briefe Summe of the Principles of Religion.[76] She adapts her preparation for the Eucharist from William Attersoll's *Badges of Christianity* and concludes with a redaction of John Andrewes's "To all Christian sinners, that desire repentance" from *Andrewes Humble Petition.*[77] A "token of my love and affection to you all" (st. 4), the manuscript is a mother's legacy – a meager "portion" but one "more of worth / than gold or silver mine" (st. 152–3).

As Ann Montagu weaves together the voices of her sources with her own, she demonstrates and embodies the processes of Puritan reading and practice and their roles in creating the godly subject. The central idea of the work is summarized in the answer to the first question posed in Hall's catechism to the question, "How many things are required of a christian?" The answer is, simply, "too knowlidg and practis" (fol. 248).[78] Ann Montagu's original poem repeatedly stresses the crucial need for the godly to "take account" in a continual process of self-examination: no less than a dozen times in 640 lines of verse does she direct her children to "reed and practise" (st. 1, 3, 4, 132, 147, 160), "meditate" (st. 41, 67, 113), and "calle to minde" (st. 89). This self-study is essential to the effort "to get full assurance of being with Christ"; as Nicolas Estwick states it in his funeral sermon for fellow Kettering lecturer, Robert Bolton, "we should study our selves, and ransacke our soules, and be of good grounds, and to have certaine evidence that our change [in death] shall be for the better."[79] Ann Montagu advises her children to "worship in feare" (st. 59), and Estwick encourages his congregation to "frequently ransacke thy heart [and] keep GODS feare fresh in thy soule."[80]

If "practis" is key to cementing the fellowship of the elect and confirming the predestined salvation of each member, "knowlidg" underscores the crucial role in self-examination of reading and hearing the Word. "By studious reading of this Booke," Bentham tells readers of *Societie of the Saints*, "thou maist know thy selfe, and understand of what company

[76] Hall, *Briefe Summe, in Works*, 799–800. I am indebted to Paula McQuade for her discovery of the source for Ann Montagu's catechism. On the flood of Protestant catechisms published in the period, see Green, *Christian's*, and on women's catechisms, see McQuade, *Maternal Catechizing*.

[77] Attersoll, *Badges of Christianity*, esp. book 3, 202–395; and Andrewes, *Andrewes Humble* Petition, sigs. $A3^{r-v}$. Attersoll's catechism, "Principles of Christian Religion," is appended to this volume (fols. $Gg3^{r}$-$Hh3^{v}$) and was enlarged and printed under this title in 1635. Andrewes was a preacher in Wiltshire and a prolific writer of religious works. See *ODNB* on both.

[78] See Hall, *Briefe Summe*, 799.

[79] Estwick, *Learned and Godly Sermon*, 32–3. On the importance of self-examination to assurance of election, see Lake, *Moderate Puritanism*, 351–68; and Green, *Print and Protestantism*, 305–71.

[80] Estwick, *Learned and Godly Sermon*, 35.

thou art."[81] Reading leads the worshipper to self-knowledge, guarantees membership in the good fellowship of the visible church, and assures enrollment in the invisible church. Hearing the Word is equally valuable: Bentham names as the fifth duty of the saints to "resolve to hear God's voice in the ministry of the Word," and insists that auditors hear the Word "not spiderlike," "not Athenian-like," "not unprofitably," "nor obstinately."[82] The resolution to read, hear, and keep the Word, according to William Perkins, defines the essence of the true religion: "The opinion and practise of the church of Rome is damnable, who barre the people of God from reading and hearing the Scripture in their vulgar tongue. For in depriving them of this . . . they barre them of their salvation."[83] Ransacking the scripture, in turn, requires us to ransack our souls. When Ann Montagu encourages her children to "pray, reade, lament thy sinnes" (st. 147), the point is not to earn salvation – she teaches them to pray, thanking God "for my election, creation, redemption, vocation, justification, and continuall preservation" (fol. 254) – but to reach assurance of election and to recognize the company of the elect.[84]

In "Letters, Prayers, and Poems," self-study is prompted by and dependent upon memory, and remembrance, in turn, is a practice governed by the unique purpose and nature of the Puritan sacraments. Ann Montagu's tour of the Sabbath, hour by hour from rising to sleep, occupies nearly a third of her poem, agreeing with Bentham's Sabbatarian view of the holy day as "a signe and meanes of mans communion with God," a call to meditate on one's readiness to partake of the Lord's supper:

For god himselfe hath this day set
unto this holy ende
remembering lest we forget
and so our god offend

(st. 51)[85]

On this day, in particular, the godly must worship in fear. Eat lightly, Ann Montagu tells her children: "Sathan loves suche belly gods . . . all they that crams themselves that day" (st. 63–4). Food dulls the wits and distracts from the self-examination needed to ensure that one receives the sacrament without sin:

81 Bentham, *Societie*, fol. ¶4v. 82 Bentham, *Societie*, 145.

83 Perkins, *Godly and Learned Exposition . . . [upon] the Revelation*, 9.

84 See Lake, *Moderate Puritans*, 151–68. MacCulloch, *Reformation*, 389–90, notes that Perkins's adherence to covenant theology required this introspection to assure election by grace.

85 Bentham, *Societie*, 141.

If you would worthily receive
examine your estate
your knowlidg faith repentance too
The danger els is greate

(st. 73)

Her redaction of William Attersoll's guidance to "what or whoever thou art that intendest to com to that heavenly banquet of christ his last supper" (fol. 250) explains the danger more fully: "In prepareing thy selfe . . . approach – but otherwise thou must know the divell is also present to enter with unworthy receivers or receiveing" (fol. 251). Her source explicates at length "the greate danger and punishment that is procured and purchased by want of this preparation. For an unworthie receiver," Attersoll writes, "is guilty of the blood of Christ."[86] It is not only the individual worshipper who must confirm her readiness to receive. In preparation for the sacrament, "masters of families" are required "to examine their people in their houses whether they can repeate the lords prayer or noe the creede and the ten commandements and in som measure understand and give a reason of them" (fol. 250). Ministers and masters – and mothers, Ann Montagu argues – lay the foundation of "knowlidg" from which "practis" proceeds.

As protection against these dangers, Lady Montagu follows Attersoll in providing a careful explication of the "trewe use of every signe" (fol. 251) of the sacrament. Her adaptation of the source is rooted in contested physical and notional space of Northamptonshire parish churches in the 1630s, where liturgical struggles between Puritans and conformists intensified in the decade before the Civil War.[87] The Kettering Lecture became a center of resistance to the Laudian enforcement of ceremonial worship, and certainly Ann Montagu's idea of the true church was aligned with that of her husband and his ministers. Puritan resistance stemmed from the perception that ceremonial worship eroded the practical divinity of the godly by stressing "the holiness of the institution" and participation in its rites as "the main criterion of membership of that church, as opposed to visible godliness."[88] Ceremonial, bodily worship – indeed, the body itself – was seen by Puritans as interfering with the spirit of grace; thus Bishop Dee's commission to create altars in Peterborough in 1637 seemed to Puritans to invite God's wrath when the plague erupted in the diocese the following year.[89] Ann Montagu's charge to eat lightly on the Sabbath and

[86] Attersoll, *Badges of Christianity*, 344. The discussion continues for four more pages.
[87] See Lake, "'Charitable Christian Hatred'"; and Fielding, "Conformists," 92–146 and 203–43.
[88] Fielding, "Conformists," 204–5. [89] Fielding, "Conformists," 126.

instead "thy soule fill full with heavenly grace" (st. 62) responds to this valuation of spirit over body. "Trusting upon that grace" (st. 64) and assured of one's election, one may partake of the sacrament as a spiritual commemoration, a feeding "in hart":

> Christ did invite all to come privatly
> in memory of his death
> to feede by faith in hart one him
> he doth himself bequeath
>
> (st. 85)

To elaborate the nature of Christ's bequest, Ann Montagu explores the dense web of signs comprising the Puritan sacrament, inspired by Attersoll's scheme.[90] There are four outward parts to the Lord's Supper: "The Minister, the Word of institution, the Signe, and the Receiver," corresponding to four inward parts: "God the Father, the Holy Ghost, Christ, and the faithfull."[91] Lady Montagu's relationship to her source is better described as inspiration than imitation: there is no verbatim copying here, as was the case in the "Cattychisme." She is clearly working from memory. As she breaks down the inward and outward parts of the sacrament, the outward sign does not simply index inward grace. Rather, the visible sacrament and its invisible meanings multiply:

> The outward parts are fower:
>
> first – the minister
> secondly – bread and wine
> thirdly – the consecration
> fourthly – the receiver
>
> These four represent 4 inwards:
>
> The minister – god the father
> The bread – the body of christ
> The consecration – the holy spirit
> The receiveing – faith
>
> (fol. 251)

In Ann Montagu's interactive sacrament, the process of reading and interpretation of the ceremony is a version of the process of reading

[90] Attersoll's scheme is not unique. See the similar model in Perkins, *Golden Chaine*, 111; and see Chapter 3 for discussion. The stress on reception of the Eucharist is a position held in common between Church of England clergy and Puritans, particularly "conforming Calvinists" such as the Montagus. See New, *Anglican and Puritanism*, 59–81.

[91] Attersoll, *Principles*, D3^{r}. The scheme is discussed at length in Attersoll, *Badges of Christianity*, 221–330.

and practicing advocated throughout the manuscript as the central duty of the godly. These processes are repeated continually. Each time the worshipper reads the scripture, each time she partakes of the sacrament, she is launched once more into a new chapter of meditation and self-scrutiny – another episode of ransacking the soul, another taking account of the inventory of sin and salvation. As the worshipper experiences each object and action, she moves through a process of reading and interpretation: indeed, the last section of Attersoll's *Principles of the Christian Religion* is entitled, "Rules of Interpretation to understand the Sacraments."[92] One reads the sacrament as if it were a text. For Perkins, in fact, textuality is the distinguishing feature of the Puritan sacrament: "every sacrament is the word of God made visible to the eye."[93]

The rules of interpretation, as Lady Montagu expresses them, rest primarily on likeness rather than essence. They are visual and tactile; they both arise from recollection and prompt memory. As the minister offers the bread and wine, she writes, so God the father offers his son; the minister's preparation of the bread and wine "calle[s] to thy remembrance" God's love in preparing his son "to be the foode of lyfe for thee;" the breaking of the bread recalls "the torments Christ suffered in his body." From remembrance, one moves to persuasion: when the minister offers the sacrament, he "must perswade thee" that God the father is offering his son. Finally, through faith and knowledge, the receiver persuades herself of union with Christ:

> When thou with thy hands request it and puttest it into thy mouth thou must with faith lift up thy soule to heaven and aprehend christ Jesus now fully perswading thy selfe that thou art in christ and christ in thee and christ with all his benefits are thine. (fol. 251)

As the godly believer, filled with "hongring desire" (fol. 250), moves from remembrance to persuasion to self-persuasion, the Puritan sacrament is refigured not as a single sign but as a dispersed collection of figures whose unity is apprehended through sensory experience. As a prompt to self-examination, the sacrament not only remembers Christ's sacrifice, but also attests to and persuades the believer and the visible church of the worshipper's election. This complex web of symbolic actions and objects thus functions as a "remembrancer" in two early modern meanings of the word. It is at once a sign of remembrance "to put you oft in mind" of Christ and a witness to salvation. If, as Perkins claims, Christ himself is a "faithful

[92] Attersoll, *Principles*, fol. D4r.   [93] Perkins, *Commentarie . . . [upon] Galatians*, 254.

witnesse," the *corpus Christi* at once a witness to salvation and the invisible substance witnessed.[94]

Ann Montagu's emphasis on sensory experience, both in Communion and in the "sweet communion" of the godly, typologically foresees Merleau-Ponty's analogy of sensation as sacramental: as "the bread is not only something sensible [but also] communicates to us the real presence of God," so through the senses we "enter into communion with the world."[95] Understanding the power of visual and tactile experience to prompt memory, Ann Montagu crafts her encounter with the sacrament with an intense concern for its appearance on the page. She transforms Attersoll's lengthy treatise into two quatrains: squares of text expressing the intertwining of objects and subjects in the visible and the invisible church. The matter of the sacrament and the manuscript are mirror images of each other.[96] In both cases, materiality is key to establishing individual and collective memory: "the shared text," as Andrew Cambers points out, "whether in manuscript or in print," played a central role in "the maintenance of godly sociability."[97] Stitched together by threads – the pinpricks of the needle still visible on every page – presented in a unique format on royal folio sheets that have been cut in half vertically, written and arranged with care, Lady Montagu's "Letters, Prayers, and Poems" is a work in which disparate, scattered parts are deliberately crafted into a unified body.

Structurally, "Letters, Prayers, and Poems" plots the observation, repetition, and self-correction of Puritan "practis." Composite, multiple, and complex, the manuscript calls itself to a stop repeatedly, only to resume its meditation in a different form, genre, or register. A dedicatory epistle opens the book, followed by the 160-stanza poem, a versification of the wisdom summed up in the catechism and the preparation for the sacrament that follow. A lengthy, multipurpose "prayer for morning or evening or any other time" is finished by a poem of five quatrains

[94] Perkins, *Godly and Learned Exposition . . . [upon] the Revelation*, 17.

[95] Merleau-Ponty, *Phenomenology of Perception*, 245–6.

[96] Montagu's scribal condensation of Attersoll's volume shares processes of Puritan writing such as sermon notation and minister's schematic reductions of doctrine (see Figure 3.4) for easy digestion by the faithful. See Hunt, *Art of Hearing*, 63 and 98–100; and Morgan, *Godly Learning*, 106–12. The British Library copy of Attersoll's *Badges of Christianity* (Shelfmark 4324.i.28) displays a reader's marginal notes throughout and summary notations on the last two pages, keyed to date of reading/writing and pagination. For example, "18 Aprille 1614: A Sacrament is nothing else but a sensible word and a sealinge up of the word within, 295."

[97] Cambers, "Reading," 815.

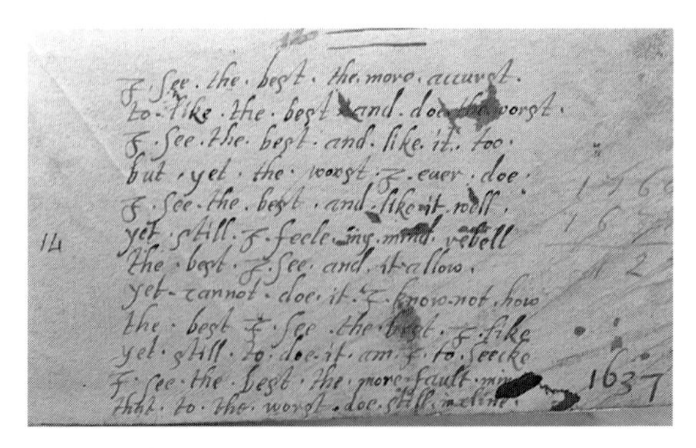
I see. the. best. the. more. accurst.
to. like. the. best and. doe the worst.
I. see. the. best. and. like. it. too.
but. yet. the. worst. I. euer. doe.
I. see. the. best. and. like it. well.
yet. still. I. feele. my. mind. rebell
the. best. I. see. and. it allow.
yet. cannot. doe. it. I. know not. how
the. best. I. see. the. best. I. like
yet. still. to. doe. it. am. I. to. seeke
I. see. the. best. the. more. fault. mine
that. to. the. worst. doe. still. incline
1637

Figure 2.5 Ann Montagu, "Letters, Prayers, and Poems," NRO Montagu MS 3, fol. 258 (detail). Northampton Record Office. By kind permission of the Duke of Buccleuch and Queensberry, KBE.

addressed to the Montagu children, ending with what appears to be the author's farewell:

> By mee your loveing mother still
> and ever your deare freinde,
> if you with care will doe gods will
> Ann Mountagu I ende
>
> (fol. 257)

But this is not the end. Followed by a short prayer of blessing for her children, another poem of eight quatrains presents "this poore work of mine" to a friend:

> my loveing friend, this book I give
> to you o reade the same
> and practice it grant, you may live
> to gloryfie gods name

"And so farwell," she ends, "I say no more / but bid you now adue / Gods grace inrich your soules with store / your freind Ann Mountagu" (fol. 258). But again the manuscript resumes: this poem is followed by a second mother's blessing, asking God to "direct them all by thy living word." Then the penultimate entry takes a new direction. In Ann Montagu's hand, a twelve-line poem of rhyming couplets is accompanied by the manuscript's date of composition (see Figure 2.5):

> I · see · the · best · the · more · accurst ·
> To · like · the · best · and · doe · the · worst ·

I · see · the · best · and · like · it · too ·
But · yet · the · worst · I · ever · doe ·
I · see · the · best · and · like · it · well ·
Yet · still · I · feele · my · mind · rebell ·
The · best · I · see · and · it · allow ·
Yet · cannot · doe · it · I · know · not · how ·
The · best · I · see · the · best · I · like ·
Yet · still · to · doe · it · am · I · to · seeke ·
I · see · the · best · the · more · fault · mine ·
That · to · the · worst · doe · still · incline · 1637
(fol. 258)

Perhaps an original work but most likely a copy, the poem is a variation on the familiar Petrarchan dilemma, "et veggio 'l meglio, et al peggior m'appiglio" ("I see the better, but lay hold on the worse").[98] Internally repetitious, reworking the same idea in six slightly different phrases, the poem is an intricately woven web in which the speaker continually tries and fails to achieve a godly state – impossible without the saving grace of God – while the poem's form embodies the same stalemate. If the poem takes a literary turn in its allusive content, the punctuation between each word emphasizes the deliberation involved in the act of writing. The pen drops to the page between each word, inscribing a halting, stilted movement that imitates the spiritual dilemma of the speaker. This deadlock is repeated by the reader, who is forced to pause, wait, and reflect between every word. While this form of composition, inserting full stops between each word, is rare in manuscript writing, it is common in carved inscriptions on funeral monuments.[99] Its usage here may suggest that the poem is a transcription of a funerary epitaph, or that the incorporated trace of monumental sculpture is an appropriate way to end this textual monument. Certainly the dating of the poem, another feature shared with funeral monuments, fixes the act of writing in a specific moment, presenting the location of writing as a space of repetition with difference; the blending of prior voices, subjects, and objects with the progressive, changing perceptions of the reading and writing selves. In this sense, the Puritan sacrament stakes out a similar location. It is a prompt to and occasion for memory based not on a simple chain of signifiers, but on a

[98] Petrarch, *Rime Sparse*, no. 264 ("I'vo pensando"), line 136.

[99] Carved inscriptions in Roman lettering often separate each word in this way: see, for instance, Blanche Parry's monument in Bacton, discussed in Chapter 6. I have been unable to find a source for the poem.

cluster of signs apprehended through repeated processes of observation, interpretation, and correction. If this penultimate poem moves toward closure of the halting manuscript preceding it, this end-stop repeats and prolongs the self-study in which the godly reader engages repeatedly throughout her life.

This equivocal closure prompts one final poem. A borrowed address "to the reader" from John Andrewes's penitential pamphlet, *Andrewes Humble Petition*, summarizes the contents of the "Letters, Prayers, and Poems." Incorporating this invitation to readership into her manuscript, Ann Montagu once again adjusts her source to emphasize the spatial placement of writing on the page. While Andrewes's book prints what is now Lady Montagu's first stanza as prose – "Reade attentively, and judge indifferently, but pray continually: receive instructions willingly, and watch the same seriously with all sedulity"[100] – the "Letters, Prayers, and Poems" creates an insistently rhyming stanza:

Reade attentively
and judge indifferently
pray continually
receive instructions willingly
and watch the same seriously
with all sedulyty
treasure them in your harts carefully
and daily meditate thereon jealously
that yee enter not into temptation carelessly

Prayer with practice
oft times on your knee
gets favour with god
as daily we see

But prayer with lips
where hart is away
returns into sinne
their soules to destroy
(fol. 259)

As she brings the buried perfect rhymes of Andrewes's prose to the surface, crafting a memorable if monotonous stanza – memorable, perhaps, because monotonous – she couples them with two ballad stanzas from Andrewes, resurrecting the form and sentiment of her original poem now

[100] Andrewes, *Andrewes Humble Petition*, fol. A3^{r}.

embodied in the borrowed text. Returning us to the first poem, the manuscript mimics the repetitious, reiterative process of Puritan taking account. The continual process of reading this book coincides with the unending process of coming to know the sanctified self.

Sharing its formal and thematic qualities with the polysemous sacrament, Ann Montagu's "Letters, Prayers, and Poems" engages in a "ritual of remembrance" infused with and defined by the sacrament.[101] The manuscript's ritual involves an art of memory, emergent in medieval mnemonics, in which memory was pictured as a wax tablet where images are inscribed upon the receptive body.[102] Reproducing a tactile process of commemoration comprised of multiple layers of reading and interpretation, Ann Montagu's text embodies the visible legacy – the trace – of an evolving, progressive materiality: the wax tablet is mirrored in both the manuscript and its writer. Through continual processes of perception, recollection, and meditation, the Puritan art of memory creates the saint.

Produced and defined through engagements with an interactional sacrament, the godly worshipper in "Letters, Prayers, and Poems" is involved in a web of perceptions and relations mirrored by the commemorative text. In Ann Montagu's manuscript, as Merleau-Ponty observes, "the perceiving mind is an incarnated body," and the body "is the fabric into which all objects are woven."[103] This insistence that knowledge and practice involve "our living immersion in matter"[104] offers the starting point for a positive reading of this fluid exchange between the body and the world as a site for the evolution of a gendered subject and a feminine art of remembrance. In *The Visible and the Invisible*, Merleau-Ponty explores the "crisscrossing of the self and the world, an enfolding where the objective and subjective continually oscillate, and where the subject emerges gradually through this process.[105] "The flesh (of the world or my own)," he writes, "is not contingency, chaos, but a texture that returns to itself and conforms to itself."[106] "If one wants metaphors," he continues, "the body sensed and the body sentient are ... one sole movement in its two phases," progressive segments like the phases of the moon.[107] Emerging in progressive acts of remembrance and interpretation of sacramental matter, conforming her flesh to the body of Christ, Ann

[101] Ezell, "Elizabeth Isham's Books," 80.

[102] Carruthers, *Book of Memory*, 18–55. Ann Montagu's manuscript can be read as an analog to Freud's "Mystic Writing Pad." For applications of this image to early modern writing, see Fleming, "Whitewash," 136, and Ezell, "Elizabeth Isham's Books."

[103] Merleau-Ponty, *Phenomenology of Perception*, 87 and 273.

[104] Grosz, "Merleau-Ponty," 15.

[105] Merleau-Ponty, *Visible and Invisible*, 133.

[106] Merleau-Ponty, *Visible and Invisible*, 146.

[107] Merleau-Ponty, *Visible and Invisible*, 138.

Montagu – author, subject, and reader – embodies the fluid, supple "texture" of godly experience in herself and in her text.

Like the tablet of wax, the Puritan sacrament also contains an evolutionary trace: the bread and wine offered, the broken body of Christ recalled, the minister's persuasion, the self-persuasion of the receiver, all displayed before the eyes and inscribed as a whole and complete unity in the mind's eye. The sacrament at once initiates and reiterates the process of self-examination that precedes and emerges from it. If Montagu men call upon the language of embodiment current in Puritan conceptions of the godly family to create permanent memory traces, Ann Montagu borrows the signs of the sacrament to craft her memorial. Her text recollects a sacrament that confirms salvation, imprinting its seal on the malleable, impressionable body of the saint. Each approach to partake – of the sacrament and of Montagu's sacramental text – is one of hundreds of scenes, acted and reenacted, where the soul reads and practices again the predestined fact of grace.

3 In Perfect Memorie

In the decade following Ann Montagu's writing of her "Letters, Prayers, and Poems," the vulnerabilities of church buildings and their fabric became starkly clear. Ornaments of ceremonial worship installed during Laudian renovations were uprooted and destroyed. As Simon Gunton laments, in the ravages afflicted on Peterborough Cathedral by Cromwell's troops in 1643, sacred and secular monuments were equally threatened: "When there was no more painted or carved work to demolish, they then rob and rifle the Tombs, and violate the Monuments of the dead," beginning with those of Katherine of Aragon and "what is left of Mary Queen of Scots" (*History*, 335). Writing to her imprisoned husband in the same year, Ann Montagu reported that parliamentary troops had also ransacked her home, Barnwell Castle:

> the souldiers soe unruly . . . got all the best things out of the house [and] hath blowne all the windoes in the halls, not one bit of them left, and great part of the parlor windoes. . .All the beds that stand in the howse are almost spoyled for they have left whole regements of cattell behinde.

"Seeing it is gods will it should bee soe let to us," she concludes, "let us undergoe with patience that which god layeth upon us."[108] She would not see her husband again; he died under house arrest in London the following year.

[108] NRO Montagu MS 191 (loose sheet). "Cattell" here must mean "insects, vermin, and the like" (*OED*).

In the last wills of the dying, remembrance retreated from the contested space of sacred sites to the social and familial networks of exchange and commemoration. The iconoclastic attack on religious objects, including funeral monuments, as Susan E. James puts it, "made it painfully clear to the entire population just how unrealistic an expectation was of perpetual remembrance encased in an ecclesiastical amber."[109] Church monuments continued to be built, of course: Elizabeth Montagu's effigy lies in Weekley, and she bequeathed £100 for her funeral, "desyring my said executor not to exceede that somme, for suche expenses are but frivylouse, hinder the livinge, and the deceased profitt nothinge."[110] Yet beyond merely disposing of her property, Elizabeth Montagu uses her will to paint a lasting self-portrait and to ensure her presence for posterity by transmitting material signs of remembrance. Like Ann Montagu's "Letters, Prayers, and Poems," Elizabeth Montagu's bequests convene a community joined in a covenant of remembrance; a godly family bound as witnesses to her life, each member contracted to fulfill her final wishes.

Elizabeth Montagu's will demonstrates how mourning and commemoration convey the legacy of pre-Reformation relationships to religious objects, images, and sacraments by turning from mystery to memory. The tokens bestowed by Lady Montagu place obligations of recollection on the receiver. The covenant they enact, in the belief that the bonds created in life will persist beyond death, is a secular version of the sacred union of the visible and invisible saints. The charge to remember transfers Catholic rituals of remembrance from the sacred to the secular as well: masses and obits performed for the sake of the soul are replaced by the obligation to keep alive the memory of the departed. Belongings are given "as a poore remembraunce of mee" or "a smale remembraunce of my love," with the charge that they be worn "for my sake." Lady Montagu's gifts embed memory in the quotidian: she bequeaths "my silver pottenger" to her sister, "desiring her to remember me when she eates her pottage." To a manservant, "a silver bottle to carry . . . when he travelles," noting "my worthye good Cosen, the first Ladye Dyer gave it to mee, and I am sure he will not so wishe the losse for her sake."[111]

[109] James, *Women's Voices*, 75. [110] TNA PROB 11/131/760, fol. 425^{r}.

[111] TNA PROB 11/131/760, fols. 425^{r-v}. See Hamling, "'An Areloome,'' on the post-Reformation will as a means of domesticating remembrance and relocating its rituals within the familial context. Lady Dyer may be the mother-in-law of Lady Catherine Dyer, attributed author of an epitaph for her husband, William: see Stevenson and Davidson, *Early Modern Women Poets*, 222–4.

The passage of property scripted by Lady Montagu's will creates a web of remembrance where a common identities and histories are forged. Objects originally bequeathed to her are passed on for memory's sake: "a paire of plate basins . . . which sometimes was the gratious kinges mothers" goes to her sister-in-law, and to her eldest son, "a great goulde ringe with a blonde stone in it, which ringe I desire maye remaine as an heirloome to the house because given, as I have heard, by King Henry the Eighth to the Lorde Chiefe Justice his grandfather."[112] Her son respected her wishes, bequeathing "the blond stone ring . . . which was my greate-grandfathers" to his eldest son in 1644.[113]

Elizabeth Montagu's legacies weave through a wide community of inheritors, uniting members of the Montagu circle in a common affection. Yet this dispersal of property is not a random scattering: Lady Montagu's inventory, recollected "in perfect memorie," is precise.[114] Her gifts are targeted and meaningful, and she interprets their signs for their recipients, inserting her lasting presence into their future uses and meanings: she leaves to her sister, "my little ringe being a death enamiled in greene; I have much loved, and mourned for my worthy daughter Wray, that gave it to mee, and with my blessing I send [it], to mourne for mee."[115] If Ann Montagu's "Letters, Prayers, and Poems" takes its shape from the polysemous sacrament at its heart, Elizabeth Montagu's legacies are infused with the trace of mystical presence, now converted to the matter of memory. When she closes her will by presenting herself as the king's "dayly poore Beadeswoman," her prayers, performed in absence of the discarded rosary, carry only the memory rather than the mystery of a sacramental past.[116] And although lacking prophetic power to enforce her will, Lady Montagu's living legacies exert their force through memory. When her bequest of £5 to the poor of six parishes was violated by "the townes (having none or very few poore) put[ting] out their five pounds to usury," the donation was repaired, in part, by her son Edward.[117] Twenty-five years later, he bequeathed 6s 8d to each of

[112] TNA PROB 11/131/760, fol. 425r. This reference to property owned by Mary, Queen of Scots, is intriguing. Edward and Elizabeth Montagu, along with other Northamptonshire gentry, were mourners at the queen's funeral at Peterborough Cathedral in 1587. See R. Prescott-Innes, ed., *Funeral*, 12 and 15.

[113] TNA PROB 11/196/404, fol. 367r.

[114] TNA PROB 11/131/760, fol. 425r.

[115] TNA PROB 11/131/760, fol. 425r.

[116] TNA PROB 11/131/760, fol. 426v. Compare, for example, TNA PROB 11/24/113, fols. 66v–67r, Katherine Styles's bequest in 1530 of "payer[s] of beades" to two female inheritors.

[117] NRO Montagu MS 186, item 10, Bentham, "Life," 10.

the same six parishes, "to be paid the nineteenth of May, which was the day of my mothers death."[118]

If Elizabeth Montagu's material legacies convene the godly family across generations, so, too, do the manuscripts emanating from the circle of literate men and women within which she lived and between whom the production and circulation of manuscripts was common.[119] Elizabeth Harington was the daughter of James Harington of Exton and Lucy Sidney, and the Montagus were actively engaged in the exchange of manuscripts with these two literary families.[120] As we might expect, the manuscripts, miscellanies, correspondence, and printed texts produced by members of this circle engage in a multigenerational conversation conducted in shared languages of spirituality and secularity.

The pattern of dispersal and recollection embodied in Ann Montagu's "Letters, Prayers, and Poems" aligns her manuscript with miscellanies: works comprised of pieces of writing that are seemingly random, usually unattributed, and contributed by different hands, sometimes over long periods.[121] The descent of these works through generations prompts not only reading and writing, but memory as well. Writing of the circulation of Catholic books of devotion, Alexandra Walsham suggests that these expensive, treasured volumes "might well be regarded as a special class of sacramental."[122] In the refashioning of the sacramental as the commemorative, manuscripts are legacies, their memorial function incarnated in their material. The vellum cover of the Bright manuscript is stamped with the Montagu arms, specifically those of Charles, Elizabeth Montagu's great-grandson, who joined this textual community more than a century after the miscellany was compiled.[123] Creating the book as an

[118] TNA PROB 11/196/404, fol. 366r.

[119] The presence of literate female members of Lady Montagu's household is suggested by a letter she wrote after her blindness, stating "For lacke of a man writter I am fain to imploy a woman secretary": see NRO Montagu MS 191 (loose sheet). Paulina Pepys was the great-aunt of the diarist Samuel Pepys, who was tutored at the Montagu house as a boy. After her death, Sidney Montagu married Anne Isham, distant cousin of Justinian Isham and his sister Elizabeth.

[120] Elizabeth's mother, Lucy Sidney, was Frances Sidney's sister; both were aunts to Robert, Mary and Philip Sidney. Her brother, John Harington, Baron of Exton, was the father of Lucy Harington Russell, Countess of Bedford, and her uncle John Harington of Stepney (1525–1582) was a poet and the father of Sir John Harington of Kelston (1561–1612), poet and translator of Ariosto's *Orlando Furioso*. On the Sidney manuscripts, see Lamb, *Gender and Authorship*, esp. 194–228; and Woudhuysen, *Sir Philip Sidney*, 356–65. On the Harington manuscripts, see Hughey, "The Harington Manuscript"; and Hughey, ed., *Arundel Harington Manuscript*.

[121] On manuscript miscellanies, see Burke, "Seventeenth-Century Women's Manuscript Writing"; and Eckhardt and Smith, eds., *Manuscript Miscellanies*.

[122] Walsham: "Domme Preachers," 120. See also Burke, "'Memorial Books.'"

[123] See BL Add MS 15232, "Poems of Sir Philip Sidney." Charles was the grandson of Henry Montagu, Earl of Manchester. The arms date from 1710–1714, when he was 1st Baron Halifax; the manuscript was compiled in the 1580s. See Woudhuysen, *Sir Philip Sidney*, 362–3.

heirloom of the house, the binding, as Christopher D'Addario observes, "suggests a desire to leave a record of the distinctly ephemeral act of reading."[124] On the second folio of the Hill manuscript, written between 1556 and 1570, the signature, "R Montague" – Ralph, Edward Montagu's grandson and the future Duke of Montagu, born in 1638 – appears written vertically in the middle of the page in an apparently childish hand.[125] Inside, thirteen poems by Thomas Wyatt and Henry Howard, Earl of Surrey are copied in the hands of Ellina and Frances Harington, grand-nieces of Elizabeth Montagu. Their signatures – practiced in different hands, some elegantly calligraphic – are scattered throughout the manuscript.[126]

On the final page of the Hill manuscript, a memorial for the Puritan pastor Edward Dering ends this largely secular collection on a sacred note.[127] Under the title, "Gilt woordes followinge that Mr. Dering spake in this life," a secretary hand describes the godly deathbed:

> The oration was by the opening of a window, at which the sun dyd shyne in upon him, the which window was opened of purpose by those that then wear with hym, who thought he had been dead because he Laye so still and moved not, then they asked him if the sun did not burne hym, who answered thus.
>
> There is but one sun that giveth light unto the earth, there is but one Son of righteousness, there is but one ffellowshipp of Saintes.

At the bottom of the page, in a clear italic, is the name, "Ellina Harrington."[128] Ellina's signature marks her not as the writer of this book of gold but as a reader. If, as D'Addario argues, "the marks of reading in the volume stand as material traces of an individual's own past and passing,"[129] what Ellina remembers is her membership in the dynasty of her ancestors and in the "ffellowshipp of Saintes." As in Ann Montagu's "Letters, Prayers, and Poems," through the processes of recollection and reiteration, and in the acts of reading, and interpretation, the godly comes to know herself. The dispersed, multiple parts of the Hill manuscript are gathered meaningfully in this last gesture of godly fellowship, where Ellina – having the last word, one that provokes a conversation across centuries – stands as a witness to the company she keeps.

[124] D'Addario, "Echo Chambers, 87.

[125] BL Add MS 36529, "Poems of Surrey, Wyatt and Others," fol. 2^{r}. This was the Ralph Montagu who, as an adult, installed paneling in the chancel of Barnwell All Saints: see Chapter 1.

[126] Frances (b. 1584) and Ellina or Helena (b. 1591) were the daughters Sir John Harington of Kelston (b. 1561), Elizabeth Montagu's cousin. See Hughey, *Arundel Harington Manuscript*, vol. I, 40. See also BL Add MS 36529, fol. 29^{v}, for the calligraphic signatures, "ffrancis Harryington" and "Ellina Harrington."

[127] On Edward Dering, see Lake, *Moderate Puritans*, 16–54; and *ODNB*. Dering (d. 1576) was a product of Cambridge's Puritan colleges Christ's and Emmanuel, and was married to Anne Locke.

[128] BL Add MS 36529, fol. 82^{r}.

[129] D'Addario, "Echo Chambers," 94.

CHAPTER 3

Innogen's Needle
Remembrance and Romance in Cymbeline

> Next him Tenantius rained, then Kimbeline
> What time th'eternall Lord in fleshly slime
> Enwombed was.
>
> – Edmund Spenser[1]

> One zealous Prayer, one Orthodoxe Sermon is a more glorious furniture, then all the precious rarities of mechanique excellencies.
>
> – Joseph Hall[2]

Puritan Shakespeare

In his Puritan book of remembrance, "The Life of Lord Edward Montagu," Joseph Bentham convenes and reanimates a lost community of Montagu ancestors, unfolding the mandate of "auncient *Stocke* and *Name* " to take account of his patron's virtues.[3] Drawing on "authentick records and credible relations" – including chronicle histories, funerary inscriptions, printed dedications, private manuscripts, and personal recollections – Bentham resurrects a body of textual authorities whose voices bleed into his. Amid shifting and simultaneous times, places, and persons, Bentham's "Life" constructs Edward Montagu as an exemplum of godly magistracy and a member of a transhistorical church. In form and content, the manuscript imagines the "scattered Apostles and dispersed Christians" now living as "members of the one and self-same body hav [ing] mutuall Society of their eternall election."[4] An invisible church, too, is incarnated in Bentham's spirited procession, joined to the living body by "invisible and [in]dissoluble" ties.[5] Bearing memory and prophecy, these

[1] Spenser, *Faerie Queene*, 2.10.51–2. [2] Hall, *Sermon*, 17–18.
[3] Speed, *Theatre*, 896; and NRO Montagu 186, item 10, Bentham, "Life."
[4] Bentham, *Societie*, 3–4. [5] Bentham, *Societie*, 215.

witnesses convey to the Montagu sons the legacy of godly ancestors and the promise of reunion in the afterlife.

In *Cymbeline*, Shakespeare convenes and reanimates the ancestors of Posthumus Leonatus who encircle their sleeping descendent, summoned by his desperate prayer for a new "audit" (5.3.121).[6] This spectral cloud of witness recites not its own history but that of a son who is at once an imprisoned St. Paul, awaiting an angel to "cancel these cold bonds" (5.3.122), and an unskilled St. John, to whom Jupiter's revelation is "senseless speaking, or a speaking such / As sense cannot untie" (5.3.241–2). This apparitional troupe makes visible the lost ancestry that has "Moulded the stuff so fair" (5.3.143) in their descendent, affirming the "internal, invisible, and [in]dissoluble bonds" uniting Posthumus to an invisible body. For Bentham the universal church enjoys the fellowship of eternal life; however, the Leonati are the ghostly remains of the eternally dead. Amid the play's sheer slippages of time and place, they are pre-Christian saints on the verge of the Incarnation. Posthumus's incorporation into this temporal heritage is predicted in difficult terms in the play's resolution: embracing the newly reconciled Innogen, he encourages her to "Hang there like fruit, my soul, / Till the tree die" (5.4.262–3).[7]

In giving visible shape to this invisible community, Shakespeare, like Bentham, calls forth a team of textual authorities whose voices inform his drama. Yet the records of the life of Posthumus Leonatus are less than authentic or credible, and their lapses bespeak the uniquely dense intertexuality of this "most bookish of plays."[8] As the Leonati recast the plot in which they are encrypted in "rhyming fourteeners," Shakespeare associates this obsolete, Elizabethan poetic form with the obsolescence of the Leonati themselves.[9] Beyond this formal appropriation, the Vision constructs a genealogy as ghostly as the figures that people it: Posthumus's father, Sicilius, shares the name but not the career of a king mentioned by Holinshed, and his mother and two brothers are anonymous.[10] Moreover, their effigies gild a redundant monument. Although their prayers stir Jupiter's descent, his divine message is that the Leonati are troubling

[6] I accept the argument that a likely misprint resulted in Innogen's name being changed to Imogen, but I am not convinced that Jachimo's name should be changed to Giacomo. My usage reflects this view. For discussion, see Warren, in Shakespeare, *Cymbeline*, 265–9. On Posthumus's vision, see Knight, *Crown of Life*, 168–202.

[7] Escobedo, "From Britannia to England," locates the play's ambivalence about English (as opposed to British) nationhood in Posthumus's rootlessness.

[8] Wilson, "'Our Bending Author,'" 68.

[9] See Warren, "Introduction," in Shakespeare, *Cymbeline*, 54–5.

[10] See Warren's note to 1.1.29, in Shakespeare, *Cymbeline*.

themselves needlessly: "No care of yours is it; you know 'tis ours," Jupiter reminds them, to unfold the future of their "low-laid son" (5.3.194–7). Unable to affect the future, these apparitions are reduced to postmen, delivering the tablet on which Jupiter's prophecy is inscribed. Materialized between an unstable history and an uncertain prophecy, the Leonati, far from affirming dynastic union, are as fleeting as a dream: sleep is their "grandsire," Posthumus claims upon waking and, rewriting his posthumous birth in their infant death, complains "they went hence so soon as they were born" (5.3.220).

This reading of *Cymbeline*'s ephemeral Vision alongside Bentham's Puritan encomium may easily be seen as wrenching the true cause the false way; on the whole, Puritans have not fared well in Shakespeare.[11] Yet the cooperation in these two passages of secular and scriptural images of fellowship reminds us that "conforming Calvinists" participated in crafting Church of England doctrine and shared an extensive body of imagery supporting adaptations of religious beliefs to political and cultural projects.[12] A reader coming to William Perkins's Puritan commentary on St. John's Revelation with *Cymbeline* in mind, for instance, will be struck by the shared vocabulary of these two works. While Robert Hill, who edited the work for printer Richard Field after Perkins's death in 1602, calls ministers "Remembrancers, to put in mind" the Lord, Cymbeline's Queen refers to Pisanio as Innogen's "remembrancer of her to hold / The hand-fast to her lord" (1.5.77–8). Hill's statement that Perkins's "worthie labours doe speake enough for him, by name . . . his Posthume," glosses Shakespeare's Posthumus as a text delivered after its author's death.[13] And Perkins's commentary on the first verse locates his work between temporal sites excavated in *Cymbeline*: "there is a great difference between an historie and a Prophesie," he explains, and later, in a conflation worthy of Shakespeare, St. John's book is "a propheticall history concerning the estate of the Church, from the time of John to the end."[14]

[11] See, for instance, Shakespeare's mockery of Puritanism in *Twelfth Night's* Malvolio and his critique of Puritan hypocrisy in the "precise" Angelo of *Measure for Measure*. On *Twelfth Night*, see Bevington, "Debate." On *Measure for Measure*, see Lake and Questier, *Anti-Christ's Lewd Hat*, 621–700; Shuger, *Political Theologies;* and Gurnis, "'Most Ignorant of What He's Most Assured.'"

[12] See Collinson, *Religion of Protestants;* Tyacke, *Anti-Calvinists:* and Lake and Questier, "Puritans;" and see Chapter 2.

[13] Hill, "Epistle Dedicatorie," in Perkins, *Lectures*, fols. ¶3ᵛ and A3ᵛ.

[14] Perkins, *Lectures*, 2 and 22. I do not claim that Hill's edition of Perkins is an unacknowledged source for *Cymbeline*, although clearly St. John's Revelation is a guiding text for Shakespeare's play: see Pettegree, *Foreign and Native*, 164, who identifies Franciscus Junius's commentary on Revelation, published by Richard Field in 1592, as a framing text for the play. I see

This chapter does not argue that Shakespeare was a closet Puritan or attempt to read his play as a religious allegory.[15] Rather, my point is that in the syncretistic blend of sources and beliefs comprising *Cymbeline*, a Puritan model of sacramentality is explored and embodied in Innogen's role as an agent of recovery and renewal of the play's spiritual and political bodies. Set within the matrix of remembrance, I argue, *Cymbeline* encounters Puritanism not primarily or exclusively as a doctrinal position in religious debate, but as a productive field of creativity for "women's work," the regenerative texts and works of Shakespeare's post-Boccaccian heroine.[16] A resourceful sister to the Montagu women, Innogen employs her needle to craft a reparative web of textualities that mends the torn fabric of *Cymbeline*.

Chapter 2 showed how the project of union conducted by the Montagu brothers exploited the imagery of dynastic union and the Pauline vision of the conjoined church body to construct monuments commemorating fraternal fellowship. Sharing the religious culture of Puritanism, however, the Montagu women created flexible, fluid textualities; monuments that exploit the multiplicity of the Puritan sacrament in an evolving, progressive ritual of remembrance where dispersed members – signs, bodies, and texts – are meaningfully recollected and unified. The Montagu women's commemorative processes of dispersal and recollection unite a community of saints through a creative and generative intertwining of the female subject, sacramental matter, and the material text.

This chapter maps the romance world of *Cymbeline* as a location of dispersal and reincorporation, processes that are embodied in Innogen's blending of subject, sacrament, and text. In Section 1, I study the conflation of femininity and materiality as it intersects with contested views of the sacrament in Posthumus's wager and in Jachimo's voyeuristic violation of Innogen's chamber. Section 2 shows how Shakespeare locates the

Shakespeare's encounter with Puritan discourses, including Perkins's, primarily in terms of the materiality of books and their international transmission.

[15] On the religious content of *Cymbeline*, see, for example, Moffett, "*Cymbeline* and the Nativity"; Geller, "*Cymbeline* and the Imagery of Covenant Theology"; and Betteridge, "Writing Faithfully."

[16] Shakespeare's primary sources for *Cymbeline's* historical dimension are Raphael Holinshed's *Chronicles* (1587) and Geoffrey of Monmouth's *Historia Regum Britanniae*. William Baldwin's *Mirror for Magistrates* (1587) and the anonymous drama, *The Rare Triumphs of Love and Fortune* (1589) inform the Welsh plot. The source for the wager plot is Boccaccio's *Decameron* 2.9. Although Boccaccio's tale was not translated into English until 1620, versions were available in French, and a German translation appeared in English as *Frederyke of Jennen* in 1560. See Bullough, ed., *Narrative and Dramatic Sources*.

period's vexed double vision attending idolatry, iconoclasm, and sacramentality in the romance setting of the lady's chamber. Jachimo's comparison of Innogen's "sense" to a monument set within the chapel of her body transforms the chamber to a chantry, where incompatible views of church ritual and furniture inflect interpretations of Innogen's secular textualities. Jachimo's abusive gaze, wandering between idolatry and iconoclasm, perceives and produces Innogen as a hybrid creature – at once a Catholic sacrament and an idol.

In Section 3, I follow Innogen into the pastoral world of Wales, where Shakespeare stages her pilgrimage as an intertextual performance, a progressive interpretation of the sacrament that is also the Word. At the center of this journey, a ritual of remembrance, at once improvised and recycled, enlivens the effigial Innogen of the chamber by mobilizing Protestant figurations of the diffusion and reincorporation of natural elements – like industrious bees in a hive – that bring forth spiritual rebirth. Shakespeare answers Jachimo's deadening imagery by moving his heroine from the sacrament of death to that of life. Embodying a wondrous essence in the fluid blending of subject, sacrament, and text, Innogen claims a recreative, generative power to mend the political and spiritual bodies of *Cymbeline*.[17]

In tracing Puritan sacramentality into *Cymbeline*, my purpose is not to suggest that the play or its author embrace a reformed theology but to demonstrate its utility as a counter to Catholicism on the spectrum of Reformation beliefs. Shakespeare makes use of contrasting views of the sacrament and its ritual performance, first, to challenge Innogen's integrity and secondly, to re-establish her as a transformational figure for the play's resolution. In the play's three plots of dispersal and recollection, pivoting around Innogen's triple role as spouse, daughter, and sister, losses and recoveries are attended by intertextual, improvisational rituals of remembrance in which resourcefulness is a primary virtue. Read as a memorial performance, the play reassembles and remembers, finally, the history of the Reformation itself: a story of international religious debate, makeshift rituals, interpretative rivalries, and innovative performances of remembrance, all attending the "enwombed" Word. This tale of recovery

[17] I agree with recent scholarship that supports an empowered Innogen. See, for instance, Lander, "Interpreting the Person," who argues that "Imogen takes audacious control of the social, ideological, and existential structures to which she must ultimately submit (although not without qualification)" (184). For views of Innogen's unqualified submission, see Frye, *Pens and Needles*, 177–90; and Mikalachki, "Masculine Romance."

is told through the reclamation and intertwining of three pliable materials: the sacrament, the book, and the viscous flesh of a woman's body.

1 A Heretical Script

Cymbeline begins with a sacrament and its failure: the covenant of Posthumus's and Innogen's marriage is sealed by the exchange of tokens, and this bond is cancelled when Posthumus enters a contract with Jachimo. Innogen seals the "hand-fast" with her mother's diamond ring, "an heirloom of the house."[18] Posthumus, in turn, places "Upon this fairest prisoner" a "manacle of love" (1.1.124–5). In the cluster of images attending this exchange, the cancellation of the bond by death, for which the imprisoned Posthumus will long in Act 5, is anticipated in Innogen's imprisonment, one that will place her, too, under penalty of death. The scene anticipates this as well: when Innogen charges Posthumus to wear her ring, "till you woo another wife, / When Innogen is dead," Posthumus's reply produces the corpse: "give me but this I have, / And cere up my embracements from a next / With bonds of death" (1.1.114–8).

The ritual exchange of tokens in *Cymbeline* engages the arts of remembrance in post-Reformation England, particularly the ways that gender intersects with commemoration. In Posthumus's play on *cerecloth* – linen treated with melted wax, used to wrap a corpse – the "embracements" he disavows will be "cered up" by his death, precipitated, we suppose, by Innogen's. Yet his suspended syntax invites the possibility that these embraces will be forestalled, rather, by the death of a second lover, "a next." All women are imagined to die with Innogen. Both possibilities invoke the figure of a shrouded female effigy, at once sealed in the grave by "bonds of death" and uncannily present in her sculptural double. Haunting images of this kind, most often of women, multiplied in post-Reformation chapels and chancels: the shrouded effigy of Alicia Dudley (see Figure 3.1) accompanies that of her mother, Alice Dudley, Duchess Dudley, on a monument erected by the duchess twenty-seven years after her daughter's death.[19] When funeral monuments no longer issued calls for prayers to improve souls' progress in the afterlife, they were initially reconceived as genealogical records and, increasingly during the seventeenth century, as memorials to the emotional bonds between the living

[18] TNA PROB 11/131/760, Will of Elizabeth Montagu, fol. 425^{r}. Wayne, "Woman's Parts," 288, notes that the ring is "the only trace of [Innogen's] natural mother."

[19] See Hurtig, "Seventeenth-Century Shroud Tombs."

Figure 3.1 William Wright, Monument for Alice Dudley, Duchess Dudley (detail: Alicia Dudley, d. 1621) (1648).
St. Mary's, Stoneleigh. Author's photograph.

and the dead.[20] While dynastic monuments contained women by stressing their role in sustaining the male line, more affective memorials often idealized their female subjects, presenting them as precious objects; most often, as commodities possessed by men. Female effigies appear with an array of luxury items – jewels, pomanders, portrait miniatures, pillows, textiles, books large and small – illustrating the literal objectification of women's bodies in death. Epitaphs use similar objects to advance their subjects as feminine ideals. Women are "mirror[s] that no breath could staine," "Jewell[s]" set in the cabinet of the grave, or "muche treasure" enclosed in a vault.[21] The intertwining of femininity and materiality enacted in these monuments implicitly guides the exchange of tokens in *Cymbeline* and becomes explicit in Posthumus's encounter with Jachimo. Throughout the wager scene, Posthumus conflates Innogen's ring with her body ("I praised her as I rated her, so do I my stone;" "I fear not my ring," 1.4.73 and 94), while Jachimo resurrects the corpse imagined in Posthumus's parting oath: "Either your unparagoned mistress is dead, or she's outprized by a trifle" (1.4.76–7).

[20] Elizabeth I, *Proclamation* (1560). On post-Reformation changes in commemoration, included increased expressions of affection, see Marshall, *Beliefs and the Dead*, 265–308.

[21] Stow, *Survey* (1633), 881 and 761; and Gough, *Description*, 33.

Although the political subplot of *Cymbeline* involves the ancient Roman Empire, the Rome to which Posthumus resorts in his exile from Britain is the contemporary city reviled as the seat of England's Catholic adversary.[22] When Innogen correctly identifies Jachimo as "a saucy stranger in [the] court to mart / As in a Romish stew" (1.6.151–2), she echoes reformed views of "Romish authority [as] either heathenish, or Popish."[23] As the embodiment of the "Romish Antichrist,"[24] Jachimo portends division within the conjoined body of the Protestant faithful, figured in Innogen and Posthumus's union. Puritan polemicist Thomas Tuke casts this monstrous severance "betwixt the head and the members" of the church as a permanent Crucifixion: "Christ may be sayd to be crucified [and] slayne continually by Romish authority."[25] This division is stated in sacramental terms by William Perkins in his rejection of the Catholic defense of transubstantiation: "If the Popish real presence be granted, then the body & blood of Christ are either severed or joyned together. If severed, then Christ is still crucified."[26]

As Posthumus enters the realm of "Romish authority," he is a severed member of the Protestant body, vulnerable to heathenish practices; Jachimo will confess in the play's resolution, "mine Italian brain/ Gan in your duller Britain operate / Most vilely" (5.4.197–9). Indeed, Philario's Roman house suggests religious divisions on a trans-European scale. In addition to Italian, French, and British nationals, a Spaniard and a Dutchman are extraneously present, included silently in the scene. While this multinationalism carries the trace of Shakespeare's sources, where the wager takes place during a meeting of merchants, mercantilism is replaced in *Cymbeline* by the international religious struggles of the Reformation.[27] The silent nationals recall Spanish Catholicism and the confessional divisions of the Catholic and Protestant Netherlands; fraught battlefields of religious severance where Englishmen had been enlisted to support the "dispersed Christians" of the Protestant side.[28] In the midst of this staging

[22] For a useful reading of the Jacobean reconciliation of Britain and Rome, see Parolin, "Anachronistic Italy."

[23] Tuke, "Translators Epistle," fol. C8r.

[24] Abbott, *Exposition*, 13.

[25] Tuke, "Translator's Epistle," fol. C8r.

[26] Perkins, *Reformed Catholicke*, 370.

[27] See Warren, "Introduction," in Shakespeare, *Cymbeline*, 35, for the argument that Shakespeare expands the wager plot into a story of international warfare; and 62 on the play's reconciliatory establishment of international peace as a mirror of James's pacifistic foreign policy.

[28] I am indebted to Jaime Goodrich for this observation. On diverse religions in Shakespeare's London, reflected in *Cymbeline's* doctrinal eclecticism, see Heal, "Experiencing Religion."

of doctrinal rivalry, accordingly, Jachimo's challenge to Posthumus is inflected with the language of idolatry. Converting women's flesh to a corrupt commodity – the "gilt or painted idols" condemned by early reformers as "wanton Harlottes" (*Homyly*, fol. 66^{r}) – he claims, "If you buy ladies' flesh at a million a dram, you cannot preserve it from tainting; but I see you have some religion in you, that you fear" (1.4.129–32). In Posthumus's response, "This is but a custom in your tongue; you bear a graver purpose I hope" (1.4.133–4), the subtle slippage between "graver" and "graven" – Jachimo as engraver of graven images – attends his heretical substitution of a true covenant by a false. "Let there be covenants drawn between's," he insists, "here's my ring" (1.4.138–41). His assurance of the contract completes the conjoined body's dismemberment by Romish influence: "my ring I hold dear as my finger," Posthumus claims, "'tis part of it" (1.4.127–8).

When Innogen's "trifle" (1.1.121) is carried abroad, it is subject to the extremes of idealization and debasement that objectify her throughout the wager scene; the commonplaces of the *querelle des femmes*, given new urgency in the doctrinal debates of the Reformation. If the positive term of this equation attends women's monumental effigies, the negative term pervades reformed polemics on idolatry, where a wanton woman was a painted sepulcher and an idol, conversely, "a strumpet with a paynted face" (*Homyly*, fol. 66^{v}). This alignment of effigies and idols occasionally prompted the destruction of monuments: the mutilated figure of Elizabeth Montagu Bertie on her mother's tomb at Chiddingly (see Figure 3.2) may bespeak the violent effects of this conflation.[29] The immediacy with which Posthumus accepts as proof the circumstantial evidence of Innogen's guilt in Act 2, scene 4, too, follows the compelling logic of the iconoclast: Innogen is either a paragon or an idolatrous cheat. "Render me some corporal sign," he demands, and as Jachimo's oath "by Jupiter" replaces Posthumus's oath to Innogen, he concludes, "she hath bought the name of whore" (2.4.120–6). The corporal sign of her birthmark completes the imagery of the idol's "tainted flesh"; it is a "stain" that proves "Another stain, as big as hell can hold" (2.4.137–8).

[29] The damage to the Jefferay monument may be the result of early modern iconoclasm or may have occurred in later unrest. The monument may have been targeted during the "Captain Swing Riots," waves of agricultural unrest that swept across Sussex in 1830: see www.coopersfarm.co.uk/church/churchguide1.htm. See also Aston, *Broken Idols*, 194–219, on the coincidence of political and economic unrest and the defacement of church monuments.

Figure 3.2 Unknown artist (Cure workshop?), Jefferay Monument (detail: Elizabeth Bertie) (1612).
Chiddingly Parish Church. Author's photograph.

As Innogen's token is abused to seal a false covenant, it is caught up in the Reformation contest between the belief in the holy essence contained in religious objects and reformed views of this faith as idolatrous. This debate becomes more complex in Innogen's chamber, where disputed interpretations of the sacrament are relocated in the room's secular imagery, and where the shifting currents of Reformation polemics are staged in and as the chamber's teeming interplay of texts. Drenched in intertextuality, the chamber revisits and revises earlier approaches – particularly by Shakespeare – to the object that is the female body. Recollections of Ovid's Philomel (2.2.44–6) and Actaeon (2.4.80–5), emblems of rape and voyeurism respectively, appear alongside echoes of Shakespeare's works: the sleeping Desdemona, like Innogen, is violated by the male gaze; a "silk and silver" tapestry, "the story / Proud Cleopatra, when she met her Roman" (2.4.69–70), replays Enobarbus's famous ekphrasis of the queen attended by "pretty, dimpled boys, like smiling Cupids" in *Antony and*

Cleopatra; and Jachimo's comparison of himself to "Our Tarquin" (2.2.12) restages the rape recounted in Shakespeare's *Lucrece*.[30]

Innogen's chamber is an allusive web of Shakespeare's authorship and a location of writing where authors and coauthors multiply. In this meta-poetic scene, Shakespeare transforms Jachimo from rapist to voyeur to writer:

> I will write all down.
> Such, and such pictures, there the window, such
> Th'adornment of her bed, the arras, figures,
> Why such, and such; and the contents o' th' story.
> (2.2.24–7)

In enriching his "inventory" (2.2.30), Jachimo's obsession with visible surfaces bespeaks both "the blyndnes of false superstition" (*Homyly*, fol. 36^{v}) that constitutes idolatry and the "mad blind Zeal" of iconoclasm (Gunton, *History*, 335) – conjoined twins in a sacramental debate that also influenced visual and monumental forms. While the idolater's desire to animate the object mistakenly attributes divine essence to dead matter, the iconoclast destroys not the inanimate object but that whose lingering power he fears. In Innogen's chamber, the results of this symbiosis are to destroy the goddess and produce a heretical scripture. Thus Innogen's bracelet, "As slippery as the Gordian knot was hard," slithers from her arm, casting her as Eve before "the tempters of the night" (2.2.9) from which her prayer cannot protect her.[31] Her andirons, "two winking Cupids / Of silver, each on one foot standing, nicely / Depending on their brands" (2.4.89–91), resonate with the twin anacreontics that close *Shakespeare's Sonnets*, where Cupid's brand ignites the "love-kindling fire" of syphilis.[32] And the tapestry of Cleopatra – "a piece of work / So bravely done, so rich, that it did strive / In workmanship and value" (2.4.69–71) – witnesses women's sensuality and seductiveness. If the textualities of Innogen's chamber bespeak her self-creative sovereignty,[33] Jachimo's obscene gaze usurps these licensing narratives. His inventory lists the immaterial

[30] Shakespeare, *Antony and Cleopatra*, 2.2.197–248, at 208. Frye, *Pens and Needles*, 160–90, reads *Othello* and *Cymbeline* together, drawing out the connections between Desdemona's handkerchief and Innogen's textualities.

[31] Innogen's prayer echoes the "Collect for Aid Against all Perils," the third collect in the Order of Evening Prayers: see BCP (1604), fol. A8^{r}.

[32] Shakespeare, *Shakespeare's Sonnets*, no. 153, line 3.

[33] See Frye, *Pens and Needles*, 177–82, for the argument that Innogen's textualities establish her as a subject. See also Ziegler, "My Lady's Chamber."

Figure 3.3 Unknown artist, Monument for Alice Spencer, Countess of Derby (detail: cherub) (before 1636). St. Mary's, Harefield. Author's photograph.

things – objects consumed by the eye and dissolved into word and memory – that he will submit in evidence of Innogen's infidelity.

Jachimo's inventory, like Posthumus's conflation of embracement and entombment in the scene of parting, alludes to the rituals surrounding death and burial. Jachimo rises from the chest in a false resurrection like a malignant spirit haunting a tomb: "O sleep, thou ape of death," he prays, "lie dull upon her, / And be her sense but as a monument, / Thus in a chapel lying" (2.2.31–3).[34] In this figuration, Innogen's consciousness becomes a monument set within the chapel of the body. The flicker of "sense" is doubly encrypted, in the effigy and in the chapel where it lies. As the scene progresses, Shakespeare enlarges the crypt to encompass the chamber. Jachimo's exclamation, "fresh lily! / And whiter than the sheets!" (2.2.15–16) imagines a monumental effigy wrapped in her shroud; a beautiful corpse crafted to be looked upon (Figure 3.1). The "Golden cherubins" decorating the ceiling of the chamber (2.4.88) frequently adorn funerary monuments (see Figure 3.3), while the wax taper left burning (with the others in the candlelit indoor theatre) transforms the chamber into a chantry.[35]

[34] The association of Jachimo's emergence from the trunk with resurrection is explicit in Shakespeare's source, where the villain remains in the trunk for three days. See Anon., *Frederyke of Jennen*, fol. B3^{r}; reprinted in Bullough, *Narrative and Dramatic Sources*, vol. VIII, 69.

[35] The late medieval will of Katherine Styles, TNA 11/24/113, bequeaths "by the same space vii yeres two tapers brennyng and to stand over my tombe and grave" and "xii torches at my burying and monnethis mynd whiche I have redy in my house" (fols. 66^{v}–67^{r}). In the Reformation, "money given or bequeathed to obits and dirges, or to the finding of torches, lights, tapers, and lamps," was redirected as charity for the poor: see James, *Women's Voices*, 25–6; and see "Royal Injunction of Queen Elizabeth I, 1559," in Frere and Kennedy, eds., *Visitation Articles*, vol. III, 17. The return of

As he itemizes the possessions left behind by a senseless corpse, Jachimo composes a probate inventory that glosses the memorial architecture of Innogen's chamber.[36] She is a recumbent effigy in a private chapel; a rich movable, as Jachimo puts it, "Above ten thousand meaner moveables" (2.2.29), objectified – idealized to death – by the luxury items surrounding her. Most enigmatic among these items is "Th'adornment of her bed, the arras." Critics often assume that Jachimo refers here to the "tapestry" of Cleopatra that he describes to Posthumus at their reunion in Philario's house (2.4.69–76). However, referring the object to probate inventories in the period suggests that the arras *is* the adornment of Innogen's bed.[37] "Arras coverlets" appear frequently among the bedding of householders, routinely differentiated from "hangings." In 1524, Joan Thurcrosse bequeaths "a covering of aris havyng the picture of our Lady ridyng into egypte wroughte on it."[38] The probate inventory for Katherine Bowcher, widow (d. 1614), includes under "beddinge," "fower Arras Coverletts whereof one is wrought with selke."[39] The chamber of Francis Baylie, clothworker (d. 1620), contained, among other things, "one fether bed, fower fether boulsters . . . fower Carpetts, one payre of Andyrons, [and] one arras Coverlett."[40] The "Inventory of all the beddinges and other moveables" in Cardinal Reginald Pole's chambers at his death in 1558 includes "a coverlet of Arras woorke," ten more "coverlets of Arras," fifty-eight "coverlets of tapestre," "a coverlet of Imagery woorke," and "one coverlet of tapestre that hangeth without the chamber] doore."[41] The multiple functions of arras coverlets as bedspreads, bed hangings, and wall coverings are startlingly expressed in Thomas Wood's 1491 bequest of "his best Arras bed" to Holy Trinity, Hull, "to cover his grave at the

tapers as accessories in night funerals during the Jacobean period carried the memory of a repudiated Catholic practice: see Gittings, *Death, Burial and the Individual*, 180; and Harding, "Choices and Changes," 391–2.

[36] For a valuable treatment of household probate inventories, see Orlin, "Things with Little Social Life"; and on guild inventories, see Giles, "'A table of alabaster."

[37] Critics have found Jachimo's slippage from "arras" to "tapestry" troubling: see, for example, Olson, "Before the Arras," who sees Jachimo's switch in terminology "as analogous to the central acts of translation and transformation in the play" (51).

[38] Borthwick, 9, fol. 272^{v}. I am indebted to Elisabeth Salter for this source, and for the Latin will of Agnes Bedford, Borthwick 2, fol. 418^{r}–419^{v} (dated 1459), which also bequeaths an arras coverlet with bedding. Salter confirms, in conversation, that she has found the distinction between arras bed coverings and hangings widespread in late medieval wills she has examined.

[39] George, et al., *Bristol Probate Inventories*, 20.

[40] George, et al., *Bristol Probate Inventories*, 31.

[41] TNA SP 12/1, fols. 20^{r}–29^{r}, "Inventory of . . . Card[inal Pole]."

anniversary of his death, and to be hung among other worshipful beds at the feast of St. George."[42]

Complementing these documentary sources, two literary images of the arras coverlet resonate with Innogen's bedspread. Spenser's *Epithalamion* covers the newlywed Elizabeth Boyle, "twixt sleep and wake" on her wedding night with lilies and an arras later borrowed by Shakespeare to display Innogen: "Lay her in lillies and in violets, / And silken courteins over her display, / And odourd sheetes, and Arras coverlets."[43] Homer's Helen, in Chapman's treatment the matronly hostess in Menelaus's household, puts her guests to bed with an arras coverlet cast "aloft":

> Then Argive Hellen made the handmaid go,
> And put faire bedding in the Portico;
> Lay purple blankets on, Rugs warme and soft;
> And cast and [*sic*] Arras coverlet aloft.[44]

A household Helen also attends Innogen in her chamber: "Who's there?" the startled Innogen asks, "My woman Helen?" (2.2.1). In Chapman's portrayal, Helen takes on the twin roles of victim and wife, roles also played by Innogen and Lucrece, and by way of Shakespeare's *Lucrece*, she is Innogen's precursor in ravishment. Shakespeare's Helen, like Jachimo's Cleopatra, is also subject of ekphrasis in "a piece / Of skilful painting, made of Priam's Troy," before which the poem places the distraught Lucrece.[45] Innogen's inventory of bedding and movables links her in a chain of intertextual allusions to the violated Helen and Lucrece, and to the objects of sexual pleasure, Cleopatra and Elizabeth Boyle. The unspoken contents of the arras's story seem to be the inscrutable degrees of willingness and resistance, innocence and experience, of the woman in bed.

2 Bell, Book, and Candle

Imagining Innogen's chamber as a chapel that mirrors the "Holy Temple" of her flesh (*Homyly*, fol. 21^r) opens up a new set of analogies for the

[42] Quoted in Kermode, *Medieval Merchants*, 150. Kermode assumes that Wood refers to bed hangings.
[43] Spenser, *Epithalamion*, lines 302–4.
[44] Chapman, trans., *Homer's Odyssey*, 55. I see Spenser's *Epithalamion* as a source for Shakespeare's imagery in Innogen's chamber. Chapman's *Odyssey* was printed as much as five years after *Cymbeline* was first performed. Although Shakespeare may have seen Chapman's work in manuscript, I am not insisting on Chapman's influence on Shakespeare.
[45] Shakespeare, *Lucrece*, lines 1366–1569, esp. line 1367. On the ekphrasis, see Belsey, "Invocation."

textiles and objects in Innogen's room, relocating the scene's "translations" within the Reformation's contested sacred spaces.[46] In parish churches, stocks of hangings, plate, candles, statuary, and vestments were dispersed following the Edwardian injunctions until their widespread recollection under Archbishop of Canterbury William Laud.[47] Inspired by "the beauty of holiness," Alice, Duchess Dudley, donated to her home parish of St. Giles-in-the-Fields – a church consecrated by then Bishop of London Laud after its rebuilding in 1631 – taffeta hangings bordered with silk and silver; embroidered altar cloths in velvet, cambric, and damask; two books embossed with gold; altar cushions embroidered with gold; a Turkish carpet; a carved wood screen; a pair of organs with a gilded case; altar rails; silver and gold plate; five bells; and "the great Bell in the Steeple: which, as oft as it ringeth, sounds her Praise." Except for the bell and plate, Robert Boreman lamented in her funeral sermon, "all the forenamed Ornaments of the Church (being counted Superstitious and Popish) were demolished and sold (under the Pretense of relieving the poore) by the Deforming-Reformers (as they were called) in the late bloody Rebellious times."[48]

Private chapels in country houses followed the more or less conformist beliefs of their owners and enjoyed more license in and greater longevity of their decorative programs.[49] Joseph Hall praises the "comely whiteness" of the Earl of Exeter's chapel, where wall paintings were whitewashed during the renovation in 1623 and the "glorious furniture" of the medieval chapel dissolved to writing, imagination, and memory:

> Imagine the Altar never so gay, the Imagerie never so curious; the Vestments never so rich; the Pillars, Walls, Windowes, Pavement, never so exquisite; yet I dare boldly say, this present glory of this House in this comely whitenesse, and well contrived coarctation, is greater then the former . . . One zealous Prayer, one Orthodoxe Sermon is a more glorious furniture, then all the precious rarities of mechanique excellencies.[50]

46 Frye, *Pens and Needles*, 185, notes that "translating" referred in the period to the process of cutting down and refashioning textiles.

47 See Whiting, *Reformation*, on changes in church interiors and fabric from the Edwardian Reformation to the Civil War. The Visitation Articles provide essential information on Church of England buildings: see Frere and Kennedy, eds., *Visitation Articles*; and Fitcham, ed., *Visitation Articles*.

48 Aston, *Broken Idols*, 259–358 at 263; and Boreman, *Mirrour of Christianity*, 22–4.

49 See Ricketts, "Evolution," for an excellent and copious study of private chapels to which my discussion is greatly indebted. The dissertation was published posthumously as Ricketts, *English Country House Chapel*, but the publication omits a great deal of material on interior decoration. For this reason, I refer to the dissertation rather than the printed book.

50 Hall, *Sermon*, 17–18.

Yet recoveries were as common as reformations. When the chapel at Haddon Hall, seat of the earls of Rutland, was renovated in 1624, the medieval stained glass windows depicting the Crucifixion, the Annunciation, and the saints and apostles were retained.[51] Ceilings and carved bosses were painted with choirs of angels, as is the ceiling of Innogen's chapel. Sanctioned by the Old Testament description of Solomon's temple, where the *sanctum sanctorum* was guarded by angels, latter-day cherubim attended the Christian Holy of Holies, the altar.[52] In 1535, Henry VIII paid £451 "for gylttyng and garnesshing of the vought" in the Chapel Royal at Hampton Court "wyth angells holdyng schochens wyth the Kynges armes and the Quenes, and wyth great pendantts of boyes playing wyth instruments."[53] When John Cosin, Bishop of Durham, renovated the episcopal chapel of Aukland Castle more than a century later, he had installed "myters and cherubims heads over the Communion Table."[54] Tapestries showing Old Testament scenes, such as the meeting of Solomon and Sheba, or Judith presenting the head of Holofernes (see Plate 2), as well as images of saints and the life of Christ – nine "Hangings of rich arras with golde of the Passion" at Wilton House, for example – commonly appear in the postmortem inventories of noble homeowners.[55] These textiles were both valuable and flexible, since they could be removed from chapels and rehung elsewhere in the house.[56] Such relocations between sacred and secular settings sometimes involved entire decorative programs. In 1573, a bedroom at Burghley House vacated by the death of William Cecil's first wife, Mary, was renovated as a chapel. Despite its converted use, the room was not repainted; traces of the grotesque work decorating Mary's apartment survive in the chapel today.[57] Among parishioners, too, disallowed church fabric could be translated to secular use: John Wright converted banners that previously adorned St. Lawrence, Tallington, into "cloths for to hang his hall with."[58]

A blending of sacred and secular functions occurred in "chapel chambers," rooms peripheral to the main chapel whose inventories listed beds

[51] Ricketts, "Evolution," vol. I, 209. On the persistence of Catholic imagery and objects in parish churches and in private chapels, see Dolan, "Gender."

[52] See 1 Kings 7:23, "And within the oracle he [Solomon] made two cherubims of olive tree, each ten cubits high." See also Aston, *Broken Idols*, 320–58, on cherubim and the Reformation debates surrounding them.

[53] See Law, *History*, 360.

[54] Quoted in Ricketts, "Evolution," vol. I, 224; and see Aston, *Broken Idols*, 332–3, for Cosin's defense of angelic ornament.

[55] Ricketts, "Evolution," vol. I, 189, 225 and 187.

[56] Ricketts, "Evolution," vol. I, 179.

[57] Ricketts, "Evolution," vol. 1, 32.

[58] Quoted in Whiting, *Reformation*, 82.

along with devotional items. "The chapel chamber at Hengrave," Annabel Ricketts writes, "was furnished as a bed chamber, but traces of a direct link to the chapel by means of a squint which overlooked the altar, indicates that ... a dual function was likely."[59] In 1598, Paul Hentzner visited Hampton Court and described Queen Elizabeth's chapel chamber in terms that provide a tantalizing gloss to that of Shakespeare's Innogen:

> The Chapel of this Palace is most splendid, in which the Queen's Closet is quite transparent, having its windows of crystal. We were led into two chambers ... which shone with tapestry of gold, silver, and silk of different colours. [Here] is besides a small chapel richly hung with tapestry, where the Queen performs her devotions. In her bed-chamber the bed was covered with very costly coverlids of silk. At no great distance from this room, we were shewn a bed, the teaster [canopy] of which was worked by Anne Bullen and presented by her to her husband Henry VIII.

Among the "curiosities" in the adjacent hall were "the History of Christ's passion, carved in mother of pearl," and "the true portrait of Lucretia."[60]

The site of concentrated adornment and debate in both parish churches and private chapels was the altar. In early Tudor country house chapels, decorative programs were planned to "culminat[e] in a crescendo of colour and texture at the east end or chancel."[61] The inventory of Hengrave Hall, drawn up after the death of Sir Thomas Kitson in 1603, shows this recusant family's integration of decoration approved by Elizabethan injunctions – the "long old Turkey carpit which lyse upon ye aulter," for instance – with Catholic remainders, including "a table of Our Lady" and an east window depicting the Creation, life of Christ, and Last Judgment.[62] In parish churches before the Reformation, textiles supporting "ritually important functions" included altar cloths with frontals (for the high altar and for secondary altars in mortuary chapels); canopies above the high altar's pyx; houseling cloths, for communion; cushions, to support books used during the mass; cloths to protect and decorate the Easter sepulcher; chrisom cloths, used in baptism; a pall or hearse cloth – usually embroidered – for funerals; processional banners; and hangings, often

[59] Ricketts, "Evolution," vol. I, 49. She notes that approximately 70% of sixteenth-century inventories of chapel chambers list beds among their contents. A squint, or hagioscope, is "a small opening, cut through a chancel arch or wall, to enable worshippers in an aisle or side chapel to obtain a view of the elevation of the host" (*OED*).

[60] Hentzner, *Journey*, 80–1. [61] Ricketts, "Evolution," vol. I, 181.

[62] Ricketts, "Evolution," vol. I, 275–6.

bearing donors' arms, for the pulpit.[63] The translation of these materials across the blurred doctrinal borders of the early Reformation is apparent in an altar frontal at Winchcombe that reused discarded medieval copes for an embroidered scene of saints, patriarchs, and the Crucifixion; tradition holds that it was worked by Katherine of Aragon.[64] Near the end of Elizabeth's reign, her maid of honor Blanche Parry donated an embroidered altar cloth to her home parish in Bacton, a translated gown from the queen's wardrobe.[65] Guided by the Laudian resurrection of sacred signs and objects, parishioners bought "a carpet-cloth for the communion table" in St. Martin, Leicester, in 1628, and Elizabeth Cuddon donated an altar cloth of lace linen to St. John the Baptist, Shadingfield, in 1632.[66]

The altar and its ornamentation were at the heart of ecclesiastical dispute within the religious politics of the Jacobean church. The early reformed position that sacraments were essentially commemorative – signs of remembrance only – undermined their necessity in affirming, let alone conferring, grace.[67] When the Hampton Court Conference restricted the performance of private baptism to "lawful ministers," for instance, it reflected the belief that the presence of God's grace in the sacrament demanded elevated ceremonial and sacerdotal engagement.[68] A similar view of the Eucharist lay behind the embellishment of the altar as the specific site of God's presence in the church. The Laudian retrieval of screens, altar rails, and painted cherubim resurrected the Catholic chancel, a Holy of Holies exclusively entered by priests. At St. Giles-in-the-Fields, "the *sanctum sanctorum* [was] separated from the chancel by a large skreene" – donated by Alice Dudley – "in the figure of a beautifull gate," carved with statues of three saints, "all set above with winged cherubims."[69]

For Puritans, such renovations were at least inconvenient, since the elevation and seclusion of the altar by rails and screens disrupted the communal worship by the body of believers – the practice initiated in

63 See Whiting, *Reformation*, 71–84, esp. 73. See also Gunton, *History*, 58–65, for the 1539 inventory of Peterborough; and Peacock, ed., *English Church Furniture*, for "A List of the Goods Destroyed in Certain Lincolnshire Churches, A.D. 1566."

64 According to Whiting, *Reformation*, 71, "copes were by far the most expensive items in the inventory." The attribution to Katherine of Aragon is based on the fact that her emblem, the pomegranate, is stitched around the edges of the frontal.

65 Richardson, *Mistress Blanche*, 62. The altar cloth is preserved at Bacton. See Figure 6.1.

66 Whiting, *Reformation*, 83.

67 For insightful discussions, see Milton, *Catholic and Reformed*, 196–206; and Beckwith, "Stephen Greenblatt's *Hamlet*," 261–7.

68 See Sawyer, ed., *Memorial*, vol. II, 13–16; and see Chapter 2.

69 Dobie, *History*, 106.

Elizabeth's first Royal Injunctions, which charged that "altars be clean taken away and that there be no monument of them left" and in their place, Communion tables should be set at the center of chancels.[70] More pressingly, the ornamentation of the altar veered dangerously close to the idolatrous worship of the transubstantiated host. Moderate Puritans accepted these embellishments as "things indifferent"; Joseph Hall concedes the accessories of ceremonial worship by treating them in allegorical terms:

> [L]ooke unto the furniture: What is the Altar whereon our sacrifices of praier and praises are offered to the Almightie but a contrite heart? What the golden Candlesticks, but the illumined understanding, wherein the light of the knowledge of God, and his divine will shineth for ever? What the Tables of Shew-bread, but the sanctified memorie, which keepeth the bread of life continually?[71]

Radical reformers, however, equated ornamentation with idolatry. Henry Cawdrey protests that "if we should bow toward or before [the altar] with those religious respects of more holiness, or more special presence of Christ in it . . . we should be superstitious, if not Idolatrous."[72] To worship the altar is to worship mere furniture, and its ostentation renders it a painted sepulcher. While Perkins expresses the conforming Puritan view that "We holde and believe a presence of Christs bodie and bloode in the Sacrament of the Lord's Supper: and that no fained, but a true or reall presence,"[73] he is at pains to deny transubstantiation and to clarify the manner of this presence as "first in respect of the signes, secondly in respect of the communicants":

> when the elements of bread and wine are present to the hand and to the mouth of the receiver, the very same time the bodie and bloode of Christ are presented to the minde: thus and no otherwise is Christ truly present in the signes. The second presence is in respect of the communicants, to whose beleeving hearts he is also really present.[74]

Perkins accordingly develops a scheme of the Eucharist as a cluster of signs, acts, and effects, each with a sensible and a spiritual aspect. "The Ministers action is fourefold," he writes, and "the action of the receiver, is double,"

[70] See "Royal Injunction of Queen Elizabeth, 1559," in Frere and Kennedy, eds., *Visitation Articles*, vol. III, 27–8.

[71] Hall, *Contemplations*, 237–8.

[72] Cawdrey, *Superstitio Superstes*, 26.

[73] Perkins, *Reformed Catholicke*, 183.

[74] Perkins, *Reformed Catholicke*, 84.

and he supplies a chart of the relations within the sacrament to affix them more firmly in worshippers' memories (see Figure 3.4).[75]

This multifaceted sacrament and the afterlife of liturgical debate and practices that prompted its creation permeate Innogen's chamber. If Innogen is an effigy lying in a chapel, referring this monumental display to the ritual performance of the Eucharist associates her corpse with the *corpus Christi*. Early-Elizabethan visitation articles prescribed for the altar "a decent and simple table . . . covered with a fair carpet, and a fine linen table-cloth upon it."[76] While by the 1630s "the communion-table" should be "enclosed and ranged about with a rail of joyners and turners work, close enough to keep out dogs from going in and profaning that holy place from pissing against it or worse," the table was still covered with "a carpet of silke or such like, and a fayre lynnen cloth belonging to the same."[77] The "corporal" used during the mass – "a faire white linnen cloth," as the 1604 Book of Common Prayer calls it – represents the shroud wrapped around Christ in the sepulcher, now covering his body in the sacrament.[78] The use of luxurious "carpet-cloths" to adorn the altar translates the arras coverlet from secularity to sacramentality. Adorned by a linen sheet and arras coverlet, Innogen is a sacrament on the altar, surrounded by candles, attended by cherubim aloft.

As was true of her early modern counterparts represented in monumental sculpture, Innogen's femininity and her materiality collude to push the female effigy at once toward idealization and idolatry. The distracted eye of idolatry colludes with the blurred vision of iconoclasm. The extremes of sanctity and idolatry are played out by Innogen's celestial cherubim, on the one hand, and infernal "winking Cupids" decorating her fireplace, on the other. Her slippery bracelet recalls the "brazen serpent" erected by Moses, as William Perkins reports, "to be a type, signe or image to represent Christ crucified" – but it is one easily turned into its opposite: "when the people burned incense to it," Perkins recalls of the Old

[75] Perkins, *Golden Chaine*, 111.

[76] See Frere and Kennedy, eds., *Visitation Articles*, vol, III, 165; vol. III, 371; and vol. III, 109. Carpets are frequently represented as covering tables in Tudor and Stuart portraiture, Holbein's *Ambassadors* (1533) and the anonymous *Somerset House Conference* (1604) being familiar examples. My association between the arras coverlet and the carpet is based on their similar decorative forms, textures, and uses.

[77] Fitcham, ed., *Visitation Articles*, vol. II, 195; and vol. II, 1. For articles requiring carpets and linen cloths for the Communion table in the early Jacobean period, see Fitcham, ed., *Visitation Articles*, vol. I, 31 and 99.

[78] BCP (1604), fol. P4^v^. Etymologically, corporal combines the Latin and *corpus* (body) and *pallium* (pall), literally meaning "to cover": see *OED*.

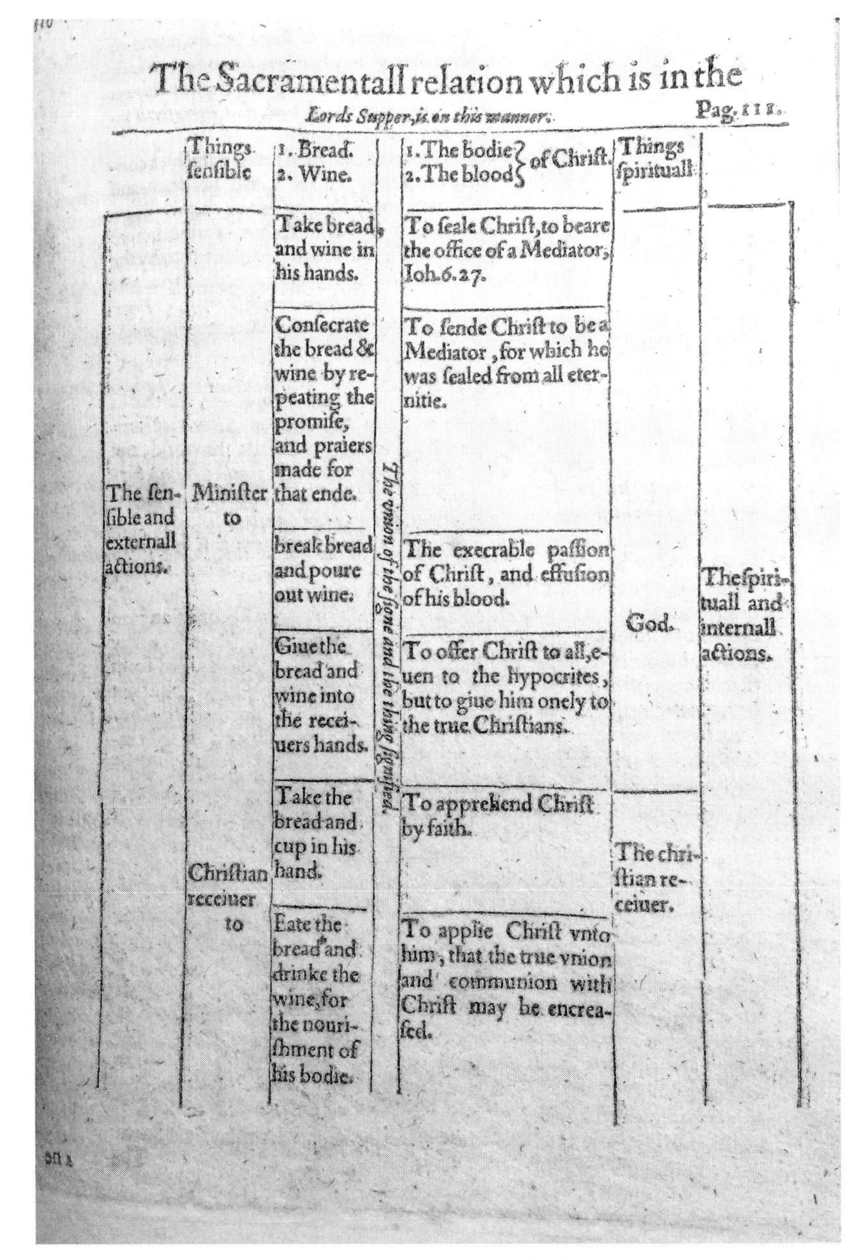

The Sacramentall relation which is in the *Lords Supper, is on this manner.* Pag. 111.

		Things ſenſible: 1. Bread. 2. Wine.		1. The bodie / 2. The blood } of Chriſt.	Things ſpirituall	
The ſenſible and externall actions.	Miniſter to	Take bread, and wine in his hands.	*The vnion of the ſigne and the thing ſignified.*	To ſeale Chriſt, to beare the office of a Mediator, Ioh. 6. 27.	God.	The ſpirituall and internall actions.
		Conſecrate the bread & wine by repeating the promiſe, and praiers made for that ende.		To ſende Chriſt to be a Mediator, for which he was ſealed from all eternitie.		
		break bread and poure out wine.		The execrable paſſion of Chriſt, and effuſion of his blood.		
		Giue the bread and wine into the receiuers hands.		To offer Chriſt to all, euen to the hypocrites, but to giue him onely to the true Chriſtians.		
	Chriſtian receiuer to	Take the bread and cup in his hand.		To apprehend Chriſt by faith.	The chriſtian receiuer.	
		Eate the bread and drinke the wine, for the nouriſhment of his bodie.		To applie Chriſt vnto him, that the true vnion and communion with Chriſt may be encreaſed.		

Figure 3.4 William Perkins, *A Golden Chaine* (Cambridge: John Legate, 1600), 111. © The British Library Board. Shelfmark 3557g16.

Testament icon, "Hezekias brake it in pieces."[79] Jachimo's abuse of Innogen's bracelet, similarly, transforms this sign of the sacrament into an idol. As the "corporal sign" that Posthumus seeks, the Innogen of the chamber is thornily duplicitous. Yet when her corporal – the tainted remnant of an idolatrous ritual – transmutes into the "bloody cloth" intended to prove Innogen's sacrifice (5.1.1), it seems to retain a trace of sacramental power in the hands of the repentant worshipper, Posthumus. The relic is a second Veronica, endowed with real presence and transformational effect, becoming, as does the worshipper, "less without and more within" (5.1.33).

If Jachimo's iconoclastic vision violates the sacrament, his perversion also demonizes the communicant. As Ann Montagu warns those intending to take Communion, "the divell is also present to enter with unworthy receivers or receiveing."[80] "An unworthie receiver," William Attersoll menacingly states, "is guilty of the blood of Christ."[81] Jachimo is the devil haunting the sacrament – "hell is here," he confesses (2.2.49) – and he misconstrues and perverts the spectacle of the altar. In his incursion into the Holy of Holies, Jachimo renders Innogen a vacant movable entombed in a desecrated chapel, one whose worship "is superstitious, if not Idolatrous." She is vainglorious furniture.

In this intricate chapel chamber, as William Perkins puts it, "every sacrament is the word of God made visible to the eye."[82] Jachimo's conversion of things into words in his commemorative inventory participates in the tissue of material and intertextual translations in which the chamber is enmeshed. His design "To note the chamber" (2.2.24) requires a portable writing technology, probably a wax or gesso tablet, where one inscribes erasable characters on the waxed surface.[83] This probability is confirmed by Jachimo's implicit description of the device: "Why should I write this down," he asks, "that's riveted, / Screwed to my memory?" (2.2.43–4). One of several competing figurations of memory imagined remembrance itself as a wax tablet where impressions were inscribed.[84] In Jachimo's alignment of the wax tablet, screwed to its wooden frame, with the images screwed to his memory, writing is the ephemeral remainder of memory, progressively inscribed in an evolving material. Dispersed in multiple layers of reading and interpretation,

[79] Perkins, *Reformed Catholicke*, 171 and 178. Perkins cites John 3:14 on the serpent as a type for Christ, and 2 Kings 18:4 on the object as idol.
[80] NRO Montagu MS 3, fol. 251. [81] Attersoll, *Badges of Christianity*, 344. See Chapter 2.
[82] Perkins, *Commentarie . . . [upon] Galatians*, 254. [83] See Wakelin, *Scribal Correction*, 278–9.
[84] Carruthers, *Book of Memory*, 18–55. See Chapter 2.

superimposed on each other, the script of Jachimo's tablet captures – or, rather, imprisons – the "sense" of Innogen's chamber and its occupant as the petrified essence of the sacrament's "sanctified memorie."

The vulnerability to erasure implicit in the wax tablet consumes Innogen, whose image is conjoined with the wooden frame in a crucifixion that counters Jachimo's false resurrection. As the nails of crucifixion become the rivets and screws of memory, Jachimo also takes possession of Innogen's union with Posthumus: Perkins's material figuration of marriage, which sees man and wife as "two boords joyned together with glue" evocatively captures the divorce decreed by Jachimo's tablet.[85] As prurient voyeurism transmutes into the illicit desire of idolatry, it performs an iconoclastic destruction of the licensed bond.

The contest of sacramental signs and rituals played out in Innogen's chamber produces an equivocal Eucharist, accommodating both true and false views, eliciting the skewed vision of idolatry and inviting the blind passion of iconoclasm. As *Cymbeline* leaves this scene of sacramental failure behind, we are led to wonder what it would mean to approach the signs and rituals of remembrance in a world set apart from the Reformation struggles that so vex Innogen's chapel chamber. How might we retrieve the pastorals of Christ's Passion: the garden of Gethsemane, with its authentic Lord's Supper; or the Garden Tomb, where we may find an empty grotto whose occupant has risen and returned, momentarily, to the world?

3 Innogen's Needle

William Perkins, in another posthumous work – which, like his commentary on St. John's Revelation, was edited by Robert Hill and printed by Richard Field – includes candles among "all such merchandize of waxe, &c., as the Papists use to maintaine their superstitions and Idolatrie."[86] While wax tapers were associated with funerals and Catholic chantries, they also embellished the altar during the ritual of Communion; accessories, in the eyes of Puritans, to the dead idol of the Catholic sacrament. John Deacon numbers among the "Romishe Reliques as helpe to hold up the kingdome of Antichrist . . . Vestments, Copes, wax Tapers, with tenne hundred suche trifilng toyes."[87] William Buchanan – in a work translated from Latin by Robert Hill and printed by Richard Field – censures the use of "vaine ceremonies of annointing, shaving, wax candles and such

[85] Perkins, *Christian Oeconomie*, 10. [86] Perkins, *Satans Sophistrie Answered*, 95.
[87] Deacon, *Treatise [Nobody is my Name]*, fol. L3r.

toyes," which idolatrously transform "the ordination of ministers into a sacrament."[88]

Yet against this idolatrous matter, figurative deployments by reformers compared the impression of a seal on wax to the seal of election. Perkins writes:

> we perceive that election which is in God as concerning us, as wee gather the pattern by the picture: like as by the similitude of the forme of a seale, fashioned in wax, we doe easilie understande, what is the very forme and fashion of the seale. Therefore it is manifest, that it is the maner of God, by the effectes of his election and predestination imprinted in us.[89]

What is imprinted is the Word of God: "When [the worshipper] findes the Scripture imprinted in his heart, as the signe of the seale is in the waxe . . . his heart is transformed into Scripture, as the waxe is into the similitude of the seale."[90] Thomas Tuke, editing Perkins's treatise on predestination, enlivens the image: "the Spirit of God abideth in [the faithful], who is busy within the hive of their hearts as a Bee, and worketh them like waxe.[91] Like the seasonal unfolding of the natural world, this transformation is an evolving process, the continual working of one material into another. God's spirit, through the stirrings of the internalized Word, molds and fashions the Christian from within.

Identified with the sacrament in her chapel chamber, Innogen plots a course of dispersal and recollection as she moves beyond, one that maps the multiplicity of the Puritan sacrament onto the structure and operation of romance. Unlike her predecessor, Boccaccio's Zinevra, whose romance voyages script a random cartography of late-medieval mercantilism, Innogen's journey into the pastoral landscape of Wales is directed and focused by *Cymbeline's* sacramental subtext. In Wales, an extended ritual of

[88] Buchanan, *Institutions*, 568.

[89] Perkins, *Case of Conscience*, 44–5. Innogen is associated with election at 3.4.110, where she imagines herself as "th'elected deer" standing defenseless before the hunter. In the same scene, she casts herself as a sacrificial lamb (3.4.97) in a displacement of the overt sacramentality of Shakespeare's source, where the heroine "caryed with her a lytell lambe that she was wonte to play withall," which is slaughtered to stain the cloth. See Anon., *Frederycke of Jennen*, fols. C1^{v}-C2^{r}; reprinted in Bullough, *Narrative and Dramatic Sources*, vol. VIII, 71. The word, "election," is also used in *Cymbeline* at 1.1.53 and 1.6.175, referring to Innogen's choice of Posthumus.

[90] Perkins, *Godly and Learned Exposition of Christs Sermon in the Mount*, 468. The imagery of the soft wax of the heart is widespread and crosses confessional divides: see, for example, Church of England clergyman Harvey's *Schola Cordis*, Epigram 26, which figures the heart as a wax table: "In the soft table of thy heart I'll write, / A new law, which I'lll newly indite. / Hard stony tables did containe the old / But tender leaves of flesh shall this infold."

[91] Thomas Tuke and Francis Calcot, "Dedicatory Epistle," in Perkins, *Christian and Plaine Treatise*, fol. A2^{v}.

remembrance corrects the petrified essence imposed on Innogen in the chamber scene, replacing that monumental figure with natural images of the body's dissolution. If Innogen's suspension between life and death involves her in a material sense with nature, she is also involved with and quickened by the spiritual inflections given to the natural world by reformed exegetes.

In the same way that Innogen's corporal – her linen sheet as shroud – is transmuted to a penitential token of the Crucifixion in Posthumus's hands, the legacies of the chamber's textualities are redeemed as instruments joining characters and episodes across the last two acts of *Cymbeline*. The corrective reinterpretation of the chamber's textualities begins in Act 3, scene 2, when Innogen revises Jachimo's heretical tablet with "young Cupid's tables," "clasped" by waxen seals. "Good wax, thy leave" she exclaims, addressing the seal on Posthumus's letter, "Blest be / You bees that make these locks of counsel!"(3.2.34–5). As the scene continues, the imagery of wax is reworked. Innogen's charge to Pisano, "speak thick — / Love's counsellor should fill the bores of hearing / To th' smothering of the sense—"(3.2.55–7) associates love's counselor with the waxen "locks of counsel" sealing Posthumus's letter. The image of earwax locates the wax of blessed bees within the body, incorporated through hearing, smothering the sense but enlivening the spirit. The "thick speech" manufactured in the hive of the heart, to adapt Tuke's image, works Innogen like wax, transforming her to Scripture. Shakespeare sets this incarnated Word against Posthumus's heretical texts. "The scriptures of the loyal Leonatus / All turn'd to heresy?" Innogen complains, "Away, away, / Corruptors of my faith" (3.4.82–4).

This transitional imagery sets the stage for the play's restorative ritual of remembrance performed in Wales, at the site of a natural grave that contrasts starkly with the mortuary chapel created and desecrated by Jachimo. When her brothers lay Innogen (as Fidele) to rest, they perform a ritual that is improvised, yet recycled; natural, but framed by supernatural intimations. The juxtaposition of this makeshift ritual with traditional rites of burial and commemoration indicts the ineffectuality and corruption of the Catholic liturgy. Impromptu, open-ended, resourceful, and collaborative, the ritual opens up possibilities for marvelous interventions and unexpected recoveries. Innogen's processual, ephemeral monument in Wales marks the play's turn toward redemption and renewal.

With the sounding of Belarius's "ingenious instrument" (4.2.187), not heard since the death of the brothers' nurse, Euriphile, Innogen's death is announced and preparations for her burial commence. An equivocal sign of the supernatural quality of the scene of burial and resurrection, this "Solemn music" (4.2.186.s.d.) emphasizes the retrieval of earlier funeral rites in laying Innogen to rest "by good Euriphile, our mother" (4.2.234), "sing[ing] him to th' ground / As once our mother; us[ing] like notes and words, / Save that Euriphile must be Fidele" (4.2.236–8). The substitution of one name, one corpse, for another is glossed later in the scene, when the decision to bury Cloten alongside Fidele leads Guiderius to reason, "Thersites' body be as good as Ajax' / When neither are alive" (4.2.254–5). If there is irony in this claim that one body or name – one subject – can substitute for another in death, the idea is not advanced derisively. Rather, the recovery and reuse of an improvised rite, in which differences between lives and deaths become unimportant, connects Innogen not only to the nation of the dead who have also passed through this porous threshold, but to an organic and ecosystemic notion of death as a phenomenon aligned with seasonal loss. As Rosi Braidotti puts it, "that which we fear most does not lie ahead but is already behind us." This "impersonal death" is "the precondition of our existence, of the future."[92] What strikes us at first as ironic in the Arviragus's and Guiderius's ritual turns instead toward accommodation and acceptance of an impersonal death:

> Fear no more the heat o'th' sun,
> Nor the furious winter's rages,
> Thou thy worldly task hast done,
> Home art gone and ta'en thy wages,
> Golden lads and girls all must,
> As chimney-sweepers, come to dust.
> (4.2.259–64)

This impersonal death is also implicit in the brothers' closing prayer over Innogen's body, "Quiet consummation have, / And renown'd be thy grave" (4.2.281–2). The idea of consummation echoes the language but not the sense of the Book of Common Prayer's "Order for the Burial of the Dead," which offers a communal prayer for "perfect consummation and bliss" with God.[93] The finality of Innogen's quiet consummation, by contrast, is the undisturbed ground of the grave itself. The addition of the wish for renown in the prayer – particularly in light of the unlikelihood that the unmarked grave of a wrongly identified corpse can achieve renown in any conventional sense – decenters the idea of spiritual transcendence, moving instead toward, as Braidotti puts it, "the intelligence of radically

[92] Braidotti, *Posthuman*, 95 and 99.
[93] See Warren's note to 4.2.281 in Shakespeare, *Cymbeline*; and BCP (1552), fol. 123^{r}.

immanent flesh that states . . . that the life in you is not marked by any master signifier and it most certainly does not bear your name."[94] Innogen's consummation is the decorous dissolution of the body as it "come[s] to dust" (4.2.264) – as all bodies inevitably must. In the wide berth of impersonal death, the nurse Euriphile is no less fondly remembered for having been mistaken for mother (3.3.103–5).

The monument constructed by Guiderius and Arviragus is an anti-monument, engrafted on a recovered rite to recall and overturn traditional ceremonies. Thus the lyrical song of mourning performed by the brothers is spoken, not sung: "I cannot sing," Arviragus complains. "I'll weep, and word it with thee, / For notes of sorrow out of tune are worse / Than priests and fanes that lie" (4.2.241–3). This difficult simile may suggest that tuneless notes are "worse" both for the collected mourners – a small congregation, in this instance – and for the departed. The invocation of "priests and fanes" (temples) would locate the performance in the chantry by alluding to the Catholic faith that prayers for the dead can influence the progress of the soul in the afterlife, a superstition akin to idolatry for Protestants. Engaging traditional ceremonies both in advance of the brothers' performance and at its close, Shakespeare uses Reformation liturgical debates as foils for this improvised ritual. Thus the brothers lay the body "with his head to th'east," countering the topography of Christian burial without further considering Belarius's "reason for 't" (4.2.246–7). The simplicity and sincerity of this maverick rite shames "Those rich-left heirs that let their fathers lie / Without a monument" (4.2.227–8), and resonates, too, with the reformation of funeral rites that prompted the majority of Protestant testators to will explicitly that they be laid to rest without the "vain ostentation or pomp" associated with Catholic funeral masses. In 1618, as we have seen, Elizabeth Harington Montagu insisted that her executors see her buried without "frivylouse" ceremonies that "hinder the livinge, and the deceased profitt nothinge."[95]

From this anti-monumental ceremony, two wonders emerge. Setting aside conventional rituals, Shakespeare stages a renaissance of remembrance. The first miracle is the song itself, a lyric performance of extraordinary beauty and affect that replaces religious and liturgical figurations with those of the natural, seasonal cycles of birth and death. In form and content the poem inscribes the passage of time that inevitably leads to

[94] Braidotti, *Posthuman*, 99. [95] TNA PROB 11/131/760, Will of Elizabeth Montagu, fol. 425^r.

death: since they last performed this rite as boys, the brothers' "voices / Have got the mannish crack" (4.2.236–7). The verses are, appropriately, spoken over a monument made of flowers rather than marble, not over an alabaster effigy but one of flesh and blood – one seasonally dormant:

> Thou shalt not lack
> The flowers that's like thy face, pale primrose, nor
> The azured harebell, like thy veins; no, nor
> The leaf of eglantine, who not to slander
> Outsweetened not thy breath. The ruddock would
> With charitable bill—O bill sore shaming
> Those rich-left heirs that let their fathers lie
> Without a monument!—bring thee all this.
> (4.2.221–8)

Associated with process, evolution, and metamorphosis, this anti-monument reverses and rewrites the deadening tomb erected in Innogen's chamber. What is imagined in this act of remembrance is the body's gradual merger with earth: "Yea," Arviragus concludes, "and furred moss besides, when flowers are none, / To winter-ground thy corpse" (4.2.229–30).

The blending of the body with the natural world in death – the progressive dissolution of bodies and their memorials to dust – predicts a future of repeated performances of commemoration; a very human process of remembrance in which the departed are recalled in the death of others, in each renewed work of mourning.

But there is a second wonder, of course, emerging from Shakespeare's virtuoso performance. Standing outside orthodox rites of dying, Innogen's funeral in Wales situate her at the borders of the human. Innogen's funeral figures her "being-in-the-world," as Merleau-Ponty would say, and she awakes as a vital, material subject for whom death, in Braidotti's formulation, "is another phase in a generative process."[96] Innogen's transient interment imagines the fluid exchange between her flesh and the "flesh of the world;" an evolving materiality typologically aligned with Merleau-Ponty's sacramental "communion with the world," which restores and recreates the subject.[97] If Innogen is disanimated by Jachimo's transformation of her sense into insensible stone, her passage through a second sleep is a regenerative transformation. Her resurrection occurs within a natural, evolving ritual that blurs borders between subjects, objects, and others.

[96] Braidotti, *Posthuman*, 88.

[97] Merleau-Ponty, *Visible and Invisible*, esp. 88 and 144; and *Phenomenology of Perception*, 245–6.

Her body becomes viscous – as if composed of the wax produced by spiritual bees – and porous, as the limits between the body and world become imperceptible.[98] She is involved in natural, spiritual, familial, and memorial networks whose revelations depend upon her wondrous rebirth. Remembrance is fused to pliant, evolving matter.

The iconoclastic association of feminine matter with the body in death is reversed in Innogen's resurrection, where natural figurations of spiritual regeneration – the malleable wax of the Christian body, worked by the internalized hive – are mobilized. When Innogen awakens to find the beheaded body of Cloten, the tableau richly alludes to the Crucifixion and the mourning of Christ by the three Maries; the sorrowful female body of the church laments the loss of her head.[99] The Orphic overtones attending Cloten's death ("I have sent Cloten's clotpoll down the stream," 4.2.185) place the body of Christ – whether embodied or remembered in the Eucharist – at the heart of familial (and thus, political) restoration in *Cymbeline*.[100] Yet as she arises from the grave, Innogen turns from the sacrament of Christ's death to the sacrament of renewal and rebirth. She consigns to earth the dismembered trunk to which she has been engrafted in a second death: as Lucius reasons, "nature doth abhor to make his bed / With the defunct, or sleep upon the dead" (4.2.358–9). Leaving behind this crucified body – a corpse that nature abhors – in resurrected flesh, she names the trunk "Richard du Champ" (4.2.378) and repeats her self-christening as Fidele (4.2.380). With these acts of naming, Shakespeare again performs a sacramental intertextuality in his allusion to the printer, Richard Field.[101] If every sacrament is a visible Word, each ritual performance involves a web of material and immaterial texts that are repeated, relearned, and renewed. In this baptismal moment, Innogen reaffirms her faith as she repeats the name, Fidele, adopted on her entry to the cave (3.6.58). She is named and renamed as she reenters the temporal realm of history. At the same time, she turns away from the body in death ("of the field") to plot a course of recreation and reconciliation.

In two complementary figurations, Innogen imagines and enacts this fluid merger of the materials – sacramental, textual, and feminine matter – involved in her funeral and reawakening. Hearing that Cloten has drawn on the exiled Posthumus, Innogen exclaims, "I would they were in Africa

[98] Tuana, "Viscous Porosity." [99] Arbery, "Displaced Nativity," 165.

[100] See Armitage, "Dismemberment of Orpheus," 132; and Hunt, "Dismemberment," 419–21.

[101] "Fidele" is an anagram of "Fielde," while "Richard du Champ" reflects the translation of Field's name, often printed on his foreign editions. See Kirwood, "Richard Field"; and Pettegree, *Foreign and Native*, 146–75.

both together, / Myself with a needle, that I might prick the goer-back" (1.1.168–70). Again, as Pisanio describes Posthumus's departure, she swears:

> I would have broke mine eye-strings, cracked them, but
> To look upon him, till the diminution
> Of space had pointed him sharp as my needle:
> Nay, followed him, till he had melted from
> The smallness of a gnat, to air. (1.3.17–21)

Both of these aspirational images point to the limits of Innogen's abilities to influence the play's political sphere. She would, but cannot, intervene in the swordplay between two adversaries, and she can only follow the exiled Posthumus with her eyes rather than accompanying him or calling him back. Yet both of these invocations of the needle suggest Innogen's creative capacity to weave together the plot of *Cymbeline* by recollecting the remnants of other texts and signs, recalling and thereby resurrecting the patterns and forms of romance. Both interventions of Innogen's needle figure the expansive, imaginative landscapes of the genre – the emptiness of Africa and the vast horizon into which Posthumus disappears – sewing into the fabric of *Cymbeline* the memory of the world traversed by Boccaccio's Zinevra and her translational descendants. Wielding her needle, Innogen controls and repossesses the textualities of her chamber, restoring their capacity to bestow upon her agency and transformational power. Measuring the distance between herself and Posthumus, Innogen's needle becomes an instrument of discrimination and judgment; like the crosshair of a sight, it enables a true vision so difficult in Jachimo's and Posthumus's idolatrous views of Innogen. Her keen insight reduces Posthumus from needle, to gnat, to air, plotting his course in exile from Innogen's elected partner, to a memorial trace contained in her bracelet, to the thin air of his vanished covenant.

Innogen's needle points toward a productive intertextuality embodied in the play's sacred book, Jupiter's prophecy, deposited on the breast of the sleeping Posthumus by the "fairies that haunt [the] ground" of his cell (5.3.227). The appearance of the prophetic tablet amid a company of fairies – in this case, the departed Leonati – links Jupiter's monumental text to the monument of Innogen's chamber, haunted by the diabolical "fairy" Jachimo, and to her anti-monument in Wales, which her brothers predict, "With female fairies will . . . be haunted" (4.2.218). If the tomb is haunted by fairies in the world of *Cymbeline,* Posthumus's sleep reiterates Innogen's, both in her chapel chamber and in her Welsh grave.

As Posthumus rises to the revealed Word of God, he begins the process of interpretation and correction that will lead to reunion with Innogen.[102]

Emerging from the site of entombment, Jupiter's tablet is at once the Old Testament tablet of Moses and the rare book of the New Covenant. As a sacramental text – a Word that is also a sacrament – God's book is a book of remembrance. Yet the imperative to interpret this sacred text is challenged not by its obscurity – although it is, indeed, obscure – but by the possibility that this sacrament may itself be an idol: "A book? O rare one," Posthumus pleads, "Be not, as our fangled world, a garment/ Nobler than that it covers" (5.3.227–9).[103] Through intertextual exchange, however, Jupiter's tablet becomes Fidele's: the rare book of New Testament sacramentality, a text of true faith. At the heart of this sacramental text is the Word enfleshed, "a piece of tender air" (5.3.253).

The imaginative landscape sketched by Innogen's needle outlines the cooperation and communion that will restore the bodies of marriage and the commonwealth; it points toward the "consociation of our persons" that Robert Hill describes as the fellowship forged by the sacrament, "a confederation of our affections and concatenation of our wils."[104] Unfolding Jupiter's prophecy, the soothsayer explains its central figure of consociation: "a lion's whelp shall, to himself unknown, without seeking find, and be embraced by a piece of tender air" (5.4.436–8). The image is most often read as embodying the typological completion of the Old Covenant (the lion figuring the Tribe of Judah) in the New (the tender air of the Holy Spirit).[105] As the redemptive Christian narrative underpinning the plot rises to the surface, the soothsayer's interpretation depends on a tortured etymology. "The piece of tender air," he explains, is Cymbeline's "virtuous daughter, / Which we call '*mollis aer*'; and '*mollis aer*' / We term it '*mulier*'" (5.3.447–9). The immediate source for this etymological sleight of hand is Henri Estienne's *World of Wonders*, translated by the author and printed by Richard Field in 1607. There, the etymology appears as part of Estienne's condemnation of the extravagant "cunning" of Catholic exegesis and ceremonial worship. Conflating,

[102] Beckwith, *Shakespeare and the Grammar of Forgiveness*, 104–26, sees Posthumus's reformation as a ritual of confession.

[103] Crumley, "Questioning History," reads Jupiter's text as underscoring the fallibility of textual exegesis, relating this interpretive error to the play's engagement with the rival histories of Rome and Britain.

[104] Hill, *Communicant Instructed*, 230. Hill's preparation for Communion was first published as a catechism in 1608, and presents a scheme of the sacrament that is very similar to Perkins's.

[105] Moffet, "*Cymbeline* and the Nativity," 216; and Geller, "*Cymbeline* and the Imagery of Covenant Theology," 250.

as does *Cymbeline*, "the ancient Latinists" with contemporary Catholics, Estienne derides their "good dexteritie in giving Etymologies of ancient latin words":

> witnesse the notation of Mulier, quasi mollis aër. But now we are to prosecute other subtill speculations, concerning matters of greater moment. And first, what braines may we thinke had they, which coyned so many quaint questions . . . [T]hey make a nose of waxe of them.[106]

In charging Catholic exegetes with "making a nose of wax" of the scriptures, Estienne employs a figuration frequently used by Calvin: "by this wee may see how Satan hath possessed the papists," Calvin writes, "when as they say, that the word of God is . . . a nose of wax, which a man may turne what way he listeth."[107] For Estienne, this exegetical malleability parallels the "apish trickes and turnings used in the Mass."[108] Etymology is a form of idolatry.

Shakespeare's allusion to Estienne's work imports into *Cymbeline* a "world of wonders" not of secular romance but of textual circulation and spiritual debate. By way of wax, this subtext returns to Jachimo's wax tablet, complementing his dispossession of Innogen; thus, the heir becomes simply air.[109] Yet by way of the swirling stock of Richard Field's shop, Estienne's text imports into Shakespeare's play the productive social and textual exchanges of the international Reformation. Field's apprenticeship in the London shop of French expatriate Thomas Vautrollier and his subsequent marriage to Vautrollier's widow, Jacqueline, placed Field in close affiliation with French Huguenot printers, including Estienne, many of whom escaped religious persecution in the multicultural liberty of Blackfriars.[110] Carrying associations with "French culture and with international Protestantism," as Douglas Bruster points out, *A World of Wonders* engages Innogen's French wordplay and *Cymbeline's* encounter

[106] Estienne, *World of Wonders*, 292–3.

[107] Calvin, "The xiiii. Sermon upon the hundredth *and nineteenth* Psalme," in Calvin, *Two and Twentie Sermons*, fol. 115^{r}.

[108] Estienne, *World of Wonders*, 293.

[109] Howard, "Introduction to *Cymbeline*," in Greenblatt, et al., eds., *Norton Shakespeare: Romances and Poems*, 244.

[110] See Heal, "Experiencing Religion," 64–7 on the Dutch reformed and French Huguenot communities in London. Bruster, "Shakespeare's Lady 8," presents a similar argument based on Field's use of the printer's mark on the title page of his 1594 edition of Shakespeare's *Lucrece*, which was adapted from Huguenot printers such as Estienne and Vautrollier and therefore carried associations with international Protestantism. The image appears in Estienne's *World of Wonders* and a variation of it, identified as, "Lady 1a" by Kirwood, "Richard Field," 33, appears twice in Perkins, *Lectures*, at 340 and 373.

with the literary skirmishes of international religious debate.[111] Thus, for example, Field's edition of Perkins's commentary on the Revelation bespeaks the wide translational career of Perkins's Puritan writings within the international religious conversation staged in *Cymbeline*.[112] Glossing the Spanish and Dutch nationals in Philario's house are 185 Dutch imprints of Perkins's works, twice as many as any other Puritan writer's, and a Spanish translation of his *Reformed Catholicke* printed in London and Amsterdam, "probably for proselytizing purposes in the Spanish Netherlands."[113] *Catholico reformado* was printed in 1599 "En casa de Ricardo del Campo."[114]

Another layer of intertextual exchange lies behind the etymology as well, one that calls forth a subtext of Innogen's chamber, Shakespeare's *Lucrece*. The derivation of *mulier* from *mollis aer* was first presented in William Caxton's 1474 translation of a French source, *The Game and Playe of the Chess*. Shakespeare returns to the inaugural moment of English print – a textual recovery that parallels *Cymbeline's* politico-historical engagement with the remote British past – to retrieve the etymology in a passage that finds its way into *Lucrece*:

> For the women ben likened unto softe waxe or softe ayer and therfore she is callid *mulier* whyche Is as moche to saye in latyn as *mollys aer*. And in english soyfte ayer. And hit happeth ofte tymes that the nature of them that ben softe and mole taketh sonner Inpression than the nature of men that is rude and stronge.[115]

"For men have marble, women waxen minds," as Shakespeare's *Lucrece* adapts the passage, excusing women for the false impressions forced upon them by men.[116] At once the air of resurrection, the malleable text at the center of doctrinal debate, and the soft wax of femininity, Innogen embodies the dense "intertwining (*entrelacs*)" of the sacred subtext of *Cymbeline*, its romance meanderings, and the recollection of Romano-British history informing its project of nation-building.[117] If she is a page,

[111] Bruster, "Shakespeare's Lady 8," 79.

[112] Perkins's works were translated into Dutch, Spanish, German, Latin, French, Czech, and Welsh: see *ODNB*.

[113] Patterson, *William Perkins*, 194; and see van der Haar *From Abbadie to Young*, vol. I, 96–108.

[114] Perkins, *Catholico reformado*.

[115] Caxton, *Game*, n.p. Caxton's source was the French translation by Jean de Ferron of Jacobus de Cessolis's thirteenth-century Latin treatise. This was long considered the first book printed in England, but Knowles, "Caxton," demonstrates that it was the second.

[116] Shakespeare, *Lucrece*, line 1240

[117] Merleau-Ponty, *Visible and Invisible*, 117.

she is a table of wax, and her needle is the stylus with which she scripts the evolutionary matter that enacts a consociation of persons, reuniting the severed bodies of *Cymbeline*.

A Mark of Wonder

Marked by two monuments for a living woman, *Cymbeline* plays out the petrifying violence of idolatry and iconoclasm and resurrects the female subject in a productive, regenerative incorporation of the sacrament that is also the text. The monument marking Fidele's death in Wales, made of flowers rather than stone, embodies one of two forms of memory traversing *Cymbeline*. Associated with process, evolution, and inevitable change, this version of remembrance stands in sharp contrast to the chantry erected by Jachimo, and to the monumental chronicles informing the pseudo-history of *Cymbeline*. Understanding the counter-narrative associated with Innogen's circuitous journey toward Milford Haven requires one to remember the imperial histories against which she travels. She is on a counter-course with the invading troops of Romans led by Julius Caesar, who entered Britain there, and also with the plot of British Empire. At Milford Haven, Henry Tudor began his successful campaign to inaugurate the Tudor monarchy and, as fate would have it, the reign of the Stuart king who would embody a united Great Britain.[118]

Against the centripetal monuments of chronicle history, *Cymbeline* sets the malleable tablet of Jupiter: a nose of wax. The movement of *Cymbeline*, following in the wake of its heroine, is from permanence to ephemerality. The Queen's potions do not kill but only produce the transient image of death; the soothsayer's truths are equivocal. Stately memorials are present only in their absence; fathers lie without monuments, and the monuments of antiquity scatter like petals before the marvelous return of long-dead ancestors, the astonishing descent of an antique god. The sacrament explored in *Cymbeline* is multifaceted and interrelational, and the imperative to approach this Word through repeated, revisionary acts of interpretation binds remembrance to pliable matter. Throughout *Cymbeline*, this submerged sacramental plot of scattering and recollection, dispersal and reincorporation, enables the unfolding of the prophecy promising a world

[118] Parolin, "Anachronistic Italy," 192–3; and see Warren, "Introduction," in Shakespeare, *Cymbeline*, 62.

of wonder. We understand that Innogen's sacramentality will be displaced by the "enwombment" of the true sign; a woman's wondrous work of a different order. The play looks toward the venter that will enable the true sign and sacrament to don the mantle of "fleshly slime." As *Cymbeline* fades to dark, this is a horizon toward which Innogen's needle only points.

PART II

"Monuments of Antiquitie"

CHAPTER 4

"The grave is but a Cabinet"
Remembrance and Recreation in Post-Reformation London

> Min herte is growen into Ston,
> So that my lady therupon
> Hath such a priente of love grave,
> That I can noght miselve save.
> – John Gower[1]

> [T]o save his life, [Noah] is commaunded to go into the grave & willingly to deprive himselfe of the aire and of vitall spirite. For the onely stinche of dung beeing without aire, and the place also so full farssed and stufte up, might the fourth day have killed all the living creatures that were in the Arke.
> – Jean Calvin[2]

A Closett of Raryties

In 1662, Hester Tradescant worried that her neighbor Elias Ashmole, by way of a secret door he had made "out of his Garden into my Orchard," would "com into my House as[oon] as the breath was out of my Body, & take away my Goods."[3] The goods in question were rare indeed: Hester was the widow of John Tradescant the younger, who had bequeathed to her the "Closett of Raryties" amassed by his father, an enormous collection that he maintained and increased until his own death in 1662.[4] A deed signed three years earlier had given the collection to Ashmole, but the couple attempted to rescind the document, which, Hester claimed,

[1] Gower, *Confessio Amantis*, in *Complete Works*, vol. II, book 1, lines 553–56. All subsequent citations are to book and lines in this edition unless otherwise indicated and appear parenthetically.
[2] Calvin, *Commentarie ... [upon] Genesis*, 189.
[3] Bod Rawlinson D. 912. During the dispute, Ashmole moved to the South Lambeth property adjacent to Hester's. See Leith-Ross, *John Tradescants*, 137–56.
[4] TNA C7/454/1, Ashmole v. Tradescant, 1662. See Swann, *Curiosities and Texts*, 27–54.

Tradescant had signed when he was "distempered"; that is, "in his drincke."[5] Tradescant's true intentions – to ensure the integrity of the collection in perpetuity – were reflected, Hester argued, in his last words: "I give, devise, and bequeath my Closett of Rarities to my dearely beloved wife Hester Tredescant dureing her naturall Life, and after [her] decease . . . to the Universities of Oxford or Cambridge, to which of them shee shall thinke fitt."[6]

Hester Tradescant's fears were not unfounded. Shortly after Tradescant's death, Ashmole's successful Chancery claim supported the 1659 deed and thus his right to the collection, but only after Hester's death.[7] In the sixteen years that she lived, while Hester continued to trade in rarities and build the collection, Ashmole persistently demanded possession, acquiring a portion of the "Ark," as Tradescant's collection was known, in 1674.[8] When Hester was found drowned in a pond in her South Lambeth garden four years later, Ashmole at last took complete control of the collection, transporting it in its entirety from her house to his within days of her death. He, in turn, bestowed it upon the University of Oxford, creating the museum that was his legacy and claim to immortality: as his epitaph remembers, "durante Musaeo / Ashmoliano Oxon. nunquam moriturus" (as long as the Ashmolean Museum at Oxford endures, he will never die).[9]

If Ashmole exploited the closet of rarities, as Marjorie Swann argues, to "harness wonder as a political and social asset," Hester Tradescant did so as well.[10] Since Tradescant's son and heir had died in 1652, the bequest to Hester both preserved the rarities that the couple together had acquired and ensured Hester's occupation and estate. Not only did she increase the collection but, trading on the period's fascination with the rare and marvelous, she also continued to make it available to public view for a fee of sixpence.[11] These repositories of the fabulous, wondrous, rare, and monstrous – indeed, as John Tradescant the elder put it, "Any thing that Is strang" – were tourist attractions in England and across Europe, offering firsthand spectatorship of objects whose strangeness often defied

[5] TNA C7/454/1; and TNA C7/541/2, Ashmole v. De Critz.
[6] TNA PROB 11/308/88, fol. 152^r.
[7] Swann, *Curiosities and Texts*, 43–5, argues that Ashmole claimed ownership to the collection based on his part in publishing the catalogue.
[8] In July 1667, William Corten recorded items acquired from Hester: see Leith-Ross, *John Tradescants*, 146–7.
[9] Epitaph, Monument for Elias Ashmole, in Allen, *History . . . of Lambeth*, 124.
[10] Swann, *Curiosities and Texts*, 26.
[11] MacGregor, "The Cabinet of Curiosities," 204; and Leith-Ross, *John Tradescants*, 101. The Tradescants hired a curator to show the collection: see Leigh, *Transproser Rehears'd*, 123.

explanation and whose stories often stretched belief.[12] When German student Georg Christoph Stirn visited Tradescants' Ark in 1638, he saw, among other wonders, "a hand of mummy," "a cup of an East Indian alcedo, which is a kind of unicorn," and "a scourge with which Charles V. is said to have scourged himself."[13] Despite the seeming randomness of this assembly of rarities, "*wunderkammern* were not assembled by chance or caprice": rather, as Lorraine Daston and Katherine Park observe, artifacts "belonged to recognizable genres and were linked by hidden assumptions and aims."[14] Thus the Ark's contents were strikingly similar to those observed by Swiss traveler Thomas Platter in Sir Robert Cope's cabinet four decades earlier. Platter's account of a day's outing in 1599 London passes easily from his attendance at a bearbaiting in Southwark to a viewing of Cope's collection of rarities in Kensington.[15] There, he saw "an embalmed child (Mumia)," "a unicorn's tail," and "the bauble and bells of Henry VIII's fool." "The city of London," Platter concludes, "is brimful of curiosities."[16]

Circumscribed by dexterous narratives spun by the collector, curiosities enmesh the viewer in the strangeness of things past, suggesting the resistance of artifacts to reuse and foretelling the innovative recycling that put them to work in post-Reformation constructions of individual and cultural identities. Hester Tradescant's struggle to control her legacy stages the rivalry of competing claims to commemoration, a monumental project that is integral to collecting itself. The cabinet, like any monument, elicits remembrance in perpetuity – of the collector and of the world recollected in her rarities – by exploiting the immanence and perennial power of the wondrous artifact. Like monuments, cabinets craft narratives of the past, publicly displayed to assert their continued relevance to the present and to predict a future that is beyond control. As Jennifer Potter puts it, the story of collecting is one of "self-definition and cultural innovation"; of "ingenuity at a time of rapid and profound change."[17]

[12] BL Add MS 6703; quoted in Leith-Ross, *John Tradescants*, 86. See also Peck, *Consuming Splendor*, 152–87.

[13] See Schaible, "Geschichte der Deutschen in England," 453, for a translation of Stirn's German account from Bod MS Add. B. 67.

[14] Daston and Park, *Wonder*, 272–73.

[15] On Cope's collection, see Peck, *Consuming Splendor*, 156–58. Cope (d. 1614) was a friend of Sir Robert Cotton and his collection anticipates the Ark: see MacGregor, "Cabinet of Curiosities," 202.

[16] Platter, *Thomas Platter's Travels*, 169–75. For an early new historicist reading of Platter, see Mullaney, *Place of the Stage*, 60–87.

[17] Potter, *Strange Blooms*, xxiii. See also Swann, *Curiosities and Texts*.

Like monuments, too, *wunderkammern* are theaters of memory, "overly complex and prone to confusions of fact and fiction."[18] From their earliest articulations, the narratives supporting English collections and the antiquarian retrieval of texts and monuments asserted memory's centrality to the preservation and recreation of cultural histories. Sir Robert Cotton's vast library of medieval manuscripts and his collection of Brito-Roman antiquities and epitaphs worked together to transform the classical and medieval past into the materials of "antiquarian literacy."[19] Elias Ashmole's fervent desire to possess Hester Tradescant's cabinet was paralleled by his tirelessness in compiling a chorography of his home county: his *Antiquities of Berkshire* is a textual collection of monuments and inscriptions, a repository of commemorative artifacts.[20] Capturing "Homer's Iliad in a nut[,] / A world of wonders in one closet shut," as the Tradescants' epitaph puts it, cabinets embody remembrance as, in Sarah Beckwith's words, "a place of absolute plentitude and catastrophic loss."[21] Their commemorative performances, moreover, are fundamentally theatrical: as actors on a barren stage offer mere "motes and shadows" of valuable but vanished realities, the cabinet's rarities occupy a stage that represents the world in fragments and remains.[22] Set within a poetics of wonder that joins the romance of travel to its literary and dramatic representations, cabinets stage a world brimful of curiosities.

Chapter 1 of this study examined a cabinet of memory created by Sidney Montagu to commemorate his son, Henry, who drowned at the age of three. The manuscript box installed at Barnwell All Saints preserves and rehearses the relics of Henry Montagu's brief life as witnesses to his predestined fate and as tokens supporting his father's superstitious retrieval of the boy's figure and memory. As sacred objects bleed into secular memorials, belief and superstition collaborate to attribute to secular objects an aura of the sacred.

[18] Hallam and Hockey, *Death, Memory and Material Culture*, 32. See also Bolzoni, *Gallery of Memory*, 246–49; and see Mullaney, *Place of the Stage*, 15–20, on Stow's *Survey* as a memory theater.

[19] Summit, *Memory's Library*, 167.

[20] Ashmole, *Antiquities of Berkshire*. Ashmole acquired property in Berkshire through his marriage to Lady Mary Mainwaring.

[21] Beckwith, "Present of Past Things," 364, summarizing Nora, "Between Memory and History." For the epitaph, see Allen, *History . . . of Lambeth*, 142. The anonymous epitaph was inscribed on a blue granite stone and installed in 1773. It covered the tomb until the restoration of 1852. The 1773 ledger stone is now in the Ashmolean Museum. See MacGregor, "The Tradescants, Gardeners and Botanists," 15; and see Marshall, "The Tradescants," 512.

[22] Shakespeare and Wilkins, *Pericles*, 4.4.21.

Situated in post-Reformation London, bordered by the South Lambeth of Tradescants' Ark and the Southwark of John Stow's *Survey of London*, this chapter follows what Alexandra Walsham has called the "the reformed relic culture" in cabinets of curiosities and in the commemorative career of a remarkable medieval survivor, the tomb erected by John Gower in St. Mary Overie.[23] Focusing on the structural and conceptual affinities between cabinets and monuments, I align Stow's reclamation of Gower's monument and memory with the processes and values guiding collectors' reclamations of relics and rarities. Both the chorographer's and the collector's negotiations between past and present involve cultivations of narrative and belief in its restorative power. Their stories are performed in pieces – artifacts, epitaphs, effigies – that engage the senses in contradictory ways, producing incongruities that are reconciled only by willingness to believe.[24] Casting compilers not as historians but as "remembrancers," the chorography and the cabinet are centrally preoccupied with "the aesthetic transfigurations wrought by death," in Patrick Mauriès's phrase.[25] They replace decayed remains with monumental figurations of the beautiful, mysterious, and rare. Operating in the realm of imagination, they replace history with a remembered story of the past.

Calling to mind Thomas M. Greene's description of the "archaeological" and "necromantic" metaphor lying at the heart of the early modern humanism, "*disinterment*, a digging up that was also a resuscitation or a reincarnation or a rebirth," my argument in this chapter is that within monumental projects, every act of remembrance is simultaneously an act of recreation.[26] In the theoretical *wunderkammer* of this chapter, I show how experiences of early modern materials – the cabinet, the tomb, the book – viewed through the lens of remembrance shift focus away from history, where meanings are fixed and finalized, toward the evolving, unfinished processes of memory and its renewal of objects, individuals, and beliefs across time. Replete with mysteries, the curiosities contained in this chapter demonstrate the persistent power of past things to influence and create meanings in and of the present.[27]

[23] Walsham, "Skeletons," 131. See also Woolf, *Social Circulation*, 193–7.

[24] See Harris, *Untimely Matter*, 95–118, for a useful account of Stow's narrative historiography.

[25] Mauriès, *Cabinets of Curiosities*, 119. See also Gordon, *Writing Early Modern London*, 110–54, who notes that "in 1571, the City [of London] created the new post of Remembrancer" (124).

[26] Greene, "Petrarch," 206.

[27] The *wunderkammer* has been associated with new historicism's treatment of material culture and religion: see Mullaney, *Place of the Stage*, 60–87; and Greenblatt, "Resonance and Wonder," expanded in Greenblatt, *Marvelous Possessions*. The image has been used to criticize new

Section 1 of this chapter begins in the north aisle of Southwark Cathedral – William Shakespeare's London parish – "where," as Thomas Berthelette reported in 1532, "somewhat after the olde facion [John Gower] lieth right sumptuousely buried."[28] I argue that the commemoration of Gower by one of his first commentators, John Stow, exploits strategies akin to those of collectors to fashion and embed the relic "John Gower" in the cathedral's changing cartography and in London's cultural memory. As Stow beautifies Gower's remains, he negotiates the shift from pre- to post-Reformation rituals of remembrance, creating a secular, present-tense poet by reimagining the city's religious and cultural past and Gower's foundational place within it. His concern is not the spiritual afterlife of the Catholic Gower, but the poet's immanent body and its involvement in the webs of interrelations binding Southwark's living community to the alien nation of the dead. Attending the porous threshold between the living and the dead, the tomb gives visible shape to the tale told in Gower's *Confessio Amantis*, where the self is restored and sustained by recollection and the present materializes amid rituals and artifacts that imaginatively reconfigure the past.

Section 2 explores the memorial processes of collecting in the Tradescants' Ark. These collectors, like Stow, recycle relics and beautify remains, setting them within narrative frames that create a stage for continual performances of remembrance. Glossed by the stories generated by the collector, the contents of cabinets, like Gower's tomb, are vital and immanent, repeatedly disinterred and resurrected. In a realm where, as Daston and Park argue, "the wonders of nature remained wondrous even after explanation," the Tradescants' violent ransacking of the natural world incongruously preserves enchantment.[29] The Ark situates its creators and

historicism by Harris, "New New Historicism's *Wunderkammer* "; and Marotti and Jackson, "Turn to Religion," 175. My view is aligned with recent scholarship focusing less on the rupture in beliefs and more on continuous confessional and cultural spectra through which pre-Reformation artifacts and practices were conveyed to and reinvented in the post-Reformation world. See, for example, Harris, *Untimely Matter*; Summit, *Memory's Library*; Beckwith, "Stephen Greenblatt's *Hamlet*"; Walsh, "'A Priestly Farewell"; and Walsham, "Skeletons." See also Curran and Kearney, "Introduction," 354, on historical phenomenology's emphasis on "how meaning accrues from the way sensing bodies experienced and perceived objects" as a means to resist "the material turn's tendency to treat objects as bearers of prosthetic meaning."

[28] Thomas Berthelette, "To the Reader," in Gower, *Jo. Gower de confessione amantis* (1554), fol. *iii^{r}. Subsequent references are to this edition unless otherwise noted and appear parenthetically. This is a reprint of Berthelette's 1532 edition, dedicated Henry VIII. Southwark obtained cathedral status in 1905; in Gower's lifetime, it was the priory of St. Mary Overie, and was renamed St. Saviour's after the dissolution. See Thompson, *Southwark Cathedral*; and Walsh, "Shakespeare in Stained Glass."

[29] Daston and Park, *Wonder*, 228.

visitors amid "a weird tangle of animals, environments, and vital materiality" where distinctions between life and death, art and nature, past and present dissolve within a secular worship of the "wonder-inducing variety," as Laurie Shannon calls it, of the recollected world.[30]

Outlining a poetics of wonder that permeates post-Reformation recollections of the pre-Reformation past, this chapter anticipates the next, where the commemorative strategies explored here are mapped onto William Shakespeare's and George Wilkins's *Pericles.* Criticisms of the weaknesses of *Pericles* have generally held that Gower appears in the play as an emblem of archaism and the incommensurability of "mouldy tales" and their Catholic heritage to post-Reformation audiences.[31] Chapter 5 argues, instead, that *Pericles* engages in a monumental intertextuality where a renewed approach to the antique English poet and his plot treats them as familiar relics linking Gower's era to Shakespeare's. Gower's archaizing octosyllabics, introduced by Wilkins in the first scenes of *Pericles*, offer a structural and poetic starting point for Shakespeare to enrich and enliven Gower's authorial performance and his own. In this collaborative work, Shakespeare responds to his coauthor Wilkins but, more pressingly, to the need to produce a story to mobilize the transformative and generative power of objects and texts across time. In this project, his collaborator and model is the "memorial writer," John Gower.[32]

1 A Curious Littell Cheste

Dedicating his printed edition of John Gower's *Confessio Amantis* to King Henry VIII in 1532, Thomas Berthelette begins with an image of a book in a box:

> Plutarke writeth, whan Alexander had discomfite Darius the kynge of Perse, amonge other jewels of the saide kynges, there was found a curious littell cheste of great value, which the noble king Alexander beholding saide: This same shall serve for Homere (fol. *ii^{r}).

Perhaps anticipating the subject of Gower's Book VII, Aristotle's instruction of Alexander, the image compares Alexander's "greate love and favour . . . unto lernyng" (fol. *ii^{r}) to Henry's own, noting, consequently,

[30] Campana and Maisano, *Renaissance Posthumanism*, 3; and Shannon, *Accommodated Animal*, 22.
[31] The claim of the moldiness of *Pericles* was famously made by Ben Jonson, "Ode to Himself (Come leave the loathed stage)," in Jonson, *New Inn*, sig. H2^{r}.
[32] Summit, *Memory's Library*, 190.

Berthelette's hesitancy to present his paltry gift. As he explains his boldness in doing so, however, the book itself transmutes into a curious chest of great value. Unable to give the king "the most goodliest & largest cite of al the worlde," Berthelette offers instead the work of "that excellente clerke the morall John Gower," a book that is itself a little world:

> And who so ever in redynge of this warke, doth consider it well, shall fynde, that it is plentifully stuffed and fournished with manifolde eloquent reasons, sharpe and quicke argumentes, and examples of greate auctoritiee, perswadynge unto vertue, not onely taken out of the poetes, oratours, historie writers, and philosophers, but also out of the holy scripture (fol. *ii^{r}).

Confessio Amantis is, for Berthelette, a copious collection of tales and *exempla* gathered by an expert "compiler," one whose linguistic variety, moreover, has stuffed and furnished the English language with a "pleintie of english wordes and vulgares" (fol. *ii^{r}).[33]

If Berthelette casts Gower's book as a world of wonders, he offers his edition as a textual monument to this consummate collector. Returning to the "bokes that be written" (fol. *iir) – specifically, a manuscript copy of *Confessio Amantis* in Duke Humfrey's library – Berthelette claims to correct the mistakes of Caxton's 1483 printed edition, thereby setting Gower before readers "in his owne shappe and likenes" (fol. *iii^{r}).[34] Berthelette's monumental portrait of Gower's shape and likeness is further augmented by a description of the sculptural effigy on Gower's monument. Gower "prepared for his bones a restynge place," Berthelette reports, "in the monasterie of saynt Marie Overes . . . in the chapel of saynt John." There, he occupies a sumptuous, if archaic, tomb befitting "this worthy olde writer" (fol. *ii^{v}-*iii^{r}).

Gower's volume and his monument are equally replete with a wealth of precious meanings, and Berthelette's descriptions of both share the perspectival shifts that govern the cabinet of curiosities: the book and the tomb alike are closets of plentitude. This aesthetic aligns the imagery of boxes, books, monuments, and cabinets with classical understandings of memory, transmitted through the medieval period to the early modern in works like *Confessio*

[33] When Stow and Berthelette venerate Gower as a compiler – a collector of ancient tales and exempla – they celebrate him as a methodological precursor: antiquarian Stow and printer Berthelette, likewise, collect, compile, and convey. For Gower and for his editors and historians, compilation is a fruitful form of composition: both are derived from the Latin *componere*, to collect or compile, but also to write or compose: see Traupman, ed., *New College Latin and English Dictionary*. Thus Caxton describes *Confessio Amantis* as the "book was maad and compyled by Johan Gower": see Gower, *Confessio Amantis*, ed. Caxton, fol. 1^{r}.

[34] Berthelette's edition is based on Bod MS 294 and corrects Caxton's *Confessio Amantis* (1483). The precision of his textual recovery is of primary importance in Berthelette's paratexts, where he imagines the reader "conferringe both the printes, the olde and myn together" (fol. "ii^{r}).

Amantis. Deploying this architectural analogy between the mind and the world, Augustine describes "the spacious palace of memory, where there are treasures of countless images," while Bartholomeus Angelus more precisely locates the diminutive "celle" of memory as the one of three "chambers" of the brain that "holdeth and keepeth in the treasure of the minde."[35] This embodiment of the abstract idea of memory in the concrete structure of the cell or cabinet is reflected in the boxes-within-boxes commonly found in post-Reformation collections. Tradescants' Ark, for instance, contained "An ancient anointing Box of guilt-brass" (Tradescant, 40), "A little box of straw and silke" (41), and, inscribing and condensing the protracted, foundational narrative of New Testament faith, "A little box with the 12 Apostles in it" (37). As Patrick Mauriès notes, "boxes and caskets were themselves contained within drawers: drawers which together formed – on the architectural model resembling a monument in miniature – the elements or furnishings of the cabinet of curiosities."[36]

The Gower monument shares the structure of memory's "Chinese boxes" (see Figure 4.1).[37] The tomb enclosing the poet's remains is set within the chapel of St. John. In three compartments above the recumbent effigy are three female Virtues (Charity, Mercy, and Piety). Seven panels, perhaps alluding to the seven Christian virtues, decorate the front of the tomb.[38] On the wall next to the monument, as Berthelette states, "hongeth a table, wherin appereth, that who so ever praith for the soule of Johan Gower, he shall so oft as he so doth, have a M. and D. daies of pardon" (fol. *iii^{r}). The promise contained on the plaque is echoed at the close of many of Gower's manuscripts: Sir Robert Cotton's copy of *Vox Clamantis*, for instance, concludes with Gower's "Orate pro anima," and it made its way into print in Caxton's 1483 edition.[39] The architecture of the monument associates Gower's books with his tomb as well. Like the "rare piece of hollow-carved worke in fashion of a Book" held in the Ark (Tradescant, 38), there appear, "Under [Gower's] head," as John Stow writes in 1592, "the likenesse of three bookes, which he compiled: the first *Speculum meditantis* in French, the second *Vox clamantis* in Latine, the third *Confessio amantis* in English (see Plate 3)." With the care of a collector, Stow remarks that Gower's English work "is extant in print,"

[35] Augustine of Hippo, *Confessions*, 10:8:12; and Bartholomeus Angelus, *Batman uppon Bartholome*, fols. D2^{v}–D3^{r}.

[36] Mauriès, *Cabinets of Curiosities*, 35.

[37] See Bolzoni, *Gallery of Memory*, 239–40.

[38] Hines, Cohen and Roffey, "Iohannes Gower," 26. The panels may also allude to the structure of *Confessio Amantis*, where Amans confesses and is absolved of the seven deadly sins.

[39] Summit, *Memory's Library*, 190. The manuscript is BL Cotton Tiberius A.iv, fol. 174^{v}. See also Gower, *Confessio Amantis*, ed. Caxton, fol. 211^{v}. For discussion, see Echard, "Last Words."

Figure 4.1 Unknown artist, Gower Monument (before 1408), Southwark Cathedral. Author's photograph. Reproduced by permission of the Dean and Chapter of Southwark Cathedral.

his Latin work, "I have faire written," but the French text, "I have not seene."[40] By 1603, Stow can be more precise about his own library and the status of Gower's recovered works: "*vox clamantis* with his *Cronica tripartita*, and other in latine and French never printed, I have and doe possesse, but *Speculum meditantis*, I never saw, but heard thereof to be in Kent."[41]

The pride in ownership that Stow displays toward Gower's works responds to the promotion of Gower's books and his reputation on his monument itself, a decorative program dedicated to preserving Gower's memory as a founding father of English letters. Stow's veneration, however, is enacted across the cultural and confessional divide of the Reformation. Gower's casket is a profoundly medieval structure, encoding traditional rites of commemoration within a Catholic cartography of the afterlife. Gower's request for intercessory prayers on the tablet hung beside the monument was part of a larger program of remembrance: Berthelette reports that "in the chapell of sainte John ... he hath of his own foundacion, a masse daily songe. And moreover he hath an obite yerely doen for hym within the same churche, on fridaie after the feaste of the blessed pope saynte Gregorie" (fol. *iii^r).[42] In addition to founding the chantry and financing commemoration in perpetuity, the texts of Gower's monument offer prayers for the soul's progress in the afterlife. Each of the three Virtues offers an intercessory prayer on Gower's behalf. As Stow reports, following Berthelette:

> Besides in the wall were painted three virgins crowned, one of the which was written Charity, and held this devise. *En toy qui filz de Dieu le pere sauve soit, qui gist sous ceste pierre.* The second Mercie with this devise: *O bon Jesu fait ta merci alme dont le corps gist icy.* The third Pitie with this devise. *Pour ta pite Jesu regard; Et met cest alme in sauvegarde.*[43]

[40] Stow, *Annales*, 518. [41] Stow, *Survay* (1603), 411.

[42] This passage was printed without emendation in 1554: in the Marian edition no correction was necessary. The turn toward Protestantism may account for the fact that no new edition of Gower's poem was printed until 1857: see Machan, "Thomas Berthelette," 144.

[43] Stow, *Annales*, 518, following Berthelette, fol. *iii^r. Hines, Cohen, and Roffey, "Iohannes Gower," 36, translate as follows:

Charity:	In Thee who are the Son of God the Father may he who lies beneath this stone be saved.
Mercy:	O Good Jesus, show Thy mercy to the soul whose body lies here.
Piety:	For your pity, Jesus, take heed, and place this soul in [Thy] safe-keeping.

The allegories were most recently repainted in 1950. On changes to the monument, see Walsh, "Shakespeare in Stained Glass;" Thompson, *Southwark Cathedral*, 201–9; Gower, *Complete Works*, vol. IV, xviii-xxiv; and Hines, Cohen and Roffey, "Johannes Gower."

In his will, furthermore, Gower provides payments to the prior and canons of St. Mary Overie for prayers at his funeral and payments for intercessory prayers to all of Southwark's churches and hospitals, including Bedlam. He bequeaths ornaments and tapers for masses in the chapel of St. John, along with two vestments of silk, and a new chalice, "all which are to be kept for ever for the service of the said altar."[44]

The Catholic rites promoted in Gower's self-commemoration inevitably rendered his monument vulnerable during the Reformation. Sometime after the surrender of the priory to the crown and its renaming as St. Saviour's in 1539, the chapel of St. John was dismantled: the tomb was now highly visible in the north aisle, both an anachronism and an invitation to violent reformations.[45] Thus Stow's 1592 description of the three Virtues and their devices reveals that he is seeing what is no longer there: "All which is now washed out, and the image defaced, by cutting off the nose and striking off his handes, because they were elevated towardes heaven."[46] With a keen ability to read both texts and images, St. Saviour's iconoclasts found Gower's piously folded hands, "elevated toward heaven," as well as the Virtues' devices to constitute the special pleading of intercession.

Stow may have remembered having seen the painted iconography of the monument prior to its whitewashing, but he was certainly relying on earlier published accounts to supply details that had been lost.[47] Although Stow's rescue of the monument's imagery may be tinged with nostalgia, he seems not to long for the old religion and its abandoned rites.[48] Rather, he engages the artifact, its subject, and its ephemeral decorations with a method approximating the collector's, sorting through remains, providing a narrative to accommodate the spaces and times through which the relic has passed. Like Berthelette, Stow's concern is with the "facion" of the tomb: the relative truth or falsehood of the doctrine governing its design is less at stake than the changing interpretative and aesthetic attitudes

[44] John Gower, "Testamentum," in Todd, *Illustrations*, 88–90. Gower's will, proved October 24, 1408, survives as Lambeth Palace Library, "Register of Archbishop Thomas Arundel, 1396–97, 1399–1414," fols. 256^{r}–7^{r}. For Macauley's English translation, see Gower, *Complete Works*, vol. IV, xvii–xviii.

[45] See 1 Edw. VI, c.14, 1547, "Act for the Dissolution of Chantries" (1547), in Tanner, ed., *Tudor Constitutional Documents*, 103–7. See also Kreider, *English* Chantries, 186–210; and on St. John's Chapel, see Walsh, "'A Priestly Farewell,'" 93–4.

[46] Stow, *Annales*, 518.

[47] Stow's description is very close to Berthelette's, but he had John Leland's account available and corrected Leland's biography of Gower and description of the monument. See Bale, *Scriptorum illustrium*, 524–5; and Gower, *Complete Works*, vol. IV, x and xxn2.

[48] See Collinson, "John Stow"; and Archer, "Nostalgia."

influencing responses to it. His reading is "post-confessional," in Betteridge's terms, in reaching back to a moment when religion was a source of union rather than division.[49] Stow's description stages, as it were, the remembrance of the Catholic iconography banished from the monument: he presents the "motes and shadows" of authentic Catholic rites. At the same time, his reinscription of the ritual renews and recreates it, relocating the sacramental past within the secularity of the commemorative text.[50] Stow repositions Gower to chart both the permutations in and the persistence of the communal experience of his tomb.[51]

In reclaiming the whitewashed imagery of Gower's tomb, moreover, Stow's account, like the monument itself, displaces corporeal remains with a beautiful image and figure. Although Gower's self-authored epitaph celebrates the soul's departure from the body ("Spiritus exutum se gaudeat esse solutum," ["The naked soul rejoices all in its release"]),[52] Stow lovingly records the adornments and colors beautifying the corpse: "The haire of his head aburne, long to his sholders, but curling up, and a small forked beard, on his head a chapelet, like a coronet of foure Roses, an habite of purple, damasked downe to his feet, a collar of Esses, gold aboute his necke."[53] This preservation of the effigy affirms the wonder of the artifact and arrests Gower's shape and likeness in Stow's vivid poetry. Sequestered in the covers of his book, reduced to the black and white of the page, the visual distractions of Gower's monument are mediated, relieved of their threatening alignment with the colors and images of idols. While the idolatry implicit in the Catholic rituals of remembrance for which Gower ardently pleas are embedded in the brightly painted tomb, Stow's conversion from artifact to text offers instruction to post-Reformation viewers on how to look at the pre-Reformation tomb. The exemplum of iconoclasm provided by Stow enables the retrieval and renewal of the artifact: the *Survey* presents the fact of iconoclasm as an authorizing story, one aspect of the accumulated content of the relic as it is recycled for readers. Stow's repossession of Gower and the Virtues' outlawed scripts transforms the saintly relic to a token of remembrance:

[49] Betteridge, "Writing Faithfully."

[50] On the lingering sacramentality of post-Reformation relics, see Walsham, "Skeletons;" and Mauriès, *Cabinets of Curiosities*, 12–24.

[51] See Gordon, *Writing Early Modern London*, 116–17, for the argument that Stow's monumental inscriptions restore community by "performing a textual version of the duties once paid to the parish dead in the bede roll."

[52] From the monument; translation by Echard, "Last Words," 99. Stow records the epitaph for the first time in *Survay* (1603), 411–12.

[53] Stow, *Survay* (1603), 411.

a translation – a benevolent iconoclasm – performed through preservation rather than destruction.

Stow recreates Gower's monument as a secular rarity, placing it in the increasingly secularized environment of St. Saviour's, where a changing ecclesiastical cartography after the Reformation prompted innovative reclamations of church space. The Lady Chapel – the site of the Easter Sepulcher, a stone coffin holding the remains of one of St Mary Overie's monks, and a piscina – was converted into a "Spritual Court" for the trials of seven Protestant martyrs during Queen Mary's reign.[54] This legal appropriation was followed by a "wretched, base, and unworthy . . . abuse" of this "faire & beautifull Chappell" decried by Anthony Munday in his continuation of Stow's *Survey*, when the space was "leased and let out, and this House of God made a Bake-house":

> Two very faire doores, that from the two side Iles of the Chancell of this Church, and two that thorow the head of the Church . . . went into it, were latch't, daub'd, and dam'd up: the faire Pillars were ordinary posts, against which they piled Billets and Bavens; in this place they had their ovens, in that a Bolting-place, in that their Kneading-trough, in another (I have heard) a Hogs-trough . . . Some part of the Bake-house was sometime turned into a Starch-house.[55]

In 1551, St. Saviour's vestry records note a lease to "Hemsley Ryelle, for iiijd. a year to set his carts" in the churchyard, and two years later, "the 'Olde chapel behind the chancel" was leased "for the benefit of the School."[56] The recycling of church interiors and fabric for secular purposes was not isolated to St. Saviour's. William Whittyngham, Dean of Durham, ordered the cathedral's medieval stone coffins, like the one in the Lady Chapel at Southwark,

> to be plucked up, and appointed them to be used as troughs for horses to drink in, or hogs to feed in. All the marble and free-stones also that covered them and other graves, he caused to be taken away and broken, some of which served to make pavement in his house.[57]

Stow records a similar renovation of the Augustinian priory transferred to William Paulet, Lord Treasurer, in 1538:

[54] See Thompson, *Southwark Cathedral*, 47–60, who discusses the fabric of the Lady Chapel and the 1555 trials of Lawrence Saunders, Robert Ferrar, Rowland Taylor, John Bradford, John Philpot, John Hooper, and John Rogers.

[55] Stow, *Survey* (1633), 885. Merritt, "Reshaping of Stow's 'Survey,'" 52–88, notes Munday's greater emphasis than Stow's on religious difference, a tendency that may explain the outrage of his account. See also Moore, "Succeeding Stow."

[56] Quoted in Thompson, *Southwark Cathedral*, 50.

[57] Wood, *Athenae Oxonienses*, vol. I, 449.

> The Friers Church hee pulled down ... The other part, namely the Steeple, Quire, and side Isles to the Quire adjoyning, he reserved to household uses, as for stowage of corne, coal, and other things; his son the heir Marques of Winchester, sold the Monuments of Noblemen (there buried), great number ... and in place thereof made faire stabling for horses.[58]

At Aswardbie, in Lincolnshire, "all the mas bookes and all bookes of papistrie were torne in peces in Anno primo Eliz and sold to pedlers to lap spice in."[59] At St. Paul's, as Richard Bancroft's visitation of 1598 reveals, "Carpenters leased some of the vaults; trunk makers occupied parts of the crypt and cloisters ... the chapel beneath the far end of the south side was let to a glazier; [and] the 'muche unglased' chapel of St Katherine intermittently served as a schoolroom."[60]

Clearly, post-Reformation churches were not merely sites of iconoclasm, but of recycling and reuse as well. In Stow's revivification of Gower's monument, aesthetic concerns far outweigh religious ones: although marked by the visual signs of the monument's passage through the history of religious differences, the "John Gower" reclaimed by Stow follows Gower's own self-commemoration on the monument: "Hic jacet J. Gower Arm. Angl. Poeta celeberrimus ac huic sacro edificio benefac. insignis" ("Here lies John Gower, Esquire, a most famous English Poet and distinguished benefactor of this building").[61] For Stow, Gower is first and foremost "a famous Poet," his likeness resting on those of his books, memorialized together in the place where he wrote them.[62] Gower's value as the local genius of Southwark was affirmed in 1615, when repairs to the monument unearthed the poet's long buried epitaph. It rematerializes in Munday's 1618 edition of the *Survey of London*, where Gower's "very faire Tombe" stands "in the North Ile of the Church" – the dismantled chapel of St. John forgotten. Banished, too, is the specter of iconoclasm that defaced the effigy and erased the Virtues and their intercessory scripts: Munday prints their devices without qualification. The communal reclamation of Gower as poet and member of the *contemporary* church body resonates in the note that the monument was "Noviter constructum impensis Parochiae, Anno Domini 1615" (Newly built at the expense of the parish, A. D. 1615).[63]

[58] Stow, *Survey* (1633), 184. For discussion, see Bonahue, "Citizen History."
[59] Peacock, ed., *English Church Furniture*, 33. [60] Quoted in Crankshaw, "Community," 82–3.
[61] From the monument; translation Hines, Cohen, and Roffey, "Johannes Gower," 36.
[62] All three of Gower's major works were indebted to the holdings of the priory's library: see Allen, "John Gower and Southwark," 118.
[63] Stow, Survay (1618), 780.

When Berthelette and Stow preserve and convey the memory of Gower's monument and its scripts, they continue a project begun by Gower. Two additional bequests to St. Mary Overie merge Gower's two roles as poet and benefactor. He bequeaths, first, a large, new missal ("unum missale grande et novum eciam") for use in services in the chapel of St. John and, secondly, a martyrology:

> Item lego Priori et Conventui quendem magnum librum sumptibus meis noviter compositum, qui *Martilogium* dicitur, sic quod in eodem specialem memoriam scriptam secundum eorum promissa cotidie habere debeo.
>
> (Item: to the Prior and Convent, I give a certain large book newly composed at my cost, called *Martilogium*, on the condition that I have in the same a special memorial [read] daily, according to their promises.)[64]

The *Martilogium*, like the missal, had a liturgical use in monastic churches. Containing "not only the brief notices of saints and martyrs which were read on the day preceding their celebration," the martyrology also included "the records of obits of the members of the chapter and of their benefactors."[65] Gower's provision that his recorded memorial should be read daily speaks not only to his confidence in intercession, but also to the importance of a written record to script his inclusion in the company of saints. Both the missal and the martyrology are "new" creations, produced, like the tomb erected "in loco ad hoc speciliter deputato" (in the place specially appointed) in Gower's lifetime, in preparation for death.[66] All three commissions were intended to improve the state of Gower's soul in the afterlife and to promote his presence as a member of the communal church body, a permanent, vital fixture in the living map of the cathedral.

Gower's liturgical books share with his *Confessio Amantis* the view of memory as the means by which the individual composes, remembers, the self. As the work begins, Amans's heart, petrified by the sight of the beloved, has become a tomb on which she engraves his epitaph (1.553–6). Gower's frametale leads Amans through confession to absolution: Genius, the priest of Venus, compiles stories and exempla to "drawe into remembrance" (Pro. 69) the seven deadly sins. The act of confession relies on the imaginative retrieval and reassessment of the past, a process achieved through narrative: tale-telling in *Confessio Amantis* is the means

[64] Gower, "Testamentum," in Todd, *Illustrations*, 89. I wish to thank Jaime Goodrich for her help with the translation. Gower's missal survives as BL Add MS 59855, among twenty-eight surviving manuscripts from St. Mary Overie's monastic library: see Kerr, *Medieval Libraries*, 180–1.

[65] Procter and Dewick, "Introduction," in *Martiloge in Englysshe*, v.

[66] Gower, "Testamentum," in Todd, *Illustrations*, 88. On the likelihood that Gower's tomb was erected before his death, see Hines, Cohen, and Roffey, "Johannes Gower," 33.

by which memory is activated and, in turn, actualizes spiritual renewal in the present. It is only at the poem's close, accordingly, when Genius's "ensamples" (8.2137) have restored the lover to himself that Amans is christened: Venus "axeth me what is mi name," the speaker reports, and he answers, "'Ma dame,' I seide, 'John Gower'" (8.2320–21). Addressing the poet by his proper name, Venus presents a token of remembrance, which, like Gower's Southwark monument, conveys a sacramental past into a secular present. "A Peire of Bedes blak as Sable" bearing the motto "*Por reposer* " (8.2902–7) underscores the interrelation of the commemorative object and the penitential subject in bringing forth poet Gower and foretells the eternal repose of the "olde" author (8.2916) on his monument. Amans's stone heart, "graved" by the beloved, becomes the poet's stone effigy, merging with the memory of his works: "tarie thou mi Court nomore." Venus advises, "Bot go ther vertu moral duelleth, / Wher ben thi bokes, as men telleth, / Whiche of long time thou hast write" (8.2924–7).

Amans's absolution and Gower's monument in Southwark both enable the self-composition of the poet "John Gower." If Gower's project of self-commemoration inserts his legacy into the unfolding plot of Christian time as experienced in St. Mary Overie, Stow's recovery and conveyance of Gower's memory responds to the poet's commemorative project and its continuation in the scribal transmission of Gower's works. The final folio of a late-fifteenth-century copy of *Vox clamantis* inscribes Gower's "Orate pro anima" alongside his self-authored epitaph on the Southwark monument.[67] The manuscript borrows the imagery of the tomb as well: it is "beautified with his armes," as Stow writes of the monument, "and the likenes of Angels."[68] Yet the scribe presents, finally, an image of a coffin draped in a decorative pall – not yet the sculptural effigy of Gower's finished monument, but a body in transit between life and death. As Sian Echard has argued, these "last words" form "part of a process of ongoing revision" of poet Gower, one that may not have corresponded to his desires.[69] Composing the self – collecting the remnants of the past that create and renew the present – is a perilous process. Beyond the protection of the tomb, in the afterlife of commemoration, meanings become contested, and artifacts deprived of their sacramental aura are profoundly at risk. As if proving this rule, Gower's repose in his Southwark tomb was itself imperiled by ongoing

[67] Glasgow University Library, Hunter MS 59, fol. 129^{r}. See Echard, "Last Words," on the complexities of Gower's self-commemoration and its scribal transmission.
[68] Stow, *Annales*, 518, describes the angels as accompanied by "posies in Latine."
[69] Echard, "Last Words," 101.

revision: in 1832, when the monument was removed from the north aisle following a fire in the cathedral, the poet's remains disappeared. Gower's translation from sacred to secular relic was completed when "the old sexton," William Thompson reports, "used to show visitors a bone, which he said was taken from the tomb" of John Gower.[70]

2 "Out-landish Fruits"

As part of an exhibition entitled "Bones to Bronze: Extinct Species of the Mascarene Islands," the Gallery Pangolin, Gloucestershire, displayed several contemporary bronze sculptures of a dodo, reanimating the creature once held in Tradescants' Ark (see Figure 4.2). The remains of the Tradescant dodo – "the head and one foot, and unique soft tissue in the form of skin and traces of feathers" – were transferred to the Oxford Museum of Natural History in the 1860s.[71] The artist captures a connection between the creature and the viewer that registers resistance to the species' demise: we might catch a glimpse of a dignified smile on the dodo's face, and we are compelled to meet the dodo eye to knowing eye. This sculptural effigy is one in a long history of resurrections of the dodo, curiosity heightened, no doubt, by the species' extinction as early as the 1690s.[72] The decomposed remains mark the disappearance of the marvel with which visitors to the Ark viewed this most famous and rare of its objects, hung from the ceiling to defy nature: as Tradescant's catalogue, *Musaeum Tradescantianum*, notes, the "Dodar, from the Island Mauritius ... is not able to flie being so big" (4).[73] Elided from this narrative are the ravages wrought by European travel and exploration on the native inhabitants, human and animal, of new worlds. The dodo was hunted as game and as marvelous cargo: Emmanuel Altham wrote to his brother in Essex in 1628, "You shall receve ... a strange fowle which I had at the island Mauritius, called by the portingalls a Dodo, which for rareness thereof I hope will be welcome to you."[74] Sir Hamon L'Estrange

[70] Dollman, *Priory Church*, xxivn2, records this oral communication from Thompson.

[71] See www.gallery-pangolin.com/exhibitions/bones-to-bronze-extinct-species-of-the-mascarene-islands; and Nowak-Kemp and Hume, "Oxford Dodo, Part 1."

[72] See Nowak-Kemp and Hume, "Oxford Dodo, Part 2," on the dodo's reconstructions and displays since the nineteenth century. For representations of the dodo, and on the species' extinction, see Hume, "History of the Dodo."

[73] Nowak-Kemp and Hume, "Oxford Dodo, Part 1," based on the lack of evidence of mounting on the remaining foot, conclude that the dodo was suspended from the ceiling of the Ark.

[74] Quoted in Nowak-Kemp and Hume, "Oxford Dodo, Part 1"; and see Hume, "History of the Dodo," 68–9. The dodo was first sighted by Dutch sailors in Mauritius in 1598.

Figure 4.2 *Dodo Head* by Nick Bibby.
Photo: Steve Russell Studios. Courtesy Gallery Pangolin.

reports that, walking in London in 1638, "I saw the picture of a strange fowle hung out upon a cloth canvas," and went in to see the living creature, which "the keeper called . . . a dodo," confined in a chamber and fed pebbles.[75]

The artist's bronze reproduction bestows upon the dodo an aura that extends its life and resurrects its mystery. In doing so, it suggests the chief features of the poetics of wonder governing the Tradescants' project more broadly. A beautiful substitute for the decayed remains, the sculpture embodies the covetous art of collecting and its production of stories that repossess objects uprooted and installed in the cabinet of wonders. The history of the creature's acquisition is mediated, if not erased, in imaginative reconfigurations of its past and its present embeddedness in "the nebulous domain of the marvelous."[76] The dodo's bronze effigy displaces

[75] BL Sloane MS 1839, fol. 54^{r}. [76] Daston and Park, *Wonder*, 159.

and improves the remains, recreating the fragile body as an immortal monument – but one that remembers the violence wrought on the nonhuman by the human.

Mediating the phenomenal world with a blend of memory and narrative, cabinets set in sharp focus the dynamic interrelations of subjects and objects. Collectors are masters of ceremony, orchestrating the experience of the collection. In the realm of the cabinet, appearances become meaningful only when glossed by the collector's tales. A stone is not merely a stone: it may be "A piece of Stone of the Oracle of Apollo," or a fragment of "Saint John Baptists Tombe" (Tradescant, 43). What one sees in the theater of curiosities is absolutely dependent upon what one hears. While collections cultivate narrative, the tales they tell vary according to the motives of individual collectors and the nature of their projects. Cabinets were "knowledge environment[s] that integrated artifacts and texts," and at this rich intersection, innovative technologies developed to manage the treasures stored within them.[77] As Paula Findlen observes, "the catalogue is an early modern invention. Inventories record the contents of a museum. They quantify its reality." Catalogues, by contrast, are "repositories of multiple intersecting stories;" self-conscious, interpretive, and crafted, they provide not an index of reality but a second nature of invention.[78] Sir Robert Cotton collected Roman antiquities in support of a new history of the national past intended, as William Camden put it, "to restore antiquity to Britain, and Britain to his antiquity."[79] While antiquarians, as Jennifer Summit has shown, were engaged in "a romance of the archive," the Tradescants' Ark sought to situate identity – individual and cultural – within an ever-expanding cartography of early modern seafaring and discovery. Awash in the romance of travel, the Tradescants conveyed a wealth of treasures home to flourish in a newly global London.[80]

Although less scholarly, the Tradescant cabinet was no less industrious than Cotton's, nor were the narratives authorizing it any less ambitious. The texture of the Tradescants' project is suggested by the books associated with their cabinet, many fewer than Cotton's, certainly, but tellingly selected. Indian books made of "Phillyrea [and] Grasses" and "Indian paper made of Straw, Rinds of trees with large margents full of figures

[77] Nelson, "Museum as Knowledge Environment." [78] Findlen, *Possessing Nature*, 36.

[79] Camden, *Britain [Britannia]* (1610), fol. *4^{r}. On archaeological antiquarianism, see Woolf, *Social Circulation*, 221–56; and Sharpe, *Sir Robert Cotton*, 17–47. See also Summit, *Memory's Library*, 136–96, for a brilliant and exhaustive discussion of Cotton's library and its influence.

[80] Summit, *Memory's Library*, 175.

and diverse colours" (41) were tokens of the Tradescants' travels to America.[81] These inscrutable manuscripts joined other mysterious texts in the Ark: "Rolls of the Barkes of Trees wherein are graved the China, Arabian and Eastern languages" (39); "a Book of all the Stories in the glass-windowes of Sancta Sophia, lim'd in vellum by a Jew" (41); "the Turkish Alkaron in a silver box" (43); "Jewes Philacteries with the Commandments in Hebrew" (37). The extent of the Tradescants' readership of these works is not certain: like the hollow likenesses of Gower's books on his Southwark monument (see Plate 3), they are artifacts in the Ark's commemorative library. Books are rarities – cabinets within the cabinet – valuable despite one's inability (at present) to access their secrets. Perhaps the most enigmatic example of this elision of textual content is "A copper Letter-case an inch long, taken in the Isle of Ree, with a Letter in it, which was swallowed by a Woman, and found" (54).

Some manuscripts in the Ark's collection, however, document the close involvement of the Tradescants' activities with the textual narratives that alternatively anticipate and record them. A thirteenth-century bestiary (see Figure 4.3), a rare repository of the wondrous diversity of beasts, preserved the memories of exotic creatures and predicted those materialized in the Ark, from "an Alegator or Crocodile from Aegypt" to "A natural dragon above two inches long" (Tradescant, 6).[82] Perhaps in imitation of the bestiary's inclusive record of the creaturely, the Tradescants commissioned a "Book of Mr. Tradescant's choicest Flowers and Plants, exquisitely limned in vellum by Mr. Alex: Marshall" (41). The manuscript was a textual monument to the primary purpose and contribution of the Ark: the importation into England of a hundreds of varieties of plants from all parts of the world. Nearly three-quarters of Tradescant's catalogue is devoted to a list of the trees, shrubs, flowers, and "Out-landish Fruits, and the like" with which the Tradescants, like pre-lapsarian Adams, "dresse[d] /

[81] The younger Tradescant visited Virginia three times, returning with over 200 species of native plants and a variety of rarities, most notably "Powhatan, King of Virginia's habit, all embroidered with shells, or Roanoke" (47). The elder Tradescant, through association with the Virginia Company, was a friend of Captain John Smith, who bequeathed one-fourth of his library to Tradescant: see TNA PROB 11/160/168. Smith published his traveler's tale at the request of Sir Robert Cotton in 1630: see Smith, *True Travels*, fol. A4^{r}.

[82] Bod MS Ashmole 1511, "The Ashmole Bestiary." Stirn's account of his tour of the cabinet in 1638 notes the presence of "Isidor's MS. of de natura hominis," perhaps responding to the illumination in the bestiary (fol. 95^{v}) depicting Isidore writing this work: see Schaible, "Geschichte der Deutschen in England," 453. The bestiary was given to the Ark by Sir Peter Manwood, who appears as a benefactor in Tradescant, *Musaeum Tradescantianum* (180): see Poole, "A Manuscript," 221–2; and Hassall and Hassall, *Treasures*, 65–8.

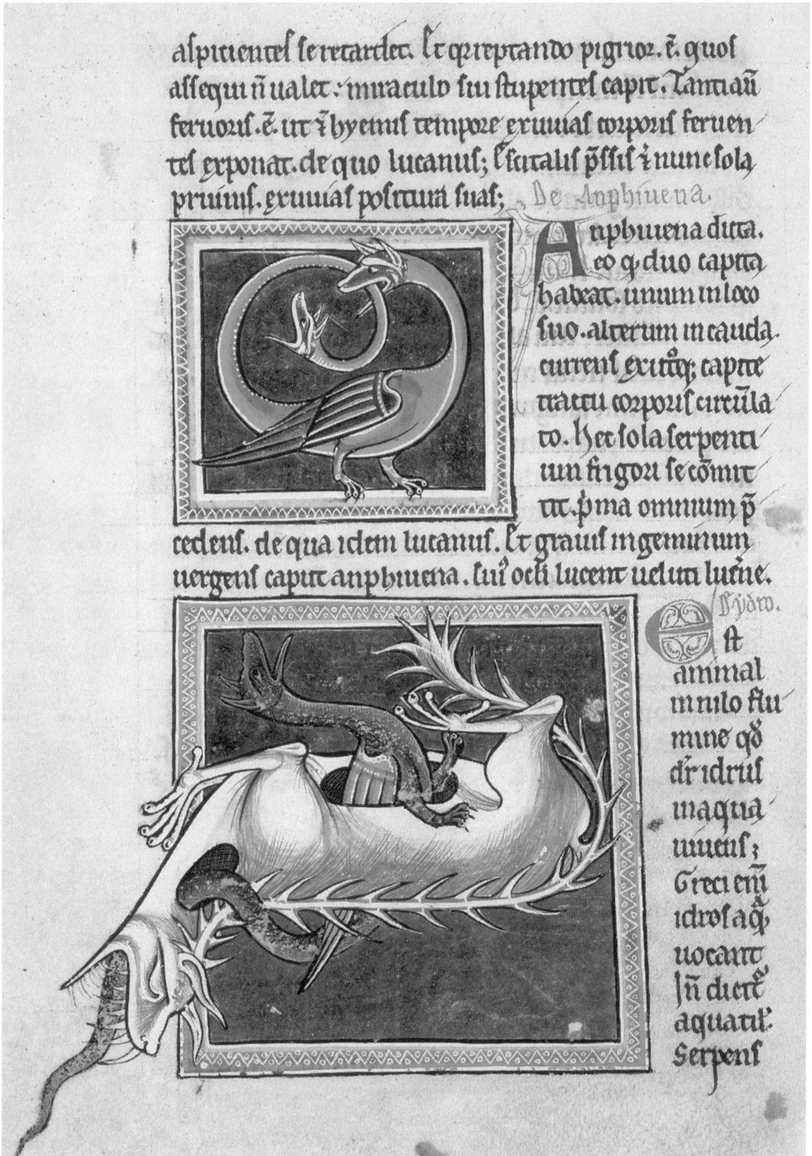

Figure 4.3 "The Ashmole Bestiary" (thirteenth century), "De amphivena" and "De ydro."
The Bodleian Libraries, The University of Oxford. MS, Ashmole 1511, fol.81ᵛ.

Figure 4.4 "Tradescant Orchard" (after 1611), "Amber Plum."
The Bodleian Libraries, The University of Oxford.
MS. Ashmole 1461, fol. 86^{r}.

The worlds great Garden" (a3 and A4).[83] A manuscript of watercolors depicting garden fruits associated with John Tradescant the elder notes, below a resplendent image, "The Amber plum which . J.T. as I take it brought out of France and groueth at Hatfeld: ripe Septem: the .8'"(see Figure 4.4).[84] The younger Tradescant swore allegiance to "the Mystery of Gardeners of the City of London" in 1634, and was later painted by his kinsman Thomas de Critz, shovel in hand, planted with an air of ephemerality in his garden (see Figure 4.5).[85] A manuscript account of the elder Tradescant's "Viag of Ambusad" to Russia in 1618 records his retrieval of literally outlandish botanical samples for transplantation in England. "On monday," he writes, "I had on of the Emperor's boats to cari me from iland to iland to see what things growe upon them whear I found single Rosses wondros sweet withe many other things whiche I meane to Bringe

[83] This catalogue is based on John Tradescant the elder's *Planatarum in Horto* (1634), which listed 750 plants; reprinted by Leith-Ross, *John Tradescants*, 220–38. The elder Tradescant also wrote a list of plants he had received between 1629 and 1633 in his copy of botanist John Parkinson's *Paradisi*; printed by Leith-Ross, *John Tradescants*, 211–17.

[84] Bod MS Ashmole 1461, fol. 86^{r}. The italic hand is not Tradescant's, and it is not known who painted the watercolors. The volume was bound for Ashmole. Both Tradescants were gardeners to the great, their employers including Robert Cecil, George Villiers, and Charles I and Henrietta Maria.

[85] Leith-Ross, *John Tradescants*, 110–11.

Figure 4.5 Thomas de Critz (attrib.), John Tradescant the Younger as a Gardener.
Image WA1898.10 © Ashmolean Museum, University of Oxford.

with me."[86] His harvesting extended to "a Strang Bird . . . which was taken alive & put to my Custody. But Dyed within two dayes After," and "5 fowles . . . Great to the Bignes of a fescent the wings whit the bodies green the tayles Blewe or Dove Coller," which he unsuccessfully springed, stating disappointedly, "I would have Given 5s for one of their skins."[87]

This series of representations of the Ark's enterprises situates the Tradescants unnervingly between exploitation and inclusion. The fantastic creatures of the bestiary hunted, killed, and preserved in the Ark or the living foliage reduced to two-dimensional shades on a calfskin page suggest, in Laurie Shannon's phrase, a "disanimation" that signals the end of the "more creaturely and less human exceptionalist vision of cosmopolity;" a time "before the human" when "early modern humanity [was] relatively ecosystemic."[88] As Merleau-Ponty states this idea, "before reason, humanity is another corporeity."[89] In this interpretation, the metaphor of the Ark seems especially apt since the story of Genesis marks

86 Bod Ashmole MS 824, fol. 179^{v}; printed in Leith-Ross, *John Tradescants*, 59–71.
87 Bod Ashmole MS 824, fols. 178^{r}–9^{r}.
88 Shannon, *Accommodated Animal*, 225; and Shannon, "Eight Animals," 477.
89 Merleau-Ponty, *Nature*, 208. Both Shannon and Merleau-Ponty locate the division between human and nonhuman in the dualism of Descartes's *cogito*.

the moment at which humanity moved from mutuality with creatures to supremacy over them: "And the fear of you and the dread of you shall be upon every beast of the earth, and upon every fowl of the air, upon all that moveth upon the earth, and upon all the fishes of the sea; into your hand are they delivered" (Genesis 9:2).[90] Certainly, on the most basic level, the Tradescants exploit their sanctioned sovereignty over the diverse animals and objects of the created world.

Yet to view the Tradescants' project simply as one of disanimation is to miss the intimacy binding the collector to the rarities – animate and inanimate, natural and artificial – that the collection passionately preserves. John Tradescant the younger, enmeshed in greenery, shares and embodies the productive vitality of the garden he tends. The Ark's materializations of the bestiary's menagerie posits, in Shannon's terms, "a 'hoste' of creatures [that] partake in a remembered creation"; an Edenic "species-memory" that speaks to the "ensouledness" of human and nonhuman.[91] In this tissue of interrelation between subject and artifact – "fields in intersection," as Merleau-Ponty writes, where "the human is to be taken in the *Ineinander* [intertwining] with animality and Nature" – figurations of porosity, intertwining, entanglement, and hybridity multiply, constituting the contents of the cabinet and its vision of the world.[92] The wondrous tokens with which the Ark was replete – "divers sorts of Ambers with {Flies, Spiders} naturall" (36), "Several Landskips . . . naturally wrought in stones" (38), or "Blood that rained in the Isle of Wight" (44) – were especially valued for their intertwining of human and nonhuman, art and nature; a fusion which blurred – and finally dissolved – the boundaries between natural wonders and those of human craftsmanship.[93] Acknowledging creative agency in nature, collectors were mutually involved – cocreators with "ensouled nature" – in the production of wonder.[94] In the realm of the marvelous, as Daston and Park write, "Bedrock assumptions were shaken and the intensity of wonder was correspondingly seismic."[95] The collector and visitors to the Ark confronted mysterious, hybrid artifacts spun in an intricate web of wonder.

[90] See Shannon, *Accommodated Animal*, 59–66 and 272–84.

[91] Shannon, *Accommodated Animal*, 50, 75, and 100. See also Wolfthal, "Beyond Human, 245, on the belief, which may inform the Tradescants' botanical enterprises, that "human entanglements with plants [were] magical [and] potent."

[92] Merleau-Ponty, *Visible and Invisible*, 227; and Merleau-Ponty, *Nature*, 208; and see Memon, "Merleau-Ponty," for discussion.

[93] See Daston and Park, *Wonder*, 255–301.

[94] Daston and Park, *Wonder*, 298.

[95] Daston and Park, *Wonder*, 266–7.

It is within this tissue of expectations and aspirations that the Ark preserves the material remains of religious practice. Relics are juxtaposed to enhance the diversity and relativism of belief: "The Idol of Osiris ... which the Aegyptians worshipped" (42) appears alongside "Nunnes penitential Girdles of Haire" (48); an "Indian Conjurer's rattle, wherewith he called up Spirits" (42) is displayed near "S. Francis in waxe under glasse" and "a small piece of wood from the cross of Christ."[96] The Tradescants' juxtaposition of relics stages religious difference, including the divisions of the Reformation, in much the same way that Stow enlists the intercessory past of Gower's tomb in the commemorative performance of the *Survey*. Discussing an object in the Cotton collection – a piece of the skull of Thomas à Becket – Jennifer Summit reads the medieval relic as "no longer an object of belief, but a specimen in the history of belief."[97] The sacred token is desacralized in an iconoclasm enacted, much like Stow's recovery of Gower, not through destruction but through preservation. Like Gower's Catholic tomb relocated in Stow's chorography, the skull is converted from relic to secular artifact in the antiquarian's collection.

Although the relics of the Ark are similarly "desacralized" and, as Walsham argues, "denuded of religious aura," they are not emptied of mystery.[98] The Ark preserves artifacts that challenge the authenticity of religious rituals but nonetheless affirm the potency of their accessories – both Christian and "pagan" – to move and amaze. As the Ark appropriates religious mystery, turning relics to tokens of cultural memory, it replaces the relic's sacred aura with its commemorative "capacity," Walsham writes, "to open a window into a past that was slipping into oblivion."[99] The Ark views the European religious past through a veil of memory rather than in the clear light of history. At the same time, it subsumes and domesticates religious difference – of non-European beliefs as well as the relics of primitive and Catholic Christianity – by embedding them in the realm of wonder.

In an act of coauthorship with the agency of the material, the collector accesses the occult connections that enliven his cabinet, asserting a creative and recreative sovereignty to acquire, preserve, and narrate the world's diversity. "The collector was never far from the realm of necromancy," Patrick Mauriès writes, "engaged as he was in bringing the dead back to life or consigning living things to death."[100] Certainly the most concise tokens

[96] See Schaible, "Geschichte der Deutschen in England," 453–4.
[97] Summit, *Memory's Library*, 168 and 178. [98] Walsham, "Skeletons," 142.
[99] Walsham, "Skeletons," 142. [100] Mauriès, *Cabinets of Curiosities*, 119.

of this transcendent will to power are the funerary accessories and bodily remains that the Tradescants and other collectors lovingly resurrected.[101] If Cotton could boast Becket's skull, the Ark held a "hand of a mummy," "a human bone weighing 42 pounds," and items acquired from tombs – a lachrymatory and Roman burial lamps among others.[102] The removal of human remains or funereal relics from the site of burial replaces history – the life of the individual commemorated in the tomb – with a collective memory of "impersonal death."[103] In a revised ritual of remembrance, relics are imbued with a renewed, if secular, aura that instructs the amazed viewer in the aesthetic value – the rarity – of these grotesque acquisitions. The cabinet aims not merely "to halt the passage of time, to freeze the ineluctable progress of life or history," as Mauriès writes, but, more importantly, "to replace it with the fragmented, controllable, circular time frame," the repetitious rhythms of fairy tales and myths.[104] Thus among the ruins of ransacked tombs, the Ark also displays "an Orange gathered from a Tree that grew over Zebulon's Tombe" (43): an icon that argues the renaissance, at once natural and supernatural, of the world's irrepressible vitality. In the collection, the object becomes, once again, a mystery, a prompt to memorial reconstruction, and the irresistible matter with which to craft a wondrous tale.

If the figuration of the cabinet as an Ark suggests the tragic division of the human from the creaturely, it also enables the recreative sovereignty claimed by the Tradescants. The Ark is the ship of Noah; an encyclopedia of nature's wealth, tirelessly compiled and preserved from the deluge of time in a single vessel. But at the same time, the Tradescant collection imitates the Ark of the Covenant: God's coffer, carrying an ancient book – a book of genesis – alongside tokens that affirm the occult origin of the text. According to St. Paul, "the golden pot that had manna, and Aaron's rod that budded" – a biblical precursor to the fruitful tree sprung from Zebulon's grave – were enclosed and revered in the Ark along with "the tables of the covenant" (Hebrews 9:4). At once Noah, the collector of rarities, and Aaron, whose branch

[101] The Ark's display of human remains and funereal relics parallels John Bargrave's collection, which also contains accessories of Roman burials and a mummified finger. Bargrave bequeathed his collection to Canterbury Cathedral in 1680, where it is preserved. See "The Bargrave Collection," www.canterbury-cathedral.org/bargrave/. The catalogue is Canterbury Cathedral Archives, Lit. Mss. E16a; printed as Bargrave, *Catalogue of Dr. Bargrave's Museum*. The John Bargrave Collection, http://drc.usask.ca/projects/bargrave/about.php, part of the Digital Ark project, contains a wealth of information documenting the activities of seventeenth-century collectors.

[102] Schaible, "Geschichte der Deutschen in England," 453.

[103] Braidotti, *Posthuman*, 95; and see Chapter 3.

[104] Mauriès, *Cabinets of Curiosities*, 119.

miraculously blooms – the prophetic Tradescants oversee a site of hallowed preservation, redemption, and recreation.

The Garden Tomb

In the Bodleian Library, there is a manuscript catalogued as "The Confession of Hester Tradescant."[105] Far from enacting the ritual of confession and absolution experienced by Gower's Amans, Hester appears to "acknowledge & confess ... that I have very much wronged Elias Ashmole ... by severall false slanderous & defamatory speeches & Reportes & otherwise tending to the diminution and blemishing of his Reputation & good Name."[106] Hester confesses to five violations, from claiming that "Ashmole robd me of my Closet of Rarities & cheated me of my Estate," to the petty infraction of piling "a great heape of Earth and Rubbish" against Ashmole's garden wall.[107] The document, written in Ashmole's hand and signed before a justice by Hester and seven witnesses, speaks to the acrimony of Hester's struggle with Ashmole. Forced to submit, she may well have felt that her legacy had indeed been stolen.

Among the witnesses to her confession was Thomas de Critz the younger, Hester's kinsman and one of three in the family of painters responsible for the unusually large group of Tradescant portraits that survive.[108] It seems likely that the inclusion in the Ark of "Materialls of Dyers and Painters" (Tradescant, 34–6) reflects Hester's engagement with the De Critz workshop, perhaps her familiarity with grinding ingredients and mixing colors. Four portraits of Hester are extant, and both of her stepchildren, John III and Frances, are subjects of individual likenesses. Two portraits of the elder Tradescant – one as he lay in his deathbed – were finished posthumously, and Hester's husband was commemorated in his various roles: at work in his garden; receiving a cache of exotic shells from merchant Roger Friend; as husband and partner with Hester in a double portrait; and as a grieving father, posed beside a moss-covered skull following the death of his son and heir. In each of the Tradescant portraits, directly or indirectly, the main subject is the Ark. The paintings were part

[105] Bod Rawlinson MS D. 912, fol. 668r. The title is supplied by the John Bargrave Collection, http://drc.usask.ca/projects/bargrave/public_msitem.php?id=72. A loose sheet in the manuscript volume calls the document "Mrs Tradescant's Submission."

[106] Bod Rawlinson MS D. 912, fol. 668r.

[107] Bod Rawlinson MS D. 912, fols. 668r–9r.

[108] Eleven portraits of the Tradescants by Thomas de Critz (d. 1653) and his sons Emanuel and Thomas are extant. For the family connection between Hester and the De Critz's, see Poole, "Outline."

of the collection, thus Ashmole acquired them and transferred them to Oxford, where they remain. But the images themselves also recall the cabinet. The double portrait of Hester and her husband was made to commemorate the publication of *Musaeum Tradescantianum* in 1656.[109] In the joint portrait of Hester and her stepson (see Figure 4.6), the boy hands Hester what at first appears to be a book. But looking again, we see that he presents to his stepmother a box containing a jewel (see Plate 4).[110] Placed between the two subjects, embodying the interrelations of the Tradescants with each other and their mutual involvement with the rarities of the Ark, the subject of the painting is the jewel: a rendering in pearls and gemstones of the stalks and stems growing in the Tradescants' garden. In blurring the boundaries between art and nature, between human and nonhuman virtuosity, the jewel is a succinct and remarkable figuration of the vitality of the cabinet and its keepers.[111]

Hester's final commission in 1662 also conforms to the cabinet's commemorative processes as it beautifies the body of death and preserves the memory of the Ark in a perennial monument. In the churchyard of St. Mary's Lambeth, where three generations of John Tradescants were buried and where Hester would join them in 1678, she erected a monument to the Ark (see Figure 4.7).[112] Framing each of the panels carved on the tomb's four sides are sculptural trees with branches thick with leaves. The eastern panel shows the ruins of ancient civilizations: Corinthian columns, Roman arches, and obelisks lie broken on the ground. On the opposite side, the Nile runs through an ancient Egyptian landscape where the Ark's crocodile lingers on the shore among the cabinet's exotic shells.

[109] See Leith-Ross, *John Tradescants*, 172–3.

[110] The portrait is inscribed, "Aetis: 37. Septembris Anno Domini 1645; Aetis 12 A.D. 1645; and: 124 Sr John Tradescant his Second Wife, and Son." Ashmole donated it to the Ashmolean in 1683.

[111] See Bovilsky, "Shakespeare's Mineral Emotions," on the perceived vitality of minerals as "registering a uniquely early modern belief in the likeness of subject and object" (262). On her husband's death, Hester inherited a miniature containing his likeness, another rarity worthy of the cabinet, which she would have worn as a token of remembrance. The image is based on Thomas de Critz's portrait of Tradescant as a gardener (see Figure 4.6) and was probably commissioned by the sitter. Tradescant appears wearing it in the 1656 double portrait with Hester. See Fumerton, "Secret Arts," on the memorial aspects of miniatures and their relationships to the privacy and publicity of cabinets and sonnets.

[112] The Parish of Lambeth granted Hester permission to erect the monument on May 12, 1662. The first burial in the churchyard, at which time the family vault was constructed, was that of Jane, the younger Tradescant's first wife, in 1635: see Leith-Ross, *John Tradescants*, 110 and 144. The monument in its present state was recarved in 1852 based on drawings of the original. It is signed, "C. P. White & Son, Vauxhall Bridge." See note 118.

Figure 4.6 Thomas de Critz (attrib.), Hester Tradescant and her Stepson, John, 1645.
Image WA1898.14 © Ashmolean Museum, University of Oxford.

On the third side, the Tradescant coat of arms appears – heraldry that the family assumed but to which they were not entitled.[113] On the fourth, a seven-headed hydra rises menacingly above a skull (see Figure 4.8).

[113] Leith-Ross, *John Tradescants*, 116. The arms are also printed in *Musaeum Tradescantianum*, fol. $A4^{v}$.

Figure 4.7 The Tradescant Tomb (detail: Nile scene) (1662/1852). Author's photograph. Courtesy of the Garden Museum.

Figure 4.8 The Tradescant Tomb (detail: Hydra) (1662/1852). Author's photograph. Courtesy of the Garden Museum.

Like the foliage, antiquities, and crocodile carved on the tomb, the hydra alludes to the Ark. The monument recovers the imagery and text of the medieval bestiary to import a spiritual allegory into its memorial program. The bestiary explains:

> Est animal in nilo flumine quod dicitur idrus in aqua vivens . . . Hic idrus satis est inimicus cocodrillo, et hanc habet naturam et consuetudinem, ut cum viderit cocodrillam dormientem in littore, vadit aperto ore et involuit se in luto quo facilius possit in faucibus eius illabi. Cocodrillus igitur subito vivum eam transglutit. Ille vero dilanians omnia viscera eius, non solum vivus sed et exit illesus.
>
> ([The hydrus] is an animal living in the water of the Nile . . . This hydrus is a worthy enemy of the crocodile and has this nature and habit: when it sees a crocodile sleeping on the shore, it enters the crocodile through its open mouth, rolling itself in the mud to slide more easily down its throat. The crocodile, therefore, instantly swallows it alive. But the hydrus, tearing open the crocodile's bowels, crawls out again unharmed.)

The allegory is unfolded as follows:

> Sico ergo mors et infernus figuram habent cocodrilli, quorum inimicus est dominus iesus christus. Nam assumens humanam carnem descendit ad infernum et dirumpens omnia viscera eius, eduxit eos qui iniustae tenebantur ab eo. Mortificavit enim ipsam mortem, resurgens ex mortuis, et illi insultat propheta diccens: O mors ero mors tua, morsus tuus ero inferne.
>
> (Thus the crocodile symbolizes death and hell; their enemy is our Lord Jesus Christ. For taking human flesh, he descended into hell, and, tearing open its bowels, he led forth those where were unjustly held there. He destroyed death itself by rising from the dead and through the prophet, mocks death, saying, 'O death, I will be thy plagues; O grave, I will be thy destruction.')[114]

The images on the Tradescant tomb recycle the medieval source to script, in the visual and material lexicon of the cabinet, the promise of resurrection.

Hester may or may not have been the author of the monument's symbolism, although clearly it is not coincidental that the Tradescant crocodile roams the banks of the Nile immediately adjacent to its eternal enemy. Seventeenth-century sources renewed the emnity between the pair, making more resonant and available the medieval contest: Adriaen

[114] Bod MS 1511, fol. 81^{v}–82^{r}. The text is derived from Isidore of Seville, *Etymologies*, 256 and 243–4. The allegory is from Anon., *Physiologus*, 88. The passage concludes by quoting Hosea 13:14. See James, *Bestiary*, for classifications of bestiaries. I am indebted to Jaime Goodrich for her approval of this translation.

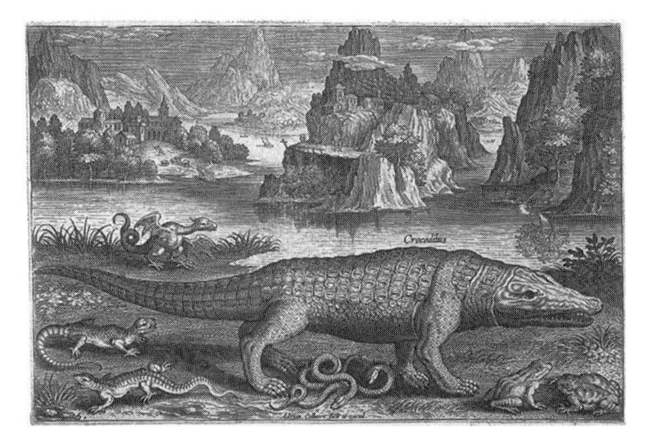

Figure 4.9 Adriaen Collaert, "A Crocodile with Other Reptiles on the Bank of a River," Wellcome Library no. 42140i. (Creative Commons CC BY 4.0).

Collaert's engraving of a crocodile beside the Nile (see Figure 4.9) depicts a hydrus in pursuit in the background, assuming a shape somewhere between the embodiments of the bestiary and the tomb. The version of the creature chosen to decorate the monument, moreover – the "dragon" whose ability to grow multiple heads, the bestiary claims, is "fabulosum"[115] – cultivates a narrative of the collection, offering a fabled ancestor to the dragons of the Ark whose materiality augments the tomb's transcendental allegory with an assertion of "radically immanent flesh."[116] In converting the closet of rarities to a sculptural memorial in the panels of the tomb, Hester both remembers and prolongs the Ark and its creatures on her own terms, rather than on Ashmole's. Like the figure of a skull falling obliquely between the viewer and Holbein's ambassadors, the effigial traces of the Ark's vitality enmesh the Tradescants' remains in a tissue – both remembered and real – of generative works, days, and things.[117]

Hester's memorial was itself viewed as a wonder: engravings and drawings of the monument were produced and circulated immediately after its

[115] Bod MS 1511, fol. 82ʳ: "Idra draco multorum capitum . . . Hec latine excedra dicitur quia uno ceso tria capita crescebant, sed hoc fabulosum est" ("The hydra is a dragon with many heads . . . It is called *excetra* in Latin because when one head is cut off, three more grow back. But this is only a story.") The conflation of the hydrus and the hydra is ubiquitous in medieval sources.

[116] See Braidotti, *Posthuman*, esp. 99; and see Shannon, *Accommodated Animal*, 49–50, for the view that the materiality of creaturely life mitigated early modern uses of animals simply as allegories.

[117] See Introduction, 16.

construction and for a century afterward.[118] But in the world beyond the cabinet, works of memory are vulnerable. When the tomb fell into ruins, it was on the basis of these precise engravings that the monument and its imagery were restored in 1773 and again in 1852.[119] In this ongoing revision, Hester's last word was lost. When the monument was repaired in 1773, an inscription was omitted:

> This monument was erected at the charge of Hester Tradescant, the relict of John Tradescant, late deceased, who was buried the 25th of April 1662.[120]

If the text was obscured on the monument, though, it persisted in Hester's will, where she identifies herself as "widdow Relict and Executrix of John Treduscant late deceased."[121] Hester as relict – widow – but also relic – remains, a surviving trace, a survival – supplies the quintessential figuration of the cabinet.[122] A jewel in the cabinet of the grave, set within the garden filled with outlandish fruits, in a tomb that embeds a world of wonders, the figure asserts the protection, preservation, and refinement of matter by memory and the unfolding course of time to which objects inevitably return. Yet this return is not submissive. The remains of memory, the survivors, reconfigure the past, embellishing it with an amazing tale. In doing so, they remake the present and shape an unimaginable future.[123]

[118] The monument was remarkable for being one of the first built in the churchyard rather than in the church building. Samuel Pepys commissioned a pen and brown ink drawing, now at Magdalene College, Cambridge, MS PL 2972/226a and b, which shows the Nile scene with crocodile as the west side and the adjacent hydra in perspective. See A. W. Aspital, ed. *Catalogue of the Pepys Library at Madgalene College Cambridge, Vol III, Prints and Drawings, Part i: General* (Woodbridge: Boydell and Brewer, 1980), 19; and see The John Bargrave Collection, http://drc.usask.ca/projects/bargrave/public_image.php?id=2163, for the image. Hollar produced an engraving in 1677 that was reprinted with the portraits of the Tradescants from *Musaeum Tradescantianum* in 1793, now National Portrait Gallery, NPG D28374. See Pennington, *Descriptive Catalogue*, 264. Hollar's image underscores the parallel between the catalogue as a printed monument and the tomb.

[119] Tanswell, *History . . . of Lambeth*, 164–66.

[120] Allen, *History . . . of Lambeth*, 142, prints the inscription and states that it was omitted in the 1773 renovation. It was originally inscribed on the top stone "of good black Marble," according to John Aubrey: see MacGregor, "Tradescant's Rarities," 14n105, and see 14–15 for the tomb's renovations in 1773 and 1852. The attribution was retrieved in 1852 and now reads, "The tomb was originally erected on this site in the year 1662 by Hester, relict of John Tradescant the younger" (quoted from the monument).

[121] TNA PROB 11/356/545, fol. 429r. [122] See *OED*.

[123] Since 1977, St. Mary's Lambeth and the surrounding grounds have housed the Garden Museum, a contemporary memorial to the Tradescants where Hester's monument is the centerpiece of a garden modelled on the elder Tradescant's design at Hatfield House. See "The Garden Museum," www.gardenmuseum.org.uk.

CHAPTER 5

Shakespearean Reliquaries
Pericles *and the Ark of Wonder*

> Her husband (yet without a sinne)
> was not a stranger, but her kin,
> That her chaste Love might seeme no other,
> unto a husband then a brother.
> Keepe well this pawne, thou marble chest,
> till it be cal'd for, let it rest:
> For while this Jewell here is set,
> The grave is but a Cabinet.
>
> – Epitaph for Anne Littleton[1]

> Thou that findest this arche . . . lete this corps be honourably sepultured and buryed the whiche thynge yf thou do not I pray to the heuenly goddes that thou mayst be the last of thy lygnage and that thou mayste dye as a cursed creature & that thou mayst never fynde ony that wyll bury the.
>
> – *Kynge Appolyn of Thyre*[2]

Glorious Caskets

On John Gower's monument in Southwark Cathedral, the poet's effigy is accompanied by three "Virgins," as John Stow calls them, who themselves have patiently endured death and resurrection (see Figure 4.1). Charity, Mercy, and Piety were shrouded in whitewash during the Reformation and were restored in 1615 at the expense of the parish.[3] If the Virgins attending Gower were absent-present in his memorial, so, too, were his attendants in life. Gower's effigy appears alone on a monument whose symbolism had recently become legible: "conspicuous" tombs such as Gower's "were often

[1] Stow, *Survey* (1633), 762.
[2] Heinrich Steinhöwel, *Kynge Appolyn of Thyre*, trans. Robert Copland (London: Wynkyn de Worde, 1510), sig. D4^{v}.
[3] Stow, *Survey* (1618), 780. See Chapter 4 for discussion.

associated with men who died without an heir, so that the assertion of the lineage in fact coincides with its effective demise."[4] Certainly the iconography of Gower's tomb asserts that the three texts he compiled, whose likenesses appear on the monument, were offspring substituting for his absent heir (see Plate 3). Yet in the passage of this literary lineage to posterity, the trace of another heir can be discerned. When he was nearly seventy years old, Gower married Agnes Groundolf, "possibly a poor girl," Rosamund Allen speculates, "who the priests recommended as a servant to save her from life in the brothels."[5] Although Agnes's effigy does not accompany Gower's on his tomb and no monument for her survives, John Leland reported in the mid-sixteenth century that Gower's wife "is buried in the same place [as her husband], but in a lower tomb." In John Bale's loose papers, alongside a verse affirming the immortality of the poet's writings, Gower's epitaph for his widow is preserved:

> Quam bonitas, pietas, elemosina, casta voluntas,
> Sobrietas que fides coluerunt, hic iacet Agnes.
> Uxor amans, humilis Gower fuit illa Joannis:
> Donet ei summus celica regna Deus.

> (Here lies Agnes, whom goodness, devotion, charity, chaste inclination,sobriety and faith cultivated; she was the loving and humble wife of John Gower; may the supreme God grant her the heavenly kingdom.)[6]

The lower tomb of this "uxor Amans" passively cultivated by virtues has disappeared in the surrender of artifact to memory.

The displacement of Agnes, a survivor of the brothel to whom Gower bequeathed all his worldly goods, by the three other-worldly Virgins supporting her husband in death uncannily suggests the careers of the women of William Shakespeare's and George Wilkins's *Pericles*.[7] A shadow St. Agnes in the brothel at Mytilene, Marina is one of the play's three

[4] Hines, Cohen, and Roffey, "Iohannes Gower," 39; citing Gittos and Gittos, "Motivation and Choice," 143–67.

[5] Allen, "John Gower and Southwark," 140.

[6] See Gower, *Complete Works*, vol. IV, xxi, for Macauley's translation of Leland's account; and see vol. IV, lix for the Latin verses from Bale. For the epitaph in English, see Allen, "John Gower and Southwark," 139. A "lower tomb" may refer to marked burial in the cathedral floor.

[7] I am not arguing the direct influence of the monument on *Pericles*, although its presence in Southwark Cathedral means that Shakespeare certainly was familiar with the tomb and its iconography. Rather, I argue that the trinity of female figures on the monument emerges from an established and familiar pool of devotional (Catholic) imagery that also informs Shakespeare's use of female intercessors (particularly Marina) to convey Gower's medieval tale to a post-Reformation audience.

female heirs.[8] Among minor alterations to their source, Gower's *Confessio Amantis*, Shakespeare and Wilkins multiplied the father-daughter couple by three. The incestuous alliance that initiates Pericles's wandering leads him to marriage with Thaisa, sole heir of Simonides, and finally to the reversal of his fortunes and of the play's moral trajectory when his sole heir, Marina, "beget'st him that did thee beget" (5.1.185). As Michelle Dowd has argued, the proliferation of female heirs in *Pericles* is closely imbricated with the structure of the romance as it overlays the fluidity attending the failure of primogeniture onto its dilative, episodic plot.[9] The "seafarer" and "sojourner" Marina embodies the currents of the play's "whirring" action as it crests and falls in Gower's tale (3.1.41; 4.2.129; 4.1.19). A second change Shakespeare made to his source further underscores Marina's role as a figuration of the nomadic travels leading to the plot's resolution, while removing the taint of sexual corruption the name carried in *Confessio Amantis*. Gower, too, had changed the name of his heroine to Thaise, thus associating her with a well-known prostitute of the Southwark stews.[10] Reassigning this name to Marina's mother, Shakespeare flirts with the lingering theme of incest, a subtext that similarly troubles the epitaph for Anne Littleton that prefaces this chapter, in which the subject's "chaste Love" is affirmed and disturbed by the claim that her husband is also her brother: kin without sin.[11]

In the production and transmission of the wonder that is the *raison d'être* of romance, and of the cabinet of curiosities, women play a central part. Hester Tradescant's collaborative project of collection and her struggle to retain her inheritance, discussed in Chapter 4, speak to the collaborative script enacted in *Pericles*, where Shakespeare cultivates three "women of wonder" through whom Gower's wondrous tale "seems to live" (4.4.7).[12] Moreover, a conflation of femininity and monumentality is central to this transmission. The figure of Hester Tradescant as a "relict" – both survivor and relic, creating and contained within the monument she erected for her male kin – is anticipated in the hybridity of *Pericles*'s female heirs; they are at once wondrous closets, and the contents of the coffers they embody. When the remnant and survivor, Marina, appears as

8 See Helms, "Saint in the Brothel"; and Cooper, "'This worthy olde writer,'" 109.

9 Dowd, *Dynastic Inheritance*, 163–208; see also Cooper, "'This worthy olde writer,'" 110.

10 Olsson, *John Gower*, 218.

11 On the centrality of the incest theme to *Pericles*, see especially Nevo, *Shakespeare's Other Language*, 33–61; and to *Confessio Amantis*, see Scanlon, "Riddle of Incest"; and Watt, "Gender and Sexuality."

12 See Clubb, *Italian Theatre*, 65–89.

"Patience gazing on kings' graves and smiling / Extremity out of act" (5.1.129–30), Pericles's awakening foreshadows like effects of the recreative gardens and creatures carved on the Tradescant tomb (see Figure 4.7).[13]

A maritime adventure of seemingly endless crossings, *Pericles* is, paradoxically, a play of enclosures. Caskets, coffers, coffins, and chests – along with the claustrophobic spaces of the ship's hold and the brothel – merge seafaring, commemoration, and restoration across the play's turbulent passages. Structurally, Gower's eight choruses parcel and compartmentalize the embedded action, and on three occasions, further entomb performance in dumb shows, dioramas where the "motes and shadows" (4.4.21) of enactment are enclosed. This chapter argues that the drama attending the compilation of the Tradescants' Ark and its passage to posterity highlights the themes held in common between *Pericles* and the cult of curiosity. The limitless seascape of travel and discovery that produces the marvels of the cabinet also propel the plot of *Pericles*, both conveying, like memory itself, "absolute plentitude and catastrophic loss."[14] The stage, like the cabinet, condenses a vast world of wonders in a "wooden O," in impersonations that recall a remote reality, an elsewhere.[15] The confluence of remembrance and loss in the cabinet, as in the romance, is expressed in a preoccupation with beautiful remains: a conflation of physical beauty (for Shakespeare, the beautiful female body) with death. In both cases, moreover, the temporal blurring of past and present realities relies upon commemorative narratives, myths of origin and transmission, and belief in their restorative power. For the collector – or the playwright, or the singer of "a song that old was sung" (1.0.1) – sight and hearing collude, casting matter as the marvelous in dexterous stories that confer mystery and provoke wonder. In Shakespeare's innovative retrieval and reuse of past things – both "ancient Gower" and his twice-told tale (1.0.2) – remembrance is an act of recreation. Gower's disinterment is a renaissance.

Section 1 of this chapter focuses on the effigial female figures of Antiochus's daughter and Thaisa to show how *Pericles* engages the dependence of the eye on the ear that underpins the poetics of wonder. While the vexed alignment of sight and certainty is played out in spectacles of death and commemoration, the play's preoccupation with unburied corpses and unstable monuments underscores the threat to memory and identity posed

[13] See Hecksecher, "Shakespeare," 36–56, for the visual analogues for Marina's embodiment of Patience.

[14] Beckwith, "Present of Past Things," 364.

[15] Shakespeare, *Henry V*, Pro. 14.

by faulty judgment and foul show. If monuments are material thresholds of remembrance binding the living to the dead – artifacts that embody the intertwining of bodies and things – *Pericles* troubles these connections, cutting its protagonist adrift in a self-forgetful isolation of which the play's unstable monuments are figures.[16] In the living tombs of Antiochus's daughter and Thaisa, "the aesthetic transfigurations wrought by death" blend bodies and their enclosures, both prompting Pericles's visual and epistemological lapses, and embodying the interplay between narrative and spectacle – the ear and the eye – introduced by Gower's choruses.[17]

Section 2 turns to the play's cabinet of curiosities, Cerimon's closet, where wonder is perfected and where the cooperation between the senses becomes a matter of text. Aligning the creative sovereignty asserted by Cerimon with Gower's, I argue that the multilayered enclosures circulating through the world of *Pericles* enable the intertwining of actors and narrators of which the romance consists. Gower's emergence as a "maker" in and of *Pericles* relies upon Shakespeare's metrical virtuosity in scripting his speech. In Gower's choruses – circumscribed texts, like books in boxes – Shakespeare amasses the variety of poetic texts comprising the theatrical script. The rarities collected in Gower's choruses are not the performances of the play's embedded action, but the polytemporal meters and styles with which the story is told. The result is a textual intertwining of poet Shakespeare and a newly contemporary Gower. Poetic form is a generative work of remembrance and recreation.

This section concludes with a reading of Gower's epitaph for Marina in Chorus 5 as the point of climax of the play's interactions between sight and hearing, and as a turning point in the relationship between Shakespeare and coauthor Gower. In Section 3, I argue that in this transformational moment, Gower recedes from his role as storyteller and is replaced by Shakespeare's "fresh new seafarer," Marina (3.1.41). At once a new creation and a container of "most clear remembrance" (5.3.12), Marina is a memorial writer, but one for whom memory is "multi-directional," reaching into the past to restore lost bonds and, aided by imagination, moving forward and outward to forge new ties between bodies, ideas, and worlds – both on stage and off.[18] Making Gower's wondrous, twice-told tale her own, Marina emerges as at once a subject and a cure from the fluid currents of relations through which she passes.

[16] See Butler, "Merleau-Ponty," on the futility of attempts to escape the intertwining of self and world.
[17] Mauriès, *Cabinets of Curiosities*, 119. [18] Braidotti, *Posthuman*, 118.

Cabinets of curiosities, like church interiors and the monuments they hold, are theaters of memory: dynamic, regenerative networks embracing artifacts, the histories they embed, and the subjects who experience them. Like Tradescants' Ark, *Pericles* situates its narrators, characters, and audience amid fluid seascapes and alien environments where distinctions between life and death, art and nature, and past and present are strategically blurred. Imagining Shakespeare's and Wilkins's *Pericles* as such a structure, this chapter responds to critical assessments that see the play, on the one hand, as profoundly ahistorical, dissociated from its context, and, on the other, as a "mouldy tale" unable to accommodate an ancient narrator who interrupts the action and impedes the marvel that the play intends to produce.[19] Yet the narratives of the cabinet and the romance depend not on historical fact but on memorial reconstruction. In theatrical terms, of course, memorial reconstruction is commonly called forth to explain the origins of play texts that are clearly flawed. The apparent textual corruption of *Pericles*, which has resulted in radically different editions of the play, challenges close readings of passages that may or may not be authentic to either author, Shakespeare or Wilkins.[20] Memory errs, and textual infirmities are in need of surgical repair. In narrative terms, however, memorial reconstruction produces inventive, fantastic stories of origin that gloss otherwise unremarkable or inscrutable appearances. Memory, in the cabinet of curiosities, is a source of wonder and instruction, a guide to deciphering images and artifacts that cannot be understood by the eye alone. If *Pericles* is ahistorical, it is because it is a memorial reconstruction in both senses, at once vulnerable to error and replete with marvels. "Assuming man's infirmities" (1.0.3), poet Gower launches a textually and visually complex, multilayered, and composite work: a series of boxes within boxes and texts within texts whose commemorative "purchase is to make men glorious" (1.0.9).

Gower's tale is steeped in the infirmities attending living time, set in a world across whose threshold the poet passes easily: "I life would wish," he affirms, "and that I might / Waste it for you like taper light" (1.0.15–16). If Gower is a transient apparition, as luminous and fading as candlelight, Shakespeare lends his reincarnated coauthor immortality – but of a

[19] See, for example, Mullaney, *Place of the Stage*, 135–51; and Zurcher, "Untimely Monuments." For *Pericles* as a moldy tale, see Jonson, *New Inn*, sig. H2r; and on Gower as a figure of "Brechtian alienation," see Nevo, *Shakespeare's Other Language*, 68; and Knowles, "'Wishes Fall Out,'" 14.

[20] See the reconstructed text by Gary Taylor and Macd P. Jackson available in Shakespeare, *Pericles*, ed. Warren. See also Gossett in Shakespeare and Wilkins, *Pericles*, 38–44, and her discussion of the play's creation, editing, and production history, 1–106.

theatrical sort. Removing the relic from history, *Pericles* ensconces Gower in memory; a productive, recreative engagement with the past that reconfigures the present. In the choruses of *Pericles*, Gower's remains are beautified by the compiler Shakespeare, not as "specimens of temporal otherness" but as a vital cocreator.[21] Recovering Gower as a skillful English poet, Shakespeare engages in a ritual of remembrance like Stow's. His innovation renews and rejuvenates not only Gower's story but also Wilkins's nascent script.[22] Shakespeare, Gower's heir, returns to the textual origin, *Confessio Amantis*, to embark upon a new romance of cultural memory.

1 Ships' Wooden Sepulchres

The opening moments of *Pericles* consist of a scene of visual seduction situated between frame tale and performance, as Gower's prologue glosses but cannot govern Pericles's wayward eye. The episode at Antioch is indebted to *Confessio Amantis* not only in Gower's retelling of the Apollonius of Tyre story in Book 8, but also in the frame tale of the medieval text.[23] Pericles, like Amans, falls victim to the faulty eye. As Gower's textual double in *Confessio Amantis* complains to his confessor:

> Mi fader, ye, I am beknowe,
> I have hem cast upon Meduse,
> Therof I may me noght excuse:
> Min herte is growen into Ston,
> So that my lady therupon
> Hath such a priente of love grave,
> That I can noght miselve save.
> (1.550–6)

Amans's petrified heart becomes a tombstone on which the *donna petrosa* engraves his epitaph in the process erasing his memory of himself. The imagery joining femininity to the stony interiority of self-loss, and to the tomb that marks it, is repeated and corrupted in the incest story that closes

[21] Summit, *Memory's Library*, 182, describing Camden's integration of fragments of medieval verse into his *Britannia*. See Lynch, "Authority of Gower," on the interplay between Shakespeare and Gower; and Jones, "'The quick and the dead,'" who sees Shakespeare's Gower, as I do, as "a hybrid of archaic alterity and iconic familiarity" (209).

[22] Like most critics, I consider Wilkins to be the author of Acts 1 and 2 of *Pericles*, with Shakespeare appearing in 3.1. See Gossett, in Shakespeare and Wilkins, *Pericles*, 54–80; and Vickers, *Shakespeare's Co-Authors*, 291–332. For a complication of the theory of dual authorship, see Edwards, "Approach."

[23] See Hillman, "Shakespeare's Gower."

Confessio Amantis and opens *Pericles*. Since Shakespeare's and Wilkins's Gower censures the "Bad child, worse father" (1.0.27) of Antioch in advance of the action, Pericles's erring vision is clear in his initial description of Antiochus's daughter:

> See where she comes, apparelled like the spring,
> Graces her subjects, and her thoughts the king
> Of every virtue gives renown to men;
> Her face the book of praises, where is read
> Nothing but curious pleasures.
>
> (1.1.13–7)

Antiochus's daughter, promising "curious pleasures," is a rarity badly in need of a gloss. An inept reader, Pericles shares both the desire for and the imagery of Antiochus's daughter with her incestuous father.[24] Yet the equation of her beauty with death is overdetermined, and the scene is replete with captions that are difficult to overlook. By way of Antiochus's comparison of his daughter to the Hesperides, she becomes both Eve and the fatal fruit she purveys (1.1.28). The "speechless tongues and semblance pale" of "martyrs slain in Cupid's wars" advise with "dead cheeks" not to attempt her (1.1.36–8), and Pericles ventures merely to touch her "upon [his] life" (1.1.87). If the daughter's association with death is obvious to the audience throughout the scene, it eventually becomes apparent to Pericles as he unravels the riddle, an embedded text that transfers semiotic transparency to the princess's body: "Fair glass of light, I loved you, and could still, / Were not this glorious casket stored with ill" (1.1.76–7). A dead and deadening reliquary of corrupt remains, Antiochus's daughter, like the Medusa that transforms Amans, brings forth the grotesque monument of the lover's death; Shakespeare's Gower makes this inescapably clear when he "*Points to the heads displayed above*" (1.0.42 s.d.).

The image of Antiochus's daughter as a glorious casket interring decayed remains participates in the reformed suspicion of artful surfaces, which left sumptuous monuments, like Gower's Southwark tomb, vulnerable to iconoclasm.[25] When Puritan Thomas Achelley misreads Cyriac of Ancona's amber inclusion of a fly as an "Amber Box, which proffered a glosing and beautiful show . . . yet had nothing with in it but a thing of

[24] See Bishop, *Theatre of Wonder*, 96–9, on the scene's problematic mingling of Pericles's and Antiochus's views of the daughter.

[25] Finkelstein, "Politics of Gender," 321, sees the taboo of incest as a metaphor for seduction by visual signs. On vision in the play more broadly, see Hanna, "Christian Vision."

nought," he censures the ostentation with which death is masked and beautified.[26] Shakespeare's and Wilkins's figuration of the daughter as both a beautiful tomb and the decayed corpse it encloses remarkably revises Gower's original representation of a violated and victimized daughter who "evere wissheth after deth" (8.333). *Pericles* embeds a reformist view of the collusion of bodily corruption with spiritual death in the daughter's mortuary form, sharing Achelley's vocabulary when Antiochus confesses in an aside, "I will gloze with him" (1.1.11). This revisionary treatment of the Catholic source, rather than demanding that we attribute a Protestant perspective to the play generally – or indeed to either of its coauthors – occurs in relation to a creature whose hybridity and liminality figure the blending of religious beliefs evident in *Pericles* and in Shakespeare's late plays more broadly. Situated between beliefs and embodying the complex intertwining of apparent opposites – life and death, beauty and corruption, truth and falsehood, human and nonhuman – the daughter's resistant legibility within the frame of starkly opposed religious views urges a collapse of these definitive categories and beliefs. Antiochus's daughter seems to demand a fluid cooperation of Catholic and reformed approaches to imagery and corporeality.[27] Thus, the report given by Pericles of his misadventure both preserves the potency of Catholic reliquaries and their saints, and summarizes the violence wrought in Antioch as an idolatry repaid by the hero's iconoclastic disdain: "Her face was to mine eye beyond all wonder. / The rest—hark in thine ear—as black as incest" (1.2.73–4).[28]

While both Antiochus and his daughter "gloze" (1.1.111) – one with an infected speech that masks a murderous intent, and the other with an infected beauty that kills – *Pericles* also explores a restorative form of "glosing" in its pre-confessional narrator, Gower. In an argument for religious syncretism in *Pericles*, Brian Walsh calls attention to Gower's role as a point of concentration for the play's religious hybridity: resurrecting the medieval poet and his Catholic plot, Shakespeare calls upon this figure to "stand i' th' gaps" (4.4.8) between Catholic and Protestant beliefs. The play's improvised and occluded rituals (Pericles's offstage rites for Thaisa, for instance) invite us to decide, "based on where individual

[26] Achelley, *Key of Knowledge*, sig. B8^{v}-C1^{r}. See Introduction.

[27] The scene was most likely authored by Wilkins. For views of Shakespeare's syncretism, with which I agree, see Mayer, *Shakespeare's Hybrid Faith*; Hunt, "Syncretistic Religion"; and Betteridge, "Writing Faithfully."

[28] Implicit in negotiations between sight and hearing in *Pericles* is the reformed reliance on both reading and hearing the word in self-examination. See Hunt, *Art of Hearing*.

playgoers fall along the traditional and reformed religious spectrum . . . what a 'priestly farewell' means and what shape it takes."[29] Set within the interpretative matrix of remembrance, the reincarnated Gower is not only a figure for religious hybridity; he is also the Gower of Berthelette and Stow, one of the founding fathers of English letters. The Gower of *Pericles* is a "memorial" poet in two senses: his corpus points to the central role of memory in the Catholic rite of penance, and to the place of memory in sustaining the ties between the living and the dead. This duality is consistent with readings by Shakespeare's contemporaries. As Jennifer Summit points out, John Weever's *Ancient Funeral Monuments* (1631) treats Gower as a "master of the epitaph," a writer who "secures the afterlives of his subjects and himself not through intercessory prayer or other superstitious practices but through the durable writing of the monumental epitaph."[30] In *Pericles*, Gower reappears as both a relic retrieved in the borrowed plot and the "remembrancer" of that tale. Accordingly, when the dangerous sights of Antioch spill over their frame, Gower is called upon to reconcile the eye to the ear ("Your ear unto your eye I'll reconcile," 4.4.22). He ends his prologue with two lines of iambic pentameter – an intimation of his ability to compete in "latter times / When wit's more ripe" (1.0.11–12) – that call upon viewers to submit "to the judgment of your eye / My cause, who best can justify" (1.0.41–2).

The dangers of foul show that prompted reformers to censure theatricality more broadly may inform Shakespeare's exploration of the relative merits of spectacle and narrative in *Pericles*.[31] Yet these two structural poles of the play merge from the start. While Gower's prologue suggests that the audience's eye is capable of a judgment more sound than Pericles's, it simultaneously undermines that suggestion by predicting and explaining the action that follows. The narrative gloss intended to restrain and instruct the eye is made redundant – or perhaps it is the scene that is unnecessary – since the performance ultimately confirms the fact of incest that Gower has already revealed. As poet Gower stands in the gaps, he stands between the audience and the action, blurring direct visual

[29] Walsh, "'A Priestly Farewell,'" 89; and see 96–102 on Gower's intermediary status between Catholicism and Protestantism. See also Werth, "Great Miracle," who sees in *Pericles* "a split religious palimpsest" (203); and Appleford, "Shakespeare's Katherine," who argues for Shakespeare's "conscious Catholicization" (152) of Reformation history in *All is True*. For readings of the religious subtext of *Pericles*, see Dean, "Pericles's Pilgrimage"; Bicks, "Backsliding at Ephesus"; and Finkelstein, "*Pericles*."

[30] Summit, *Memory's Library*, 189–90.

[31] See Barish, *Anti-theatrical Prejudice*, 80–154; and on the intersection of anti-theatricality and gender, see Levine, *Men in Women's Clothing*.

experience and filtering it through the lens of his remembered tale. As Anne Barton writes, "planes of reality are made to shift and blur" between Gower's narrative frame and the theatrical performance within it.[32] Rather than erecting an opaque barrier between the audience and the performance, however, these exchanges offer a rarified view, producing a double vision like that attending Antiochus's duplicitous daughter and prompting reparative performances by her theatrical doubles, Thaisa and Marina. Thus, Antiochus's malevolent glosing prefaces Simonides's benevolent "dissembling" (2.5.22), as his daughter's incestuous feeding on her mother's flesh (1.1.65–6) is replaced by Thaisa's healthy cannibalism, "wishing [Pericles] my meat" (2.3.31). Both Gower's choruses and the women of *Pericles* "obliterat[e] a boundary, inviting misinterpretation as substance rather than shadow."[33] Like amber inclusions – fair glasses of light where included remains are transformed to rarities, or rarities to remains – they are at once wondrous containers, and the essences, good or ill, contained.

The relationship between narrative and spectacle that accompanies Gower's presence in *Pericles* borrows from the *Confessio Amantis* an understanding of storytelling as memorial and restorative. "Love, which that blind was evere / Maketh all his servants blinde also" (8.2130–1), Gower's Genius explains to Amans, and his exemplary tales "drawe into remembrance" (Pro. 69) the lover's true identity – that is, the poet "John Gower" (8.2321) – of which he has lost sight. Pericles's interpretive lapse at Antioch repeats Amans's and is repeated throughout his play: although he escapes the death suffered by the suitors, a protracted career of flawed perceptions and stony melancholy ensues. He mistakenly assumes, for instance, that the jocular dissembling of "the good Simonides" (2.1.96) is a trap; he midjudges Thaisa's death; and he is tricked by the foul show of Marina's cenotaph. The loss of self that follows Pericles's sight of Antioch's glorious casket foretells his melancholic despair in misreading these signs.

Pericles's self-loss is figured in the play's many images of the deprivation of burial and funeral rites and the severing of bonds between the living and dead signaled by the absence of commemoration. If the commemorative work of the monument is to affirm social identity – as Marina's false executor, Dionyza, puts it, to "express / A general praise to her and care in us / At whose expense 'tis done" (4.3.43–5) – the refusal of burial signals a failure akin to Pericles's lapse of vision and memory, his episode of self-forgetting, at Antioch. The suitors' heads, displayed "without covering save

[32] Barton, "'Enter Mariners wet,'" 201–2. [33] Barton, "Enter Mariners wet," 190.

yon field of stars" (11.38), are at once a perishable monument and a memorial to the subjects' anonymity. They recall only the fatal vision that transformed them into nameless effigies, a serial martyrdom registered by Antiochus's daughter: "Of all 'ssayed yet, mayst though prove prosperous; / Of all 'ssayed yet, I wish thee happiness" (1.1.60–1).[34] The unstable monuments of *Pericles* are adrift in currents that erode the bonds between bodies. In due course, the "shrivelled up" corpses of Antiochus and his daughter are deemed unworthy of burial: "for they so stunk / That all those eyes adored them ere their fall / Scorn now their hand should give them burial" (2.4.9–12). The starving survivors of the dead at Tarsus "Have scarce strength left to give them burial" (1.4.49) until the famine is relieved by Pericles and the memory of the unburied dead is displaced by the monument built "to remember" Pericles and "to make him glorious" (2.0.13–4). When Pericles washes ashore at Pentapolis, he expresses the dependence of identity on burial in his confession, "What I have been I have forgot to know," and his immediate request, "For that I am a man, pray see me buried" (2.1.69 and 75). Pericles is able "somewhat to repair" himself with the chance recovery of "part of my heritage / Which my dead father did bequeath" (2.1.118–20). In its capacity to convey remembrance and confer identity, the armor is a portable monument awash in play's ever-changing seas.[35]

So, too, is Thaisa's coffin. Her burial at sea provides the clearest staging of this threat to remembrance. The transient monuments of *Pericles* speak to a world at sea, where identities are unfixed and contingent, and where memory – of the past and of oneself – is easily compromised. The abrupt curtailment of a traditional rite bestowing Thaisa "hallowed" to her grave displaces the chapel housing a permanent marble sepulcher with a fluid seascape where an evocative natural monument is envisioned: "the belching whale / And humming water must o'erwhelm thy corpse, / Lying with simple shells" (3.1.59–64).[36] The use of this naturalism to challenge the flawed commemoration of traditional monuments parallels Innogen's funeral in Wales, which indicts the failed sacramentality of her chamber in *Cymbeline*.[37] While Innogen's rites suggest the dissolution of porous

[34] Bishop, *Theater of Wonder*, 96, notes that the suitors' open eyes suggest the daughter's coercive theatricality.

[35] See Dowd, *Dynastic Inheritance*, 188–9, who sees the armor as reconstituting lineage; and see Stallybrass, "Hauntings."

[36] See Walsh, "'A Priestly Farewell,'" 86–9, for a compelling reading of this episode.

[37] See Chapter 3 for discussion.

borders between body and earth, staging the intertwining of her flesh with "the flesh of the world," Thaisa's body, entombed in her "coffer" (3.4.2), is wildly aestheticized: she is a jewel set in the cabinet of the grave.[38] Enmeshed in precious artifacts, her body becomes a site for the blending of art and nature, a breathtaking translation of flesh to rarity. "Her eyelids," Cerimon claims, are "cases to those heavenly jewels / Which Pericles hath lost," with "fringes of bright gold" (3.2.97–99). Thaisa's hybridity as both living creature and artifact – a replication and correction of that of Antiochus's daughter – is implicit in Lychorida's description of Marina as "a piece / Of your dead queen" (3.1.17–18), more fragment than flesh. As this beautiful relict is cast overboard, she is encrusted with tokens and texts that collude to make her legible. She is "Shrouded in cloth of state, / Balmed and entreasured with full bags of spices" (3.2.63–4); buried with jewels retrieved from Pericles's "casket" and "satin coffer" (3.1.65–7); and named in Pericles's makeshift epitaph, which brokers burial to preserve the memory threatened by the nomadic grave. "Besides this treasure for a fee," it concludes, "The gods requite his charity" (3.2.67–74).

Despite the contingency of Thaisa's sea burial, the episode gives visible shape to the body enmeshed in the crafted diversity of the material world. This involvement embeds a sacramental plot; a plot of bodies swallowed and reborn.[39] The typology of Jonah woven through the play carries the imagery of entombment and resurrection staged in the creaturely world – in an animate sea – which undergirds the wonder of Thaisa's awakening and Pericles's restoration at the play's close.[40] If Calvin sees Noah's entry into the Ark as a descent "into the grave," Thaisa's casket, "caulked and bitumed" (3.1.70–1), shares the pitch of the Ark. It is a chest of resurrection and genesis; a box containing a world, traversing the waters of a providential sea.[41]

[38] Merleau-Ponty, *Visible and Invisible*, 144.

[39] See Merleau-Ponty, *Phenomenology of Perception*, 246, for the analogy between the sacrament and sensation.

[40] See Dean, "Pericles's Pilgrimage," who reads the typology of Jonah in this scene, in Marina's experience in the brothel (a St. Marina who, like Jonah, was swallowed and vomited up), and in Pericles's restoration.

[41] Calvin, *Commentarie . . . upon Genesis*, 189; and see Shakespeare and Wilkins, *Pericles*, 287n71. The story of Noah is also referenced in *Pericles* 1.1.117, when Pericles is given forty days to answer Antiochus's riddle: see Gossett, in Shakespeare and Wilkins, *Pericles*, 189n117. See Dean, "Pericles's Pilgrimage"; Hunt, "Shakespeare's *Pericles*," 306; and Roychoudhury, "Mental Tempests," 1034.

2 A Secret Art

At the center of *Pericles*, Shakespeare embeds a cabinet of curiosities. In his closet, amid a world of wonders, Cerimon practices a "secret art" (3.2.32) that gives him access to and control of the hidden powers of nature. "Hundreds call themselves your creatures," he is told, "who / By you were restored" (3.2.44–5). Cerimon is at once a collector and magus, "bringing the dead back to life," as Mauriès writes, "or consigning living things to death."[42] His closet, like any cabinet of curiosities, is a site of fluid exchanges between art and nature, being and nonbeing, human and nonhuman. Bodies encrypting the causes and meanings of their lives and deaths are preserved and explained; "authorities," like epitaphs, permit their stories to be told (3.2.33). In this space where Cerimon exercises interpretative and recreative authority, the chief rarity, of course, is Thaisa (3.2.92). She both enters and figures the cabinet where remains are transformed to rarities. Her reawakening – described by onstage spectators as "strange" and "most rare" (3.3.104–7) – stages the cooperation of ear and eye: the dramatic scene is a prolonged ritual accompanied by music, crafted to captivate and create wonder.[43] While retaining traces of the mystery of Catholic rites, Cerimon's secret art is textual and exegetical: he is able to correct the "too rough" and erroneous judgment of those "that threw her in the sea" (3.2.78–9).[44] A skilled and practiced reader, Cerimon can see the "fire of life" in the body and rekindle it (3.2.82). Like the resurrected Gower, Cerimon stands in the gap between life and death, and his secret art has the capacity, promised by Gower, to reconcile the eye to the ear.

The entrance of Thaisa's little world, the ark of wonder, into the little world of Cerimon's closet takes part in a "game of Chinese boxes," in Lina Bolzoni's metaphor, that cabinets of curiosities commonly play.[45] In Ben Jonson's *Entertainment at Britain's Burse*, performed at the opening of London's New Exchange in 1609, the list of commodities for sale reads like the catalog of a collection: while Tradescants' Ark lists "a nest of 52 wooden-cups turned within each other as thin as paper" (37), Jonson's inventory includes "China boxes, China Cabinetts, Caskets ... Christal

[42] Mauriès, *Cabinets of Curiosities*, 119.

[43] Hart, "Cerimon's 'Rough' Music,'" sets the scene's music in a religious context that associates it with the restorative images of music throughout the play.

[44] Cerimon's secret art has been associated with Catholic rituals: see Bicks, "Backsliding at Ephesus."

[45] Bolzoni, *Gallery of Memory*, 239–40.

globes" and more.[46] If the availability of these exotic items reflects London's increasing activity in global travel and trade, the fascination with embedded boxes and caskets offers a succinct figure for the containment of and control over an ever-expanding world. The discoveries of the cabinet, glossed by the collector's tales, domesticate a world of wonders even as they work to enhance and preserve their strangeness. In *Pericles*, the rich circulation and intersections of multilayered enclosures – coffer, coffin, casket, and chest – figure the multiplicity of the world of romance. As Suzanne Gossett notes, *Pericles* demonstrates a confusion between "coffer" (a container for money or valuables) and "coffin" (a chest for a dead body) unusual in Shakespeare's corpus. "By the later seventeenth century," she writes, "the meaning 'a chest, case, casket or box' for *coffin* seems to have been reduced to a book box."[47] While Gossett attributes this confusion to "either the reporter or the compositor," the maintenance of these multiple meanings throughout *Pericles* returns us to Berthelette's edition of *Confessio Amantis*, certainly the edition that Shakespeare and Wilkins used.[48] In Berthelette's paratexts, a "curious littell cheste" (fol. *ii^r) in which, we're told, Alexander kept his treasured copy of Homer, is a figure for Gower's book itself, a world "plentifully stuffed and fournished" with stories compiled from a collection of authorities. In *Pericles*, this imagery invites an equation between Cerimon's creative sovereignty, "Making man a god" (3.2.31), and poet Gower's. Both are "makers," composing the stories of the cabinet and of the play.

This authorial power and prerogative take on new dimensions in Cerimon's closet, when they become a matter of text. As Thaisa's coffin is opened to reveal the beautiful corpse, the wondrous sight demands a narrative gloss to instruct the eye and to ensure remembrance. The caption is provided by Pericles's epitaph, written hastily in the tempest but read only now:

> Here I give to understand,
> If e'er this coffin drives a-land,
> I King Pericles have lost,
> This queen, worth all our mundane cost.
> Who finds her, give her burying.
> She was the daughter of a king.
>
> (3.2.67–72)

[46] Jonson, *Key Keeper*, 8 [47] Gossett, in Shakespeare and Wilkins, *Pericles*, 286–7n67.

[48] Following Berthelette's 1554 reprint, *Confessio Amantis* was not published again until 1857: see Machan, "Thomas Berthelette," 144.

In scripting the epitaph, Shakespeare adopts Gower's octosyllabics, retrieving the meter used by Wilkins in Gower's choruses and in the play's first embedded text, the riddle at Antioch. By inserting Gower's material text emphatically into this scene of restoration, Shakespeare places himself between ear and eye; between, that is, the sensory experience of the reader and that of the spectator. When we *hear* Gower's jaunty octosyllabics, the book where we might *read* his verse materializes in the scene. Yet the epitaph both is and is not Gower's: as Thaisa's flesh blends with and the silk, jewels and spices in which she is enmeshed, Shakespeare and Gower as authors blend to eulogize a living woman, to create an epitaph that is also a "passport" (3.2.65). Similarly, the choruses of Shakespeare's authorship exploit the resonance of metrical variation, progressively working to reconcile ear and eye by imagining "secret art" as the art of poetry. Gower's metrical magic is displayed in the heightened sophistication of his subsequent performances.[49] Working with Gower as coauthor, Shakespeare stages an intervention of textuality into the theatrical unfolding of his play, one that uses the poet Gower effectively to recycle and renew his medieval tale. The play beautifies Gower's ashes as his textual remains grow increasingly sophisticated and accomplished – increasingly Shakespearean.

The framing structure of *Pericles* is fundamental to this textual intervention. Gower's choral episodes capture, like books in boxes, the ongoing action, and performances are embedded "texts," to use Gower's description ("Pardon old Gower: This 'longs the text," 2.0.41), set within the narrative frame. It must be no accident that the action of *Pericles* is parceled into seven sections, perhaps borrowing the seven-part division that notionally structures *Confessio Amantis*, or that the Gower of *Pericles* presents eight choruses, the number of books in the medieval source.[50] Gower's association with his material book is underscored by the woodcut printed on the title page of Wilkins's *Painfull Adventures of Pericles* depicting the poet reading from the volume lying open on the lectern before him. As the title page equivocally and elliptically tells us, the story was "lately presented by the worthy and ancient Poet John Gower."[51] Of the five choruses written

[49] See Hoeniger, "Gower and Shakespeare," for a reading of Gower's metrical innovations throughout his choruses. Hoeniger's associated argument for Shakespeare's single authorship is untenable: see Thomas, "Problem of Pericles."

[50] Gossett, in Shakespeare and Wilkins, *Pericles*, 82. *Confessio Amantis* follows the seven-part structure in Amans's confession and absolution for the seven deadly sins. However, book 7, on Aristotle's education of Alexander, results in the work's division into eight books.

[51] Wilkins, *Painfull Adventures of Pericles*, sig. A1^r.

Upon the Birth and
death of his deere sonne Henry
Mountagu Sr. Sidney
Mountagu knight.
Anno Dni 1627

Good May brought thee to a world of flowers
But Aprill drownd thee in so many Showers
Wensonday baptis'd thee Christian
Thursday returnd thee to Ascend againe

Et genus et proavos et quæ non fecimus ipsi
Vix ea nostra voco

1627

Plate 1. Sidney Montagu, "Upon the Birth and death of his deere sonne, Henry Mountagu, S[i]r Sidney Mountagu, Knight. Anno D[omi]ni 1627." Barnwell All Saints. Author's photograph.

Plate 2. Flemish workshop, "Judith Presenting the Head of Holofernes" (before 1589). Boughton House.
By kind permission of the Duke of Buccleuch and Queensberry KBE.

Plate 3. Unknown sculptor, Gower Monument (detail).
Author's photograph. Reproduced by permission of the Dean and Chapter of Southwark Cathedral.

Plate 4. Thomas de Critz (attrib.), Hester Tradescant and her Stepson, John, 1645 (detail: jewel).

by Wilkins, all in octosyllabics, two contain dumb shows that are, in effect, "letter cases": the second and third dumb shows enact little more than the arrival of letters (2.0.16 and 3.0.14), texts occluded in the silence of these theatrical parcels that must be read for us in Gower's surrounding commentary.[52] The rigidity and redundancy of Wilkins's choruses are deadening, and the last that is likely of Wilkins's authorship (Chorus 7) seems to predict the return of Gower's ashes to the tomb at the play's close: "Now our sands are almost run / More a little, and then dumb" (5.2.1–2). The casket containing Gower and his book, it appears, is soon to be sealed.[53]

Shakespeare's three choruses (Chorus 5, 6, and the Epilogue), by contrast, are enlivened by interplay between Gower and Shakespeare as coauthors and between Gower as narrator and as actor in his narrated plot. Like a creature in an amber inclusion, Gower is involved in the luminous matter of Shakespeare's play. The merger of authors and texts is wonderfully demonstrated by Gower's sixth chorus (5.0), which is thematically linked to Wilkins's octosyllabic lines extolling Marina's talents above those of her envious companion in Chorus 4:

> Be't when she weaved the sleided silk
> With fingers long, small, white as milk;
> Or when she would with sharp needle wound
> The cambric, which she made more sound
> By hurting it; or when to the lute
> She sung, and made the night-bird mute,
> That still records with moan; or when
> She would with rich and constant pen
> Vail to her mistress Dian; still
> This Philoten contends in skill
> With absolute Marina.
>
> (4.0.21–31)

Shakespeare takes the occasion to outdo Wilkins when the accomplished 'modern' poet Gower celebrates Marina's creative dexterity. The chorus is presented in alternately rhymed iambic pentameter lines, creating implied quatrains:

> Marina thus the brothel scapes, and chances
> Into an honest house, our story says,
> She sings like one immortal and she dances

[52] Tradescant, *Musaeum Tradescantianum*, 54, lists letter cases made of copper and "rinds of trees and grasses."

[53] Lake, "Rhymes in *Pericles*," argues, based on nasal assonances, that Wilkins is entirely responsible for Gower's Chorus 7 (5.2).

As goddess-like to her admired lays.
Deep clerks she dumbs; with her nee'le [she] composes
Nature's own shape of bud, bird, branch or berry
That even her art sisters the natural roses.
Her inkle, silk, twin with the rubied cherry.

(5.0.1–8)

In Shakespeare's handling, the intricacy of the poetic form parallels Marina's virtuosity in representing nature's beauty. The intertwining of rhyming lines mirrors the artful interlacing crafted by Marina's needle. In these metapoetic lines, Gower and Shakespeare collaborate as coauthors, "making" and controlling nature with a secret art. Yet Marina does so as well: as nature's twin sisters, Marina's compositions take part in the wondrous conflations of artistic and natural virtuosities at which cabinets – and poetry – excel.[54] Coauthors multiply in the chorus – Wilkins and Shakespeare, Gower and Marina – one embedded in the next like nesting dolls.

As Shakespeare plays with his collaborators' meters, he advances a poet of his own making, Marina. The exchange and transformation between the cocreators of *Pericles* take place in the shadow of a monument. In the second episode of mistaken death and burial in *Pericles*, Shakespeare meditates on the distance between "the real olde usance" (*Confessio Amantis*, 8:1522) and the ripeness of later wits – that is, between Gower's authorship and his own – while at the same time interrogating liturgical and theatrical performances of remembrance. Marina's cenotaph at Tarsus is spectacularly displayed within the first of Gower's choruses performed entirely in iambic verse. The poetic form blends modernity and memory: as Marina is mourned in the obsolete dramatic device of the dumb show, Gower's authorship becomes the main subject of the chorus. Gower asserts his creative power to control time, space, and scene: "Thus time we waste and long leagues make short . . . / Making to take our imagination / From bourn to bourn, region to region" (4.4.1–4). He calls attention to the theater as a space of seeming rather than being, where mere motes and shadows, more ghostly than Gower himself, perform.[55] The chorus implicates both the spectacle of Marina's false tomb and the dumb show in

[54] See Chapter 4 for discussion.

[55] See Mayer, *Shakespeare's Hybrid Faith*, who associates this phrase with ghosts, thus locating theatricality within Reformation debates about images and the disappearance of Purgatory. Thus the question of where Gower's spirit (like that of Hamlet's father) has come from is a point of contact between Gower's Catholic intercessory machinery and the hybrid rituals of remembrance performed in *Pericles*.

which it appears, arguing the utter dependence of vision on the narrator who "stands i' th' gaps to teach you / The stages of our story" (4.4.8–9). This instruction involves Gower's reading of another occluded text, like those extrapolated from the two dumb shows preceding. Here Gower, "the master of epitaphs," supplies Dionyza's epitaph, a text whose instability troubles the spectacle and its memorial reconstruction:

> The fairest, sweetest and best lies here,
> Who withered in her spring of year:
> She was of Tyrus the King's daughter,
> On whom foul death hath made this slaughter.
> Marina was she called, and at her birth
> Thetis being proud swallowed some part o' th' earth.
> Therefore the earth, fearing to be o'erflowed,
> Hath Thetis's birth-child on the heavens bestowed;
> Wherefore she does, and swears, she'll never stint,
> Make raging battery upon shores of flint.
>
> (4.4.34–43)

The object of much critical debate, the epitaph appears profoundly flawed: Thetis the sea nymph is confused with Tethys, wife of Oceanus; the imagery of the flood switches between the figurative and apparently literal; and the verse form, too, begins with Gower's tetrameters and switches to pentameter after line four. At the same time, however, the poem resonates with Marina's elemental affiliation with water and continues the play's engagement with the flood of Genesis. Most compelling, perhaps, is the failure of the proposed alternative to satisfy the genre's purpose; to confirm identity and ensure memory. Eliding Marina's identification as "of Tyrus the King's daughter" (4.4.36), the Oxford editors replace the last eight lines of the epitaph with a simpler couplet printed in Wilkins's *Painfull Adventures*:

> The fairest, chastest, and most best lies here,
> Who withered in her spring of year:
> In nature's garden, though by growth a bud,
> She was the chiefest flower: she was good.[56]

Unaccompanied by either an effigy or a name, the epitaph creates an unstable monument, one of the impermanent memorials that permeate the world of *Pericles*. Shakespeare enhances the uncertainty of commemoration when he departs from his source, confining Marina's memorial to

[56] Warren, in Shakespeare and Wilkins, *Pericles, Prince of Tyre*, ed. Warren, scene 18, lines 34–7.

text without the aid of an image: in *Confessio Amantis*, by contrast, Gower tell us that "After the real olde usance, / A tumbe . . . With an ymage unto hir liche / Liggende above therupon / Thei made" (8:1522–30). The anonymous monument – appropriately, a cenotaph – repeats the anonymity of the unburied suitors at Antioch. There is no body here.

If surgical corrections of the epitaph respond to the errors of memorial reconstruction, however, the generative, inventive capacity of memorial reconstruction as a poetic device is also demonstrated in this scene. The imagery of the longer epitaph resonates with that of "several of Shakespeare's Sonnets,"[57] drawing ancient Gower more firmly into the contemporary coterie surrounding Shakespeare. Although the shift in meter from octosyllabic to decasyllabic verse in the fourth line "may indicate textual revision or confusion," it fits cleverly with Shakespeare's larger strategy of manipulating the meters of Gower's choral performances to align the two poets and their projects more closely.[58] Performed first in Gower's archaic meter and then in more modern feet, the epitaph exemplifies the polytemporality of the poet's presence in *Pericles*: his reincarnation in the play not as an antique rarity but as a vital coauthor and collaborator.

Chorus 5 and its deceptive display of Marina's cenotaph argue the need for narrative gloss to mediate "foul show." From this moment forward, however, Gower's moral, memorial poetry is appropriated by Marina; a sojourner, like Gower, who carries the poet's commemorative script into performance. A "maker" herself – composer of "admired lays" and embroidered textualities that blend art and nature – Marina, like Gower, passes through the action primarily as a container of memory and narrative. She embodies the inner coherence of the self that Amans retrieves in the confessional performance of *Confessio Amantis*, and she allows Pericles to repeat Amans's restorative voyage. This fresh new seafarer is a monument in motion, entombed neither in the cenotaph nor in the confines of Gower's ancient book.

3 Absolute Marina

In *Pericles*, metrical variations enable the intricate intertwining of poetic voices. Poetic form moves internally between individual poets and their thoughts, and externally between the poet and the world. In a play that exploits poetry's processual, kinetic figure, metrical feet move across the

[57] Gossett, in Shakespeare and Wilkins, *Pericles*, 345n43.
[58] Gossett, in Shakespeare and Wilkins, *Pericles*, 344–5n34–43.

spaces between sensation and thought, reconciling ear and eye by aligning the senses with the author's expression and intent. Poetry's words and measures are enmeshed in networks of inscriptions, revisions, rehearsals, and meanings – within both discrete parcels of verse and their inclusions in the unfolding romance plot.

Marina is a poet of process. Her Word – tinged with traces of confession and penance yet pivoting toward marvelous novelty – shares the hybridity and intertwining of its twin fathers: "But to have divinity preached there," a patron of the brothel muses, "did you ever dream of such a thing?" (4.5.4–5). She is a pre-confessional saint in the brothel and a post-confessional voyager; a nomadic poet tracing and creating the expansive imaginative map of the play's far-flung shores. For Marina, reconciliation is a collective project achieved by convening a body of believers in the kinship of a family or a church: shared belief in the wonder of the tale.

Like Gower, Marina rehearses a twice-told tale. If Amans is the penitential double of the poet "John Gower," Marina's confessional poetry, similarly, tells the story of her life. She is a self-authoring subject, one brought into being through a continuous process of "autopoiesis or self-styling," to adapt Braidotti's terms, as she navigates the threatening straits, literal and figurative, through which she passes.[59] Marina's intertextual performances involve her in processes of creation by compilation, where fragments of other texts, bodies, and sites are recollected and worked into a new fabric; she embodies the creative process of *Pericles* itself. As a "piece" of her mother, Marina carries the fleshly trace of a commemorative bond. Pericles describes her "eyes as jewel-like / And cased as richly" (5.1.101–2), renewing Cerimon's figure of Thaisa's eyelids as caskets containing jewels. Yet Marina's legacy is one of movement rather than stasis: while Thaisa, released from her coffin, is an object passively "placed" by Cerimon in the tomb-like temple of Diana (5.3.67), Marina resumes her seafaring in the "lasting storm" that is her life (4.1.18).[60]

Marina's generative, interrelational self-styling is figured in her entry into the play. As she strews flowers on Lychorida's grave, she crafts an ephemeral monument – a textuality that lies "as a carpet" on the grass (4.1.18) – but one that rejuvenates the unstable monuments strewn across the play. The image returns to and expands Marina's earlier virtuosity in needlework whose flora and fauna "twin" nature's artistry. Here, the affinity between the girl born of and named for the sea and the natural

[59] Braidotti, *Posthuman*, 30.
[60] For a more productive view of Ephesus, see Hart, "'Great Is Diana.'"

landscape of remembrance characterizes Marina's nomadic journey as one that charts the multiple relations in which embodied subjects are embedded – indeed, in *Pericles*, the currents in which they are engulfed. She plots an evolving, creative intertwining with the creatures and environments of a plentiful world. Thus Marina's repetition of her story to Leonine is an exercise in intertextuality. She cites Lychorida as the source for her small epic, Marina's "Iliad in a nut":[61]

> When I was born the wind was north . . .
> My father, as nurse says, did never fear
> But cried, 'Good seamen!' to the sailors,
> Galling his kingly hands with haling ropes
> And clasping to the mast endured a sea
> That almost burst the deck.
>
> (4.1.47–55)

In the fantastic dimensions of her tale – we may hear a note of incredulity in Leonine's question, "When was this?" (4.1.56) – Marina's self-authorship shares the creative and recreative processes of Cerimon's closet, where mysteries and their stories produce and preserve wonder. Marina's self-conscious honing of her wondrous tale continues in her encounter with Pericles at the play's close. "If I should tell / My history," she begins, "it would seem like lies / Disdained in the reporting" (5.1.107–9). And she goes on to spin her narrative from the threads left loose by other narrators: "My mother was the daughter of a king," she tells him, "Who died the minute I was born, / As my good nurse Lychorida hath oft / Delivered weeping" (5.1.148–51). This self-authored rarity, as we might expect, is herself the object of "general wonder" (4.0.11), a maid "gazed on like a comet" (5.3.80). As she co-opts and cleanses the brilliant transparency of Antiochus's daughter, a fair casket stored with ill, Marina also rewrites Wilkins's deadening riddle of incest – leaving behind its wooden octosyllabics as well – with an incarnational riddle of creation and renewal: she is "not of any shores," she claims, "Yet I was mortally brought forth and am / No other than I appear" (5.1.102).

Marina's self-authorship as she moves through the scattered sites of the play's alien nations responds to Gower's unsettled, liminal positionality. Both of these poets are travelers before whose feet borders seem to dissolve. They are both free from the limits of time and place. They are entombed – in the grave, or the brothel, or the pirate's hold – yet elude

[61] See Roychoudhury, "Mental Tempests," 1014, on Marina's "personal mythology of sea birth."

confinement. Indeed, all of the graves of *Pericles* are cenotaphs. From the sedimentary remains of Wilkins's Gower, Shakespeare creates a memorial poet whose kinetic self-crafting gives shape to the whirling world of romance. Memory, for Marina, enables "nomadic transpositions," in Braidotti's term – a creative and critical interweaving of the complex, diverse entities populating the sites through which she passes and with whom she is, momentarily, enmeshed.[62]

If Marina embodies the generative and transformational nature of memory, she ensures the wonder of her tale through the depth and breadth of her imagination. The expansiveness of her imagery mirrors the expansiveness of the plot she navigates. Her wish "that these / Pirates . . . had but o'erboard thrown me / For to seek my mother" (4.2.59–61) imagines the sea as a space where lost relations might fortuitously be found.[63] Marina's figurations in the brothel divide and finally dissolve (for herself, at least, if not for her coinhabitants) the structure whose "very doors and windows savour vilely" (4.5.114–5). Her sermons convert customers, most importantly Lysimachus. The governor initially misreads Marina as a "creature of sale" defined by her position, but he is "altered" (4.5.109) by Marina's self-recollection that culminates in a flight of fancy:

> For me
> That am a maid, though most ungentle Fortune
> Have placed me in this sty, where since I came
> Diseases have been sold dearer than physic—
> O, that the gods
> Would set me free form this unhallowed place,
> Though they did change me to the meanest bird
> That flies i' th' purer air!
>
> (4.5.100–107)

Transformed by Marina's ascendant desire, Lysimachus is also converted from prose to poetry, a formal reflection of Marina's debasement in the brothel and the transcendence imagined in her figure of a bird rising into purer air.[64]

Marina's self-branding as a rarity by means of a miraculous tale displaces Gower's poetic sovereignty over the world of *Pericles*, placing the memorial

[62] Braidotti, *Transpositions*.

[63] Dean, "Pericles's Pilgrimage," 135–6, argues that Shakespeare's Marina is in part based upon St. Margaret of Antioch, who was also known as St. Marina.

[64] The scene's use of verse at this conversionary moment recalls Spenser's *ars poetica* in *Shepheardes Calender*, "October": "O pierless Poesye, where is thy place? / . . . Then make thee winges of thine aspyring wit, / And, whence thou camst, flye backe to heaven apace," (lines 79 and 83–4).

reconstruction of narrative within the action rather than framing it. She is a narrator whose tale-telling itself cures and restores, calling the listener to self-remembrance. Her skill is that advocated by Diana in her miraculous appearance to Pericles: "Reveal how thou at sea didst lose thy wife . . . And give them repetition to the life" (4.1.240–2). The recollection of his story at Ephesus, enabled by Marina's clear remembrance, further prompts Pericles to demand from Thaisa "Can you remember what I called the man?" and her correct recollection is "still confirmation" of "this great miracle" (5.3.52–55, 59), a tale which "would seem like lies." When she assumes the effigial role of "Patience gazing on kings' graves," Marina is a monumental and memorial writer. In self-styling throughout the last acts of *Pericles*, she writes her own epitaph, replacing Dionyza's foul show and joining loose ends of the interlaced plot in a skillful needlework that creates and preserves the wondrous ties that bind. A remembrancer enmeshed in the animate world of *Pericles*, Marina's life story argues that, in Braidotti's astute phrase, "Life as virtual suicide is life as constant creation."[65]

If Marina's virtuosity leads to the play's resolution, though, the outcome is marked by mortuary images that stage the family romance as a post-mortem: "O, come," Pericles encourages the recovered Thaisa, "be buried / A second time within these arms," and Marina crafts the jarring trans-plantational image, "My heart / Leaps to be gone into my mother's bosom" (5.3.43–5). In the temple of Diana, the women of *Pericles* seem to face a future of reinterment. It remains for Gower to renew the moral of the story in the play's closing couplet: "So on your patience evermore attending, / New joy wait on you. Here our play has ending" (Epilogue 17–18). In Gower's incantation, the patience inscribed within Marina's effigy and the joy with which Pericles and Thaisa are reunited extend past the embedded action and move outside the frame to the audience beyond. Neither Gower nor the flickering, theatrical shadows he has convened face a permanent grave. Provisionally entombed in porous monuments, "out of act," the quiet dead of *Pericles*, like costumes and props returned to the theatrical trunk, wait patiently for the next performance, the next reincarnation, the resurrection to come.

A Bok for Engelondes Sake

Beginning his *Confessio Amantis*, Gower asserts the monumental and commemorative functions of writing:

[65] Braidotti, *Posthuman*, 97.

Of hem that writen ous tofore
The bokes duelle, and we therfore
Ben tawht of that was write tho:
Forthi good is that we also
In oure tyme among ous hiere
Do wryte of newe som matiere,
Essampled of these olde wyse
So that it myhte in such a wyse,
Whan we ben dede and elleswhere,
Beleve to the worldes eere
In tyme comende after this.
(Pro. i.1–11)

The dead, residing "elleswhere," survive through the books that continue to "duelle" among the living. Past things "beleve" – in the Middle English sense, to remain, to survive – in the ears of future generations.[66] Gower the relict, the survivor, is the author of a book made, he claims "for Engelondes sake, / The yer sextenthe of kyng Richard" (Pro. i.24–25). Commissioned by a king whose reign would end in deposition, Gower's book registers the insecurity of future events, political and poetic:

What schal befalle hierafterward
God wot, for now upon this tyde
Men se the world on every syde
In sondry wyse so diversed,
That it welnyh stant al reversed.
(Pro. i.26–30)

The uncertainty of the "tyde" – the oceanic ebb and flow of the times on which *Confessio Amantis* launches forth – will be realized in the Lancastrian revision that removes all references to Richard during the ascendency of Henry Bulingbrook. In the shifting allegiances of its paratexts, Gower's poem is "a book of all that monarchs do" (*Pericles*, 1.1.95).[67]

The unpredictable seascape traversed by Gower's book is spatial and temporal. Compiling ancient, alien stories into his "newe" English work, *Confessio Amantis* charts the passages between past and present; old stories and new; "diversed" worlds and selves; confessional and cultural reversals and renewals. The seascape of romance in *Pericles* follows a similarly diverse course, wandering liberally through a pre-Christian world ruled by Diana; a Pauline cartography of the primitive Christian church; Old

[66] See Glossary, in Gower, *Confessio Amantis*, vol. III, 566.
[67] See Gower, *Complete Works*, vol. II, xxi-xviii, on the date and circumstances of Gower's writing *Confessio Amantis* and the changes made in light of the ascension of Bulingbrook as Henry IV.

Testament typologies; Catholic saints; and Roman lamps lighting an absent tomb.[68] The storm assaulting Pericles is "a tempest which his mortal vessel tears" (4.4.30); a shipwreck that threatens to drown him, "yet he bears it out" (4.4.31). Pericles sets sail for the sake of his country, having "scaped the land to perish at the seas" (1.3.28), and his recovery forever forestalls his journey home. He will rule in Pentapolis, and his son-in-law in Tyre. The ship's cabin, the depths of the hold, the modest vessels cut adrift – these are the most resoundingly fragile and fluid of monuments in the world of *Pericles*. In recording their voyages, Shakespeare and Wilkins draw upon a swirling pool of past stories to tell their tale anew.

For John Tradescant the elder, the return voyage from Archangel as a member of Sir Dudley Digges's "Viag of Ambusad" in 1618 was governed by fair and foul winds, good and ill fortune, fair sailing and violent tempests that provoked the terror of perishing at sea:

> On Friday morning being the 23 of August the wind came fayre to the Northeast . . . On Satterday midnight the wind changed East & so continewed all that day with a great storme . . . That [Sunday] night & Mu[n] day we had a marvelus great storme that put us to leeward . . . On Thursday mornyng being x of September, thanks be to God, the wind cam to West Norwest . . . On Tewsday the 22 [September] we landed at Saynt Katherins neer London whear, God be thanked, we ended our viage having no one man sick, God be thanked.[69]

Tradescant's litany of changing winds shares with *Pericles* and its poets the romance of travel and the horror of "lay[ing] . . . in ships' wooden sepulchres," the vagaries of fortune that lead to new discoveries and return the seafarer and his collected treasures, miraculously, back to native shores.[70] In Tradescants' Ark, natural and artificial rarities strove to surpass each other in wonder, and the landscape was remade by "Out-landish Fruits" transplanted from overseas to beautify England's gardens. This ingenious project, "Making man a god," reached wide to gather, domesticate, and preserve a world of wonders.

While the collector exercised power over the life and death of curiosities in his cabinet, his omnipotence did not extend beyond that marvelous box. When John Tradescant III died at the age of 19, the future of the Ark was in peril. Although his sister Frances survived, the prospect of bequeathing

[68] Gossett, in Shakespeare and Wilkins, *Pericles*, 285–6n62.

[69] Bod Ashmole MS 824, fols. 181^r–2^r.

[70] Donne, "Satire III," in *Complete English Poems*, lines 17–18. See Schoulson, *Fictions of Conversion*, 6–10, for a reading of Donne's poem (which bears the manuscript title "Of Religion") as registering the instability of the post-Reformation's culture of religious change.

her father's and grandfather's remarkable legacy to this sole, female heir seemed, for reasons unknown, likely to doom the collection to drowning in oblivion.[71] The shifting seas on which the passage of property to the female heir inevitably embarked caused the Ark to change course, finally to lay the foundation for one of the nation's foremost cultural monuments, the Ashmolean.

Like the collector, voyager, and tale-teller Tradescant, the poets of *Pericles* – Gower and Cerimon, Shakespeare and Marina – preserve the stories of their passages and convey the rarities recovered from remote places and times to refashion and recreate their native shores, imprinted with the traces of their passing feet. Their fantastic voyages and recoveries return England to itself. This book made for England's sake imagines a world newly transformed by the poetry of wondrous rebirth, by the power of remembrance to awaken the dead.

[71] See Leith-Ross, *John Tradescants*, 137–40.

CHAPTER 6

"Chain'd up in Alabaster"
Awakening Remembrance in The Winter's Tale *and* Comus

Here lies the envy'd, yet unparalell'd Prince,
Whose living vertues speak (though dead long since)
If many worlds, as that fantastick framed,
In every one, be her great glory famed.
1643.

– Anne Bradstreet[1]

Not so diligently is Ceres ... said to have sought her daughter Proserpina, as I seek for this idea of the beautiful, as if for some glorious image, through all the shapes and forms of things (for many are the shapes of things divine): day and night I search and follow its lead eagerly.

– John Milton[2]

Calling Shapes and Beckning Shadows

In John Milton's *Maske Presented at Ludlow Castle, 1634*, two brothers, "without blame / Or our neglect," they maintain, lose their sister in the woods, leaving her, if not vulnerable, then "unowned."[3] In the Lady's absence, they reassure themselves that her "hidden strength," her Chastity,

[1] Bradstreet, "In Honour of that High and Mighty Princess, Queen Elizabeth, of Most Happy Memory," in *Tenth Muse*, 203.

[2] Milton, *Complete Prose Works*, vol. I, 326–7. I am indebted to Martin, "Non-Puritan Ethics," 215, for bringing this passage to my attention.

[3] Milton, *A Maske* (1645), in *Complete Works*, line 407. The masque survives in two manuscripts and three printed versions: the Trinity manuscript (Trinity College, Cambridge, MS R. 34) represents Milton's autograph composition and revisions of the work before its first publication (by Henry Lawes) in 1637 and subsequent printings in the 1645 and 1673 *Poems*. The Bridgewater Manuscript (BL Loan MS 76) is a copy (possibly by Lawes) of the masque as it was performed in 1634, with numerous changes and omissions from Milton's Trinity version. The 1637 printing of the masque returned to the order of Milton's holograph manuscript, restored deleted passages, removed some lines, and added new material. Subsequent printed volumes are close to the 1637. Both manuscripts are transcribed and printed in Milton, *Complete Works* (Trinity, 300–331; and Bridgewater, 332–60). For good critical commentary on the various versions, see Evans and Fishman, *Miltonic*

will preserve her and render her unassailable. "A thousand liveried Angels lacky her," the Elder Brother asserts, who cast the beam of "solemn vision" on her outward shape and turn "the unpolluted temple of the mind" toward "the souls essence, / Till all be made immortal" (455–62). Lust, however – the "defilement" of a woman's "inward parts" – has the opposite, mortal outcome: "The soul grows clotted with contagion, / Imbodies, and imbrutes till she quite loose / The divine property of her first being" (466–9). There follows a remarkable vision of these "imbruted" female souls whose embodiment of sin is apparent in their refusal to accept the modest disembodiment of death:[4]

> Such are those thick and gloomy shadows damp
> Oft seen in Charnell vaults and Sepulchers
> Lingering, and sitting by a new made grave,
> As loath to leave the body that it lov'd,
> And link't it self by carnal sensuality
> To a degenerate and degraded state.
>
> (470–5)

Wedded to the body, these unchaste shadows haunt the tombs where their remains lie decaying, swayed by a "carnal sensuality" that denies the spiritual longing that is a prerequisite to salvation. Trapped in the threshold between body and spirit, these shapes are "weighed down" and "dragged back into the visible world," by the corporeal, which, as Milton's source, Plato's *Phaedo*, explains, "is burdensome and heavy and earthly and visible."[5] They are spectral doubles of the marble effigies they attend, yet textured like them, thick and damp. When Milton's Second Brother responds with delight at his brother's ghost story, he uses a pun that links the petrifying logic implicit in this dualistic view of female corporeality with the paralyzing magic of the necromancer, Comus: "How charming is divine Philosophy!" (476).

In the "blind mazes" of the same "tangl'd Wood" (181), where "A thousand fantasies / Begin to throng into [her] memory / Of calling shapes and beckning shadows dire" (205–207), the unowned Lady is suspended in a similar living death. "Set in an inchanted Chair" (656 s. d.), "In stony

Moment, 39–70; Brown, *John Milton's Aristocratic Entertainments*, 132–52 and 171–8; and Marcus, "John Milton's *Comus*."

[4] In the Trinity Manuscript, "sepulchers" replaces the half-written "~~monume~~," a telling revision that may suggest Milton's awareness, if not endorsement, of the Puritan association of monuments with corrupt matter.

[5] Plato, *Phaedo*, in Plato, *Euthyphro, Apology, Crito, Phaedo, Phaedrus*, 81c–81d. See Savage, "*Comus* and its Traditions."

fetters fixt and motionless" (819), she firmly resists the temptation of the sorcerer's charmed cup. The Lady, like the embodied shadows haunting her brothers' imagined sepulchers, lingers between spirit and matter; she is a demi-effigy, threatened with permanent entombment: "If but I wave this wand," Comus warns, "Your nervs are all chain'd up in Alabaster, / And you a statue; or as Daphne was / Root-bound, that fled Apollo" (659–62). Yet if the exchange between her brothers elevates divine philosophy, men's intellectual stronghold, over the embodied sexuality (pure or impure) that defines the feminine, the Lady's career in Comus's enchanted chair seems to script instead a reconciliation of mind and matter within a (temporarily) "unowned," self-authored female body. While her "corporal rinde" is "immanacled," the "freedome of [her] minde" remains her own (663–4). In her temperate resolve, the Lady is a *donna petrosa.*

This chapter takes the blending of word and image in church monuments as a starting point for exploring figures of "marmorization" – bodies comingled with, turned into, or experienced as stone – in Shakespeare's *The Winter's Tale* and in Milton's *Maske Presented at Ludlow Castle, 1634.*[6] As matter wedded to the body and its unique site of interment, funeral monuments and their texts are validated and authorized by proximity, an assurance expressed in the ubiquitous guarantee, "here lies." Yet the unstable and vulnerable matter of post-Reformation monuments and the loss of traditional rituals of remembrance undermined this faith in presence as a guarantor of the mnemonic efficacy and effectiveness – the truth value – of commemoration. In a poetics of proximity commonly adopted in printed epitaphs in the period, for instance, the author insists, often falsely, upon the physical space of interment as the situation of the poem. Anne Bradstreet, writing in New England forty years after the death of Queen Elizabeth I, nonetheless ends her elegy for the queen with two epitaphs that erect a textual monument recalling and replacing the distant chapel in Westminster Abbey.[7] In imitation of Cyriac of Ancona's collections of classical inscriptions, Giovanni Gioviana Pontano's *De tumulis*, one of the earliest printed anthologies of contemporary epitaphs, creates a textual gallery where the reader moves from one monument to the next.[8] A century later, William Camden's visitor's guide to the tombs of Westminster Abbey typifies the

[6] I adapt this geological term for the transformation of limestone into marble (see *OED*) as a figuration of the blending of flesh and stone.

[7] Bradstreet, "In Honour of that High and Mighty Princess, Queen Elizabeth," 203.

[8] Pontano, *De tumulis, in Opera* (1505).

genre in British antiquarianism, where the fluid relationship between "literary" epitaphs and "authentic" ones is adapted to preserve vulnerable stone monuments and their inscriptions.[9] This fluidity often makes it impossible to determine the factual or fictional provenance of printed epitaphs: thus Camden's *Remains* concludes a chorographic collection of inscriptions with a series of poems chosen "to shew the fertility of our modern wits." Some, clearly were never intended for monumental inscription; some are linked to specific sites; but most, including a Latin "epitaphium" for Jane Paulet, Marchioness of Winchester, may or may not have appeared on vanished monuments.[10]

At the heart of the "pseudo-inscriptional epitaph"[11] is the real or threatened absence of a permanent memorial; an absence, I argue, that is deeply involved with seismic changes in beliefs and literacies in the post-Reformation moment. Margaret W. Ferguson describes the "shifting and plural phenomenon" of literacy as a site of social performance and contest "surrounded and often constituted by interesting lies, as well as by highly interested constructions of evidence on the part of writers from various historical eras including our own."[12] The poetics of proximity embodies and interrogates the "interesting lies" of authorship and readership, where *deixis* – the lie of "here lies" – reminds us of the absent ritual, object, or text; the truth that is no longer, or never was, there. The anonymous epitaph "made" at the sea burial of Sir Francis Drake wittily exposes this buried truth: "On whom an epitaph none can truly make, / For who can say 'Here lies Sir Francis Drake.'"[13] At the same time, pseudo-inscriptional epitaphs often index more ephemeral textual performances and improvisational rituals of remembrance, conferring the permanence of print on epitaphs pinned to the pall of the deceased, recited at the funeral, or posted near the site of interment. John Eliot's epitaph for the Marchioness of Winchester commemorates the transformational moment

[9] Camden, *Reges, Reginæ* (1600). Enlarged editions were printed in 1603 and 1606. And see Guthke, "Talking Stones," 27.

[10] Camden, *Remains*, 413 and 415. This fifth edition, continued by John Philipot, also prints Camden's essay "Of Epitaphs," 360–5. Basing House, where Jane Paulet died, was under siege during the Civil War and the monuments in the church severely damaged: see Victoria County History, *Hampshire*, vol. IV, 115–27.

[11] Scodel, *English Poetic Epitaph*, 88. See also 86–101 for Scodel's useful commentary on the genre.

[12] Ferguson, *Dido's Daughters*, 3, 7, and 10. I am indebted to this excellent and provocative exploration of literacy as imbricated with gender and political change. I consider the shift in beliefs from the old religion to the new as akin to the rise and fall of empires which, as Ferguson argues, prompt pressing renegotiations among competing literacies: see 31–82.

[13] Herbert, *Witts Recreation*, sig. Bb5^{r}.

in which religious ritual is displace by literate performance when he compares "The blots of Inck that from my pen do fall" to "hired mourners, at a Funerall." "Let others then sad *Epitaphs* invent / And paste them up about thy moniment," Eliot insists, "I see one writ in every Readers Eye."[14]

This chapter argues that the spatial and temporal migrations of remembrance from place to print involve exchanges between subjects and objects that take shape in Shakespeare's and Milton's hybrid, marmoreal female figures.[15] What is remembered in the poetics of proximity are liturgical and improvisational rituals of remembrance that have been transformed by the changing literacies attending the ascendency of print. Bodies that blend flesh and stone offer succinct figurations of this transformational work. As they anticipate effigies enlivened and set free by an awakening word, they register the complexities of the unions of subjects and objects, mind and matter, and truth and falsehood in the exodus of cultural memory from place to print.

As gendered beings, moreover, these figures allow us to interrogate the processes by which subjects come into being in their intertwining with matter. The hybrid figures examined in this chapter invite us to approach the abstract idea of the gendered subject in materials that visualize relationships of interiority and exteriority, mind and body, and self and world. Set in the notional threshold between the phenomenal and ethereal, monuments conjure subjects on the verge of matter. While the marmoreal forms examined here affirm materiality, they also insist that the body is never simply object or subject, but an instrument through which the world of objects is perceived and the means by which subjects become self-aware and self-authoring. Accordingly, this chapter is hybrid in its methodology, situating these complex female figures contextually in relation to the changing field of literacy, and also offering a corporeal feminist view of these women as both material ("imbodied") and nonessential ("unowned") subjects.

Section 1 of this chapter reads the epitaphs of two monuments erected for Blanche Parry, and the occluded epitaphs of Shakespeare's *Winter's Tale* as works that share the fluidity between truth and fiction attending

[14] Eliot, "An Elogie," in *Poems*, 39. Edward Hoby's Latin eulogy for his stepfather Lord John Russell is noted in his commonplace book as having been pinned to the pall during the funeral in 1584. It was later inscribed on Russell's monument in Westminster Abbey. See Add MS 38823, fol. 48^{r}. On the custom's transatlantic migration, see Hammond, *American Puritan Elegy*, 11–41.

[15] Scodel, *English Poetic Epitaph*, 88, notes that "the epitaph is part of a spatial monument, the elegy of a temporal ritual."

the movement of memory from place to text. In a remote parish church, Parry erected a monument to herself and her sovereign, Elizabeth, but she was ultimately buried in a tomb commissioned by her nephew in St. Margaret's Westminster, where her memory is contained by orthodox social and religious norms. By defining her cenotaph spatially rather than temporally, Parry creates a productive, imaginative memorial to herself and her monarch that maps corporeal enclosure – not entombment but virginity – onto the monumental form. In doing so, Parry evades the oppressive gendering of the Westminster tomb. I follow this oscillation between self-authorship and subordination into Paulina's recreation of her sovereign, Hermione, in Shakespeare's *Winter's Tale*, reading the play's suppression of epitaphic sources as central to the crisis of belief that precipitates tragedy, and to the reparative comedy of Hermione's reanimation. Shakespeare grounds this wondrous awakening on two unspoken epitaphs, indexed but absent texts – like Mamillius's winter's tale itself – in order to stage not the "triumph of time," but time's surrender to place, when the long histories of Paulina's recollection and Hermione's silent interment give way to a spectacle at whose evidentiary center is an empty grave that only faith can fill.

Section 2 follows Mamillius's ghost story into those of Milton's *Maske* by way of two of Milton's youthful epitaphs. In these poems, Milton deploys images of marmorization to figure the stasis of embodied performance – both masque and graveside remembrance – set against the disembodied freedom of print as the young poet crafts a career in the public eye. This authorial awakening continues in *Comus*, where the Lady's stasis mirrors that of the apprentice poet, "the Lady of Christ's."[16] Although the fluid genius of the Severn, Sabrina, releases both the Lady and Milton from entanglement in matter, the unowned women of *A Maske* are ultimately calcified and coopted in a printed "drama of authorship" that transmutes their productive matter into the materiality of the book.[17]

Section 3 considers a generative, positive materiality that is Sabrina's legacy as realized in the commemorative afterlives of Alice Egerton and her grandmother, Alice Spencer, Countess of Derby. The texts and imagery of Spencer's self-authored monument exploit "interesting lies" to argue that the generative potential of women's bodies lies not in reproduction but in their capacity for creative self-styling and collective self-definition. Joining

[16] See *ODNB*. On the identification of Milton as or with the Lady, see especially Shuger, "Gums of Glutinous Heat"; and Shullenberger, *Lady in the Labyrinth*, 203–25.

[17] Coiro, "Anonymous Milton," 625.

the monumental circle of her female kin, Alice Egerton becomes a figure of plural literacies who combines body and text, a living embodiment of the fluid corporeality imagined in Milton's Sabrina.

Chapter 2 of this book associated the bequests of Elizabeth Harington Montagu with the manuscript miscellanies that passed through the hands of members of the Montagu circle, arguing that both of these practices and the artifacts associated with them constitute rituals of remembrance in their own right. The commemorative acts of reading and writing in this monumental circle displace traditional, pre-Reformation forms of remembrance with a materiality rooted not at the graveside but in the literate practice of descendants and the presence evoked by the commemorative token, the book.[18] Understanding manuscript circulation as a form of publication, this discussion interrogates the relationships between the performances of social theater and textual forms that move beyond the immediacy of these embodied practices and sites to engage wider literate audiences. Thus I am concerned with printed books that rely upon repeated acts of reading to instantiate presence, books that see both sculptural monuments and manuscripts as ephemeral, vulnerable forms. While I sketch the migration of Milton's early works from manuscript circulation to print as a vocational choice, I do not wish to suggest that the two modes of publication were exclusive.[19] Rather, I am interested in the losses attending these ephemeral forms. On this shifting ground of literate practice, what lies behind the text is not the body but its absence; the disappeared monument, the lost manuscript; the lapses of memory that printed texts pretend to repair. In Milton's *Maske*, for instance, the "calling shapes and beckning shadows" that thrust rudely into the Lady's memory transcribe a performance that did not happen: the lines were excised from the script, now the Bridgewater Manuscript, when the masque was presented on Michaelmas, 1634. When Milton restores the passage in the printed edition of 1637, he creates a false memory to fill a gap in the embodied masque – a performance haunted by a ghostly manuscript that materializes in the printed memorial three years later. In the absence of the body, the interesting lies of literacy congregate, multiply, and live in perpetuity.

[18] See Williams, "Manuscript, Monument, Memory," for a related argument.
[19] See Ezell, *Social Authorship*.

1 The Spider and the Fly

On New Year's Day, 1575, Blanche Parry presented to Queen Elizabeth, "a flower of gold Enamuled greene, with three white roses, in either of them a sparcke of rubyes, and the midst thereof a flye."[20] This whimsical jewel joins the familiar red and white of the Tudor rose with an emblem of the parasitic royal court. Insects, less Machiavellian, also decorate an embroidered silk kirtle originating in Queen Elizabeth's wardrobe, worked by Parry, perhaps with the queen and ladies of the Privy Chamber (see Figure 6.1). To a professionally embroidered floral pattern, an assortment of insects has been added, alongside a creaturely menagerie and an occasional monster of the imagination.[21] After the removal of this royal memento from court to country, it was refashioned as an altar cloth and incorporated into the religious fabric of St. Faith's, Bacton. In this small Herefordshire church, Parry also installed a memorial window in stained glass and, twelve years before her death, erected her alabaster funeral monument (see Figure 6.2). All of these objects preserve Parry's service as the Chief Gentlewoman of the Privy Chamber and Keeper of the Queen's Jewels and Books for most of the monarch's reign. On the monument, Parry kneels before the sovereign, holding a small book in one hand while with the other she offers the queen a pomander, a jewel filled with scented resin and spices.[22] When Parry retired from her post in 1587, at the age of eighty, she prepared an inventory, "A Boke of soche Jewells . . . nowe in charge of Mrs. Blaunshe Parrey," listing 628 items, among them ten books with jeweled covers, sixteen "habiliments" decorated with jewels, over thirty "great chaynes" and "bracelettes of pomander," and "a chayne of gold containing . . . sixteen amber beades with flies in them, and small linkes of golde enamelled white and red betweene them."[23]

Parry's service placed her in especially intimate relationships with the people and holdings of Elizabeth's court, and these networks of relations are interwoven into the monuments attending her death. Although a will in the hand of William Cecil, Lord Burghley, written while Parry was gravely ill in 1578, directs that she should be buried in Bacton "in the tomb [she] had prepared," the monument is a cenotaph.[24] After a funeral

[20] Goldring, Archer, and Clarke, eds., *John Nichols's The Progresses . . . of Queen Elizabeth, Volume II*, 228.

[21] See Cust, "Queen's Kirtle."

[22] Bradford, *Blanche Parry*, 29, identifies the object as a pomander. In her final will, Parry gives "my beste Diamond" to the queen: see TNA PROB 11/75/180, fol. 124^{r}.

[23] BL Royal Addendum 68, fols. 10^{r}–12^{r}.

[24] BL Lansdowne 102/94; transcribed in Richardson, *Mistress Blanche*, 151–7, at 154.

Figure 6.1 Blanche Parry (attrib.), Altar cloth (detail) (c. 1570s). St. Faith's, Bacton. Author's photograph.

Figure 6.2 John Gildon (attrib.), Cenotaph of Blanche Parry (before 1578) (detail). St. Faith's, Bacton. Author's photograph.

Figure 6.3 Unknown artist, Monument for Blanche Parry (1595/6) (detail). St. Margaret's Westminster.

financed by the queen, Parry was interred in St. Margaret's, Westminster, where a second monument was commissioned by her nephew (see Figure 6.3). Enmeshing the subject in a web of meaningful objects, the monument commemorates Parry's royal service: two books lie on the table; Parry is dressed in the queen's livery; and brilliant ropes of jewelry are carved on the capitals of the framing pilasters. In St. Margaret's, Parry would be joined by her companions in the privy chamber – Margaret Radcliffe, for whom the queen erected a monument in 1599, and Dorothy Stafford, who survived her mistress by a year – creating the sacred space as a theater of social engagement and a collective memorial for the female monarch and her female court.

Parry's two monuments and their epitaphs employ competing languages to interpret her legacy, illustrating the involvement of women's bodies in the plurality and rivalry of post-Reformation cultural literacies. As her nephew's commission, Parry's Westminster monument plays out the processes by which women are essentialized and objectified as they enter orthodox social and spiritual networks. The epitaph written by her nephew is predictable and fixes Parry's temporal passage in the place of her interment. She was:

> beneficiall to her kinsfolke / and countrymen, charitable to the poore, insomuche that she gave to the poore of Bacton, /and Newton in Herefordshiere seaven score bushells of wheate and rye yerelie forever with / divers

> somes of money to Westminster and other places for good uses, she died a maide / in the eightee two yeres of her age the twelfe of Februarye 1589.

Parry's effigy, an object among others, materializes the virtues of the virginal body entombed beneath, but also turns virginity from enclosure and unproductivity toward nurture and fertility. Her maiden body is imagined as pure but porous: a passive tablet for the inscription of fidelity and chastity, but also a productive source from which charity pours forth.

If Parry's Westminster monument bases her biography on the presence and nature of the body entombed at the site, Parry's cenotaph in Bacton adorns an absence with a crafted narrative of feminine interrelationality and self-authorship. Representing not a single woman but two, the monument renders permanent a living relationship. Neither of the monument's subjects was, in fact, dead when the structure was erected.[25] Although the building of one's tomb in one's lifetime is a technicality for the post-Reformation faithful taught to "live to die," what is commemorated at Bacton is not death but the vibrant social fabric of the queen's female court, remembered in the productive display of its material remains.[26] With the altar cloth and stained glass window, the cenotaph forms a commemorative web that transforms the chapel into a gallery. In this reimagined space, Parry's monument to two maidens displays a self-created image of femininity, achieved by controlling, in death as in life, one's appearance and effects. As it embellishes Elizabeth's body, the monument gives shape to the social, sexual, and spiritual ties binding Parry's memory to her monarch's life. Conferring upon Elizabeth the royal treasures Parry safeguarded during her lifetime, representing the queen as Gloriana, Parry creates her own memory in this recreative act.[27] The Bacton cenotaph does not commemorate absence but is a perennial performance of presence enabled by its situation in a closed theatrical space on an empty stage. In this remote location – set in the Welsh Marches just west of the River Severn, where Parry had been born and raised in "a bilingual, cultured

[25] Parry's final will, TNA PROB 11/75/180, fol. 123^{v}, requests burial at St. Margaret's near her nephew John Vaughan "yf yt please god to call me neare London" Her burial at Bacton depended on whether the queen would predecease her, which may have necessitated Parry's relocation from court to country.

[26] The formulaic "live to die, die to live" is ubiquitous in the period: Walmsey, "'Live to die,'" 2, notes that it was "often engraved on mourning rings."

[27] Richardson, *Mistress Blanche*, 143–7, attributes the monument to John Gildon of Hereford, noting that Parry's is the first example of the iconography of the queen as Gloriana.

Welsh household" – the church becomes an unimaginable space of feminine self-creation and fellowship.[28]

The visual tissue of interrelations tying subject to monarch weaves verbally through Parry's self-authored epitaph. Elizabeth Hallam and Jenny Hockey argue that memorial inscriptions, bound to matter, are implicitly incomplete, since memorial writing "refers to the transformation from material body to spiritual entity – it instantiates difference, separation, and distance."[29] Refusing to look beyond the moment of death, Parry's epitaph resides wholly in lived time and secular space. It clings insistently to materiality, situating its speaker in relation to the female companion with whom she shared her life and continues to share the afterlife:

I · PARREHYS · DOUGHTER · BLAENCHE · OF · NEWE · COURTE · BORNE
THAT · TRAEYND · WAS · IN · PRYNCYS · COURTS · WYTHE · GORGIOUS · WYGHTS
WHEARE · FLEETYNGE · HONOR · SOUNDS · WYTHE · BLASTE · OF · HORNE
EACHE · OF · ACCOUNTE · TOO · PLACE · OF · WORLDS · DELYGHTS
AM · LODGYD · HEERE · WYTHE· IN · THYS · STONYE · TOOMBE
MY · HARPYNGER · YS · PAEDE · I · OWGHTE · OF · DUE
MY · FRYNDS · OF · SPEECHE · HEERE · IN · DOO · FYNDE · MEE · DOMBE
THE · WHCHE · IN · VAENE · THEY · DOO · SO · GREATLEY · RHUE

. . . .

I · LYVDE · ALLWEYS · AS · HANDMAEDE · TO · A · QUENE
IN · CHAMBER · CHIFF · MY · TYME · DYD · TOOVERPASSE
NOT · DOUBYINGE · WANTE · WHYLLSTE · THAT · MY · MYSTRES · LYVDE
IN · WOMANS · STATE · WHOSE · CRADELL · SAWE · I · ROCKTE

. . . .

PREFERRYNGE · STYLL · THE · CAUSES · OF · EACHE · WIGHTE
AS · FARRE · AS · I · DOORSTE · MOVE · HER · GRACE · HYS · EARE

. . . .

SOO · THAT · MY · TYME · I · THUS · DYD · PASSE · AWAYE
A · MAEDE · IN · COURTE · AND · NEVER · NO · MANNS · WYFE
SWORNE · OF · QUENE · ELLSBETHS · HEDD · CHAMBER · ALLWAYE
WYTH · MAEDEN · QUENE · A · MAEDE · DYD · ENDE · MY · LYFFE

The extraordinary suspension between noun and verb in the epitaph's opening sentence qualifies the truth of its claim, while the notion that death has robbed Parry of speech is also proven false by her first-person account of lifelong service to the queen. The repetitions of the words "handmaede," "maede in courte" "wyth maeden queen," "a maede dyd

[28] See Richardson, *Mistress Blanche*, 7–24 at 7.
[29] Hallem and Hockey, *Death, Memory, and Material Culture*, 171.

ende my lyffe," assert an identity between Elizabeth and Parry in their mutual refusal to enter into the sexual economy that would translate them from maids to wives. Parry's and Elizabeth's virginity is promoted to preserve their identity as subjects rather than objects; self-possessed rather than the possessions of others.

The pervasive pun on the word "maede" in the Bacton epitaph – virgin, maid of honor, maker of the tomb – preserves the political and sexual networks controlled and evaded by the female sovereign and her closest advisor, one who saw the infant princess's cradle rocked and who exercised the power to "move her grace hys ear." Parry's fashioning of the monarch as a living woman in stone at once embraces the materiality of women's bodies and refuses the essentialism asserted by Parry's Westminster monument: the effigies, in Clare Colebrook's terms, are "an expression of matter itself – separate, vibrating . . . and unproductive."[30] Reading her shared virginity with Elizabeth at once as a material vacancy and a generative site of alternative materialities, Parry fixes and finalizes the monument's two maiden bodies and the epitaph that falsely fills an empty grave. Women are made, and are made sovereign, by remaining "no manns wyfe." In the contested inheritances of post-Reformation literacy, Parry's autopoiesis overturns the subordinating narrative of reproduction that extends to the virginal remains of her Westminster tomb. Like a fly enclosed in amber, the monarch lives immaculate in her alabaster effigy. The epitaph veiling a vacancy is a text of poetic faith.[31]

If Parry's Bacton memorial publishes a text to gloss an absent body, *The Winter's Tale* erects monumental bodies built on unpublished, occluded scripts. Bodies are printed texts in *The Winter's Tale*: all three of the play's children are said to be "copies" or "prints" of their parents, and Leontes, in his delusional misreading of Perdita, wishes to see her burned like a heretical book.[32] Subject to the same misreading, Hermione is infamously "published" (2.1.98) and "on every / Post proclaimed a strumpet" (3.2.99–100), abuses that expose her to the marketplace of the popular press and align her with the subjects of Autolycus's ballads, "very pitiful, and as true" (4.4.279). Indeed, the crisis of faith at the heart of *The Winter's Tale* is a crisis of literacy. Shakespeare merges text and flesh to question the truth-value of print, troubling "a textual paradigm of knowledge" resulting from the rise in

[30] Colebrook, "On Not Becoming Man," 76.
[31] For a similar reading of *The Winter's Tale*, see McCoy, "Awakening Faith."
[32] Shakespeare, *The Winter's Tale*, ed. Orgel, 1.2.121; 2.3.98–9; and 5.1.124. All citations are to this edition and appear parenthetically. See Lees-Jeffries, *Shakespeare and Memory*, 177, on Perdita as a banned book.

literacy in the early modern period. "Combined with the increased use of print technology," Hallam and Hockey write, this epistemological shift worked "to define textual forms of memory as 'objective' and 'rational' with memories or impressions derived from sense as 'subjective' and 'non-rational.'"[33] Shakespeare exploits the assumed credibility of print to explore the profound uncertainties of post-Reformation belief. Exploiting figurations of literacy throughout the play, he challenges the relationship between readers and texts in an increasingly literate culture where print inspires faith and confers truth. "I love a ballad in print," the gullible Mopsa says, "for then we are sure they are true" (4.4.258–9).

If Autolycus's abusive "traffic [in] sheets" (4.3.23) demonstrates Shakespeare's derision of misplaced confidence in the objectivity and rationality of print, Leontes's abusive misreading of Hermione pushes the subjective and nonrational qualities of sensory impressions to their violent extremes. Subjected to Leontes's groundless accusations, Hermione expresses her lack of proficiency in this new idiom: "you speak a language I do not understand" (3.2.78). Even the sacred text inscribing the direct speech of Apollo is easily, if temporarily, dismissed: despite Dion's report of the "ceremonious, solemn and unearthly" ritual attending the Delphic pronouncement (3.1.4–7), Leontes categorically declares, "There is no truth at all i'th' oracle . . . this is mere falsehood" (3.2.137–8).

Literacy in *The Winter's Tale* is a site of contested competence, "a shifting and plural phenomenon," as Ferguson argues, "surrounded and often constituted by interesting lies." Hybrid in scene, mood, and genre, *The Winter's Tale* is performed in competing tongues whose subjectivity indexes an absent, floating referent. Bohemia and Sicilia are as interchangeable as "twinned lambs" (1.2.66), despite the fact that the play's perspectival multilingualism gives Bohemia a shore.[34] With judgment fixed "in the level of [one's] dreams" (3.2.79), the complicity of physical and mental faculties in deciding truth or falsehood is the central problem of the play, a vexed mixture of sense and knowledge summarized in Leontes's memorable image of the sway of mind over matter:

> There may be in the cup
> A spider steeped, and one may drink, depart,
> And yet partake no venom, for his knowledge
> Is not infected; but if one present

[33] Hallam and Hockey, *Death, Memory, and Material Culture*, 32.

[34] Orgel, "Introduction," in Shakespeare, *The Winter's Tale*, 37–9, reads the shore of Bohemia as a joke that resonates with the play's unreality and theme of gullibility.

Th'abhorred ingredient to his eye, make known
How he hath drunk, he cracks his gorge, his sides
With violent hefts. I have drunk, and seen the spider.
(2.1.39–45)

Knowledge is tied to vision in Leontes's figure, as it is in the play's frequent discounting of "old tales" as fabulous, having "matter to rehearse though credit be asleep and not an ear open" (5.2.60–2). Paulina's stage management of Hermione's awakening stakes its truth-value on the eye: "That she is living / Were it but told you, should be hooted at / Like an old tale" (5.3.115–7). Yet Paulina relies upon embodied speech to validate vision: "it appears she lives, / Though yet she speak not" (5.3.117–8).[35] Beyond exploring of the rival claims of eye and ear, as Shakespeare and Wilkins do in *Pericles*, *The Winter's Tale* is troubled by the imperfect interdependencies of subjects and objects and their indeterminate effects. In the world of *The Winter's Tale*, subjects and objects are intertwined: the "common inner framework" uniting them, for Merleau-Ponty, is produced neither by subject nor object, but is the "Being" or "flesh" that is between them.[36] While the chiasm serves Merleau-Ponty in disposing of "the objectivist ontology of the Cartesians," the pre-Cartesian cartography of *The Winter's Tale* – where the human is "another corporeity" – turns the chiasmic twist of mind and matter toward the chasm of uncertain truth and unstable faith.[37] If merely seeing the spider can infect the otherwise healthy body, belief – whether sound or "weak-hinged" (2.3.118) – constitutes truth: faith alone creates the world one sees, hears, and knows. When Camillo describes "the fabric of [Leontes's] folly, whose foundation / Is piled upon his faith" (1.2.424–5), he imagines Leontes as a firm but flawed monument to false belief.

Textual cenotaphs – monuments built on thin air – pervade *The Winter's Tale*, most obviously Mamillius's winter's tale itself, a "sad tale" of "sprites and goblins," appropriately situated in "a churchyard" (2.1.25–30). This phantom narrative – the bare bones of a story – haunts the play – a provocative absence around which images of monuments, graves, effigies, and epitaphs congregate. Paulina, the play's remembrancer, gives us a taste of the sixteen trying years of ghostly innuendo to which she has subjected Leontes. In response to his wish that Hermione's "sainted

[35] Shakespeare enhances the spectacular *trompe l'oeil* of the statue's awakening with the scene immediately preceding (5.2) in which wonders are heard but not seen.

[36] Merleau-Ponty, *Visible and Invisible*, 227; and see Memon, "Merleau-Ponty," 22, for discussion.

[37] Merleau-Ponty, *Visible and Invisible*, 183; and Merleau-Ponty, *Nature*, 208.

spirit" should "Again possess her corpse" (5.1.57–8), she performs a séance:

> Were I the ghost that walked, I'd bid you mark
> Her eye, and tell me for what dull part in't
> You chose her. Then I'd shriek that even your ears
> Should rift to hear me, and the words that followed
> Should be, 'Remember mine.'
>
> (5.1.63–7)

She calls on Leontes's "first queen's ghost," advising him that he will marry only "when your first queen's again in breath" (5.1.80–3) – an event both foreshadowed and forestalled in her grim acknowledgment that Perdita's recovery "is all as monstrous to human reason / As my Antigonus to break his grave / And come again to me" (5.1.41–3). It is symptomatic of the macabre tenor of this winter's tale that the wondrous and the monstrous are conjoined.

Paulina's continual remembrance of the place of Hermione's corpse and her implications that the queen may be "again in breath" – suggestions made available to Leontes's imagination and then cruelly withdrawn – call- to mind an unseen monument with an invisible epitaph. "Prithee, bring me / To the dead bodies of my queen and son," Leontes asks, vowing:

> One grave shall be for both. Upon them shall
> The causes of their death appear, unto
> Our shame perpetual. Once a day I'll visit
> The chapel where they lie, and tears shed there
> Shall be my recreation.
>
> (3.2.232–8)

While the grave is the site of Mamillius's burial, the monument built above it is Hermione's cenotaph. The appearance of the monument and its confessional epitaph at this moment of the play is a remainder from Shakespeare's source, Robert Greene's *Pandosto*. Shakespeare's unnecessary retention of the detail serves to preclude – and thereby enhance the wonder of – his radically revised climax: this tale, we are meant to understand, will end as Greene's had done, with mother and son entombed together in a grave from which they do not break. Pandosto's rites of burial, indeed, effectively curtail that possibility: he "caused his wife," Greene writes, "to bee embalmed, and wrapt in lead with her young sonne . . . erecting a rich and famous Sepulchre, wherein hee intombed them both." Greene supplies the epitaph, "ingraven on her Tombe in letters of Golde," envisioned but not performed by Shakespeare's Leontes:

> The Epitaph.
> Here lyes entombde Bellaria faire,
> Falsly accused to be unchaste:
> Cleared by Apollos sacred doome,
> Yet slaine by Jealousie at last.
>
> What ere thou be, that passest by,
> Curse him that causde this Q[u]eene to die.[38]

In Greene's fiction, the epitaph's claim to authenticity is rooted in its proximity to the corpse. Its truth is guaranteed by its placement on the monument itself and by the rituals with which the corpse was laid to rest. In this poetic interlude in Greene's prose, the monument and its script are situated in a coherent ecclesiastical space, framed on one side by a suitable royal burial (embalming, a coffin of lead, and a sumptuous monument) and on the other by repentant obsequies: "Pandosto," Greene writes, "would once a day repaire to the Tombe, and there with watry plaints bewaile his misfortune."[39] While Greene makes use of the poetics of proximity to enhance the verisimilitude of his fiction, Shakespeare exploits the strategy to achieve precisely the opposite effect. The awakening of Hermione's effigy robs the grave, lifting the curtain to expose the literal and figurative emptiness of Greene's epitaph. Shakespeare's refusal to display the monument or its text before the audience, as he does so prominently in *Pericles*, advances the absence of proximate bases for belief as *The Winter's Tale's* chief preoccupation and theme.[40]

The reprised memory of Hermione's monument in the play's closing scene transforms her troublesome cenotaph into a figuration of the uncertainty pervading *The Winter's Tale*. "Come," Paulina encourages the Lazarus-like Hermione, "I'll fill thy grave up" (5.3.100–1), resurrecting the image of the tomb that she has literally kept before Leontes's eyes for sixteen years. A moment later, the realization of Paulina's protracted illusion dawns upon Leontes: "I saw her, / As I thought, dead, and have in vain said many / A prayer upon her grave" (5.3.139–41). In the confused commemorative and performative space of the statue's awakening, we cannot know what Leontes saw when (as he thought) he saw Hermione dead, or what purpose his many "vain" prayers have served or, indeed, to whom they were offered. When the marble monument is replaced by the marmoreal queen, we have, it seems, drunk and seen the

[38] Greene, *Pandosto*, sig. C3^{v}. [39] Greene, *Pandosto*, sig. C4^{r}.
[40] Shakespeare and Wilkins, *Pericles*, 4.4.32–43; and see Chapter 5 for discussion.

spider. Seduced to surrender reason to belief, we yield to the sway of unpredictable, potent matter.

As Hermione's unoccupied tomb is displaced by her statue, her stoniness is relocated to her audience, whose silence and immobility convey their astonishment: "I like your silence," Paulina, states, "it the more shows off / Your wonder (5.3.21–2). Underlying the virtuosity of the scene – both Shakespeare's and that of his collaborator, Paulina – is another occluded epitaph. In Vasari's *Lives of the Artists*, Shakespeare would have read the epitaph of Giulio Romano, which commemorates the artist's godlike mastery of illusion: "Videbat Juppiter corpora sculpta pictaque / spirare, et aedes mortalium aequarier coelo / Julii virtute Romani" ("Jupiter saw sculpted and painted bodies breathe and the homes of mortals made equal to those in heaven through the skill of Giulio Romano").[41] Crafting her effigy of Hermione, Paulina assumes Romano's skill as an illusionist yet insistently calls attention to the materiality of the figure's carving and coloring. "The statue is but newly fixed," she insists, "the colour's / Not dry," and again, "The ruddiness on her lip is wet" (5.3.47–8 and 5.3.81–2).[42] While this increases the wonder of Hermione's awakening, Paulina's verbal coloring also recalls her shaded testimony of Hermione's death:

> I say she's dead; I'll swear't. If word nor oath
> Prevail not, go and see: if you can bring
> Tincture or lustre in her lip, her eye,
> Heat outwardly or breath within, I'll serve you
> As I would the gods.
>
> (3.2.201–5)

Although "it is required," Paulina claims, "You do awake your faith" (5.3.94–5), the scene's recollection of this false appearance and its retrieval of Hermione's cenotaph share the chiaroscuro of Autolycus's trade in false sheets and "hallowed" trinkets (4.4.598).[43]

The Romano epitaph is a spectral monument, an absent body around which the final scene of *The Winter's Tale* pivots from the infected appearances of artifice toward the vital creativity of natural virtuosity. Shakespeare's ekphrastic performance in bringing the statue to life pits art against nature and finally joins these rivals in an art that is itself Nature

[41] Vasari, *Le Vite*, 861; translation in Leonard Barkan,"Living Sculptures," 656.

[42] See Meek, "Ekphrasis," 389–414, for a similar argument.

[43] See Meek, "Ekphrasis," 404; and Lees-Jeffrey, *Shakespeare and Memory*, 142 and 188 on Autolycus's merchandise and ballads in relation to the play's negotiation with remembrance.

(4.4.97). The scene stages a Vasarian *paragone* when Paulina's incantatory poetry surpasses Romano's illusionist skill by producing a real woman rather than a mere imitation of life.[44] Blurring and finally dissolving the borders between flesh and stone, Paulina, like a collector of curiosities, fuses the creative agency of natural wonders and of human craft: Hermione is engrafted by "ensouled nature" to the marble of her statue.[45] The hybrid figure of the woman-as-stone merges human and nonhuman creativity in a generative and interactive web that joins Paulina and her creation. The scene performs a story of feminine materiality and mutuality that allows the plays women to establish themselves as "unowned" subjects – that is, material but nonessential – rather than objects owned by men. This cannot last: Hermione is returned to Leontes; Perdita will marry Florizel; and Paulina's imagined future as a lone "old turtle" (5.2.132) is curtailed by her surprise betrothal to Camillo. Still, for a moment, in a chapel that is also a gallery (5.3.10; 5.3.86), Paulina insists upon a necromancy akin to the collector's in the fantastic world of the cabinet: "If you can behold it, / I'll make the statue move indeed, descend / And take you by the hand," (5.3.87–9). Like Blanche Parry at Bacton, Paulina is the maker of the spectacle, fabricating the living figure of the queen by blending art and nature, and commemorating a lifetime of fellowship. Her assertion of ownership, "for the stone is mine" (5.3.58) suggests an intimacy and involvement with a rarity that is also a valued subject.

Paulina, like Parry displaces biological reproduction – the sanctioned form of women's creative agency – by embracing the "multiple potentialities of the body," as Braidotti puts it, emergent from the generative cartography of her own and Hermione's shared "location."[46] Although Leontes complains of a lack of verisimilitude in Hermione's statue, since she "was not so much wrinkled, nothing / So aged as this seems" (5.3.28–9), Hermione's wrinkles register the passage of time that is likely to preclude the possibility of reproduction. Hermione's pregnancy is at the heart of the play's crisis: her visible "burden" seems to prompt Polixenes's opening lines, "Nine times the watery star hath been / The shepherd's note since we have left our throne / Without a burden" (1.2.1–3), and to propel Leontes toward irrational jealousy. Released from the prospect of conception, she "hangs about" Leontes's neck, a creature uncertainly "pertain[ing] to life" (5.3.112–3). The new Hermione is a woman but barely a wife.

[44] See Gurr, "Bear"; and on the *paragone*, see Barkan, "Living Sculptures," 655–6.

[45] See Daston and Park, *Wonder*, 255–301, at 298; and see Chapter 4.

[46] Braidotti, *Posthuman*, 73.

Marked by the passage of time, she re-emerges from the closed circle of fellowship with Paulina, "a collectively shared and constructed and jointly occupied spatiotemporal territory," in Braidotti's terms – a space of harmonious engagement that is virtually unimaginable.[47] "Make it manifest," Polixenes desires, "where she has lived / Or how stolen from the dead" (5.3.113–4). The sites of "preservation" of Hermione and her daughter (5.3.124 and 5.3.127), places as "fantastick framed" as the shore of Bohemia, are the final mysteries of the play. They are mysteries that blend time and place, as epitaphs promise to do.

The spectral epitaph on Hermione's unoccupied tomb constitutes a deprivation that is repaired by the abundance of Bohemia, a pastoral world ruled by the lost heir, Perdita. The losses of Sicilia – the play's winter – are countered by the fecundity of Bohemia's spring. Playing Proserpina to Hermione's Ceres (4.4.116–8), Perdita's return to Sicilia effectively overwhelms time with place. Despite the appearance of Time as chorus in *The Winter's Tale* (4.1), the play's resolution involves a spatial figuration of perennial return, one that emulates and replaces Paulina and Hermione's shared location. In the reunion of mother and daughter, a poetics of proximity trades winter for spring, death for life.[48] Perdita's ritual commemoration performed during the sheepshearing foreshadows this reincorporation.[49] Noting her lack of the royal flowers appropriate to Florizel, "my sweet friend / To strew him o'er and o'er," Perdita cancels the mortuary figure of burial with one of natural entanglement. She will bedeck him "Not like a corpse—or if, not to be buried / But quick and in mine arms" (4.4127–32). In Bohemia, a corpse is a body living or dead, living and dead. Imagining Hermione as such a corpse – a woman not to be buried but quick, a living woman enmeshed in matter – Perdita and Paulina together practice an art that can make stones speak.

2 The Shapes of Things Divine

Mamillius's unspoken winter's tale, like Hermione's unscripted epitaph, is the absence at the heart of the play, around which the action congregates. Its churchyard, replete with goblins and sprites, materializes in the

[47] Braidotti, *Nomadic Subjects*, 15.

[48] Orgel, "Introduction," in Shakespeare, *The Winter's Tale*, 45–6, sees the Proserpina myth as the foundational subtext of the play, which may account for Shakespeare's switching the kingdoms of Bohemia and Sicily. See also Shullenberger, "Girl, Interrupted," which relates Proserpina, by way of an allusion to Perdita, to the "changing" women of the masque, including Sabrina.

[49] Shakespeare and Wilkins, *Pericles*, 4.1.12–6.

unfolding plot and places of *The Winter's Tale*. Yet, like Hermione's statue, these are spirits entangled in the material world. Defying the reasonable, if implausible, tale of Hermione's secret retirement for sixteen years, evidence of her death seems to be supplied when Antigonus is visited by her ghost:

> I have heard, but not believed, the spirits o' th' dead
> May walk again: if such thing be, thy mother
> Appear'd to me last night, for ne'er was dream
> So like a waking.
>
> (3.3.15–18)

Antigonus's literacy, if not his faith, is challenged when he wrongly surmises that "Hermione hath suffer'd death, and that . . . this being indeed the issue / Of King Polixenes, it should here be laid" (3.3.41–3). By displacing Hermione's speech from the inscriptional site of the grave to the spectral evidentiary field of the surrounding play, Shakespeare traces the migration of remembrance from traditional rites of burial, set in proximity to the body, to their ungrounded textual apparitions. Uprooted from place, Hermione's spirit is an "old tale" in which Antigonus "superstitiously" believes (3.3.39) – an epitaph more false than true.

Ghosts coinhabit the bleak cartographies of *The Winter's Tale* and Milton's *Maske Presented at Ludlow Castle, 1634* with figures of marmorization. Together, they describe the literacies of textual and embodied remembrance in the tenuous coupling of the "bright aëreal Spirits" of the book (*Maske*, 3) and the *terra firma* of the tomb. The fascination of boys with ghost stories provides Milton as well as Shakespeare a means to explore epistemological uncertainty as a spiritual phenomenon in all its senses. Hermione's spirit waits in the porous threshold between the cenotaph and her materialization in Paulina's chapel, while Milton's brother share the tangled woods with "stubborn unlaid ghost[s] / That break [their] magick chains at curfeu time" (44–5); figures akin to the specters "link't by carnal sensuality" to their sepulchers (74), who are, in turn, linked to the chaste Lady entangled in the marble of the magician's chair. The implicit dualism pervading these images is dissolved as divisions between mind and matter are blurred by female subjects whose vitality is wholly intertwined with their materiality. They share the effects of the "phantom limb," as Merleau-Ponty describes them: a phenomenon that illustrates how the perceiving mind is enmeshed and embodied (and, we may want to add, engendered) in corporeal and sensory relations. The phantom limb is not perceived as dead flesh or lost matter, nor does it posit a mere memory or image of embodiment. It is, rather, "quasi-present."[50] It reveals the intertwining of body and mind in response to material prompts that speak to the limb and stresses the tenacity of embodied experience, its resistance to retreat into an incorporeal past or future. Milton's "thick and gloomy shadows damp" that haunt the grave share this tenacity as they balance between air and earth. We might see Hermione's haunting of Antigonus, furthermore, as his experience of a phantom limb. The specter, like an epitaph cut adrift from the grave, is quasi-present; the materiality of its memory is a bridge linking viewer to phenomenon, or reader to text, spanning an unfathomable void in between.

Such funereal displacements appear in much of Milton's early poetry, where they bridge the distance between performance and print. In the poetry leading up to Milton's entry into print with *A Maske* in 1637, as Thomas N. Corns notes, "Milton's favored literary form ... was the funeral elegy," where he "persistently evoke[s] an image of the place and mode of burial."[51] Milton's "Epitaph for the Marchioness of Winchester" shares with Ben Jonson's elegy on the same subject a blend of spiritual and marmoreal figurations that trouble the relationship between poem and place. "What goodly Ghost besprint with Aprill dew," Jonson begins, "Hails me so solemnly to yonder Yeugh?" The marchioness's unlaid ghost calls upon Jonson to grieve for her, yet she renders him speechless, transforming both body and text into the marble on which she herself inscribes her epitaph: "Alas, I am all Marble: write the rest . . . I who would her Poet have become, / At least may beare th'inscription to her Tombe."[52] Milton, by contrast, imagines the marchioness's spirit ascended and enshrined in heaven: "clad in radiant sheen," she is "No Marchioness, but now a Queen" (73–4). It is the poet himself who lingers near the tomb.: "This rich marble doth enterr / The honour'd Wife of Winchester." Milton stresses the rituals of remembrance at the graveside with deictic repetition:

> Here besides the sorrowing
> That they noble House doth bring,
> Here be tears of perfect moan
> Wept for thee in Helicon.

[50] Merleau-Ponty, *Phenomenology of Perception*, 98.

[51] Corns, "Milton Before Lycidas," 32. Corns argues against the retrospective reading of Milton's early poetry, including *Comus*, as Puritan, convincingly demonstrating a more ecumenical approach to religion in these works. The most influential interpretation of Milton's Puritanism in the 1620s and 1630s is found in Marcus, *Politics of Mirth*, 169–212.

[52] Jonson, "Elegy on the Lady Jane Paulet," in *Jonson's Execration*, sig. C4^{v}-D1^{r}.

Among these poetic tears are Milton's own verses, strewn like Perdita's flowers on the corpse: "And some Flowers, and som Bays, / For thy Hears to strew the ways, / Sent thee from the banks of Came."[53] Given the long circulation of Milton's epitaph in manuscript, it is tempting to imagine that the poem might have been pinned to the pall or posted near Paulet's grave.[54] Whether or not this was the case, the poem makes use of these improvisational rituals to license the circulation, eventually in print, of text beyond place. The published epitaph, for Milton, displaces the immediacy of the authentic, inscriptional epitaph, compensating for the displacement of rituals of remembrance to the practices of readership. Jane Paulet's death and its circumstances (she died giving birth to a stillborn son) enable Milton to inscribe this transformative moment in the imagery of marmorization:

> The haples Babe before his birth
> Had burial, yet not laid in earth,
> And the languisht Mothers Womb
> Was not long a living Tomb.[55]

Becoming a living tomb, Paulet is imagined as Niobe, a figure both flesh and stone whose petrified maternal body is firmly fixed to place, but fluid: frozen in "her stony grief," Ovid writes, "her vitals are stone. But still she weeps, [and] tears trickle from the marble."[56] As a living monument, Paulet-as-Niobe blends nature and culture, moving the essentialist image of the maternal body toward the objects and rites of commemoration, the material of social exchange. The living tomb provides a figure of the poet's work as well: as the mother's body becomes the child's tomb, Milton builds a rich marble monument for Paulet herself.[57]

The poet turned to stone is the foundational figuration of Milton's first published poem, "On *Shakespear.* 1630," printed anonymously in the Second Folio of Shakespeare's *Works* in 1632. The speaker discounts the

[53] Milton, "Epitaph on the Marchioness of Winchester," in *Complete Works*, lines 1–2 and 53–9. See Frost, "No Marchioness but a Queen,'" 13, for the likelihood that Milton composed the poem while he was at Cambridge.

[54] The epitaph was first printed in Milton, *Poems* (1645), 23–6. A copy in BL Sloane MS 1446, fols. 37^{v}–38^{v}, indicates that it was circulating in manuscript.

[55] Milton, "Epitaph," lines 31–4. Paulet died of an infection, which probably also killed her child, as a result of having an abscess on her cheek lanced: see Parker, "Milton and the Marchioness," 547–50. Eliot, "Elogie," 38, mourns for "those two blessed souls, whose bones there lye," indicating that Paulet was buried with her son.

[56] Ovid, *Metamorphoses*, 6:305–12.

[57] See Schwartz, *Milton and Maternal Mortality*, 91–141, at 121.

need for material monuments for Shakespeare's "honour'd Bones" and "hallow'd reliques," arguing instead:

> Thou in our wonder and astonishment
> Hath built thy-self a live-long Monument.
> For whilst to th'shame of slow-endeavouring art,
> Thy easie numbers flow, and that each heart
> Hath from the leaves of thy unvalu'd Book,
> Those Delphick lines with deep impression took,
> Then thou our fancy of it self bereaving
> Doth make us Marble with too much conceaving.[58]

The inclusion of the date in Milton's title, which appears in all printed editions of the poem, insistently marks this poem as pseudo-inscriptional; that is, the epitaph identifies itself specifically as a printed text, set in a textual chapel, where a distinctly textual rite of remembrance is performed. The poem is replete with the language borrowed from *The Winter's Tale*, most obviously retrieving the wonder and astonishment with which the onstage spectators witness, in motionless silence, Paulina's conjuring.[59] However, Milton has in mind not a theatrical spectacle, but Shakespeare's "unvalu'd Book." Responding to the unspoken, occluded texts of *The Winter's Tale*, Milton describes a communal act of reading – "*Our* wonder," "*our* fancy" – that makes marble of the literate world. Milton's epitaph, removed from proximity to the body interred, commemorates the *poet* Shakespeare whose epitaphic lines are inscribed on every heart. Milton celebrates the transformations of Shakespeare's admirers to a "live-long Monument," a living tomb; a marmorization wrought by the wondrous act of reading. Yet, the heart inscribed, the body turned to stone does not result in the end of poetry: rather, Milton's poem echoes infinitely, permanently, in print. The "new sense of *textualized* memory," in Scott Newstock's description, attending the printed epitaph mimics as it displaces the inscriptional epitaph whose claims to presence and permanence, here and in *The Winter's Tale*, are proven false.[60]

If the severance of text from place is a condition of authorship in "On *Shakespear*. 1630," Milton's *Maske* documents his progress from occasional poet to published author; a transition most prominently figured in

[58] Milton, "On Shakespeare. 1630," lines 7–14. *Complete Works* (530–1) also prints the Second and Third Folio versions. The title in the Second Folio is "An Epitaph on the Admirable Dramaticke Poet, W. Shakespeare."

[59] See Stevens, "Subversion and Wonder," for a detailed reading of *The Winter's Tale* as subtext for the poem's "rhetoric of wonder."

[60] Newstok, *Quoting Death*, 31.

marmorization. Milton follows the lead of *The Winter's Tale*, where Shakespeare stakes his display of poetic virtuosity on Paulina's illusionist art of coaxing flesh from stone. In *A Maske*, Milton crafts a similar scene in Sabrina's release of the Lady from her marble chair, using that image to enliven his poetic skill and its move from the ephemeral performance of the masque to the permanence of a printed memorial. Milton fills the landscape of the masque with multiple figures of hybridity and marmorization, from "root-bound Daphne" (661–2) to the "unconquered Virgin," Minerva, whose "snaky-headed Gorgon shield ... freez'd her foes to congealed stone" (447–8). Comus's wood is the site of graves and caves whose walls, like Niobe's, are porous and vital – from "grots, and caverns shag'd with horrid shades" (429), to "dark sequester'd nook[s]" (500), to "Rifted rocks whose entrance leads to hell" (518). On this "inchanted isle" (417), stones themselves are animate and transformational.

Indeed, the Lady enters the masque by calling upon one such figure of lively stoniness, "Sweet Echo, sweetest Nymph that liv'st unseen" (230):

> Can'st thou not tell me of a gentle Pair
> Tha likest thy Narcissus are?
> O if thou have
> Hid them in some flowry Cave,
> Tell me but where.
>
> (237–40)

When the Lady addresses Echo – a mythic prototype, like Niobe, of a woman's fusion with stone – Milton violates poetic convention by presenting a silent Echo.[61] As Stephen Orgel puts it, "The Lady, singing to Echo is literally singing to herself."[62] As a woman "chain'd up in Alabaster," Echo can only predict the crisis to be faced by the Lady. As a woman who "liv'st unseen," she is a figure for the lingering voice and memory in the absence of a body; she makes present not the body but its residual trace, its epitaph. Intertwined with stone, Echo casts the masque's caves and grottos as natural doubles of the charnel houses and sepulchers where imbruted spirits linger.

Milton's image of spirits loath to leave the body behind provides a template with which to read the comingling of female flesh with matter throughout *Comus*. The intemperance and immodesty of these thick, damp ghosts, mired in "carnal sensuality," reside in their refusal to accept

[61] See Ovid, *Metamorphoses*, 3:359–401, for Echo's transformation.
[62] Orgel, "The Case for *Comus*," 40.

disembodiment in death. The Lady fused to stone, Daphne turned to bark and branches, and unseen Echo are similarly mired in matter: their hybridity both anticipates and forestalls the body's disappearance, an absence marked only by a lingering voice. What is elided in the Elder Brother's vision of chastity's immortal essence (462–3), after all, is the fact of disembodiment – an event threatened by Comus's "hellish charms." As the Attendent Spirit warns, "He with his bare wand can unthred the joynts, / And crumble all thy sinews" (614–5). If women are stubbornly threaded to materiality, men – overcoming base matter with an ascendent mind – simply fall apart.[63]

In a Spenserian source that lies behind Milton's *Maske*, the voice that lingers, substituting and compensating for the lost body, is poetry itself. The persistence of poetry in the absence of the bodily trace is the subject of Spenser's *Teares of the Muses*, the second poem in his 1591 *Complaints*, dedicated as a "simple remembrance" to Alice Spencer, Countess of Derby – Spenser's kinswoman and Alice Egerton's grandmother and namesake.[64] *Teares of the Muses* puts forth an extended figuration of corporeal disintegration and the reparative work of poetry. The opening stanzas recall the Ovidian myth of the origin of amber:

> For since the time that *Phoebus* foolish sonne
> Ythundered through *Ioves* avengefull wrath,
> For traversing the charret of the Sunne
> Beyond the compasse of his pointed path,
> Of you his mournfull Sisters was lamented,
> Such mournfull tunes were never since invented.
> (8–13)

Poetry emerges at the site of interment of the cracked sinews and shattered nerves of Phaethon's body. His mother, as Ovid reports, "wandered over the whole earth, seeking first his lifeless limbs, then his bones; his bones at last she found, but buried on a riverbank in a foreign land" ("laniata sinus totum percensuit orbem / exanimesque artus primo, mox ossa requirens / repperit ossa tamen peregrina condita ripa / incubuitque loco nomenque in marmore lectum").[65] Phaethon's sisters, the Heliades, mourn over his grave until they

[63] See Carrithers, "Milton's Ludlow Mask," for the reading of Comus's spell as enacting "time, decay, and death" (35).

[64] Spenser, *Teares of the Muses*, 480. Subsequent citations appear parenthetically. The dedication is to Spencer as Lady Strange, and promotes Spenser's kinship with the countess. Marcus, "John Milton's *Comus*," 252–4, suggests that Milton's early works demonstrate nostalgia for the Elizabethan Protestant militancy associated with Alice Spencer.

[65] Ovid, *Metamorphoses*, 2:335–8. Phaethon's grave bears the epitaph, carved by the Naiads who buried him: "HIC • SITUS • EST • PHAETHON • CURRUS • AURIGA • PATERNI / QUEM

are transformed into poplars: "Still their tears flow on," Ovid concludes, "and these tears, hardened into amber by the sun, drop down from the new-made trees. The clear river receives them and bears them onward, one day to be worn by the brides of Rome" ("inde fluunt lacrimae, stillataque sole rigescunt / de ramis electra novis, quae lucidus amnis / excipit et nuribus mittit gestanda Latinis").[66] Spenser conflates the Heliades with the Muses, and thus their complaint is for the decline of poetry, and, by extension, the "degenerate and degraded state" of the material world. This condition is figured in scattered and recollected remains of Phaethon, and in the hybrid materials – both the Heliades and their amber tears – marking his burial. "Streaming teares / That could have made the stonie heart to weepe" (110), Spenser's Clio laments the failure of poetry to create "light / Of things forepast, nor moniments of time" (103–4), while Polyhymnia complains that men "have mard the face of goodly Poësie, / And made a monster of their fantasie" (557–8). Anticipating the "wild rude and wanton antick" of Comus's monstrous rout, Urania laments that men, "like brute beasts doo lie in loathsome den, / Of ghostly darkenes, and of gastlie dreed" (531–2). For Euterpe, the landscape is filled with "the fearfull howling" of "fowle Goblins and Shreikowles" (283–4), akin to the "calling shapes and beckning shadows" that assault Milton's Lady. Finally, in despair, the Muses "all their learned instruments did breake." "The rest untold," the speaker concludes, "no living tongue can speake" (599–600).

In the Spenserian complaint, images of ruination – broken verse, broken instruments, and broken bodies – signal the overwhelming of poetic imagination by degenerate matter. Yet in *Teares of the Muses*, the amber produced by the Heliades's tears is the material remainder of their lost, mournful song, which, in turn, supplants the lost body of Phaethon. While the sisters are rooted to the place of burial, their amber tears are fluid and unbounded, caught in the current of the river. These hybrid female figures and their poetic tears are the graves of memory and the wellsprings of authorship. Their voices are swallowed in matter, but their tears become the poet's song.

The memory of the Heliades enters Milton's *Maske* in the Spenserian turn toward Sabrina, whose invocation, the Attendant Spirit reports, "once of Meliboeus old I learnt / The soothest Shepherd that ere pip't on plains" (822–3).[67] With her arrival, Milton energizes, as Lewalski and Haan point

• SI • NON • TENUIT • MAGNIS • TAMEN • EXCIDIT • AUSIS ("Here Phaethon lies. In Phoebus car he fared, / and though he greatly failed, more greatly dared") (2:380–1).

[66] Ovid, *Metamorphoses*, 2:364–6. [67] See Guillory, *Poetic Authority*, 68–93.

out, "the transformative power of song and poetry."[68] A local genius, Sabrina nonetheless embodies the fluidity and hybridity of the Heliades. Rising from the river that shares her name, Sabrina is immersed in Ovidian and Spenserian subtexts:[69]

> Sabrina fair,
> Listen where thou art sitting
> Under the glassie, cool, transluscent wave,
> In twisted braids of Lilies knitting
> The loose train of thy amber-dropping hair
> Listen for dear honours sake,
> Goddess of the silver lake,
> Listen and save.
>
> (859–66).

In Milton's intertwining of the mythologies of Sabrina and the Heliades, the Severn becomes the river into which the root-bound poplars drop their tears, and the generative, transformational nature of their tears prefigures Sabrina's transformational song. "Commend[ing her] innocence to the flood" (831), the Attendant Spirit recalls, Sabrina was "dropt in Ambrosial Oils, … reviv'd / And underwent a quick immortal change" (840–41). She emerges equipped with "pretious viold liquors" (847), which, like those poured forth by Spenser's mournful muses, are healing and compensatory. Against the petrifying "balefull drugs" of Comus's mother, "Circe with the Sirens three … who as they sung, would take the prison'd soul" (253–6), Sabrina lingers to "the Songs of Sirens sweet, / By dead Parthenope's dear tomb" (878–9). The submerged caverns of the Severn are unimaginable locations of feminine communion and commemoration. Filling the waters with precious jewels and spices (molten crystal, beryl, golden ore, myrrh and cinnamon, 930–7), Milton catalogues Sabrina's crystalline figure in a virtuoso blazon that blends art and nature. He extends her fluid mobility with an image of a "sliding Chariot … / Thick set with Agat and the azurn sheen, / Of Turkis blew, and Emrauld green," which, we understand, she has parked "By the rushy-fringed bank" while she has come on "printless feet" to answer the Attendant Spirit's call (890–901). The Sabrina who "with moist curb sway[s]" (825) the border between elements and nations is, like Shakespeare's Hermione, a monument in motion.[70]

[68] Lewalski and Haan, in Milton, *Complete Works*, lxv. See also Marcus, "John Milton's *Comus*," 252.

[69] Milton, *History of Britain*, 18, explains, "Estrildis and her Daughter Sabra, she [Guendolen] throws into the River: and to leave a Monument of Revenge, proclaims, that the stream be thenceforth call'd after the Damsel's Name; which by length of time is chang'd now to Sabrina, or Severn."

[70] See Murphy, "Sabrina," for a similar reading; and see Chapter 5 for Marina's mobile remembrance in *Pericles*.

Like the amber in which she is submerged, Sabrina herself is a viscous entity. "Refusing to conform to the laws governing the solid and self-identical," as Elizabeth Grosz describes women's viscosity, Sabrina is a creature of changeable and permeable borders. She blurs divisions and dissolves oppositions – between bodies, within bodies, and between bodies and things.[71] Sabrina embodies the intertwining of the flesh with flesh of the world. "Our body is a being of two leaves," as Merleau-Ponty writes:

> from one side a thing among things and otherwise what sees them and touches them; we say, because it is evident, that it unites these two properties within itself, and its double belongingness to the order of the 'object' and to the order of the 'subject' reveals to us quite unexpected relations between the two orders.[72]

If Sabrina is able to dissolve the viscous sinews binding the Lady to her marble tomb, it is not simply because both women are virgins. Or, rather, their virginity signals their embrace of alternative materialities: the multiple potentialities of the body that reside in the fluidity and hybridity that connect them to each other and to the world.

Sabrina's ritual, like Paulina's, is a sensory and material conjuring, an embodied virtuosity. For Paulina, this artistry lies in her skillful navigation between art and nature and her management of the double takes where mind and matter crisscross. Sabrina's medicinal ceremony is emphatically material. Her embodied song weaves through a ritual of touch:

> Brightest Lady, look on me.
> Thus I sprinkle on thy brest
> Drops that from my fountain pure,
> I have kept of pretious cure.
> Thrice upon thy fingers tip.
> Thrice upon thy rubied lip.
> Next this marble venom'd seat
> Smeared with gumms of glutenous heat
> I touch with chaste palms moist and cold,
> Now the spell hath lost its hold.
>
> (910–19)

For Milton, marmorization figures the problematic miring of the body in matter, and one version of this fusion is the sexual comingling and coupling, chaste or unchaste, of bodies.[73] Sabrina's touch melts the

[71] Grosz, *Volatile Bodies*, 195. [72] Merleau-Ponty, *Visible and Invisible*, 137.

[73] See Shuger, "'Gums of Glutinous Heat,'" 1–7; and, for a contextual study, Marcus, "Milieu of Milton's *Comus*."

"gumms of glutenous heat" fusing the Lady to marble, releasing her from Comus's threat of unchastity and redeeming her from the living death that this degraded state, for seventeenth-century women, would imply. The look exchanged between Sabrina and the Lady ("Brightest Lady, look on me") reminds us of the pair's unassailable virginity, but also moves beyond the closure and immobility that orthodox views of virginity imply. Sabrina and the Lady together erase the sexually charged duplicities wrought by Comus and his wand in a productive ritual enabled by their shared sex and fluid involvement with matter. The Lady's "chast footing" (146) and Sabrina's "printless feet" (897) both figure the radiant immanence of redeemed matter.

Sabrina, "a being of two leaves," embodies a creative potential that is exploited by the poet as he migrates from place to print. The 1637 publication of *A Maske Presented at Ludlow Castle, 1634* is authorized not by the poet John Milton but by the poetics of proximity. Henry Lawes dedicates the work to John Egerton, the Elder Brother of the performance, tying it to its embodiment: "this Poem," he writes, "which receiv'd its first occasion of birth from your selfe, and others of your noble familie ... now returns againe to make a finall dedication of it selfe to you." The text is "unowned" as the Lady had been: "Although not openly acknowledg'd by the Author," Lawes reports, "yet it is a legitimate offspring."[74] Lawes promises a printed play text while offering instead a false memory and an opportunity for the poet to move from occasional writing to vocational authorship.[75] Like a pseudo-inscriptional epitaph, the printed masque feigns an affiliation with place even as it sets forth on the swift, unbounded current of print. Following Sabrina's incantatory process, Milton substitutes poetry for place, pinning his verse to the vanished monument of the masque performed at Ludlow Castle. The movement from performance to print is the movement from proximity to literacy, from the Bridgewater family to the community of readers convened by the circulation of texts.

Sabrina's ritual is an embodied performance – aural, tactile, vocal, and visual – but her living word is displaced and her recreational power coopted by the poet in the printed text. In the performance of *A Maske*, nearly forty lines given by Milton to the Attendant Spirit to "epiloguize" (975 s. d.) were instead presented as a prologue. However, when the

[74] Lawes, "Epistle Dedicatorie," in Milton, *A Maske* (1637), sig. A2^{r}.

[75] See Brown, *John Milton's Aristocratic Entertainments*, 9–10; and Evans and Fishman, *Miltonic Moment*, 40, who see the period between performance and print as transformative, with *Comus* as "the most unstable" of all of Milton's works.

printed masque comes to a close, the epilogue is restored and expanded, permitting the Attendant Spirit to appropriate Sabrina's luscious poetry as he describes his departure to the "happy climes that ly . . . / Up in the broad fields of the sky" (977–9). The speech disembodies Sabrina's glittering materiality, relocating it to the ethereal realm of "liquid ayr" scented by "musky wing," "cedar'n alleys," and "balmy smels" (980–96). The epilogue overwhelms the poetics of proximity and its embodied rituals with an unembedded literacy, a free-floating sign that forges ties not among the assembled audience and authors but between the unseen reader and the anonymous text.

If Milton trades on the transformational poetics of proximity enacted in *A Maske* to underwrite his appearance in print, one addition to the 1637 imprint returns print to place with particular resonance for Alice Egerton and her siblings. When the Attendant Spirit's epilogue is restored, so, too, is an image of inconsolable feminine complaint:

> (List mortals if your ears be true)
> Beds of Hyacinth and roses
> Where young Adonis oft reposes
> Waxing well of his deep wound,
> In slumber soft, on the ground
> Sadly sits th'Assyrian Queen . . .
> (997–1002)

When John Egerton's wife, Frances Stanley Egerton, died in March 1636, in the moment between the performance of the masque and its publication, a flood of epitaphs and memorials in print and manuscript was unleashed. Thomas Fowler offered a Latin "inscription for my ladies Monument," relying on proxmity to the tomb to publish his fame.[76] The modesty of the countess's grave was celebrated as a sign of her chaste maternity: John Carter's funeral sermon, preached in the presence of the countess's body, claims that her memory lives not in a marble effigy but in "her children . . . her walking images."[77] Robert Codrington, pouring poetic "teares . . . on your blest Daughters honoured hearse" presented a manuscript to Frances's mother, Alice Spencer, Countess of Derby. Free from the limts of place, Codrington convenes an audience of literate mourners to breathe new life into the countess's marmoreal corpse:

[76] Hunt MS EL 6844, fol. 1^{r}. See also Hunt MS EL 6845, which transcribes the Latin inscription engraved on the countess's monument in the Bridgewater Chapel, Little Gaddesden.

[77] Hunt MS EL 6883," 28–9. For discussion, see Wilkie, "'Such Daughters,'" 287–97.

'Tis life alone to be her Monument,
Which needs not Graves Art, for every Sigh
Shall better speake her Epitaph, and dye.[78]

3 Conspicuous Orbes

Around the time that fifteen-year-old Alice Egerton played the Lady's part in Milton's *Maske*, her grandmother, Alice Spencer, Countess of Derby, commissioned two commemorative works in radically different temporal registers: one a masque, as Stephen Orgel points out, "that most ephemeral of Renaissance genres," the other an alabaster and marble monument, erected in the chancel of St. Mary's, Harefield.[79] In Milton's *Arcades*, performed at Harefield in 1633, Spencer appears seated in "shining throne" (15), a heavenly prefiguration of the Lady's installment a year later in Comus's enchanted chair:

Mark what radiant state she spreds,
In circle round her shining throne,
Shooting her beams like silver threds.
This this is she alone,
Sitting like a Goddes bright,
In the center of her light.

(14–19)

This "princely shrine" (36) is embedded at the center of a harmonious universe, whose music inspires the Genius of the Woods to celebrate the countess:

then listen I
To the celestial Sirens harmony,
That sit upon the nine enfolded Sphears
And sing to those that hold the vital shears
And turn the Adamantine spindle round,
On which the fate of gods and men is wound.

(63–8)

As Spencer's grandchildren, dressed as shepherds, approach this "rural Queen," (94), the Genius encourages them to "attend toward her glittering

[78] Hunt MS EL 6850, fols. A1^{r} and F2^{v}-F3^{r}.

[79] Orgel, *Authentic Shakespeare*, 49. The monument was completed in Spencer's lifetime: TNA PROB 11/174/28, fol. 90^{v}, requests burial "in the Tombe which I lately made." The identity of the sculptor is not certain: Esdaile's attribution to Maximilian Colt in 1934 has been refuted by White, *Biographical Dictionary*, 235.

state. / Where ye may all that are of noble stemm / Approach, and kiss her sacred vestures hemm" (81–3). The masque is a monumental but mobile genealogy. As the countess's silver threads intertwine with the Fates' adamantine strands, *Arcades* celebrates the interwoven fabric of the family and its feminine source. Spencer is a wondrous, resplendent spider at the heart of her web.

Spencer's monument at Harefield attempts to freeze this ephemeral performance in stone (see Figure 6.4). Although twice widowed, Spencer chose to be buried accompanied by her daughters' effigies. Kneeling on the tomb's base, they are the coheirs of Ferdinando Stanley, Earl of Derby: Anne, Lady Chandos and later Countess of Castlehaven, Elizabeth, Countess of Huntingdon, and Alice Egerton's mother, Frances, Countess of Bridgewater.[80] Elizabeth and Frances predeceased their mother, and both were buried in graves free of portraiture with their husbands.[81] Only Anne Stanley survived her mother; she was the widow of the Earl of Castlehaven, who was executed in 1631 for sodomy and sexual crimes against his wife and stepdaughter.[82] When Milton's Elder Brother maintains, "Vertue may be assailed, but never hurt, / Surpriz'd by unjust force, but not enthrall'd" (588–9), the lethal implications of this logic lie in its reversal. The woman assailed and conquered offers proof of her wantonness. If *Comus* glosses the Castlehaven scandal, it does so with this formula that blames the victim, Anne Stanley, whose rape cannot but speak her "imbruted" vice.[83] Having suffered a social death long before her corporeal demise in 1647, Anne was buried in an unmarked grave near her mother's opulent tomb at Harefield.[84]

The monument's epitaphs and effigies both demonstrate Spencer's tempering of historical record with poetic license. Although the central epitaph records Spencer's marriage to Ferdinando Stanley, it makes no mention of her second, troubled marriage to Thomas Egerton. It also elides Anne Stanley's disastrous second marriage to Castlehaven; we are told simply that, "Anne, the eldest, married Grey, Baron Chandos."[85] If the monument's text manages Spencer's and her daughters' memories with

[80] On the Stanley women, see Wilkie, "'Such Daughters." On their patronage, see Fogle, "'Such a rural queen.'"

[81] Elizabeth Stanley Hastings died January 20, 1633, and was buried in St. Helen's Churchyard at Ashby-de-la-Zouch. See Wilkie, "Such Daughters," 291. Her funeral sermon, [Fletcher], *Sermon*, was printed three times before 1636.

[82] See Anon., *Arraignment*; and Herrup, *House in Gross Disorder*.

[83] See, for instance, Breasted, "*Comus* and the Castlehaven Scandal"; Mundhenk, "Dark Scandal"; and Marcus, "John Milton's *Comus*," 241–54.

[84] Wilkie, "'Such Daughters,'" 323–4. [85] From the monument.

Figure 6.4 Unknown artist, Monument for Alice Spencer, Countess of Derby (before 1636).
St. Mary's, Harefield. Author's photograph.

interesting lies, the effigies do so as well. All three daughters and their seventy-nine-year-old mother are youthful and virginal, adorned with the flowing locks of maidenhood. Representing four maidens rather than four wives, the effigies join the Stanley women in a mutual avoidance of the translation from maid to wife. The effigies embrace the materiality of women's bodies but refuse a grounding in essentialism.

The Spencer monument exempts the Stanley women from the marital and sexual relations that would disrupt their participation in the shared location of female fellowship. With the fearlessness of her granddaughter as she harrowed the venomed marble of Comus's chair, Spencer binds her own and her daughters' flesh to stone assertively and affirmatively. Set eternally in a web of alliance, the four women commemorated at Harefield are earthbound, rooted in redeemed matter, but framed between earth and heaven. The adoring grandchildren of the *Arcades* are transmuted into cherubim dotting the ceiling and architrave above the Stanley women's virginal bodies (see Figure 3.3). "The Daughters," Thomas Gainsford writes, [are placed] "in one circle with the Mother . . . moove[ing] together like faire Planets in conspicuous Orbes."[86] If the tomb is a cartography, it is a map of the stars.

Alice Egerton's orbits after *Comus*, at first glance, seem inconspicuous. Milton's fiction and his Lady's reality both involve the return of the unowned woman to her father's ownership, where, as one of eight sisters, "nature's coyn" (*Maske*, 739) would stretch only so far. While her grandmother, Alice Spencer, bequeathed "a Jewell besett with Diamonds" to Alice Egerton, she left a dowry of £3,000 to another granddaughter and namesake, Alice Hastings.[87] Alice Egerton's marriage would not take place for another eighteen years after she thwarted Comus's advances. "Canonical literary history" concerning Alice's career after *Comus*, as Sarah C. E. Ross has pointed out, may involve a number of interesting lies.[88] In June 1652, at the age of thirty-three, Alice Egerton became the third wife of Richard Vaughan, Earl of Carbery. Her married life was a song of echo: like her father, Carbery was appointed president of the Welsh Marches, which brought Alice back to Ludlow after the Restoration. And like her uncle, he was embroiled in scandal when, in 1672, he was removed from

[86] Gainsford, *History of Trebizond*, sig. L4^{r}. [87] See TNA PROB 11/174/28, fols. 94^{v} and 96^{v}.
[88] Ross, "Coteries," 339–47 at 340. I am deeply indebted to Ross's ground breaking research on this subject.

office amid charges of mistreating his servants and tenants.[89] While the overwhelming critical consensus has been that she did not remain single by choice, the recovery of traces of Alice Egerton's activities in the literate circles of her extended family suggests a different story. A year before her performance at Ludlow, she had taken part with Spencer's other grandchildren in *Arcades*, where she joined Henry Lawes in a song anticipating Sabrina's "printless feet": "O're the smooth enameld green / Where no print of step hath been, / Follow me as I sing, / And touch the warbled string" (83–6).[90] After *Comus*, evidence of Alice Egerton's continued performances in the circles in which Lawes moved suggests her involvment as a student, singer, and fellow performer with her music instructor at least until her marriage. When her cousin Jane Cavendish wrote verses in "Answeare to my Lady Alice Egertons Songe of I prethy send mee back my hart," she was most likely referring to a performance of this standard lyric by Alice in the social theater of the conjoined Egerton and Cavendish households.[91] Manuscript transcriptions of domestic celebrations in the 1640s and 1650s marking auspicious occasions – sharing, in other words, the circumstances leading to the performance of Milton's *Maske* at Ludlow – feature songs by Alice and duets with Lawes.[92] Behind these occluded texts lies an Alice Egerton who is enfleshed, during a long career of engagement, in a multiplicity of interconnected networks of performance and relation.

Following Sabrina's imperceptible footsteps, Alice Egerton also migrated from place to print. She and her sister Mary were dedictees of Lawes's 1658 *Ayres and Dialogues*, where both women are addressed by their married titles but also recalled as "Daughters to the Right Honorable John Earle of Bridgewater, Lord President of Wales, &c."[93] Katherine Philips resurrects the "Chaos, that raigns" in Comus's tangled woods (*Maske*, 334) and its redemption by women of wonder in a poem addressed "To the Right Honourable Alice Countess of Carbury, on her enriching Wales with her Presence":

> As when the first day dawn'd Mans greedy Eye
> Was apt to dwell on the bright Progidy,

[89] See *ODNB*. Ross, "Coteries," 342, notes that in a duet by Alice and Lawes celebrating the birth of John and Elizabeth Bridgewater's first son in 1646, Lawes performed the part of Echo. Williams, *Shakespeare*, 169, associates the performance with the Lady's Song of Echo in *Comus*.

[90] Alice and her siblings had appeared in masques in the court of Henrietta Maria: see Williams, *Shakespeare*, 153.

[91] Ross, "Coteries," 339–42.

[92] Ross, "Coteries," 342 and Williams, *Shakespeare*, 169.

[93] Lawes, *Ayres* (1653), a2^{r}.

Till he might careless of his Organ grow,
And so his wonder prove his danger too:
So when your Countrey (which was deem'd to be
Close-mourner in its own obscuirty
And in neglected Chaos so long lay)
Was rescu'de by your beams into a Day,
Like men into sundden lustre brought,
We justly fear'd to gaze more then we ought.

The enshrined Alice Spencer of *Arcades* yields to her granddaughter's "Shrine," where "Pilgrims" may obtain from the countess "Worth to recruit the dying world again."[94] Henry Lawes's *Select Ayres* prints a remarkable song, "The Earl to the Countess of Carbery," which presents a series of figurations of the merger of bodies in marriage: "You ask my dear if I be well," the earl addresses his countess, "feel thine own pulse, and that will tell."[95]

In these published works, Alice Egerton is silent; the recipient of songs rather than the singer. She is quasi-present in her grandmother's masque at Harefield, and in the songs saved in her family's manuscripts. If she is a phantom, she is a phantom limb. Despite her disappearance, Alice Egerton speaks to a body that retains her memory as more than a fading epitaph. Her nomadic voyages beyond Milton's *Maske* remember the fluidity and freedom from ownership enjoyed by her savior Sabrina. A woman submerged, she navigates the afterlife with a vitality and "double belongingness" that she shares with the genius of the Severn.

Alice Egerton's orbital revolutions in the social constellations that comprised her life follow her to her burial. Surviving her husband by three years, she was buried in Westminster Abbey on July 19, 1689, in a sepulcher consecrated for the burial of the Hunsdon family ("Sepulturae Familiae de Hunsdon Consecretum"). The vault and the monument rising above it were commissioned for Alice's kinsman, Henry Carey, 1st Baron Hunsdon, in 1603 by his widow and heir, George, in his honor and memory, and being mindful of their own and their family's mortality ("Honoris et Memoriae ergo sibq[ue] & suis mortalitatis memores").[96] Alice Egerton shares the vault not by virtue of her marital alliance, but through the female ties binding her to her girlhood: Alice Spencer's sister Elizabeth, wife of George Carey, was interred in the vault seventy years

94 Philips, *Poems*, 31–3. See Ross, "Coteries," 344–6, on the connections between Lawes's circle and Philips.
95 Lawes, *Select Ayres*, 90.
96 Cokayne, et al., eds., *Complete Peerage*, vol. III, 8. Inscription from the monument.

before her great-niece. Neither woman's name appears on the monument, but carved on a floor slab near the sepulcher – unnoticed until one turns her back on the opulent tomb – "The Lord of Hunsdons Valt" lists twenty names of relations buried there, including "Elizabeth [Spencer] the 2nd B His Relict 1618" and "Alice [Egerton], wife of Richard 2nd E of Carbery 1689."[97] Although Alice Egerton is buried in the splendor of the tallest monument in the Abbey, she rests there silently; no epitaph attends the bracketed name etched on a stone that is easily overlooked. The Spencer coat of arms on the tomb enlists Alice and her great-aunt in the Carey nation of the dead and also draws them into the Stanley women's monumental circle. The arms are a ghostly marker of the invisible but intractable threads connecting Alice Egerton to the site of her mother's and grandmother's memorial at Harefield and to the lived relationships remembered in its vital remains.

Alice Egerton's silent grave finds its vocal complement in the plural literacies of Henry Lawes's songbooks; collections of texts that engage readers but, at the same time, prompt embodiment in performance. We must look to Lawes's published score and lyrics, put in the mouth of Richard Vaughan as he sings to his countess, for Alice's epitaph:

> When first I view'd thee, I did spy
> Thy Soul stand beck'ning in thine Eye;
> My Heart knew what it meant,
> And at the very first Kiss went,
> Two balls of Wax so run,
> When melted into one
> Mix'd now with thine, my Heart now lies,
> And much Loves Riddle as thy Prize.[98]

If this song was, in fact, performed, only the memory of the lost body lingers here. Yet Alice Egerton's hybrid form – uniting body and text, place and print – finds a resonant memorial in this brilliant figuration of the blending of living bodies into a single viscous substance, a substance between states that beckons and encloses the heart.

[97] From the slab, situated near the tomb in the chapel of St. John the Baptist. The brackets are part of the inscriptions. The slab was installed after 1708, the date of the last recorded burial.

[98] Lawes, *Select Ayres*, 90.

Conclusion
Many Worlds Fantastic Framed

> [A]bout two years ago at Vercelli . . . while I began to investigate something of eternity that must be respected in the old sacred temples, according to my custom, at that time indeed I responded to a certain ignorant priest asking what my occupation was, "Within those Pythian prophecies, I have learned how to raise the dead sometimes from the infernal regions." And when these things had been said, although I abandoned him—coarse, uncertain, and astounded—in that same place, I thought indeed that my art must by no means be abandoned.
>
> –Cyriac of Ancona[1]

> O, wonder!
> How many goodly creatures are there here!
> How beauteous mankind is! O brave new world,
> That has such people in't!
>
> – William Shakespeare[2]

In 1509, Wynkyn de Worde published a broadside elegy lamenting the death of King Henry VII (see Figure C.1). In ballad form, the author – long identified as John Skelton, but more likely Stephen Hawes – sings the praises of the monarch and ends each stanza with slight variations on the refrain, "henry the seventh alas alas lyeth dede." The attribution of the stanzas to John Skelton, poet laureate during Henry's reign, no doubt rests upon the presence of Skelton's Latin epitaph "in tabula pensili" ("Hanging

[1] Ciriaco de' Pizzicolli, *Kyriaci Anconitani Itinerarium*, ed. Mehus, 55. This is Cyriac's letter to Johannes Ricinatus (Giacomo Veneri de Racaneto), Bishop of Ragusa. The Latin reads: "nondum exacto biennio apud Vercellas . . . dum vetustis in sacris aedibus nostro de more aliquid verendae aeternitatis indagare coepissem, sacerdoti cuidam ignaro, quaenam mea ars esset interroganti ex tempore equidam respondi, mortuos quandoque ab Infernis suscitare Pythia illa inter vaticinia didici. Et haec ubi dicta, quum ibidem vulgarem, incertum, obstupescentemque reliquissem, artem vero meam haud reliquendam putavi." I am grateful to Jaime Goodrich for her translation. Jacob Burckhardt, *Civilization*,181, famously attributes to Cyriac the wish "to wake the dead."

[2] Shakespeare, *Tempest*, 5.1.181–4.

de all wrapped in wretchydnes
y pompes ſo gay & gloryous
asures and all thy ryches
y be but tranſytoryous
to moche pyteous
e that eche man whylom dred
by naturall lyne and cours
is alas lyeth dede

Of this moost cryſten kynge in vs it lyeth not
His tyme paſſed honour ſuffycyent to prayſe
But yet though that/that thyng envalue we may not
Our prayers of ſuertye he ſhall haue alwayes
And though that atropoſe hathe ended his dayes
His name and fameſhall euer be dred
As fer as phebus ſpredes his golden rayes
Though henry the ſeuenth alas alas lyeth dede

Figure C.1 John Skelton (attrib.), "Elegy on the Death of Henry VII" (London: W. de Worde, 1509).
The Bodleian Libraries, The University of Oxford.
Douce Fragm. E20 (1) (detail).

on a board") near the monarch's tomb in Westminster Abbey.[3] This ephemeral monument has not survived. It was first printed in Skelton's *Pithy, Pleasaunt and Profitable Works* in 1568 – a volume edited by John Stow – where it acquired the permanence of print.[4] But it seems to have remained in the chapel for at least a century after the king's death and the epitaph's composition: in his 1600 guide to the Westminster tombs, William Camden prints the poem from the board, apparently still *in situ* near the monument.

The broadside can be read in myriad ways, and each tells us much about the rituals of remembrance in the pre-Reformation moment of its publication. The collective, repetitive masses and obits of Catholic commemoration – the ceremonies that John Gower so aggressively pursued as he approached death and on which, he believed, his success in the afterlife depended – are reflected in the implied orality of the ballad and its shared performance. Yet these liturgical rituals are deflected as well, displaced from the graveside to the page. Glossing Skelton's orthodox Latin epitaph, perhaps implying a loose translation of it, the vernacular poem places its audience in proximity with the grave,

[3] Camden, *Reges, reginae*, sig. D1^{r}.

[4] Skelton, *Pithy, Pleasaunt and Profitable Works*, sig. Z2^{r-v}. On Stow's edition of Skelton, see Griffiths, "Text and Authority." Since the poem did not appear in the first edition of Skelton's collected works, *Certayn Bokes Compyled by Mayster Skelton* (edited by Henry Dab and printed in 1545 but surviving only in a 1563 reprint), it seems likely that Stow retrieved the text from its display near the king's tomb in the Abbey.

reproducing in print (as Camden's erudite antiquarian guide also does) the experience of witnessing the monument and its effigy in the chapel in Westminster. The passage from this quiet interior to the stir of popular readership is punctuated by the ballad's woodcut, which seems to borrow the traditional, familiar image of *Moriens* – the Dying – from medieval *artes moriendi* to represent our king in a paradoxical living death. Supplied with the accoutrements of royalty, the crown and the scepter, Henry nonetheless appears to be lying naked on his deathbed, eyes still open. This conflation of genres, perhaps, marks the thin line in the pre-Reformation between life and death, the living and the dead. To visit the tomb is in some sense to visit the deathbed, the place from which the dead will, eventually awaken and arise. Affirming this faith, the ballad returns – notionally, fictionally – to the graveside in its final stanza, resituating this improvisational rite of remembrance in its sanctioned site:

> And nowe for conclusyon aboute his herse,
> Let this be gravyd for endeles memorye
> With sorrowfull tunes of Thesyphenes verse
> Here lyeth the puyssaunt and myghty henry
> Hector in battayll/ Ulyses in polecy
> Salamon in wysdome the noble rose to rede
> Creses in rychesse Julyus in glory
> Henry the seventh ingraved here lyeth dede.

Here, on the broadside sheet as in his sepulcher, the king is "ingraved."

This book has followed a similar trajectory from the church interior to the bustling world beyond. Seeing remembrance as a concept energized and renewed specifically in the confessional changes of the Reformation, I have outlined the shape of this newly imagined idea in artifacts and writings that question the relevance of traditional beliefs to new worlds and create innovative, improvised rituals of remembrance. Carrying memories of past beliefs into new commemorative forms and sites, these works and practices reinvent early modern subjects as well, as the living are joined to the dead, and to the world, and to each other.

I end with an author who experienced and imagined "many worlds . . . fantastic framed" and made innovative use of remembrance to chart a course between them.[5] When Anne Bradstreet's collection of poems *The Tenth Muse, Lately Sprung Up in America*, was printed in London in 1650, a series of epitaphs for prominent Elizabethan figures – Guillaume du

[5] Bradstreet, *Tenth Muse*, 203.

Bartas, Sir Philip Sidney, and Queen Elizabeth herself – created, in Catherine Gray's evocative term, "a ghostly coterie."[6] Negotiating both the cultural proximity of New England to Old – an affinity described by Bradstreet as one of mother and daughter – and the confessional and physical distances between them, Bradstreet concludes her lengthy elegies with short, pseudo-inscriptional epitaphs.[7] This geographical dexterity suggests that "pieces" of Old England – quite literally, monuments and the effigies they carry – persist and reside in New, even as Bradstreet's book contains "pieces" of America transported back to native shores. Explaining his decision to publish without the author's approval, John Woodbridge writes, "I found that divers had gotten some scattered papers [and] were likely to have sent forth broken pieces to the Author's prejudice, which I thought to prevent, as well as to pleasure those that earnestly desired the view of the whole."[8] Presenting the whole, rather than broken pieces, Woodbridge hopes to prevent an iconoclasm that would deform Bradstreet's textual monument.

The strained symbiosis between the old and new worlds is set forth in Bradstreet's "Dialogue between Old England and New, Concerning Their Present Troubles. Anno 1642," where New England is figured as a "Faire Branche" of her mother's.[9] "And thou a childe, a Limbe, and dost not feele / My weakned fainting body now to reele?" Old England asks, "If I decease, dost think thou shalt survive?"[10] If New England is a limb, the absolute dependence asserted by the mother suggests that, despite distance, she is still "a piece" of the maternal body.[11] She is a phantom limb: neither perceived as dead flesh or lost matter, nor positing a mere memory of embodiment, the quasi-present phantom limb reveals the intertwining of mind and matter, of the self and the world – and of one world and another.[12] Like Milton's "thick and gloomy shadows damp" that haunt the grave (*Maske*, 469), the severed limb, New England, carries the material trace of the world she has lost.

When her *Several Poems* was published posthumously in Boston in 1678, Bradstreet's text came back home. Among its "Elegies and Epitaphs," more personal remembrances appear, and the monumental

6 Gray, *Women Writers and Public Debate*, 143–81.
7 See Wright, "Epitaphic Conventions," 243–62 for an excellent discussion of the epitaphic strategy as a means of reformulating the relationship of the living to the dead.
8 Woodbridge, "To the Reader," in Bradstreet, *Tenth Muse*, sig. A3^{v}.
9 Fuller, *Davids Hainous Sinne*, sig. A2^{r}.
10 Bradstreet, "A Dialogue Between Old England and New," in *Tenth Muse*, 181.
11 Shakespeare and Wilkins, *Pericles*, 3.1.17–18.
12 Merleau-Ponty, *Visible and Invisible*, 89.

Figure C.2 Unknown artist, Monument for Sir Thomas Dudley (1653). Eliot Burying Ground, Roxbury, MA. Photograph by Iman Khadija Berrahou.

landscape is more immediate. Like her English publication, the American volume begins with Bradstreet's dedication to her father, but now his elegy and epitaph are printed as well: "Within this Tomb," Bradstreet writes," a Patriot lyes," concluding equivocally, "And when his time with years was spent, / If some rejoyc'd, more did lament."[13] Although her mother had died in 1643, her epitaph was not printed in *The Tenth Muse*; it appears here, an epitaph without an elegy, recalling "A Worthy Matron of unspotted life / A loving Mother and obedient wife."[14] Thomas Dudley was buried in the Eliot Burying Ground in Roxbury, Massachusetts, in 1653, in a churchyard vault that, like the Tradescant monument in Lambeth, would hold the remains of male descendants (see Figure C.2).[15] A lead plaque with an inscription was once installed on the marble ledger stone, but it has long since disappeared. Whether or not it bore the epitaph written by Dudley's daughter is unknown.

[13] Bradstreet, "To the Memory of my dear and ever honoured Father, Thomas Dudley, Esq." in *Several Poems*, 219.

[14] Bradstreet, "An Epitaph on my dear and ever honoured Mother, Mrs. Dorothy Dudley," in *Several Poems*, 220.

[15] An inscribed plaque on the side of the monument indicates that Joseph Dudley (d. 1720), Chief Paul Dudley (d. 1752), and Col. William Dudley (d. 1743) are buried in the vault.

Figure C.3 North Andover Historical Commission, Monument for Anne Bradstreet (2000). Old Burying Ground, North Andover, MA. Photograph by Iman Khadija Berrahou. By permission of the North Andover Historical Commission, North Andover, MA, USA.

It is also not certain where Anne Bradstreet was laid to rest, but on the 350th anniversary of the publication of *The Tenth Muse*, a monument was placed for her in the Old Burying Ground in North Andover, Massachusetts (see Figure C.3). In an act of recovery that Bradstreet could never have foreseen, the monument is inscribed with John Norton's dedication to his elegy on Bradstreet, published in *Several Poems*:

> Mirror of Her Age, Glory of her Sex, whose
> Heaven-born-Soul leaving its earthly Shrine,
> chose its native home, and was taken to its
> Rest, upon 16th. Sept. 1672.[16]

In a new ritual of remembrance, the scattered pieces of the American woman poet – a new-world Phaethon – are gathered and commemorated, in a ceremony of celebration rather than grief.

[16] Norton, "Funeral Elegy upon … Mrs. Anne Bradstreet, in Bradstreet, *Several Poems*, 252.

Monuments are points of convergence for aesthetic, religious, political, and cultural strands within the tapestry of early modern life. They are subject to and help to guide post-Reformation conceptions and suspicions of visual images. Their epitaphs speak to the disputed contract between sorrow and consolation. Their inscriptions and heraldry render them repositories of dynastic narratives, and their effigies embody and negotiate the conventions of gender and class. Affording monuments and the remembrance they convey a central place in the literary, cultural, and confessional movements of the post-Reformation period, this book has attempted to recover and celebrate these remarkable artifacts. Coaxing these long-silent effigies to life, these chapters have charted their surprising transmigrations into expansive spaces of post-Reformation experience and expression, and traced their contours beneath the surfaces of familiar texts and works – shapes that cause us to look twice, to glimpse and possess unexpected rarities that, in turn, possess us.

Bibliography

Manuscripts

BL Add MS 6703, John Tradescant the Elder to Edward Nicholas, July 31, 1625.
BL Add MS 15232, "Poems of Sir Philip Sidney" ("The Bright Manuscript"), late sixteenth century.
BL Add MS 15632, fol. 44^{r}, "Proceedings and Order of the Privy Council upon a Petition of the Masters of Requests," August 3, 1662.
BL Add MS 28560, Sydney Mountagu, "Valida Consolatio," January 1, 1614.
BL Add MS 36529, "Poems by Henry Howard, Earl of Surrey, Sir Thomas Wyatt, and Others" ("The Hill Manuscript"), sixteenth–seventeenth centuries.
BL Add MS 38823, "The Commonplace Book of Sir Edward Hoby," c. 1582–1596.
BL Add MS 59855, "Gower Missal of Sarum Use," c. 1410–1420?
BL Cotton Tiberius A. IV, John Gower, "Vox Clamantis and Other Latin Poems," fifteenth century.
BL Lansdowne MS 102/94, William Cecil, "Notes on the Will of Blanche Parry," 1578.
BL Loan MS 76, "The Bridgewater Manuscript of John Milton's Maske Presented at Ludlow Castle," 1634.
BL Royal Addendum 68, "A Boke of Soche Jewells… Nowe in Charge of Mrs. Blaunshe Parrey," July 1, 1587.
BL Sloane MS 1446, fols. 37^{v}–38^{v}, John Milton, "Poem on Marchioness of Winchester, 1631," seventeenth century (copy).
BL Sloane MS 1839, fols. 50–91. Sir Hamon L'Estrange, "Observations on Thomas Browne's *Vulgar Errors*," 1653.
Bod MS Ashmole 824, fols. 175^{r}–86^{v}, John Tradescant, "A Viag of Ambusad Undertaken by the Right Honorable Sir Dudlie Digges in the Year 1618," 1618.
Bod MS Ashmole 1461, "Tradescant's Orchard," after 1611.
Bod MS Ashmole 1511, "The Ashmole Bestiary," Peterborough[?], thirteenth century.
Bod MS 294, John Gower, "Confessio Amantis," England, early fifteenth century.

Bod MS Carte 74, item 187, James Montagu to Sidney Montagu, Esquire, at Hemington House, June 27, 1606.

Bod MS Rawlinson D. 912, fols. 668^{r}–69^{v}, “Confession of Hester Tradescant,” September 1, 1676.

Bod MS Lat. misc. d. 85. *Codex Ashmolensis*, Bartolomeo Fonzio “Collectanea epigraphica,” Florence, late fifteenth century.

Borthwick 2, fols. 418^{r}–419^{v}. Will of Agnes Bedford, 1459.

Borthwick, 9, fols. 272–73^{r}. Will of Joan Thurcrosse, 1524.

Canterbury Cathedral Archives, Lit. Mss. E16a, John Bargrave, “Catalogue of Dr. Bargrave’s Collection,” 1676.

Church of England. Church Survey: Barnwell All Saints Church Survey, CARE 28/302, File 902, Doc. 902.1, n.d.

Glasgow University Library, MS Hunter 59 T.2.17, John Gower, “Vox Clamantis, Chronica Tripertita, Carmina Minora, and Traitié,” c. 1399–1408.

Hunt MS EL 6844: Letter from Thomas Fowler to the Earl of Bridgewater enclosing inscriptions for monument to Countess of Bridgewater. June 17, 1638.

Hunt MS EL 6850, Robert Codrington, Volume of verses in Latin and English by Robert Codrington on the death of the Countess of Bridgewater, 1636.

Hunt MS EL 6883: John Carter, “A Sermon Preached at Little Gaddesden in the Countie of Hartford: At the Funerall of the Truely Noble & Vertuous Lady Frances Stanley on of the Daughters and Coheires of the Right Honorable Ferdinand Late Earle of Derby, Late Wife of John Earle of Bridgewater the First Earle of That Familie. The 2nd of Aprill Anno Domini MDCXXXVI,” 1636.

Hunt MS HM 68179, “Epicedium to John Egerton 1st Earl of Bridgewater and His Wife Frances Stanley Egerton, Followed by Various Epithalamia and Acrosti Verses Celebrating the Marriage of Their Daughter Magdalen to Sir Gervase Cutler in 1633,” 1633.

Huntington MS EL 6845, Anon., Latin inscription for the monument to Frances Countess of Bridgewater, c. 1636.

Lambeth Palace Library, “Will of John Gower, Register of Archbishop Thomas Arundel, 1396–97,” fols. 256^{r}–57^{r}, 1399–1414.

Magdalene College, Cambridge, MS PL 2972/226a and b, “John Tredescant’s Monum.^{t} in Lamb^{eth} Church-Yrd,” unidentified artist, second half of the seventeenth century.

NRO MS, uncatalogued, Sidney Montagu, “Upon the Birth and death of his deere sonne, Henry Mountagu, Sir Sidney Mountagu, Knight, Anno Do [mini] 1627,” ca. 1627 (copy).

NRO Montagu MS 3, fol. 118^{r}, Charles Montagu to Edward Montagu, December 13, 1620.

NRO Montagu MS 6, fol. 183^{r}, Sidney Montagu to Edward Montagu, October 22, 1602.

NRO, Montagu MS 3, fols. 180^{r}–81^{r}, Edward Montagu to James Montagu, April 10, 1616.

NRO Montagu MS 3, fol. 69^{r}, Elizabeth Montagu to Edward Montagu, n.d.
NRO Montagu MS 3, fol. 102^{r}, Charles Montagu to Edward Montagu, March 21, 1618.
NRO Montagu MS 3, fol. 186^{r}, Edward Montagu to James Montagu, April 25, 1617.
NRO Montagu MS 3, fols. 235–59, Ann Montagu, "Letters, Prayers, and Poems," 1637.
NRO Montagu MS 6, fol. 183^{r}, Sidney Montagu to Edward Montagu, October 22, 1602.
NRO Montagu MS 186, item 10, Joseph Bentham, "Life of Lord Edward Montagu," early 1640s.
NRO Montagu MS 186, item 13, Edward Montagu, "Directions to my Sonne," January 12, 1620.
NRO Montagu MS 191 loose sheet, Ann Montagu to Lord Edward Montagu, n.d.
NRO Montagu MS 191 loose sheet, Elizabeth Montagu to Edward Montagu, n.d.
TNA C7/454/1 Ashmole v. Tradescant, 1662.
TNA C7/541/2, Ashmole v. De Critz 1679.
TNA PROB 11/24/113, Will of Dame Katherine Styles, August 8, 1530.
TNA PROB 11/53/261, Will of Humphrey Hales, August 8, 1568.
TNA PROB 11/74/331, Will of Frances, Countess of Sussex, December 6, 1588.
TNA PROB 11/75/180, Will of Blanche Parry, February 17, 1589.
TNA PROB 11/113/540, Will of Lady Elizabeth Russell, Dowager, June 23, 1609.
TNA PROB 11/131/760, Will of Elizabeth Harington Montagu, March 20, 1616.
TNA PROB 11/148/393, Will of Sir Charles Montagu, February 18, 1626.
TNA PROB 11/160/168, Will of John Smith, Captain of Saint Sepulchre, London, July 1, 1631.
TNA PROB 11/174/28, Will of the Right Honorable Alice Countess of Derby, Dowager of Harefield, Middlesex, January 26, 1636.
TNA PROB 11/196/404, Will of Edward Mountagu of Boughton, January 20, 1644.
TNA PROB 11/308/88, Will of John Tredescant, Gardener of South Lambeth, April 4, 1661.
TNA PROB 11/132/132, Will of James Montagu, Bishop of Winchester, April 6, 1618.
TNA PROB 11/356/545, Will of Hester Treduscant, Widow of South Lambeth, September 19, 1667.
TNA SP 12/1, fols. 20^{r}–29^{r}, "Inventory of All the Beddinges and Other Moveables of Card[inal Pole]," November 20, 1558.
TNA SP 12/13, fols. 77^{r}–79^{r}, William Cecil, "Draft Proclamation against Defacing of Monuments," 1560.
TNA SP 70/84, fols. 202^{r}–3^{v}, Sir Thomas Hoby to William Cecil, June 19, 1566.
TNA SP 70/84, fols. 200^{r}–1^{r}, Sir Thomas Hoby to Queen Elizabeth I, June 19, 1566.
Trinity College, Cambridge, Trinity MS R. 34, John Milton, "Trinity Manuscript," seventeenth century.

Primary Sources

Anon. *The Arraignment and Conviction of Mervin, Lord Audley, Earl of Castlehaven, who was by 26. Peers of the Realm Found Guilty for Committing Rapine and Sodomy at Westminster, on Monday, April 25, 1631*. London: Tho. Thomas, 1642.

Frederyke of Jennen. London: W. Copland for Abraham Vele, 1560.

The Holy Bible. London: Robert Barker, 1611.

Physiologus: A Medieval Book of Nature Lore. Translated by Michael J. Curley. University of Chicago Press, 2009.

The Rare Triumphs of Love and Fortune. London: E[dward] A[llde] for Edward White, 1589.

Abbott, George. *An Exposition upon the Prophet Jonah*. London: Richard Field, 1600.

Achelley, Thomas. *The Key of Knowledge*. London: William Seres, 1572.

Acosta, Jose de. *Naturall and Morall Historie of the East and West Indies*. Translated by Edward Grimestone. London: Valentine Sims for Edward Blount and William Aspley, 1604.

Alciato, Andrea. *Emblematum libellus*. Venice: Aldus, 1546.

Aldrovandi, Ulisse. *Musaeum metallicum in libro IV*. Bologna: Marcus Antonius Bernia, 1648.

Andrewes, John. *Andrewes Humble Petition unto Almighty God, Declaring His Repentance*. London: John Wright, 1623.

Ashmole, Elias. *Antiquities of Berkshire*, 3 vols. London: E. Curll, 1719.

Attersoll, William. *Badges of Christianity*. London: W. Jaggard, 1606.

Principles of Christian Religion. London: Thomas Cotes, 1635.

Augustine of Hippo. *Confessions*. Translated by R. S. Pine. Middlesex: Penguin, 2002.

Bacon, Francis. *Sylva Sylvarum, or A Naturall History*. London: J. Lee, 1627.

Bale, John. *Scriptorum illustrium majoris Brytannie*. Basil: Joannem Oporium, 1557.

Bartholomeus Angelus, *Batman uppon Bartholome his Booke De Proprietatibus Rerum*. Translated by Stephen Batman. London: Thomas East, 1582.

Bentham, Joseph. *Christian Conflict*. London: Philemon Stephens and Christopher Meridith, 1635.

Societie of the Saints. London: George Miller, 1630.

Bodnar, Edward W., and Clive Foss, ed. and trans. *Cyriac of Ancona. Later Writings. The I Tatti Renaissance Library*. Cambridge, MA: Harvard University Press, 2003.

Bolton, Robert. *Some Generall Directions for a Comfortable Walking with God: Delivered in the Lecture at Kettering*. London: Felix Kingston for Edmund Weaver, 1626.

Boreman, Robert. *A Mirrour of Christianity, and a Miracle of Charity*. London: E. C. for R. Royston, 1669.

Bradstreet, Anne. *The Tenth Muse, Lately Sprung Up in America*. London: Stephen Bowtell, 1650.

Several Poems. Boston: John Foster, 1678.

Brathwaite, Richard. *Essaies upon the Five Senses*. London: E. Griffin for Richard Whittaker, 1620.

Browne, Thomas. *Pseudodoxia epidemica*. London: T. H. for E. Dod, 1646.

Buchanan, William. *Institutions of Christian Religion*. Translated by Robert Hill. London: George Snowdon and Leonell Snowdon, and R. Field, 1606.

Calvin, Jean. *A Commentarie of Iohn Calvine, upon the First Booke of Moses Called Genesis*. Translated by Thomas Tymme. London: Henry Middleton for John Harrison and George Bishop, 1578.

A Harmonie upon the Three Evangelists, Matthew, Mark and Luke . . . Whereunto Is Also Added a Commentarie upon the Evangelist S. John. Translated by Eusebius Pagit. London: Thomas Dawson, 1584.

Two and Twentie Sermons of Maister John Calvin. Translated by Thomas Stocker. London: Thomas Dawson for John Harrison and Thomas Man, 1580.

Camden, William. *Britain, or A Chorographicall Description of the Most Flourishing Kingdomes, England, Scotland, and Ireland, and the Ilands Adjoyning, out of the Depth of Antiquitie [Britannia]*. London: George Bishop and John Norton, 1610.

Reges, reginae, nobiles, & alij in ecclesia collegiata B. Petri Westmonasterij sepulti, vsque ad annum reparatae saluti. London: E. Bolifantus, 1600.

Remains Concerning Britaine. London: Thomas Harper for John Waterson, 1636.

Cardano, Girolamo. *De subtilitate* (1560). Edited by John M. Forrester; with an Introduction by John Henry and John M. Forrester. 2 vols. Tempe: ACMRS, 2013.

Cawdrey, Henry. *Superstitio Superstes, or The Reliques of Superstition*. London: P. W., 1641.

Caxton, William. *The Game and Playe of the Chesse*. London: Needham, P. the Printer & Pardoner, 1474.

Chapman, George, trans. *Homer's Odyssey*. London: Richard Field and W. Jaggard for Nathaniell Butter, 1615.

Church of England, *Homyly against Peryll of Idolatry and Superfluous Decking of Churches, in the Second Tome of Homelyes*. London: Richard Jugge and John Cawood, 1563.

Cornwallis, William. *Miraculous and Happie Union of England and Scotland*. London: George Eld for Edward Blount, 1604.

Cyriac of Ancona (Ciriaco de' Pizzicolli). *Kyriaci Anconitani Itinerarium*. Edited by Laurentius Mehus. Florence: Joannis Pauli Giovannelli, 1742.

Davies, John. *The Holy Roode*. London: Nathaniel Butter, 1634.

Deacon, John. *A Treatise Intitled, Nobody Is My Name*. London: Robert Waldegrave, 1587.

Donne, John. *The Complete English Poems*. Edited by A. J. Smith. Middlesex: Penguin, 1971.

Dugdale, William. *The History of St. Paul's Cathedral*. London: Thomas Warren, 1658.

Eliot, John. *Poems, or, Epigrams, Satyrs, Elegies, Songs and Sonnets, Upon Several Persons and Occasions*. London: Henry Brome, 1658.
Engel, William E., Rory Loughnane, and Grant Williams, eds. *The Memory Arts in Renaissance England: A Critical Anthology*. Cambridge University Press, 2016.
England and Wales, Parliament, *Ordinance of the Lords and Commons Assembled in Parliament for the utter Demolishing, Removing and Taking Away of all Monuments of Idolatry [28 August 1643]*. London: Edward Husbands, 1643.
England and Wales, Sovereign, Elizabeth I, 1558–1603. *A Proclamation Against Breakinge or Defacing of Monuments of Antiquitie*. London: Richard Jugge and John Cawood, 1560.
Sovereign, James I, 1566–1625. *Basilikon doron*. London: Felix Kyngston for John Norton, 1603.
England and Wales, Sovereign, James I, 1566–1625. *Works of the Most High and Mightie Prince, James, by Grace of God Kinge of Great Britain, France and Ireland, Defender of the Faith, etc*. Edited by James Montagu. London: Robert Barker and John Bill, 1616.
Erasmus, Desiderius. *The First Tome or Volume of the Paraphrase of Erasmus upon the Newe Testamente*. Translated by Nicholas Udall. London: Edward Whitchurche, 1548.
Estienne, Henri. *A World of Wonders*. London: Richard Field for John Norton, 1607.
Estwick, Nicholas. *A Learned and Godly Sermon preached on the XIX day of December, An. Dom. MDCXXXI, at the Funeral of M. Robert Bolton*. London: George Miller, 1639.
F., J. [Fletcher, John]. *A Sermon Preached at Ashby De-La-Zouch in the Countie of Leicester: Upon the Funerall of the Truly Noble and Vertuous Lady Elizabeth Stanley ... The 9. Of February Anno Dom. 1633*. London: W.I. and T.P., 1635.
Fuller,Thomas. *Davids Hainous Sinne*. London: Thomas Cotes for John Bellamie, 1631.
Fuller, Thomas. *History of the Worthies of England*. London: J.G.W.L. and W.G. for Thomas Williams, 1662.
Gainsford, Thomas. *History of Trebizond*. London: Thomas Downes and Ephraim Dawson, 1616.
Gilbert, William. *De magnete*. London: Peter Short, 1600.
Goebel, Severin. *Pia commonefactio de passione, resurrection ac beneficiis Christi, quae in historia succinic depinguntur*. Oberursell: s.n. 1589.
Gower, John. *The Complete Works of John Gower*. Edited by G. C. Macauley, 4 vols. Oxford: Clarendon Press, 1901.
Gower, John. *Confessio Amantis*. London: William Caxton, 1483.
Gower, John. Gower, John. *Jo. Gower de confessione amantis*. London: Thomas Berthelette, 1554.
Gower, John. "Testamentum Johannis Gower." In Henry Todd, *Illustrations of the Lives and Writings of Gower and Chaucer*, 88–90. London: F. C. and J. Rivington, et al., 1810.

Greene, Robert. *Pandosto, the Triumph of Time*. London: Thomas Orwin for Thomas Cadman, 1588.

Gunton, Simon. *The History of the Church at Peterborough*. London: Richard Chiswell, 1686.

Hall, Joseph. *A Briefe Summe of the Principles of Religion*. In *Works*. *799–800*. London: Thomas Pavier, Miles Flesher, and John Haviland, 1625.

Contemplations, the Sixth Volume. London: John Haviland for Nathaniel Butter, 1622.

A Sermon Preached at the Happily-restored and Reedified Cappell of the Right Honorable the Earle of Exceter in his House, of S. Johns on Saint Stephens Day. 1623. London: F. Kyngston for George Winder, 1624.

Harvey, Christopher. *Schola Cordis*. London: H. Blunden, 1647.

Hawes, Stephen. *"Elegy on the Death of Henry VII."* London: W. de Worde, 1509.

Hearne, Thomas. *A Collection of Curious Discourses Written by Eminent Antiquaries Upon Several Heads in our English Antiquities*, 2 vols. London: W. and J. Richardson, 1771.

Hentzner, Paul. *Journey into England*. London: Strawberry Hill, 1757.

Herbert, George. *Witts Recreation*. London: Humphrey Blunden, 1640.

Hill, Robert. "Epistle Dedicatorie." In Perkins, *A Godly and Learned Exposition … [upon] the Revelation*, fols. *4^{r}–A3^{v}.

Lectures Upon … the Revelation," fols. ¶3–A4^{r}.

Hooker, Richard. *Lawes of Ecclesiasticall Politie. The fift Booke*. London: John Windet, 1597.

A Remedie against Sorrow and Feare Delivered in a funerall Sermon. Oxford: Joseph Barnes, 1612.

Isidore of Seville. *The Etymologies of Isidore of Seville*. Translated by Stephen A. Barney, W. J. Lewis, J. A. Beach, and Oliver Berghof. Cambridge University Press, 2006.

Jacobus de Voragine, *Legenda aurea sanctorum*. Translated by William Caxton. London: William Caxton, 1483.

Jay, George. *A Sermon Preacht at the Funerall of the Lady Mary Villiers, Eldest Daughter of the Right Hon[ora]ble Christopher Earle of Anglesey Who Dyed the XXI. of January 1625. at Horningold in Leicester Shire, and Was Buried the XXIIIJ. at Goadeby in the Sepulchres of Her Ancestors*. London: Thomas Harper, 1626.

Jonson, Ben. *The Key Keeper: A Masque for the Opening of Britain's Burse, 19 April 1609*. Edited by James Knowles. *Illustrated by David Gentleman*. Tunbridge Wells: Foundling Press, 2002.

The New Inn. London: Thomas Harper, 1631.

Lawes, Henry. *Ayres and Dialogues for One, Two, and Three Voyces: The First–Thirde Booke*. London: T. H. for John Playford, 1653–1658.

Select Ayres and Dialogues. London: William Godbid for John Playford, 1669.

Leech, Jeremy. *A Sermon, Preached before the Lords of the Councel, in K. Henry the Seauenths Chappell. Sept. 23. 1607 at the Funerall of the Most Excellent &*

Hopefull Princess, the Lady Marie's Grace. London: H[umphrey] L[ownes] for Samuel Macham, 1607.
Leigh, Richard. *The Transproser Rehears'd*. Oxford: Hugo Grotius, 1673.
Martial, *Epigrams*. Translated by D. R. Shackleton Bailey. *Loeb Classical Library* 94. 2 vols. Cambridge, MA: Harvard University Press, 1993.
Milton, John. *Complete Works of John Milton, Volume III: The Shorter Poems*. Edited by Barbara Keifer Lewalski and Estelle Haan. Oxford University Press, 2012.
The History of Britain. In *The Complete Prose Works of John Milton*. Edited by Don M. Wolfe, et al., vol. 5, 1–403. 8 vols. New Haven: Yale University Press, 1953–1983.
A Maske Presented at Ludlow Castle, 1634. London: Humphrey Robinson, 1637.
The Poems of Mr. John Milton. London: Ruth Raworth for Humphrey Moseley, 1645.
Montagu, Henry. *Contemplatio mortis et immortalitatis [Manchester al mondo]*. London: Robert Barker, 1631.
Montagu, Walter, *The Coppy of a Letter Sent from France by Mr. Walter Mountagu to His Father the Lord Privie Seale, with His Answere Thereunto Also a Second Answere to the Same Letter by the Faukland*. London: s.n., 1641.
Ovid. *Metamorphoses, Books I–VIII*. Translated by Frank Justus Miller. Loeb Classical Library 42. Cambridge, MA: Harvard University Press, 1916.
Metamorphoses, Books IX–XVI. Translated by Frank Justus Miller. Loeb Classical Library 43. Cambridge, MA: Harvard University Press, 1916.
Parkinson, John. *Paradisi in sole paradisus terrestris*. London: Humphrey Lownes and Robert Young, 1629.
Perkins, William. *A Case of Conscience*. Edinburgh: Robert Waldgrave, 1592.
Catholico reformado. Translated by Guillermo Massan London: En casa de Ricardo del Campo [i.e. Richard Field], 1599.
A Christian and Plaine Treatise of the Manner and Order of Predestination. Translated by Thomas Tuke. London: Felix Kingston for William Welby and Martin Clarke, 1606.
Christian Oeconomie. Translated by Thomas Pickering. London: Felix Kyngston, 1609.
A Commentarie or Exposition upon the First Five Chapters of the Epistle to the Galatians. Cambridge: John Legat, 1604.
A Godly and Learned Exposition of Christs Sermon in the Mount. Edited by Thomas Pierson. Cambridge: Thomas Brooke and Cantrell Legge, 1608.
A Godly and Learned Exposition or Commentarie upon the First Three Chapters of the Revelation. Edited by Robert Hill. London: William Islip for Cuthbert Burbie, 1606.
A Golden Chaine, or The Description of Theologie. Cambridge: John Legate, 1600.
Lectures upon the First Three Chapters of the Revelation. London: Richard Field for Cuthbert Burbie, 1604.

A Reformed Catholicke. Cambridge: John Legat, 1597.
Satans Sophistrie Answered. Edited by Robert Hill. London: Richard Field for E. E., 1604.
Petrarch, Francis. *Rime Sparse and Other Lyrics*. Translated by Robert Durling. Cambridge, MA: Harvard University Press, 1976.
Philips, Katherine. *Poems*. London: J. G. for Richard Marriott, 1664.
Pierson, Thomas. "Epistle Dedicatorie." In Perkins, *Godly and Learned Exposition . . . [upon] the Revelation*, fols. ¶3$^{r–v}$.
Plato. *Euthyphro, Apology, Crito, Phaedo, Phaedrus*. Translated by Harold North Folwer. Loeb Classical Library 36. Cambridge, MA: Harvard University Press, 1914.
Platter, Thomas. *Thomas Platter's Travels in England 1599*. Trans. Clare Williams. London: Jonathan Cape, 1937.
Pliny. *Historie of the World, Commonly Called the Naturall Historie*. Translated by Philemon Holland. London: Adam Islip, 1601.
Plutarch. *Philosophie, Commonly Called the Morals*. Trans. Philemon Holland. London: Arnold Hatfield, 1603.
Pontano, Giovanni Gioviano. *De tumulis duo*. In *Opera*, fols. G4^{r}–I8^{r}. Naples: Sigismund Mayr, 1505.
I libri delle virtu sociali. Edited by Francesco Tateo. Rome: Bulzoni, 1999.
Opere Joannis Joivani Pontani. Lyons: Bartholomew Troth, 1514.
Spenser, Edmund. *Poetical Works*. Edited by J. D. Smith and E. de Selincourt. Oxford University Press, 1912.
Shakespeare, William. *Antony and Cleopatra*. Edited by Michael Neill. Oxford Shakespeare, 2nd Series, 1994.
Cymbeline. Edited by J. A. Nosworthy. London: Arden Shakespeare, 2nd Series, 2008.
Cymbeline. Edited by Roger Warren. Oxford Shakespeare, 2nd Series, 2008.
Hamlet. Edited by G. R. Hibbard. Oxford Shakespeare, 2nd Series, 2008.
Life of Henry V. Edited by Gary Taylor. Oxford Shakespeare, 2nd Series, 2008.
The Norton Shakespeare. Edited by Stephen Greenblatt, et al. New York: W. W. Norton, 1997.
Othello. Edited by Michael Neill. Oxford Shakespeare, 2nd Series, 2008.
Lucrece. London: Richard Field, 1594.
Richard II. Edited by Anthony Dawson and Paul Yachnin. Oxford Shakespeare, 2nd Series, Press, 2011.
Shakespeare's Sonnets. Edited by Stephen Booth. New Haven: Yale University Press, 1975.
The Tempest. Edited by Stephen Orgel. Oxford Shakespeare, 2nd Series, 2008.
Shakespeare, William, and George Wilkins, *Pericles*. Edited by Suzanne Gossett. London: Arden 3rd Series, 2004.
Pericles, Prince of Tyre. Edited by Roger Warren. Oxford Shakespeare, 2nd Series, 2003.
Skelton, John. *Certayn Bokes Compyled by Mayster Skelton*. London: John Day, 1563.

Pithy, Pleasaunt and Profitable Works of Maister John Skelton. London: Thomas Marsh, 1568.

Smith, John. *The True Travels, Adventures, and Observations of Captaine John Smith*. London: John Haviland for Thomas Slater, 1630.

Speed, John. *Theatre of the Empire of Great Britain*. London: William Hall, 1612.

Steinhöwel, Heinrich. *Kynge Appolyn of Thyre*. Translated by Robert Copland. London: Wynkyn de Worde, 1510.

Stow, John. *The Annales of England*. London: Rafe Newbery, 1592.

A Survay of London. London: John Windet for John Wolfe, 1598.

A Survay of London. London: John Windet, 1603.

Survey of London. London: George Purslowe, 1618.

Survey of London. London: Nicholas Bourne, 1633.

Strype, John. *Survey of the Cities of London and Westminster*. 5 vols. London: A. Churchill, et al., 1720.

Tradescant, John, the Younger. *Museum Trandescantianum: or A Collection of Rarities*. London: John Grismond, 1656.

Tuke, Thomas. "Translators Epistle upon Predestination." In Perkins, *Christian and Plaine Treatise*, fols. $B1^r$–$F5^v$.

Ubaldini, Petruccio. *Descrittione del Rigno di Scoti*. London: John Wolfe, 1588.

Wilkins, George. *The Painfull Adventures of Pericles*. London: T. P. for Nat. Butter, 1608.

Ursinus, Zacharius. *The Summe of Christian Religion*. Translated by Henry Parry. Oxford: Joseph Barnes, 1587.

Secondary Sources

Abery, Glenn. "The Displaced Nativity in Cymbeline." In *Shakespeare's Last Plays: Essays in Literature and Politics*, ed. Stephen W. Smith and Travis Curtright, 157–78. Lanham, MD: Lexington Books, 2002.

Addleshaw, G. W. O. *The High Church Tradition*. London: Faber and Faber, 1941.

Aers, David. "New Historicism and the Eucharist." *Journal of Medieval and Early Modern Studies*, 33.2 (Spring 2003): 241–59.

Alaimo, Stacy, and Susan Hekman, eds. *Material Feminisms*. Bloomington: Indiana University Press, 2008.

Allen, Rosamund S. "John Gower and Southwark: The Paradox of the Social Self." In *London and Europe in the Later Middle Ages*, ed. Julie Boffey and Pamela King, 111–47. London: Centre for Medieval and Renaissance Studies, University of London, 1995.

Allen, Thomas. *History and Antiquities of the Parish of Lambeth*. London: J. Allen, 1827.

Appadurai, Arjun, ed. *The Social Life of Things: Commodities in Cultural Perspective*. Cambridge University Press, 1988.

Appleford, Amy. "Shakespeare's Katherine of Aragon: Late Medieval Queen, First Recusant Martyr." *Journal of Medieval and Renaissance Studies*, 40.1 (Winter 2010): 149–72.

Archer, Ian. "The Nostalgia of John Stow." In *The Theatrical City: Culture, Theatre and Politics in London, 1576–1649*, ed. David L. Smith, Richard Strier, and David Bevington, 17–34. Cambridge University Press, 1995.

Armitage, David. "The Dismemberment of Orpheus: Mythic Elements in Shakespeare's Romances." *Shakespeare Survey*, 39 (1986): 123–34.

Ashmole, Bernard. "Cyriac of Ancona." *Proceedings of the British Academy*, 44 (1957): 25–41.

"Cyriac of Ancona and the Temple of Hadrian at Cyzicus." *Journal of the Warburg and Courtauld Institutes*, 19 (1956): 179–91.

Aston, Margaret. *Broken Idols of the English* Reformation. Cambridge University Press, 2015.

England's Iconoclasts. Oxford: Clarendon Press, 1988.

Aston, Margaret. "Public Worship and Iconoclasm." In Gaimster and Gilchrist, eds., *Archaeology of the Reformation*, 9–28.

"Bargrave Collection." www.canterbury-cathedral.org/bargrave/.

Bargrave, John. *Catalogue of Dr. Bargrave's Museum, in Pope Alexander the Seventh and the College of Cardinals*. Edited by James Craigie Robertson. London: Camden Society, 1867.

Barish, Jonas. *The Anti-Theatrical Prejudice*. Berkeley: University of California Press, 1981.

Barkan, Leonard. "Living Sculptures: Ovid, Michelangelo, and *The Winter's Tale*." *English Literary History*, 48.4 (Winter 1981): 639–67.

Beckwith, Sarah. "The Present of Past Things: The York Corpus Christi Cycle as a Contemporary Theatre of Memory." *Journal of Medieval and Early Modern Studies*, 26 (1996): 335–79.

Shakespeare and the Grammar of Forgiveness. Ithaca: Cornell University Press, 2011.

"Shakespeare, Crypto-Catholicism, Crypto-Criticism." *Medieval and Renaissance Drama in England*, 19 (2006): 259–70.

"Stephen Greenblatt's *Hamlet* and the Forms of Oblivion." *Journal of Medieval and Early Modern Studies*, 33.2 (Spring 2003): 261–80.

Beecher, Donald, and Grant Williams, eds. *Ars Reminiscendi: Mind and Memory in Renaissance Culture*. Toronto: Center for Reformation and Renaissance Studies, 2009.

Belsey, Catherine. "Invocation of the Visual Image: Ekphrasis in *Lucrece* and Beyond." *Shakespeare Quarterly*, 63.2 (Summer 2012): 175–98.

Betteridge, Thomas. "Writing Faithfully in a Post-Confessional World." In *Late Shakespeare, 1608–1613*, ed. Andrew J. Power and Rory Loughnane, 225–42. Cambridge University Press, 2013.

Bevington, David. "The Debate about Shakespeare and Religion." In Loewenstein and Witmore, eds., *Shakespeare and Early Modern Religion*, 23–8.

Bicks, Caroline. "Backsliding at Ephesus: Shakespeare's Diana and the Churching of Women." In *"Pericles": Critical Essays*, ed. David Skeele, 205–27. New York: Garland, 2000.

Bicks, Caroline, and Jennifer Summit, eds. *The History of British Women's Writing, Volume II: 1500–1610*. Basingstoke: Palgrave Macmillan, 2010.

Bishop, T. G. *Theatre of Wonder in Shakespeare*. Cambridge University Press, 1996.

Bodnar, Edward W. "Athens in April 1436." *Archaeology*, 23 (1970): 96–105.

Bolzoni, Lina. *Gallery of Memory: Literary and Iconographic Models in the Age of the Printing Press*. Translated by Jeremy Parzen. University of Toronto Press, 2001.

Bonahue, Edward T., Jr. "Citizen History: Stow's *Survey of London*." *Studies in English Literature, 1500–1900*, 38 (1998): 61–85.

Bovilsky, Lara. "Shakespeare's Mineral Emotions." In Campana and Maisano, eds., *Renaissance Posthumanism*, 253–82.

Bradford, Charles Angell. *Blanche Parry, Queen Elizabeth's Gentlewoman*. London: privately printed, 1935.

Braidotti, Rosi. "In Spite of the Times: The Postsecular Turn in Feminism." *Theory, Culture and Society*, 25.6 (2008): 1–24.

Metamorphoses: Towards a Materialist Theory of Becoming. Cambridge: Polity, 2002.

Nomadic Subjects: Embodiment and Sexual Difference in Contemporary Feminist Theory. 2nd edition. New York: Columbia University Press, 2011.

The Posthuman. Cambridge: Polity, 2013.

Transpositions: On Nomadic Ethics. Cambridge: Polity, 2006.

Breasted, Barbara. "*Comus* and the Castlehaven Scandal." *Milton Studies*, 3 (1971): 201–24.

Bridges, John. *History and Antiquities of Northamptonshire*. 2 vols. Oxford: D. Prince and J. Cooke, 1791.

Brown, Cedric C. *John Milton's Aristocratic Entertainments*. Cambridge University Press, 1985.

Bruster, Douglas. "The New Materialism in Renaissance Studies." In *Material Culture and Cultural Materialisms*, ed. Curtis Perry, 225–38. Turnhout: Brepols, 2001.

"Shakespeare's Lady 8." *Shakespeare Quarterly*, 66.1 (Spring 2015): 47–61.

Bullough, Geoffrey, ed., *Narrative and Dramatic Sources of Shakespeare*. 8 vols. New York: Columbia University Press, 1975.

Burckhardt, Jacob. *The Civilization of the Renaissance in Italy*. Trans. S. C. G. Middlemore. London: George Allen & Unwin, 1878.

Burke, Victoria. "'Memorial Books': Commonplaces, Gender and Manuscript Compilation in Seventeenth-Century England." In Gordon and Rist, eds., *Arts of Remembrance*, 121–45.

Burke, Victoria. "Seventeenth-Century Women's Manuscript Writing." In Suzuki, ed. *History of British Women's Writing, 1610–1690*, 99–113.

Burnham, Douglas, and Enrico Giaccherini, eds. *The Poetics of Transubstantiation: From Theology to Metaphor*. Aldershot: Ashgate, 2005.

Butler, Judith. "Merleau-Ponty and the Touch of Malebranche." In *The Cambridge Companion to Merleau-Ponty*, ed. Taylor Carman and Mark B. N. Hansen, 181–205. Cambridge University Press, 2016.

Cambers, Andrew. “Reading, the Godly, and Self-Writing, 1580–1720.” *Journal of British Studies*, 46.4 (October 2007): 796–825.

Campana, Joseph, and Scott Maisano, eds. *Renaissance Posthumanism*. New York: Fordham University Press, 2016.

Carrithers, Gale H., Jr. “Milton’s Ludlow Mask: From Chaos to Community.” *English Literary History*, 33.1 (March 1966): 23–42.

Carruthers, Mary. *The Book of Memory: A Study of Memory in Medieval Culture*. 2nd edition. Cambridge University Press, 2008.

Chester, J. L. *The Marriage, Baptismal and Burial Registers of the Collegiate Church or Abbey of St. Peter, Westminster*. London: Harleian Society, 1876.

“Chiddingly Church,” www.coopersfarm.co.uk/church/churchguide1.html

Clubb, Louise George. *Italian Theatre in Shakespeare’s Time*. New Haven and London: Yale University Press, 1989.

Coiro, Ann Baynes. “Anonymous Milton, or, ‘A Maske’ Masked.” *English Literary History*, 71.3 (Fall 2004): 609–29.

Cokayne, George Edward, et al, eds. *The Complete Peerage of England, Scotland, Ireland, Great Britain and the United Kingdom*. 2nd edition. 6 vols. Gloucester, U.K.: Alan Sutton Publishing, 2000.

Colebrook, Claire. “On Not Becoming Man: The Materialist Politics of Unactualized Potential.” In Alaimo and Hekman, eds., *Material Feminisms*, 52–84.

Colebrook, Claire, and Ian Buchanan, eds., *Deleuze and Feminist Theory*. New York: Columbia University Press, 2000.

Collinson, Patrick. “John Stow and Nostalgic Antiquarianism.” In Merritt, ed., *Imagining Early Modern London*, 27–51.

Collinson, Patrick. *The Religion of Protestants: The Church in English Society, 1559–1625*. Oxford University Press, 1984.

“Constructing Elizabeth Isham,” Princeton Symposium on Elizabeth Isham, September 7–8, 2007, https://warwick.ac.uk/fac/arts/ren/projects/isham/workshop/

Cooke, John Daniel. “Euhemerism: A Mediaeval Interpretation of Classical Paganism.” *Speculum*, 2 (1927): 396–410.

Cooper, Helen. “‘This worthy olde writer’: Pericles and the Other Gowers, 1592–1640.” In Echard, ed., *Gower Companion*, 99–113.

Cope, Esther S. *The Life of a Public Man: Edward, First Baron Montagu of Boughton, 1562–1644*. Philadelphia: American Philosophical Society, 1981.

Corns, Thomas N. “Milton Before Lycidas.” In Milton and the Terms of *Liberty*, ed. Graham Parry and Joad Raymond, 23–36. Woodbridge: D. S. Brewer, 2002.

Corns, Thomas N., ed. *New Companion to Milton*. Oxford: John Wiley and Sons, 2016.

Coster, Will. “‘Tokens of Innocence’: Infant Birth, Baptism and Burial in Early Modern England.” In *The Place of the Dead: Death and Remembrance in Late Medieval and Early Modern Europe*, ed. Bruce Gordon and Peter Marshall, 266–87. Cambridge University Press, 2000.

Crankshaw, David J. "Community, City and Nation, 1540–1714." In *St Paul's: The Cathedral Church of London*, ed. Derek Keene, Arthur Burns, and Andrew Saint, 46–70. New Haven and London: Yale University Press, 2004.

Crumley, John C. "Questioning History in *Cymbeline*." *Studies in English Literature*, 41.2 (Spring 2001): 297–315.

Curran, Kevin, and James Kearney. "Introduction." *Shakespeare and Phenomenology*, special issue. *Criticism*, 54.3 (Summer 2012): 353–64.

Cust, Lionel. "The Queen's Kirtle." *Burlington Magazine*, 33.189 (December 1918): 196–201.

D'Addario, Christopher. "Echo Chambers and Paper Memorials: Mid- and Late-Seventeenth-Century Book-bindings and the Practices of Early Modern Reading." *Textual Cultures*, 7.2 (2012): 73–97.

Daston, Lorraine, and Katharine Park. *Wonders and the Order of Nature, 1150–1750*. New York: Zone Books, 1998.

Dean, Paul. "Pericles's Pilgrimage." *Essays in Criticism*, 50 (2000): 125–44.

De Grazia, Margreta, Maureen Quilligan and Peter Stallybrass, eds., *Subject and Object in Renaissance Culture*. Cambridge University Press, 1996.

Dingley, Thomas. *History of Marble*. Edited by John Gough Nichols. 2 vols. London: Camden Society, 1898.

Dobie, Rowland. *The History of the United Parishes of St. Giles in the Fields and St. George Bloomsbury*. London: printed for the author, 1829.

Dolan, Frances E. "Gender and the 'Lost' Spaces of Catholicism." *Journal of Interdisciplinary History*, 33.4 (Spring, 2002): 641–65.

Dollman, Francis Thomas. *The Priory Church of St. Mary Overie, Southwark*. London: F. T. Dollman, 1881.

Dowd, Michelle. *Dynastic Inheritance on the Shakespearean Stage*. Cambridge University Press, 2015.

Duffy, Eamon. *The Stripping of the Altars: Traditional Religion in England, 1400–1580*. New Haven and London: Yale University Press, 1994.

Durston Christopher, and Jacqueline Eales, eds., *The Culture of English Puritanism, 1560–1700*. Basingstoke: Palgrave, 1996.

Eales, Jacqueline. "Thomas Pierson and the Transmission of the Moderate Puritan Tradition." *Midland History*, 20 (1995): 75–102.

Echard, Sian. "Last Words: Latin at the End of *Confessio Amantis*." In *Interstices: Studies in Late Middle English and Anglo-Latin in Honour of A. G. Rigg*, ed. Richard Firth Green and Linne Mooney, 99–121. University of Toronto Press, 2004.

Echard, Sian, ed. *The Gower Companion*. Woodbridge: D. S. Brewer, 2004.

Eckhardt, Joshua, and Daniel Starza Smith, eds. *Manuscript Miscellanies in Early Modern England*. Aldershot: Ashgate, 2014.

Edwards, Philip. "An Approach to the Problem of *Pericles*." *Shakespeare Survey*, 5 (1952): 25–50.

Escobedo, Andrew. "From Britannia to England: *Cymbeline* and the Beginning of Nations." *Shakespeare Quarterly*, 59.1 (Spring 2008): 60–87.

Esdaile, K. A. *English Church Monuments, 1510–1840*. London: Batsford, 1946.
Evans, Joan. *A History of the Society of Antiquaries*. Oxford University Press, 1950.
Evans, Martin J., and J. Martin Fishman. *The Miltonic Moment*. Louisville: University Press of Kentucky, 2015.
Ezell, Margaret J. M. "Elizabeth Isham's Books of Remembrance and Forgetting." *Modern Philology*, 109 (2011): 71–84.
Social Authorship and the Advent of Print. Baltimore and London: The Johns Hopkins University Press, 2003.
Ferguson, Margaret W. *Dido's Daughters: Literacy, Gender and Empire in Early Modern England and France*. University of Chicago Press, 2003.
Fielding, John. "*Conformists, Puritans, and the Church Courts: The Diocese of Peterborough, 1603–1642*." PhD Dissertation, University of Birmingham, 1989.
Findlen, Paula. *Possessing Nature: Museums, Collecting, and Scientific Culture in Early Modern Italy*. Berkeley: University of California Press, 1994.
Finkelstein, Richard. "*Pericles*, Paul, and Protestantism." *Comparative Drama*, 44.2 (Summer 2010): 101–29.
"The Politics of Gender, Puritanism, and Shakespeare's Third Folio." *Philological Quarterly*, 79.3 (Summer 2000): 315–41.
Fitcham, Kenneth, ed. *Visitation Articles and Injunctions of the Early Stuart Church*. 2 vols. Woodbridge: Boydell, 1994–1998.
Fleming, Juliet. "Whitewash and the Scene of Writing," *Shakespeare Studies*, 38 (2000): 133–38.
"Wounded Walls: Graffiti, Grammatology, and the Age of Shakespeare." *Criticism*, 39 (1997): 1–30.
Fletcher Anthony, and Peter Rogerts, eds. *Religion, Culture and Society in Early Modern Britain: Essays in Honour of Patrick Collinson*. Cambridge University Press, 1994.
Fogle, F. R. "'Such a rural queen": The Countess Dowager of Derby as Patron." In *Patronage in Late Renaissance England*, ed. French R. Fogle and Louis A. Knafla, 3–29. Los Angeles: William Clark Library, University of California Press, 1983.
Freeman, Arthur. "The Writings of Thomas Achelley." *The Library*, ser. 5, no. 25 (1970): 40–42.
Frere, W. H., and W. P. M. Kennedy, eds. *Visitation Articles and Injunctions in the Period of the Reformation*. 3 vols. London: Longman, Green and Co., 1910.
Freud, Sigmund. "A Note Upon the 'Mystic Writing Pad." In *Standard Edition of the Complete Works*, translated by James Stratchey, vol. XIX, 227–33. 23 vols. London: Hogarth, 1961.
Frye, Susan. *Pens and Needles: Women's Textualities in Early Modern England*. Philadelphia: University of Pennsylvania Press, 2010.
Fumerton, Patricia. "Secret Arts: Elizabethan Miniatures and Sonnets." *Representations*, 15 (1986): 57–97.
Gadd, Ian, and Alexandra Gillespie, eds. *John Stow (1525–1605) and the Making of the English Past: Studies in Early Modern Culture and the History of the Book*. London: British Library, 2004.

Gaimster David and Roberta Gilchrist, eds., *The Archaeology of the Reformation, 1480–1580*. Leeds: Maney, 2003.
Gallagher, Catherine, and Stephen Greenblatt, *Practicing New Historicism.* University of Chicago Press, 2000.
"Garden Museum, The," www.gardenmuseum.org.uk
Gayk, Shannon. *Image, Text and Religious Reform in Fifteenth-Century England.* Cambridge University Press, 2010.
Geller, Lila. "*Cymbeline* and the Imagery of Covenant Theology." *Studies in English Literature*, 20 (1982): 241–55.
George, Edwin, Stella George, with Peter Fleming, *Bristol Probate Inventories, Part 1: 1542–1650* Bristol Record Society, 2002.
Gerish, W. B. "Cornybury." In *Transactions of the East Herts Archaeological Society*, 3.2 (1906): 151.
Giles, Kate. "'A table of alabaster with the story of the Doom': The Religious Objects and Spaces of the Guild of Our Blessed Virgin, Boston, Lincs." In Hamling and Richardson, eds., *Everyday Objects*, 267–76.
Gittings, Clare. *Death, Burial and the Individual.* New York and London: Routledge, 1984.
Gittos, Bryan, and Moira Gittos. "Motivation and Choice: The Selection of Medieval Secular Effigies." In *Heraldry, Pageantry, and Social Display in Medieval England*, ed. Peter Cross and Maureen Keen, 143–67. Woodbridge: D. S. Brewer, 2002.
Goldring, Elizabeth, Jayne Elisabeth Archer, and Elizabeth Clarke, eds. *John Nichols's The Progresses and Public Processions of Queen Elizabeth.* Oxford University Press, 2013.
Goodrich, Jaime. *Faithful Translators: Authorship, Gender and Religion in Early Modern England.* Evanston: Northwestern University Press, 2013.
Goodrich, Jaime. "Reconsidering the Woman Writer: The Identity Politics of Anne Cooke Bacon." In Phillippy, ed., *History of Early Modern Women's Writing*, 46–65.
Gordon, Andrew. *Writing Early Modern London: Memory, Text and Community.* Basingstoke: Palgrave, 2013.
Gordon, Andrew and Thomas Rist, eds., *The Arts of Remembrance in Early Modern England: Memorial Cultures of the Post Reformation.* London: Routledge, 2013.
Gough, Richard. *Description of the Beauchamp Chapel at Warwick.* London: J. Nichol and Son, 1809.
Gray, Catharine. *Women Writers and Public Debate in Seventeenth-Century Britain.* Basingstoke: Palgrave, 2007.
Green, Ian. *The Christian's ABC: Catechisms and Catechizing in England.* Oxford University Press, 1996.
Print and Protestantism in Early Modern England. Oxford University Press, 2000.
Greenblatt, Stephen. *Marvelous Possessions: The Wonder of the New World.* Oxford: Clarendon Press, 1992.

"Resonance and Wonder." *Bulletin of the American Academy of Arts and Sciences*, 43.4 (January 1990): 11–34.

Shakespearean Negotiations: The Circulation of Social Energy in Renaissance England. Berkeley: University of California Press, 1988.

Greene, Thomas M. "Petrarch and the Humanist Heremenutic." In *Italian Literature, Roots and Branches: Essays in Honor of Thomas Goddard Bergin*, ed. Giose Rimanelli and Kenneth John Atchity, 211–21. New Haven and London: Yale University Press, 1976.

Griffiths, Jane. "Text and Authority: John Stow's 1568 Edition of Skelton's Workes." In Gadd and Gillespie, eds., *John Stow*, 127–34.

Grosz, Elizabeth. *Volatile Bodies: Toward a Corporeal Feminism.* Bloomington: Indiana University Press, 1994.

Grosz, Elizabeth. "Merleau-Ponty, Bergson and the Question of Ontology." In Weis, ed., *Intertwinings*, 13–24.

Guillory, John. *Poetic Authority: Spenser, Milton and Literary History.* New York: Columbia University Press, 1983.

Gurnis, Musa. "'Most Ignorant of What He's Most Assured': The Hermeneutics of Predestination in *Measure for Measure.*" *Shakespeare Studies*, 42 (2014): 141–69.

Gurr, Andrew. "The Bear, the Statue, and Hysteria in *The Winter's Tale.*" *Shakespeare Quarterly*, 34.4 (Winter 1983):420–25.

Guthke, Karl S. "Talking Stones: Anthologies of Epitaphs from Humanism to Popular Culture." *Harvard Library Bulletin*, 10.4 (1999): 19–69.

Habermas, Jürgen. "Notes on Post-Secular Society." *New Perspectives Quarterly*, 25.4 (Fall 2008): 17–29.

Hallam, Elizabeth, and Jenny Hockey, *Death, Memory and Material Culture.* Oxford and New York: Berg, 2001.

Hamling, Tara. "'An Arelome to this Hous For Ever': Monumental Fixtures and Furnishing sin the English Domestic Interior, c. 1560–1660." In Gordon and Rist, eds., *Arts of Remembrance*, 59–83.

Hamling, Tara, and Catherine Richardson, eds. *Everyday Objects: Medieval and Early Modern Material Culture and its Meanings.* Aldershot: Ashgate, 2010.

Hammill, Graham and Julia Lupton, "Sovereigns, Citizens, and Saints: Political Theology and Renaissance Literature." *Religion & Literature*, 38.3 (Autumn 2006): 1–11.

Hanna, Sara. "Christian Vision and Iconography in *Pericles.*" *Upstart Crow*, 11 (1991): 92–116.

Harding, Vanessa. "Choices and Changes: Death, Burial and the English Reformation." In Gaimster and Gilchrist, eds., *Archaeology of the Reformation*, 386–98.

Harris, Johanna, and Elizabeth Scott-Baumann, eds., *The Intellectual Culture of Puritan Women, 1558–1680.* Basingstoke: Palgrave, 2010.

Harris, Jonathan Gil. *Foreign Bodies and the Body Politic: Discourses of Social Pathology in Early Modern England.* Cambridge University Press, 1988.

"The New New Historicism's *Wunderkammer* of Objects." *European Journal of English Studies*, 4.2 (2000): 111–23.

Untimely Matter in the Time of Shakespeare. Philadelphia: University of Pennsylvania Press, 2009.

Harris, Jonathan Gil, and Natasha Korda, eds. *Staged Properties in Early Modern English Drama*, Cambridge University Press, 2006.

Hart, F. Elizabeth. "Cerimon's 'Rough' Music in *Pericles*, 3.2," *Shakespeare Quarterly*, 51.3 (Autumn 2000): 313–31.

"'Great Is Diana' of Shakespeare's Ephesus." *Studies in English Literature, 1500–1900*, 43.2 (Spring 2003): 347–74.

Hassall, A. G., and W. O. Hassall. *Treasures from the Bodleian Library*. London: Gordon Fraser, 1976.

Hasted, Edward. "The History and Topographical Survey of the County of Kent, Volume 11." *British History Online*, www.british-history.ac.uk/survey-kent/vol11/pp209-288

Heal, Felicity. "Experiencing Religion in London: Diversity and Choice in Shakespeare's Metropolis." In Loewenstein and Witmore, eds., *Shakespeare and Early Modern Religion*, 57–78.

Hecksecher, William S. "Shakespeare in his Relationship to the Visual Arts: A Study in Paradox." *Research Opportunities in Renaissance Drama*, 13.14 (1970): 36–56.

Helms, Lorraine. "The Saint in the Brothel: Or, Eloquence Rewarded," *Shakespeare Quarterly*, 41.3 (Autumn 1990): 319–32.

Herrup, Cynthia. *A House in Gross Disorder: Sex, Law, and the 2nd Earl of Castlehaven*. Oxford University Press, 1999.

Hersey, George L. *Alfonso II and the Artistic Renewal of Naples, 1485–1495*. New Haven and London: Yale University Press, 1969.

Hillman, Richard. "Shakespeare's Gower and Gower's Shakespeare: The Larger Debt of *Pericles*." *Shakespeare Quarterly*, 36 (1985): 427–37.

Hines, John. *Voices of the Past: English Literature and Archaeology*. Woodbridge: D. S. Brewer, 2004.

Hines, John, Nathalie Cohen, and Simon Roffey. "Iohannes Gower, Armiger, Poeta: Records and Memorials of his Life and Death." In Echard, ed., *Gower Companion*, 23–41.

Hiscock, Andrew. *Reading Memory in Early Modern Literature*. Cambridge University Press, 2011.

Hoeniger, F. David. "Gower and Shakespeare in *Pericles*." *Shakespeare Quarterly*, 33.4 (Winter 1982): 461–79.

Hoyle, R. W. "Masters of Requests and the Small Change of Jacobean Patronage." *English Historical Review*, 52 (June 2011): 544–81.

Hughey, Ruth, ed. *The Arundel Harington Manuscript of Tudor Poetry*. 2 vols. Columbus: Ohio State University Press, 1960.

Hughey, Ruth . "The Harington Manuscript at Arundel Castle and Related Documents." *Library*, 15 (June 1934–Mar 1935): 388–444.

Hume, Julian P. "The History of the Dodo Raphus Cucullatus and the Penguin of Mauritius," *Historical Biology*, 18.2 (2006): 65–89.

Hunt, Arnold. *The Art of Hearing: English Preachers and their Audiences, 1590–1640*. Cambridge University Press, 2010.

Hunt, Maurice. "Dismemberment, Corporal Reconstruction and the Body Politic in *Cymbeline*." *Studies in Philology*, 99 (2002): 404–31.

"Shakespeare's *Pericles* and the Acts of the Apostles." *Christianity and Literature*, 49.3 (Spring 2000): 295–309.

"Syncretistic Religion in Shakespeare's Late Romances." *South Central Review*, 28.2 (2011): 57–79.

Hurtig, Judith W. "Seventeenth-Century Shroud Tombs: Classical Revival and Anglican Context," *Art Bulletin*, 64.2 (June 1982): 217–28.

Impey, Oliver, and Arthur MacGregor, eds., *Origins of Museums: The Cabinet of Curiosities in Sixteenth- and Seventeenth-Century Europe*. London: House of Stratus, 2001.

Innes, Paul. "*Cymbeline* and Empire." *Critical Survey*, 19 (2007): 1–18.

Jackson, Ken. "All is True—Unless you Decide in Advance What Is Not." *Criticism*, 54:3 (Summer 2012): 469–77.

Jackson, Ken, and Arthur Marotti, "The Turn to Religion in Early Modern English Studies." *Criticism*, 46.1 (Winter 2004): 167–90.

James, M. R. *The Bestiary*. London: Roxburghe Club, 1928.

James, Susan E. *Women's Voices in Tudor Wills, 1485–1603: Authority, Influence and Material Culture*. Farnham: Ashgate, 2015.

Jones, Andrew. *Memory and Material Culture*. Cambridge University Press, 2007.

Jones, Ann Rosalind, and Peter Stallybrass. *Renaissance Clothing and the Materials of Memory*. Cambridge University Press, 2000.

Jones, Kelly. "The Quick and the Dead: Performing the Poet Gower in *Pericles*." In *Shakespeare and the Middle Ages: Essays on the Performance and Adaptation of the Plays with Medieval Sources*, ed. Martha W. Driver and Sid Ray, 201–14. Jefferson: McFarland, 2010.

Kantorowicz, Ernst H. *The King's Two Bodies: A Study in Medieval Political Theology*. Princeton University Press, 1957.

Kelley, Shannon. "Amber, the Heliades, and the Poetry of Trauma in Marvell's 'The Nymph Complaining.'" *Studies in English Literature, 1500–1900*, 55.1 (Winter 2015): 151–174

Kermode, Jenny. *Medieval Merchants: York, Beverley and Hull in the Later Middle Ages*. Cambridge University Press, 2002.

Kerr, N. R. *Medieval Libraries of Great Britain: A List of Surviving Books*. London: Royal Historical Society, 1964.

King, Rachel. "'The Beads with which we Pray are Made from It': Devotional Ambers in Early Modern Italy." In *Religion and the Senses in Early Modern Europe*, ed. Wietse de Boer and Christine Göttler, 153–76. Leiden and Boston: Brill, 2013.

"Rethinking 'the Oldest Surviving Amber in the West.'" *Burlington Magazine*, 155 (November 2013): 756–62.

Kirwood, A. E. M. "Richard Field, Printer, 1589–1624." *Library*, 4th Series, no. 12. (June 1931): 1–39.

Knapp, Jeffrey. *Shakespeare's Tribe: Church, Nation, and Theater in Renaissance England*. University of Chicago Press, 2002.

Knight, G. Wilson. *The Crown of Life: Essays in Interpretation of Shakespeare's Final Plays*. London: Methuen, 1948.

Knoppers, Laura Lunger, ed. *Cambridge Companion to Early Modern Women's Writing*. Cambridge University Press, 2009.

Knowles, Christine. "Caxton and His Two French Sources: The *Game and Playe of the Chesse* and the Composite Manuscripts of the Two French Translations of the *Ludus Scaccorum*." *Modern Language Review*, 49.4 (October 1954): 417–23.

Knowles, Richard Paul. "'Wishes Fall Out as They're Will'd': Artist, Audience and *Pericles's* Gower." *English Studies in Canada*, 9.1 (March 1983): 14–24.

Kokole, Stanko, "Cyriacus of Ancona and the Revival of Two Forgotten Ancient Personifications in the Rector's Palace of Dubrovnik." *Renaissance Quarterly*, 49.2 (Summer 1996): 225–67.

Kreider, Alan. *English Chantries: The Road to Dissolution*. Eugene, OR: Wipf and Stock Publishers, 2012.

Lake, D. J. "Rhymes in *Pericles*.," *Notes and Queries* 16.4 (April 1969): 139–43.

Lake, Peter. *Anglicans and Puritans? Presbyterianism and English Conformist Thought from Whitgift to Hooker*. London: Unwin Hyman, 1988.

"Calvinism and the English Church 1570–1635." *Past and Present*, 114 (February 1987): 32–76.

Lake, Peter. "'A Charitable Christian Hatred': The Godly and their Enemies in the 1630s." In Durston and Eales, eds., *Culture of English Puritanism*, 145–83.

Moderate Puritans and the Elizabethan Church. Cambridge University Press, 1982.

Lake, Peter, and Michael Questier, *The Antichrist's Lewd Hat: Protestants, Papists, and Players in Post-Reformation England*. New Haven and London: Yale University Press, 2002.

"Puritans, Papists, and the 'Public Sphere': The Edmund Campion Affair in Context." *Journal of Modern History*, 72 (September 2000): 587–627.

Lake, Peter, and Isaac Stephens, *Scandal and Religious Identity in Early Stuart England: A Northamptonshire Maid's Tragedy*. Woodbridge: Boydell and Brewer, 2015.

Lamb, Mary Ellen. *Gender and Authorship in the Sidney Circle*. Madison: University of Wisconsin Press, 1990.

Lander, Bonnie. "Interpreting the Person: Tradition, Conflict, and *Cymbeline*'s Innogen." *Shakespeare Quarterly*, 59.2 (Summer 2008): 156–84.

Law, Ernest. *History of Hampton Court Palace, Volume 1: Tudor Times*. 2 vols. London: George Bell and Sons, 1903.

Lees-Jeffries, Hester. *Shakespeare and Memory*. Oxford University Press, 2013.

Leith-Ross, Prudence. *The John Tradescants, Gardeners to the Rose and Lily Queen*. London: Peter Owen, 2006.

Levin, Carole. "'Would I Could Give You Help and Succour': Elizabeth I and the Politics of Touch." *Albion*, 21 (1989): 191–205.

Levine, Laura. *Men in Women's Clothing: Anti-Theatricality and Effeminization, 1579–1642*. Cambridge University Press, 2009.

Llewellyn, Nigel. "'[An] Impe entombed here doth lie': The Besford Triptych and Child Memorials in Post-Reformation England." In *Representations of Childhood Death*, ed. Gillian Avery and Kimberly Reynolds, 52–64. Basingstoke: Palgrave, 2000.

Post-Reformation Funeral Monuments. Cambridge University Press, 2000.

Loewenstein, David and Michael Witmore, eds., *Shakespeare and Early Modern Religion*. Cambridge University Press, 2015.

Longfellow, Erica. "'Take unto Ye Words': Elizabeth Isham's 'Book of Remembrance' and Puritan Cultural Forms." In Harris and Scott-Baumann, eds., *Intellectual Culture of Puritan Women*, 122–34.

Lupton, Julia Reinhard. *Afterlives of the Saints: Hagiography, Typology and Renaissance Literature*. Stanford University Press, 1996.

"Macbeth's Martlets: Shakespearean Phenomenologies of Hospitality." *Criticism*, 54.3 (Summer 2012): 365–76.

Lynch, Stephen J. "The Authority of Gower in Shakespeare's *Pericles*." *Mediaevalia*, 16 (1990): 361–78.

MacCulloch, Diarmaid. *Reformation: Europe's House Divided, 1450–1700*. Middlesex: Penguin, 2004.

MacGregor, Arthur. "The Cabinet of Curiosities in Seventeenth-Century Britain." In Impey and MacGregor, eds., *Origins of Museums*, 201–16.

MacGregor, Arthur. "The Tradescants, Gardeners and Botanists." In MacGregor, ed., *Tradescant's Rarities*, 3–16.

MacGregor, Arthur. ed. *Tradescant's Rarities: Essays on the Foundation of the Ashmolean Museum 1683*. Oxford University Press, 1983.

Machan, Tim William. "Thomas Berthelette and Gower's *Confessio*." *Studies in the Age of Chaucer*, 18 (1996): 143–66.

Malay, Jessica, ed. *Anne Clifford's Great Books of Record*. Manchester University Press, 2015.

Marcus, Leah. "*Cymbeline* and the Unease of Topicality." In *Shakespeare: The Last Plays*, ed. Kiernan Ryan, 134–68. London and New York: Routledge, 1999.

Marcus, Leah. "John Milton's Comus." In Corns, ed., *New Companion to Milton*, 241–54.

"The Milieu of Milton's *Comus*: Judicial Reform at Ludlow and the Problem of Sexual Assault." *Criticism*, 25 (1983): 293–327.

The Politics of Mirth: Jonson, Herrick, Milton, Marvell and the Defense of Old Holiday Pastimes. University of Chicago Press, 1986.

Marshall, Edward. "The Tradescants," *Notes and Queries*, ser. 6, no. 78 (June 25, 1881): 512.

Marshall, Peter. *Beliefs and the Dead in Reformation England.* Oxford University Press, 2002.

Martin, Catherine Gimelli. "The Non-Puritan Ethics, Metaphysics, and Aesthetics of Milton's Spenserian Masque." *Milton Quarterly*, 37 (2003): 215–44.

Massey, Doreen. *For Space*. London: Sage, 2005.

Mauriès, Patrick. *Cabinets of Curiosities*. London: Thames and Hudson, 2002.

Mayer, Jean-Christophe. *Shakespeare's Hybrid Faith: History, Religion and the Stage*. New York: Palgrave, 2006.

McCoy, Richard. "Awakening Faith in The Winter's Tale." In Loewenstein and Witmore, eds., *Shakespeare and Early Modern Religion*, 214–30.

McManus, Caroline. "Queen Elizabeth, Dol Common, and the Performance of the Royal Maundy." In *The Mysteries of Elizabeth I: Selections from "English Literary Renaissance*, ed. Kirby Farrell and Kathleen Swaim, 43–66. Amherst: University of Massachusetts Press, 2003.

McQuade, Paula. *Maternal Catechizing in Early Modern England.* Cambridge University Press, 2017.

Meek, Richard. "Ekphrasis in *The Rape of Lucrece* and *The Winter's Tale.*" *Studies in English Literature, 1500–1900*, 46.2 (Spring 2006): 389–414.

Memon, Arsalan. "Merleau-Ponty, Deleuze and the Question Singular: What Marks the Difference Between Humans and Animals?" *Auslegung* 28.2 (Fall/Winter 2006): 19–35.

Merleau-Ponty, Maurice. *Nature: Course Notes from the Collège de France.* Editedby D. Seglard. Translated by R. Vallier. Evanston: Northwestern University Press, 2003.

The Phenomenology of Perception. Translated by Donald A. Landes. New York: Routledge, 2012.

The Visible and the Invisible, Followed by Working Notes. Translated by Alphonso Lingis. Evanston: Northwestern University Press, 1968.

Merritt, J. F. "The Reshaping of Stow's 'Survey': Munday, Strype and the Protestant City." In Merritt, ed., *Imagining Early Modern London*, 52–88.

Merritt, J. F., ed. In *Imagining Early Modern London: Perceptions and Portrayals of the City from Stow to Strype, 1598–1720*. Cambridge University Press, 2001.

Mikalachki, Jodi. "The Masculine Romance of Roman Britain: *Cymbeline* and Early Modern English Nationalism." *Shakespeare Quarterly*, 46.3 (Autumn 1995): 301–22.

Milton, Anthony. *Catholic and Reformed: The Roman and Protestant Churches in English Protestant Thought, 1600–1640*. Cambridge University Press, 2002.

Moffett, Robin. "*Cymbeline* and the Nativity." *Shakespeare Quarterly*, 13.2 (Spring 1962): 207–18.

Moore, Helen. "Succeeding Stow: Anthony Munday and the 1618 Survey of London." In Gadd and Gillsepie, eds., *John Stow*, 99–108.

Morgan, John. *Godly Learning: Puritan Attitudes towards Reason, Learning and Education*. Cambridge University Press, 1986.

Mosse, H. R. *The Monumental Effigies of Sussex, 1250–1650*. Hove: Combridges, 1933.

Mundhenk, R. K. "Dark Scandal and the Sun-Clad Power of Chastity: The Historical Milieu of Milton's *Comus*." *Studies in English Literature, 1500–1900*, 15 (1975): 141–52.

Mullaney, Steven. *The Place of the Stage: License, Play, and Power in Renaissance England*. University of Chicago Press, 1988.

Murphy, Erin. "Sabrina and the Making of English History in *Poly-Olbion* and *A Mask Presented at Ludlow Castle*." *Studies in English Literature, 1500–1900*, 51.1 (Winter 2011): 87–110.

Nelson, Brent. "The Museum as Knowledge Environment," *Scholarly and Research Communication*, 6.3 (2015), http://src-online.ca/index.php/src/article/view/225/439

Nevo, Ruth. *Shakespeare's Other Language*. London: Routledge, 1987.

New, John F. H. *Anglican and Puritanism: The Basis of their Opposition*. Stanford University Press, 1964.

Newstok, Scott L. *Quoting Death in Early Modern England: The Poetics of Epitaphs Beyond the Tomb*. Basingstoke: Palgrave, 2009.

Nichols, John. *Progresses, Processions and Magnificent Festivities of King James the First*. 3 vols. London: John Nichols, 1828.

Nora, Pierre. "Between Memory and History: Les Lieux de Mémoire." Trans. Marc Roudebush. *Representations*, 26 (Spring 1989): 7–24.

Nowak-Kemp, M., and J. P. Hume, "The Oxford Dodo. Part 1: The Museum History of the Tradescant Dodo: Ownership, Displays and Audience." *Historical Biology*, 2016. doi: 10.1080/08912963.2016. 1152471.

"The Oxford Dodo. Part 2: From Curiosity to Icon and Its Role in Displays, Education and Research." *Historical Biology*, 2016. doi: 10.1080/08912963.2016.1155211.

O'Connell, Michael. *The Idolatrous Eye: Iconoclasm and Theater in Early Modern England*. Oxford University Press, 2000.

Olson, Rebecca. "Before the Arras: Textile Description and Innogen's Translation in *Cymbeline*." *Modern Philology*, 108.1 (August 2010): 45–64.

Olsson, Kurt. *John Gower and the Structures of Conversion: A Reading of the "Confessio Amantis."* Woodbridge: D. S. Brewer, 1992.

Oram, William A. "The Invocation of Sabrina," *Studies in English Literature, 1500–1900*, 24 (1984): 121–39.

Orgel, Stephen. *The Authentic Shakespeare and Other Problems of the Early Modern Stage*. New York and London: Routledge, 2002.

"The Case for *Comus*." *Representations*, 81 (Winter 2003): 31–45.

Orlin, Lena Cowen. "Things with Little Social Life: Henslowe's Theatrical Properties and Household Fittings." In Harris and Korda, eds., *Staged Properties in Early Modern English Drama*, 99–128.

Parker, John. "What a Piece of Work Is Man: Shakespearean Drama as Marxian Fetish, the Fetish as Sacramental Sublime." *Journal of Medieval and Early Modern Studies*, 34.3 (Fall 2004): 643–72.

Parker, W. R. "Milton and the Marchioness of Winchester." *Modern Language Review*, 44 (1949): 547–50.

Parolin, Peter A. "Anachronistic Italy: Cultural Alliances and National Identity in *Cymbeline*." *Shakespeare Studies*, 30 (2002): 188–215.
Parry, Graham. *The Trophies of Time: English Antiquarians of the Seventeenth Century*. Oxford University Press, 1995.
Paster, Gail Kern, and Mary Floyd-Wilson, eds. *Reading the Early Modern Passions: Essays in the Cultural History of Emotion*. Philadelphia: University of Pennsylvania Press, 2004.
Patterson, W. B. *William Perkins and the Making of a Protestant England*. Oxford University Press, 2014.
Peacock, Edward, ed. *English Church Furniture, Ornaments and Decoration at the Period of the Reformation*. London: John Camden Hotten, 1866.
Peck, Linda Levy. *Consuming Splendor: Society and Culture in Seventeenth-Century England*. Cambridge University Press, 2005.
Pender, Patricia, and Rosalind Smith, eds., *Material Cultures of Early Modern Women's Writing*. Basingstoke: Palgrave, 2014.
Pennington, Richard. *A Descriptive Catalogue of all the Etched Works of Wenceslaus Hollar*. Cambridge University Press, 1982.
Pettegree, Jane. *Foreign and Native on the English Stage, 1588–1611*. Basingstoke: Palgrave, 2011.
Pevsner, Nikolaus, and Bridget Cherry. *Northamptonshire*. New Haven and London: Yale University Press, 1973.
Philips, John. *The Reformation of Images: Destruction of Art in England, 1535–1660*. Berkeley: University of California Press, 1973.
Phillippy, Patricia. "Living Stones: Elizabeth Russell and the Art of Sacred Conversation." In *English Women, Religion, and Textual Production, 1500–1625*, ed. Micheline White, 17–36. Farnham: Ashgate Press, 2011.
Phillippy, Patricia, ed. *A History of Early Modern Women's Writing*. Cambridge University Press, 2018.
Pickering, Danby, ed. *The Statutes at Large from the Thirty-Ninth Year of Q. Elizabeth to the Twelfth Year of King Charles II Inclusive*. 7 vols. Cambridge: Joseph Bentham for Charles Bathurst, 1763.
Poole, Rachael. "An Outline of the History of the De Critz Family of Painters." *Walpole Society*, 2 (1912–13): 45–69.
"A Manuscript from the Tradescant Collection." *Bodleian Quarterly Record*, 6 (1931): 221–2.
Potter, Jennifer. *Strange Blooms: The Curious Lives and Adventures of the John Tradescants*. London: Atlantic Books, 2007.
Prescott-Innes, R., ed. *The Funeral of Mary, Queen of Scots*. Edinburgh: E. and G. Goldsmid, 1890.
Richardson, Catherine. *Domestic Life and Domestic Tragedy in Early Modern England: The Material Life of the Household*. Manchester University Press, 2006.
Richardson, Ruth Elizabeth. *Mistress Blanche, Queen Elizabeth's Confidante*. Little Logaston, Herefordshire: Logaston Press, 2007.
Ricketts, Annabel. *The English Country House Chapel: Building a Protestant Tradition*. Edited by Simon Ricketts. Reading: Spire Books, Ltd., 2007.

"The Evolution of the Protestant Country House Chapel, c. 1500–c. 1700." PhD Dissertation, Birkbeck College, University of London, 2003.

Rimbault, Edward F. *The Old Cheque-Book or Book of Remembrance of the Chapel Royal from 1561 to 1744*. London: Camden Society, 1872.

Ross, Sarah C. E. "Coteries, Circles, Networks: The Cavendish Circle and Civil War Women's Writing." In Phillippy, ed., *History of Early Modern Women's Writing*, 332–47.

Ross, Sarah C. E. *Women, Poetry and Politics in Seventeenth-Century Britain*. Oxford University Press, 2015.

Roychoudhury, Suprana. "Mental Tempests, Seas of Trouble: The Perturbations of Shakespeare's *Pericles*." *English Literary History*, 82.4 (Winter 2015): 1013–39.

Salter, Elisabeth. *Six Renaissance Men and Women: Innovation, Biography and Cultural Creativity in Tudor England, c.1450–1560*. Aldershot: Ashgate, 2007.

Savage, J. B. "Comus and its Traditions." *English Literary Renaissance*, 5 (Winter 1975): 58–81.

Sawyer, Edmund, ed. *Memorial of Affairs in the Reigns of Elizabeth I and King James I*. 2 vols. London: W. B. for T. Ward, 1725.

Saxl, Fritz. "The Classical Inscription in Renaissance Art and Politics: Bartolomaeus Fontius: *Liber Monumentorum Romanae urbis et aliorum locorum.*" *Journal of the Warburg and Courtauld Institutes*, 4 (1941):19–46.

Scanlon, Larry. "The Riddle of Incest: John Gower and the Problem of Medieval Sexuality." In *Re-visioning* Gower, ed. R. F. Yeager, 93–127. Charlotte, NC: Pegasus Press, 1998.

Schaible, K. H. "Geschichte der Deutschen in England," *Englische Studien*, 10 (1881): 453.

School of Advanced Study, University of London. "Institute of Historical Research, Office Holders, Masters of Requests." www.history.ac.uk/publications/office/masters, Accessed February 2, 2018.

Schoulson, Jeffrey S. *Fictions of Converstion: Jews, Christians, and Cultures of Change in Early Modern England*. Philadelphia: University of Pennsylvania Press, 2013.

Schwartz, Regina Mara. *Sacramental Poetics at the Dawn of Secularism: When God Left the World*. Stanford University Press, 2008.

Schwartz, Louise. *Milton and Maternal Mortality*. Cambridge University Press, 2009.

Schwyzer, Philip. *Archaeologies of English Renaissance Literature*. Oxford University Press, 2007.

Schyler, Robert Livingston. "The Antiquaries and Sir Henry Spelman: An Essay in Historiography." *Proceedings of the American Philosophical Society*, 90.2 (May 1946): 91–103.

Scodel, Joshua. *The English Poetic Epitaph: Commemoration and Conflict from Jonson to Wordsworth*. Ithaca, NY: Cornell University Press, 1991.

Shannon, Laurie. *The Accommodated Animal: Cosomopolity in Shakesperaean Locales*. University of Chicago Press, 2013.

Sharpe, Kevin. *Sir Robert Cotton, 1586–1631: History and Politics in Early Modern England*. Oxford University Press, 1979.

Sheehan, Jonathan. "The Altars of Idols: Religion, Sacrifice, and the Early Modern Polity." *Journal of the History of Ideas*, 67 (2006): 649–73.

"Sacred and Profane: Idolatry, Antiquarianism, and the Polemics of Distinction in the Seventeenth Century." *Past & Present*, 192 (August 2006): 46–51.

Sherlock, Peter. *Monuments and Memory in Early Modern England*. Aldershot: Ashgate, 2008.

Shuger, Debora K. "Gums of Glutinous Heat" and the Stream of Consciousness: The Theology of Milton's *Maske*." *Representations*, 60 (Autumn 1997): 1–21.

Political Theologies in Shakespeare's England: The Sacred and the State in Measure for Measure. New York: Palgrave, 2001.

Shullenberger, William. "Girl, Interrupted: Spenserian Bondage and Release in Milton's Ludlow Mask." *Milton Quarterly*, 37 (2003): 184–99.

Lady in the Labyrinth: Milton's Comus as Initiation. Cranbury, NJ: Associated Presses, 2008.

Smith, Bruce R. *The Key of Green: Passion and Perception in Renaissance Culture*. University of Chicago Press, 2010.

Phenomenal Shakespeare. Oxford: Wiley-Blackwell, 2010.

"Phenomophobia, or Who's Afraid of Merleau-Ponty." *Criticism* 54.3 (Summer 2012): 479–83.

"Premodern Sexualities." *PMLA* 115 (2000): 318–29.

Stallybrass, Peter. "Hauntings: The Materiality of Memory on the Renaissance Stage." In *Generation and Degeneration: Tropes of Reproduction in Literature and History from Antiquity through Early Modern Europe*, ed. Valeria Finucci and Kevin Brownlee, 287–316. Durham: Duke University Press, 2001.

Stallybrass, Peter and Ann Rosalind Jones, "Fetishisms and Renaissances." In *Historicism, Psychoanalysis, and Early Modern Culture*, ed. Carla Mazzio and Douglas Trevor, 20–35. London: Routledge, 2000.

Steere, Daniel. "A Calvinist Bishop in the Court of King Charles I." In *Adaptations of Calvinism in Reformation Europe: Essays in Honour of Brian G. Armstrong*, ed. Mack P. Holt, 193–218. Farnham: Ashgate Press, 2013.

Stevens, Paul. "Subversion and Wonder in Milton's Epitaph 'On Shakespeare.'" *English Literary Renaissance*, 19.3 (Autumn 1989): 375–88.

Stevenson, Jane, and Peter Davidson. *Early Modern Women Poets, 1520–1700: An Anthology*. Oxford University Press, 2001.

Summit, Jennifer. *Memory's Library: Medieval Books in Early Modern England*. University of Chicago Press, 2008.

Suzuki, Mihoko, ed. *The History of British Women's Writing, Volume III: 1610–1690*. Basingstoke: Palgrave, 2011.

Swann, Marjorie. *Curiosities and Texts: The Culture of Collecting in Early Modern England*. Philadelphia: University of Pennsylvania Press, 2010.

Tanner, Joseph Robson, ed., *Tudor Constitutional Documents, A. D. 1485–1603*. Cambridge University Press, 1930.

Tanswell, John. *History and Antiquities of Lambeth*. London: F. Pinkton, 1858.

Thomas, Sidney. "The Problem of Pericles." *Shakespeare Quarterly*, 34.4 (Winter 1983): 448–50.

Thompson, William. *Southwark Cathedral: The History and Antiquities of the Cathedral Church of Saint Savior St. Marie Overie. 2nd edition*. London: Ash and Co., 1906.

Thrush, Andrew, and John P. Ferris, eds., *History of Parliament: The House of Commons, 1604–1629*. 6 vols. Cambridge University Press, 2010.

Traupman, John C., ed. *New College Latin and English Dictionary*. New York: Bantam, 1966.

Tuana, Nancy. "Viscous Porosity: Witnessing Katrina." In Alaimo and Hekman, eds., *Material Feminisms*, 188–213.

Tyacke, Nicholas. *Anti-Calvinists: The Rise of English Arminianism, c. 1590–1640*. Oxford University Press, 1987.

University of Saskatchewan and Canterbury Cathedral Archives. "John Bargrave Collection, The," http://drc.usask.ca/projects/bargrave/about.php. 2011.

van der Haar, Jan. *From Abbadie to Young: A Bibliography of English, Mostly Puritan, Works, Translated into the Dutch Language*. 2 vols. Jesup, GA: Kool Publishers, 1980.

Venn, J. A. ed., *Alumni cantabrigienses*. 10 vols. Cambridge University Press, 1922.

Vickers, Brian. *Shakespeare's Co-Authors: A Historical Study of Five Collaborative Play*. Oxford University Press, 2003.

Victoria County Histories. *History of the County of Berkshire*. Edited by P. H. Ditchfield and William Page. 4 vols. London: Archibald Constable, 1906–1924.

Victoria County Histories. *A History of the County of Hampshire*. Edited by William Page. 5 vols. London: Constable and Company, Ltd., 1911.

Victoria County Histories. *History of the County of Northampton*. Edited by William Page, et al. 7 vols. Oxford University Press, 1902–2013.

Wagner, Anthony and George Squibb, "Deputy Heralds." In *Tribute to an Antiquary: Essays presented to Marc Fitch by some of his Friends*, ed. Frederick Emmison and Roy Stephens, 229–65. London: Leopard's Head Press, 1976.

Wakelin, Daniel. *Scribal Correction and Literary Craft*. Cambridge University Press, 2014.

Wallace, Peter G. *The Long European Reformation: Religion, Political Conflict and the Search for Conformity, 1350–1750*. Basingstoke: Palgrave Macmillan, 2003.

Walmsley, Peter. "'Live to Die, Die to Live': An Introduction." *Eighteenth-Century Fiction* 21.1 (Fall 2008): 1–11.

Walsh, Brian. "'A Priestly Farewell: Gower's Tomb and Religious Change in *Pericles*." *Religion and Literature*, 45.3 (Autumn 2013): 81–113.

"Shakespeare in Stained Glass: The Shakespeare Memorials of Southwark Cathedral and 'Local' Bardolatry." *Borrowers and Lenders: A Journal of*

Shakespeare Appropriation, 7.1 (Spring 2012). www.borrowers.uga.edu/783058/show

Walsham, Alexandra. "Domme Preachers: Post Reformation Catholicism and the Culture of Print." *Past and Present*, 168 (2000): 72–123.

"'Like Fragments of a Shipwreck': Printed Images and Religious Antiquarianism in Early Modern England." In *Printed Images in Early Modern Britain: Essays in Interpretation*, ed. Michael Hunter, 87–109. Aldershot: Ashgate, 2010.

"Skeletons in the Cupboard: Relics after the English Reformation." *Past and Present Supplement*, 5 (2010): 121–43.

Watt, Diane. "Gender and Sexuality in Confessio Amantis," In Echard, ed., *Gower Companion*, 197–213.

Wayne, Valerie. "The Woman's Parts of Cymbeline." In Harris and Korda, eds., *Staged Properties in Early Modern English Drama*, 288–314.

Weiss, Gail, ed. *Intertwinings: Interdisciplinary Encounters with Merleau-Ponty*. Albany: SUNY Press, 2008.

Welch, Evelyn. "Public Magnificence and Private Display: Giovanni Pontano's *De splendore* 1498 and the Domestic Arts." *Journal of Design History*, 15 (2002): 211–21.

Werth, Tiffany J. "Great Miracle or Lying Wonder? Janus-Faced Romance in *Pericles*." *Shakespearean International Yearbook*, 8 (2008): 183–203.

White, Adam. *Biographical Dictionary of London Tomb Sculptors, c. 1560–1660*. London: Walpole Society, 1999.

White, Micheline, ed. *English Women, Religion, and Textual Production, 1500–1625*. Farnham: Ashgate Press, 2011.

White, Micheline. "Women Writers and Literary-Religious Circles in Elizabethan West Country: Anne Dowriche, Anne Lock Prowse, Anne Lock Moyle, Ursula Fulford, and Elizabeth Rous." *Modern Philology*, 103 (2005): 187–214.

Whiting, Robert. *The Reformation of the English Parish Church*. Cambridge University Press, 2010.

Wilkie, Vanessa. "'Such Daughters and Such a Mother': The Countess of Derby and Her Three Daughters, 1560–1647." PhD dissertation, University of California, Riverside, 2009.

Williams, Claire Bryony. "Manuscript, Monument, Memory: The Circulation of Epitaphs in the Seventeenth Century." *Literature Compass*, 11.8 (2014): 572–82.

Williams, Deanne. *Shakespeare and the Performance of Girlhood*. Basingstoke: Palgrave, 2014.

Wilson, Richard. "'Our Bending Author': Shakespeare Takes a Bow." *Shakespeare Studies*, 56 (2008): 67–79.

Wise, C. *The Montagus of Boughton and their Northamptonshire Houses*. Kettering: W. E. and J. Goss, 1888.

Witmore, Michael. "Shakespeare, Sensation, and Renaissance Existentialism." *Criticism* 54.3 (Summer 2012): 419–26.

Wood, Anthony. *Athenae Oxonienses*. Edited by Philip Bliss. 8 vols. London: F. C. and J. Rivington, et al., 1813.

Wooding, Lucy. "Remembrance in the Eucharist." In Gordon and Rist, eds., *Arts of Remembrance*, 19–36.

Woolf, Daniel. *The Social Circulation of the Past: English Historical Culture 1500–1730*. Oxford University Press, 2003.

Woudhuysen, H. R. *Sir Philip Sidney and the Circulation of Manuscripts, 1558–1640*. Oxford University Press, 1996.

Wray, Ramona. "Memory, Materiality and Maternity in the Tanfield/Cary Archive." In Phillippy, ed., *History of Early Modern Women's Writing*, 221–40.

Wright, Nancy E. "Epitaphic Conventions and the Reception of Anne Bradstreet's Public Voice." *Early American Literature*, 31 (1996): 243–62.

Yates, Frances A. *The Art of Memory*. London: Routledge and Keegan Paul, 1966.

Yule, George. "James VI and I: Furnishing the Churches in His Two Kingdoms." In *Religion, Culture and Society in Early Modern Britain: Essays in Honour of Patrick Collinson*, ed. Anthony Fletcher and Peter Rogerts, 182–208. Cambridge University Press, 1994.

Ziegler, Georgianna. "My Lady's Chamber: Female Space, Female Chastity in Shakespeare." *Textual Practice*, 4.1 (1990): 73–90.

Zimmerman, Susan. *The Early Modern Corpse and Shakespeare's Theatre*. Edinburgh University Press, 2005.

Zurcher, Aemilia. "Untimely Monuments: Stoicism, History, and the Problem of Utility in *The Winter's Tale and Pericles*." *English Literary History*, 70.4 (Winter 2003): 903–27.

Index